BARRIO AMERICA

BARRIO AMERICA

HOW LATINO IMMIGRANTS
SAVED THE AMERICAN CITY

A. K. SANDOVAL-STRAUSZ

BASIC BOOKS

New York

Parts of this book appeared in different form as "Latino Vernaculars and the Emerging National Landscape," *Buildings & Landscapes: The Journal of the Vernacular Architecture Forum* 20 (2013), 1–18; "Latino Landscapes: Postwar Cities and the Transnational Origins of a New Urban America," *Journal of American History* 101 (2014), 804–831; "*Migrantes, Negocios,* and *Infraestructura*: Transnational Urban Revitalization in Chicago," in *Immigration and Metropolitan Revitalization*, eds. Domenic Vitiello and Thomas J. Sugrue (Philadelphia: University of Pennsylvania Press, 2017). Permission to use this material is gratefully acknowledged.

Basic Books
Hachette Book Group
1290 Avenue of the Americas, New York, NY 10104
www.basicbooks.com

Printed in the United States of America
First Edition: November 2019

Published by Basic Books, an imprint of Perseus Books, LLC, a subsidiary of Hachette Book Group, Inc. The Basic Books name and logo is a trademark of the Hachette Book Group.

The Hachette Speakers Bureau provides a wide range of authors for speaking events. To find out more, go to www.hachettespeakersbureau.com or call (866) 376-6591.

The publisher is not responsible for websites (or their content) that are not owned by the publisher.

Print book interior design by Jeff Williams

Library of Congress Cataloging-in-Publication Data
Names: Sandoval-Strausz, A. K., author.
Title: Barrio America: How Latino Immigrants Saved the American City /
    A. K. Sandoval-Strausz.
Description: First edition. | New York: Basic Books, Hachette Book Group, 2019. |
    Includes bibliographical references and index.
Identifiers: LCCN 2019014405 (print) | LCCN 2019980679 (ebook) |
    ISBN 9781541697249 (hardcover) | ISBN 9781541644434 (ebook)
Subjects: LCSH: Urban renewal—United States—Case studies. | Neighborhoods—United
    States—Case studies. | Cities and towns—Study and teaching—United States—
    Case studies. | Community development, Urban—United States—Case studies. |
    Hispanic Americans—Case studies.
Classification: LCC HT175 .S25 2019 (print) | LCC HT175 (ebook) |
    DDC 307.3/4160973—dc23
LC record available at https://lccn.loc.gov/2019014405
LC ebook record available at https://lccn.loc.gov/2019980679

ISBNs: 978-1-5416-9724-9 (hardcover), 978-1-5416-4443-4 (e-book)

LSC-C

10 9 8 7 6 5 4 3 2 1

To mi madre y mi padre,
Cecilia and Ivan,
who were children in worlds on fire
before finding a home here;

to mi vida,
Cathleen,
who is extraordinary in too many ways to count
and whose very presence makes everything more fun;

and to mis hijos,
Cecilia and Lincoln,
the most beautiful children imaginable
for whose generation we need to save this world.

The foreigner residing among you must be treated as your native-born. Love them as yourself, for you were foreigners in Egypt. I am the Lord your God.

—LEVITICUS 19:34

CONTENTS

INTRODUCTION

O N A QUIET STREET IN DALLAS'S OAK CLIFF NEIGHBOR-
hood, in a second-story addition that rises behind a modest yellow wood-frame house, sits the headquarters of the
Federation of Zacatecan Clubs of North Texas. From the outside, the
clubhouse is so unassuming that you could pass right by for years
without ever knowing it was there. Upon stepping through the door,
the first thing a visitor notices is the ten-foot-wide, floor-to-ceiling display on the east wall of the clubhouse. A pair of formal brass poles are
mounted diagonally on the wall, each bearing a large flag: one of the
United States, the other of Mexico. The banners are spread wide and
carefully draped to create elegant folds in the bright fabric. In a dark
wood frame between the flags hangs the official seal of the Mexican
state of Zacatecas. The image, drawn from the original coat of arms
bestowed by Philip II of Spain in 1588, features La Virgen del Patro-
cinio, the Child in her arms, flanked by the sun and moon; beneath
her, four armored conquistadors look up in wonder.

On the walls, plaques and citations from officials in both Mexico
and the United States express appreciation for many years of charitable and benevolent work building basic infrastructure in remote communities and providing education for the young and medical care for
the old. Newspaper articles and photographs document community
events: congresses with federations from Chicago and Los Angeles,
a meeting with migrant clubs from El Salvador, years of banquets
and pageants. Posters announce past rallies and marches in support

1

of immigrant rights and in opposition to deportations that separate families. And certificates, duly signed and stamped, record the annual registrations of the federation's constituent clubs representing an array of small Zacatecan communities—Boquillo de Abajo, Tepechitlán, El Fuerte, La Concepción, Sombrerete.[1]

Manuel Rodela Rodríguez is a founder and past president of the federation. He has lived in Oak Cliff for more than a third of a century. Among the many projects he has undertaken with the city's Zacatecans is the *Monumento al Migrante Caído* (*Monument to the Fallen Migrant*), which they commissioned from a sculptor in Mexico and installed in a nearby public park to memorialize the many people who have lost their lives crossing the border. The three-ton statue is carved out of volcanic rock and displays key symbols of Mexico's Indigenous heritage, including a head in the style of the three-thousand-year-old Olmec civilization and a rendering of the Aztec god Quetzalcoatl. The monument also features the monarch butterfly, whose two-thousand-mile migration across the Americas has made it the leading symbol of *migrantes*. Rodela himself, like millions of Americans, remains a frequent border-crosser. "I visit whenever I have the opportunity. Every two or three months I go to Zacatecas." But like many migrants, it has been years since he last considered moving back. "My thinking has changed," he explains. "I have grown fond of this country, and I love it as if it were . . . " He pauses for a moment to find the right words. "For me, Mexico and the United States are one nation."[2]

Rodela was born in 1942 in the capital of Zacatecas but spent his childhood in Tepechitlán, a town of a few thousand residents nestled in a bend of the Tlaltenango River. When he was a boy, his parents decided to move the family to Ciudad Juárez, the Mexican border city located opposite El Paso, Texas. At first he showed little enthusiasm for the journey. "I didn't want to go to Ciudad Juárez or anywhere else," he recalls. "My mother would say, 'Let's go, my son, we're leaving,' and I would answer, 'No, you go ahead, I'd rather stay right here!'" The family moved nonetheless, and young Manuel came with them. As he remembers it, his family was "following the example of other people at that time, who were migrating to different cities."[3]

In Ciudad Juárez he started out selling fruit from a cart, but his musical training soon allowed him to find work as a performer. He and his brother formed a *conjunto* called Los Supremos, which a local newspaper called "the most popular youth band on the border." They were so successful, in fact, that they appeared regularly on television, playing Monday and Friday broadcasts that featured the young men dressed in matching blazers, white shirts, and bow ties. Rodela went on to study electronics at the city's Edison Institute of Radio and Television. In 1970 he married a Texas-born Mexicana, and the following year they relocated to El Paso, where they started a family and lived for more than a decade. He explored job opportunities in Los Angeles for a year before returning to Texas, settling in Dallas in 1985.[4]

BY THE TIME Rodela arrived, American cities had been in a state of crisis for more than a generation. The signs of distress were all around. On the ride to work along elevated train tracks or highway overpasses, people were confronted with bleak views of abandoned tenements and empty lots strewn with the bricks of demolished buildings. Television news broadcasts bombarded viewers nightly with stories of assaults and killings, each seemingly more gruesome and senseless than the one before. Mayors struggled to avoid municipal bankruptcy amid declining city revenues as downtown business owners relocated to the suburbs or struggled to make their worn-out storefronts appealing to the few customers who remained on once-bustling streets.

Nowhere was this clearer than in big-city industrial neighborhoods. These had led the way to American economic power and broadly shared prosperity until midcentury, but then entered a long period of decline. In 1990 the writer Stuart Dybek published *The Coast of Chicago*, a collection of short stories set in and around the city's South Lawndale neighborhood. He described an area long past its prime, one where residents had for years "walked past block-length gutted factories, past walls of peeling, multicolored doors hammered up around flooded excavation pits, hung out in half-boarded storefronts of groceries that had shut down when they were kids, dusty cans still stacked on the shelves." Dybek's basic theme—that something precious had been lost in South Lawndale that people could dimly perceive but did not know how to bring back—is most hauntingly manifested in his story "Hot Ice." It retells the local legend of a central European immigrant icehouse owner's daughter who drowns in a local pond. Her father finds her lifeless body, and in a grief-stricken trance he takes her back to his shop and encases her in a massive block of ice. There she stays, "her hair, not just blonde but radiating gold like a candle flame behind a window in winter," until decades later when the narrator and his friends miraculously find her in the long-abandoned icehouse.[5]

Two years later and nine hundred miles to the south, another community was pressed into service as a symbol of urban decay. In 1992 *Texas Monthly* magazine commissioned the journalist Grover Lewis to write a feature article about Oak Cliff, the neighborhood where he had grown up more than four decades earlier. Upon revisiting his boyhood home, he was moved to offer up an elegiac account of past decline and present blight. "The devastation was total," he wrote, "an entire neighborhood sunk in rot. The surviving houses were vine-choked, boarded up, literally atomizing in a ghastly mockery of the thriving community I recalled." Walking the length of Oak Cliff's main shopping street, Lewis continued: "I groped for terms to encompass the scope of the disaster: *systemic collapse, municipal cancer, de facto apartheid, social time bomb, a thousand points of dark.*"[6]

Descriptions like these could have been written about any number of city neighborhoods that hit bottom in the depths of the urban crisis. They were only the latest echoes of more than three decades of eulogies for the American city. In 1961 the urbanist Paul Ylvisaker observed: "The approved way to talk about cities these days is to speak solemnly, ominously, and fearfully about their problems. You don't really rate as an urban expert unless you foresee doom." And indeed, a year later the *Wall Street Journal* reporter Mitchell Gordon published an article entitled "Doomed Cities" in which he mused that "it remains to be seen whether the cities will be able to save themselves." In 1971 Norton Long, a public administration professor, speculated that cities might soon be useful only "as an Indian reservation for the poor, the deviant, the unwanted," and was seconded by the urban policy specialist George Sternlieb, who in an interview with *US News & World Report* said of cities, "We've got to have a sandbox . . . I am saying that for real because I don't want these people climbing up over the walls." And in 1977 Congressman Henry S. Reuss lamented, "Many of our cities are sick—losing population, losing jobs, losing fiscal solvency, losing the experience of the neighborhood and community, safety and attractiveness which are the reasons for their existence in the first place."[7]

But even the most pessimistic of these observers would seem prescient in the spring of 1992, when the ordeal of American cities reached a new level of severity. On April 29, Los Angeles erupted after the shocking acquittal of four police officers who had been caught on video delivering a lengthy beating to an unarmed and defenseless black motorist named Rodney King. The following five days and nights were marked by outright rebellion and riot, including dozens of assaults and killings, the imposition of a curfew, the deployment of the National Guard, and over $1 billion in property damage.

Suddenly it seemed as if the nation might be returning to the urban riots of the 1960s. One journalist saw the destruction in LA as representative of "many blighted urban communities" across America and worried that "poverty and criminality are worse; anger has metastasized . . . feral youth gangs have taken root and have at their disposal a mind-boggling arsenal of fire power." Soon the Princeton criminologist John DiIulio coined the term "superpredator"—"a young, juvenile criminal who is so impulsive, so remorseless, that he can kill, rape, maim without giving it a second thought." DiIulio, increasingly echoed by others, called these youngsters "teenage time bombs" with "absolutely no respect for human life." Looking forward, they fretted that if current trends held, "we're going to have a bloodbath when these kids grow up."[8]

THESE DIRE FORECASTS turned out to be wrong. Looking back to the early 1990s, we can see more clearly that the era's prophets of doom were describing urban America in the darkness before dawn. In the years that followed, crime rates would plummet, economic vitality would return to downtowns, and so many people would choose to move back into cities that instead of population loss, the biggest problem facing most urbanites would be a severe shortage of housing and the displacement of longtime residents from their neighborhoods.[9]

Among the most significant signs of the emerging urban renaissance was the way Latinos were dramatically transforming entire city neighborhoods. In South Lawndale, the arrival of tens of thousands of people from Mexico and other Latin American countries had already begun to repopulate and revitalize the neighborhood as they supplanted departing residents. Census figures showed that these newcomers had created the first significant population increase since the World War I era. The area soon became the most important barrio for hundreds of miles in any direction, serving as the center of a diasporic community numbering more than two million people. By the 1990s, the businesses along Twenty-Sixth Street, the neighborhood's main commercial strip, became renowned on both sides of the Rio Grande, and economic activity there was so intense that *Crain's Chicago Business* reported that it had become the most active commercial corridor in Chicago other than the Magnificent Mile. A decade later, a procession of community members, journalists, business groups, social scientists, and public officials would be lauding South Lawndale—now known as Little Village—as an example of a new and revitalized Chicago.[10]

A similar process took hold in Oak Cliff. Thanks to a strong and sustained influx of Latinos, mostly Mexicans and Salvadorans, the neighborhood had stopped losing residents and grown for the first time since the 1940s. Many of the newcomers had purchased homes in the area and opened new businesses that were reviving the commercial district. And the streets were becoming safer as the city's crime rate began a dramatic decline that would continue for two decades thereafter. Oak Cliff would soon begin to attract outside capital, draw in curious consumers from elsewhere in town, and eventually garner federal funding for a new streetcar line. A little more than fifteen years after Lewis's mournful article, the city's leading newspaper would be celebrating Oak Cliff as "the Latino downtown of Dallas."[11]

Anglo America was late in recognizing that something big was happening in Latino America. But the writers who created the boom in US Latino literature in the 1980s and 1990s saw things more clearly. Their novels were set in cities like Chicago, New York, and Miami but unfolded simultaneously in such places as Havana and Santo Domingo. When Sandra Cisneros wrote of her father's peregrinations between Chicago and Mexico in *The House on Mango Street* (1984), she was illustrating the cross-border connections that saved the Windy City from the kind of abandonment that affected so many

Percentage Hispanic in the United States, Dallas, Chicago, and the Oak Cliff and Little Village Neighborhoods

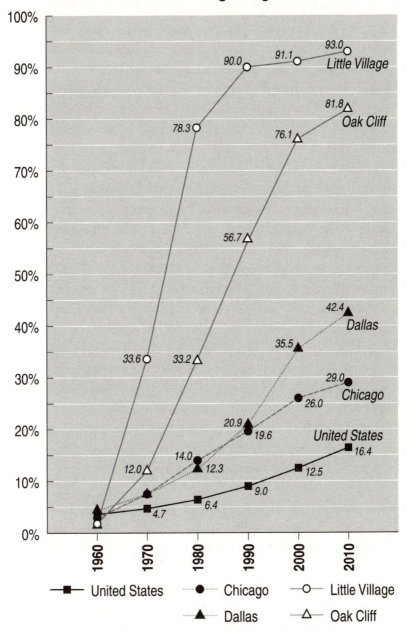

Latina and Latino newcomers helped remedy the crisis of population loss and economic devitalization. This was first on view in declining urban neighborhoods, then throughout US cities, and ultimately across the nation. Graph by Philip Schwartzberg, Meridian Mapping, Minneapolis.

industrial cities. When Cristina García's *Dreaming in Cuban* (1992) depicted a proud and industrious immigrant woman opening a small business called the Yankee Doodle Bakery, she was telling the story of countless new entrepreneurs in barrios across the country. And when Julia Alvarez's *How the García Girls Lost Their Accents* (1991) and Jaime Manrique's *Latin Moon in Manhattan* (1992) portrayed the hard but eventful lives of Dominican and Colombian immigrants to the New York City area, they showed how other newcomers from Latin America had become major participants in the resurgence of cities nationwide. It was Latina and Latino immigrant writers like these who became the true heralds of a new urban America.[12]

In retrospect we can see that earlier woeful portraits of decaying cities had become a rote narrative. These variations on the theme of "there goes the neighborhood" were sincere, but they were mostly written by people who had long since left the area. The sense of a neighborhood lost had become pervasive as the agony of the US big city spawned an entire genre of writing, one that extended from fiction to nonfiction to romans à clef in between. The genre found its novelistic exemplar in Tom Wolfe's *The Bonfire of the Vanities* in 1987, but by then urban decline as a dramatic backdrop was already so well established that it had appeared in everything from sophisticated films like *Dog Day Afternoon* (1975) and *Taxi Driver* (1976) to sensationalist science fiction movies like *Escape from New York* (1981) and *Robocop* (1986). Looking back across the decades, it is easier to see that when people set their stories in cities, they already knew what the narrative was supposed to be.[13]

THE URBAN CRISIS was not, however, just a narrative. It was a very real set of problems that afflicted the nation's cities for decades. The crisis involved a complex constellation of pathologies but is most easily understood as having five main elements: population loss, economic decline, fiscal crisis, rising crime, and the racialization of all the above.

The clearest measure of the urban crisis took the form of tens of millions of people leaving their homes in cities and moving to the suburbs. As the eminent urban historian Kenneth T. Jackson observed in 1985, of the twenty-five biggest cities in 1950, eighteen had lost population by 1980. Nationally, the proportion of Americans living in cities was falling. This represented an astounding turnabout. The United States had been urbanizing continually since its founding, and over the course of nearly two centuries of census-taking, there had not been any ten-year period with a smaller percentage of city-dwellers at the end than at the beginning, let alone three decades in a row.[14]

Jobs left the city along with people as factories, shops, and offices headed for suburbia and beyond. Manufacturers gradually relocated their production plants away from cities as they searched for low-wage, nonunion labor, tax breaks, and cheap land. Downtown retailers, from flagship department stores to car dealerships to grocers, lost business to the outlying shopping centers and malls that sprang up to cater to the fast-growing suburban populace. White-collar work also moved outward as numerous company headquarters left central business districts behind in favor of office parks and leafy corporate campuses. These changes drew pedestrians away from downtown sidewalks, sapping customers from restaurants, bars, barbershops, and other service establishments, thousands of which had to close their doors.[15]

As people and businesses departed, municipal budgets were driven deep into the red. Cities depended on various kinds of revenue to support basic services. But families who moved away paid their taxes to towns in the suburbs, and when urban property values went down, so did assessments. Meanwhile, the loss of urban manufacturing and retailing dealt a double blow by draining a key source of business taxes and fees. City governments were left with little choice but to raise tax rates to maintain essential services like schools, sanitation, firefighting, and police departments. This in turn drove even more residents and employers toward outlying towns with lower taxes, further depleting city treasuries.[16]

Crime, the fourth major aspect of the urban crisis, was its most high-profile symptom. As much as depopulation, joblessness, and insolvency all quantified the misery of the cities, at the level of individual experience the fear of being the victim of a beating or killing was the most terrifying of all urban ills. In the twenty years after 1960, the homicide rate doubled and stayed stubbornly high through the beginning of the 1990s. In those same years, the reported level of property crime tripled, sexual assault more than quadrupled, and aggravated assault soared to more than five times its 1960 rate. As a matter of statistics, these figures were appalling even before we imagine the shock and horror of all those unsuspecting and unprepared families opening their doors to somber police officers or ashen-faced clergymen.[17]

All these difficulties were interpreted through a racial lens, first and foremost by white people. They devised a racial narrative of neighborhood decline, portraying "white flight" as a reasonable response to the prospect of having black neighbors. They repeated the old racial myth that black people were just "lazy" or "shiftless," while ignoring virtually universal job discrimination and the ongoing departure of employment opportunities from cities. They fixated on black-on-white crime—even though the huge majority of victims were set on by people of the same racial background and African Americans were almost 30 percent more likely to be the targets of violent crime than whites—while ignoring endemic police violence against communities of color. And they crafted a political mythology that portrayed government assistance to the poor as wasteful spending on undeserving black people, even though whites were by far the most numerous beneficiaries of the welfare programs that were targeted for repeated cuts. In this way, prejudice compounded economic hardship, adding the dead weight of racism to a growing burden of poverty, neglect, and violence in urban communities.[18]

CONSIDERING THE SEVERITY of the urban crisis, it is hardly surprising that few people expected the recovery that was already taking hold by the mid-1990s—but interestingly, everyone seemed to agree that cities had been saved by people with lots of money. Leading research in critical sociology dwelled on the reallocation of international capital flows and the role of professionals and related workers in coordinating those flows. The most influential urban studies approach concentrated its attention on the return of the "creative class," a broad category of white-collar, intellectual, and artistic workers who were presented as the leaders of the urban renaissance. And the economics literature homed in on the lifestyle preferences of high-earning professionals, who had once formed local elites in smaller communities but increasingly clustered in the biggest cities. These explanations were certainly true in the sense that they accounted for the gradual relocation to cities of large numbers of people and vast sums of money.[19]

But they overlooked the indispensable role played by Latina and Latino migrants and immigrants, who had started to repopulate and revive declining neighborhoods at least two decades before the "back-to-the-city" movement became a significant trend among prosperous and mostly white Anglo professionals. Hispanic newcomers to US cities were more numerous than the returning yuppies who got so much attention in popular accounts of comeback cities. Moreover, the big-city lives of urban professionals would have been impossible without the kinds of work performed by Latinos and Latinas in key sectors of the urban economy, from home construction and building maintenance to restaurant food preparation and childcare.[20]

It is their stories that are at the heart of *Barrio America*. This book seeks to advance our understanding of the nation's recent history by grounding it in neighborhoods where immigrant Latinos first arrived, created communities, and gradually took on greater importance in civic, economic, and political life. It shows how a group of people who earned modest incomes and were socially marginalized, politically demonized, and sometimes undocumented managed to redeem so much of metropolitan America.

It does so by focusing on the biggest immigrant barrios in two of the nation's largest cities: the Little Village community area in Chicago and the Oak Cliff neighborhood in Dallas. These cities represent the nation's two main urban regions: the industrial North that extends from the Boston area down through New York City and Philadelphia and across Cleveland, Detroit, and the rest of the Midwest; and the Sunbelt that stretches in an arc from Florida and Georgia across Texas and into the Southwest. In Chicago, Latinos would continue to grow as a group until they constituted nearly a third of the city's population. They surpassed even that figure in Dallas, where more than four out of ten residents are Hispanic.[21]

The kinds of changes seen in these neighborhoods and their cities reflected those in many other metropolitan areas across the United States. Today, of the nation's twenty-five biggest cities, twelve have populations that are more than one-quarter Latino, including eight that are over one-third Hispanic and two that are majority-Latino.[22]

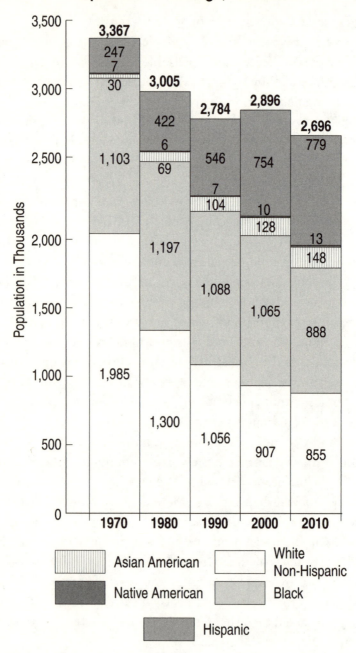

Population of Chicago, 1970–2010

Population in Thousands

| | 1970 | 1980 | 1990 | 2000 | 2010 |

3,367
247
7
30
1,103
1,985

3,005
422
6
69
1,197
1,300

2,784
546
7
104
1,088
1,056

2,896
754
10
128
1,065
907

2,696
779
13
148
888
855

Asian American   White Non-Hispanic

Native American   Black

Hispanic

If not for the arrival of hundreds of thousands of immigrants from Latin America and Asia, Chicago would have lost almost as many residents as other industrial cities like Detroit and Cleveland, which shed nearly half their populations in the fifty years after midcentury. Residual categories, rounding, and overlap mean that totals differ fractionally from components. Graph by Philip Schwartzberg, Meridian Mapping, Minneapolis.

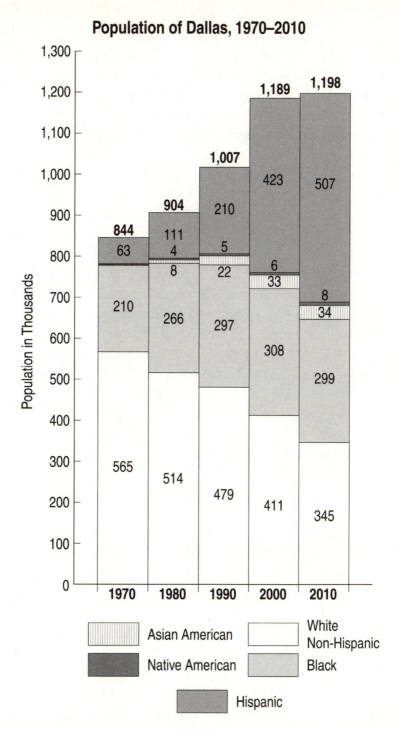

Population of Dallas, 1970–2010

Like other Sunbelt cities, Dallas continued to gain population even during the urban crisis. But this growth was so dependent on Hispanic immigrants and their children that without them, Big D would have stagnated or shrunk beginning around 1970. Graph by Philip Schwartzberg, Meridian Mapping, Minneapolis.

BARRIO AMERICA RECOUNTS this history in three parts. Part One, "There Goes the Neighborhood," surveys the years from 1950 to the late 1960s, when urban America fell from its peak of population and prosperity to the depths of crisis. Corporations began to move manufacturing and management away from cities, stripping them of employment opportunities and undercutting the gains of urban workers. Meanwhile, as black people and their allies began to dismantle Jim Crow and other forms of racial segregation through direct protest and legal action, millions of white people decided that they would rather leave their city neighborhoods than share them with African American families. Government policy also contributed to the urban crisis because a series of federal programs, including mortgage insurance, urban renewal, and highway construction, subsidized suburbanization to the tune of billions of dollars a year. As a result, cities lost millions of people and well-paying jobs along with the wealth they had produced. In these same years, however, Latin America took the opposite course. Governments fostered industrialization, creating unprecedented urban growth and rising prosperity. The cities of Anglo America and Latin America mostly developed separately, but key connections were established that would lead to large-scale migration in the decades that followed.

Part Two, "Here Comes the Neighborhood," focuses on the period between 1965 and the mid-1980s, when newcomers from Mexico and the Caribbean began to repopulate and stabilize city districts that continued to lose native-born residents. The Immigration and Nationality Act of 1965 ended decades of grotesquely discriminatory racial quotas, but as a result of political extortion it also imposed never-before-seen limits on migration across the Americas. So when Mexico's agricultural economy ran aground in the mid-1960s and more people sought employment in the United States, there were fewer ways to cross the border legally. Migrants both documented and undocumented arrived in US cities just when they were most needed: as white flight was accelerating and the Great Migration of black people from the South was ending. In Dallas these newcomers joined US-born Hispanics in repopulating Oak Cliff, buying homes and opening businesses at a time of sluggish growth across the city. In Chicago, *migrantes* flowed into the city's West Side, reinhabiting declining neighborhoods at a time when the municipal government was spending millions of dollars trying to woo professionals back to the city. In the meantime, established political machines in both cities did their best to keep Latinas and Latinos out of power, prompting them to join multiracial coalitions in hopes of securing a fair share of city jobs and municipal spending.

Part Three, "The Seeds of the Future City," deals with the years from 1986 to the mid-2010s, when immigrants from a broad range of Latin American nations expanded US barrios and helped abate the leading symptoms of the urban crisis. Across the hemisphere, new economic policies and brutal civil wars drove millions of migrants and refugees to the United States. In response, Congress passed the Immigration Reform and Control Act of 1986, a law with both intended and unforeseen consequences that intensified urban revitalization. Newly legalized immigrants invested their money and labor in their barrios, driving faster growth in urban economies, while undocumented migrants responded to heavier border enforcement by staying in the United States and bringing their families or starting new ones. These immigrants carried with them an array of city-dwelling customs that they adapted to their new environs, creating what became known as "Latino urbanism." This hybrid set of practices rejuvenated neighborhoods and restored the economic and social fabric of Anglo-designed urban spaces, most notably by driving down crime rates in and around their barrios. The rising Latino population inspired bipartisan efforts to reform the nation's immigration system, but even cautious initiatives were repeatedly obstructed by a stubborn minority who refused to recognize how much the United States depended on Latinos and other immigrants to fuel its economy and preserve its institutions.[23]

THE SUBTITLE OF this book, *How Latino Immigrants Saved the American City*, raises a few issues worth clarifying at the outset. The first of these involves identity. Latinas and Latinos have spent more than a century and a half at the center of a process of racial definition or racialization. Mexicans, Puerto Ricans, Cubans, Dominicans, and other people of Spanish linguistic heritage in the United States negotiated their social status with Anglos who defined race primarily in black and white. Because Hispanics could be of any race, their place in America remained uncertain. Like William Faulkner's *Light in August* character Joe Christmas—a man who people said might have white, black, or Mexican ancestry—Latinos were racially undefined, and many people could not figure out how to treat them without knowing for sure.[24]

In response, Latinos did their best to navigate the troubled waters of race in America. People who were mostly of mixed European, Indigenous, and African heritage identified themselves by a wide variety of terms, including *mexicano, hispano, boricua,* Spanish American, and Chicano. This process of naming turned into an elaborate dance with US officials. In 1930, for example, the Census Bureau employed "Mexican" as a racial rather than national category. From 1940 to 1960, census-takers used classifications like "persons of Spanish mother tongue" and "persons of Spanish surname." People of Latin American and Spanish heritage were first counted on the basis of nationality in the 1970 census and tallied as "Hispanics" ten years later. The term "Latino" was favored by ethnic Mexican and Puerto Rican activists in Chicago in the mid-1970s and was subsequently popularized by predominantly Cuban American advertising executives. Notwithstanding the myth of some kind of golden age before "identity politics," this all transpired in the same years that Americans were organizing around identities like Irish, Italian, Polish, Jewish, and Catholic—and of course categories like white, Anglo-Saxon, and Protestant.[25]

In this book, the terms "Latino" and "Hispanic" will be used interchangeably to refer broadly to people of Latin American ancestry living in the United States. National identifiers like "Mexican" and "Salvadoran" will also be in use, as will "Latina" to refer specifically to women. When I write about people doing things in the past, I will whenever possible use the terms they would have applied to themselves; when looking back or around analytically, I will employ the term that most precisely conveys the idea at hand. No terminology works perfectly in every situation; what we should remember is that these changing categories are themselves part of our story.[26]

The second issue involves the scope of this history. Although this book emphasizes the central role of Latinos in US urban recovery, migrants and immigrants from other parts of the world also played an indispensable part in saving the nation's cities. Hispanics have gradually become the nation's largest "minority" group, with numbers approaching sixty million people. That total encompasses people from many different nations who are bound together by a shared language or culture. But other groups of new Americans are also enormously significant, especially at the local level. Asian Americans present a strong example. They have been fewer in number, usually a bit over one-third of the Latino total. At the same time, they have been even more concentrated in cities and exceptionally important to local economies and cultures. One can see this in the expanding Chinatowns, Koreatowns, Little Saigons, Little Indias, and analogous neighborhoods nationwide. Cities have also attracted people from the Caribbean, the Middle East, Africa, and eastern Europe. In the work of urban revitalization, it has been immigrants from across the world who get the job done.[27]

These questions of identity and immigration also highlight one way this book might be misunderstood. *Barrio America* is not about racial difference. The urban crisis was frequently and mistakenly attributed to alleged African American cultural shortcomings, while Hispanics were more often characterized as hardworking and family-oriented—a thinly veiled code for "brown people good, black people bad." This book emphasizes structural characteristics like demographics, citizenship, and language more than cultural ones. This is not to say that race has not mattered: Latinos' uncertain identities sometimes advantaged them as not-black while also sometimes disadvantaging them as not-really-white. But far more important to the idea that Latinos saved the cities was that when they arrived, urban America needed saving. Black people had started migrating to cities decades earlier when others, including native-born rural whites and European immigrants, were also coming in. But by the late 1960s, as millions of whites were leaving urban areas, the Great Migration of black people was ending, so there simply were no new African Americans to compensate for the loss of population; indeed, the rising trend was black migration to the suburbs and eventually back to the South. So after 1970 immigrants from Latin America were by far the most numerous group of people arriving in US cities.[28]

Finally, this is a transnational history. It regards the United States as a nation among nations—one that is exceptional in some respects but that must still contend with many other nations, as well as with entities that transcend the nation-state, such as corporations, political movements, religious groups, and migrants. Nation-states and borders are not fading relics in an age of accelerating globalization; on the contrary, issues of sovereignty, citizenship, and the policing of frontiers have only intensified of late. But we must also recognize that the growing interdependencies among nations in the new millennium have constrained the power of governments. The United States has not been able to control migration, dictate policy to foreign governments, or, above all, contend honestly with its profound economic dependence on a foreign-born labor force.[29]

BARRIO AMERICA IS the story of how more than twenty-five million Hispanic migrants and immigrants saved vast areas of American cities, repopulating neighborhoods and revitalizing economies that had been in decline for decades. They managed this even though most had to struggle against poverty, discrimination, xenophobia, and self-defeating immigration policy. Had it not been for this influx of Latinas and Latinos, many more US cities would have suffered the kind of catastrophic population loss and economic decline that led to the abandoned buildings and ghostly downtowns featured in collections of "ruins photography" like *American Ruins* and *Lost Detroit*. These newcomers could not solve all the problems of the nation's cities, but they achieved something extraordinary in the way they used their labor, their capital, and their culture to create a new urban America.[30]

History written on a grand scale runs the risk of effacing the humanity and contingency out of which it is made. A story that involves millions of people can lose sight of actual men and women and children and their hopes and fears and plans. An account that unfolds over fifty years may underplay the importance of crucial decisions and key turning points that opened up or restricted future possibilities. A process that includes many different locations in various towns, cities, states, and nations might seem to have little regard for particularities of place. And a tale that ends with great things achieved can make it seem as if those achievements were easy or inevitable.

This history will therefore be grounded in the experiences of the people who so dramatically transformed their neighborhoods and their lives—as revealed in dozens of interviews recorded over a period of twenty years. If a journey of a thousand miles begins with a single step, a tale of migration must start with stories of people on the move. People like José Luis Loera, who grew up in a Mexico City shantytown "known as the lost neighborhood, 'Los Barrios Perdidos,' where there's no light, no water or anything. Where one needs to fight in order to survive"—and who set off for the United States because he "wanted to see if the country of liberties, expression, and everything really existed." The story must continue with people moving between nations, like the Ortiz family as they crossed the border into Texas: "There we were, like all migrants, knowing the danger of the voyage but always with hope, and the dream of seeing what it would be like to live on the other side." And it must reflect apprehension and uncertainty like that of five-year-old Rosina Magaña, who on her first day in Chicago was impressed by the look of her new neighborhood and the colors of the leaves in autumn, but who still felt anxious about the move: "I was kind of scared because, you know, it was a new world to me." [31]

PART ONE

THERE GOES
THE NEIGHBORHOOD

CHAPTER 1

NEIGHBORHOODS ON THE EDGE

"THE THINGS WE DID WERE WRONG," HE EXPLAINED many years later. "I know I violated the law, and I know that the people were a hundred percent in support. Believe me, I didn't do anything that was unusual. I wasn't a renegade. I was doing what I was delegated to do by the people in the community."[1]

More than half a century before, in 1960, Richard A. Dolejs had been working at the family business with his father and brother. The real estate firm of Andrew R. Dolejs & Sons had two offices, one located in the heart of the South Lawndale neighborhood and the other on the main street of the adjacent Lower West Side. Dolejs was deeply involved in local affairs. He was a member of the chamber of commerce, served as president of the local real estate board, and would soon be appointed secretary of the local community council. He sponsored a Little League baseball team every year and volunteered as a referee for the local boys' basketball league. And when Mayor Richard J. Daley came to visit the neighborhood, his family was prominent enough to receive the courtesy of a photo opportunity. Dolejs was, in short, a pillar of the community.[2]

Like almost all his neighbors in South Lawndale, he descended from central Europeans who had arrived beginning in the late nineteenth century and found work in the factories and railroads that surrounded the area on every side. German, Czech, and Polish immigrants had built and then filled the local Catholic parishes, established fraternal lodges and other community groups, and organized a formidable local branch of the city's political machine. They considered the neighborhood theirs, and generally liked it the way it was.[3]

But by 1961, Dolejs had a problem. His neighbors were moving out of the area faster than ever before. For decades, South Lawndale had been shedding population. This had been a gradual process of a hundred families per year buying homes in the suburbs, and local people did not think of it as a crisis. But things were reaching a boiling point. New people were moving into the area, and most of the old-timers didn't much like the look of them.[4]

In response, Dolejs set out to save South Lawndale. Some of his efforts involved a fairly well-recognized genre of good-natured real estate hucksterism. Others borrowed from a long American tradition of local boosters who tirelessly promoted the particular virtues of their communities. But he also pursued solutions of a rather different kind—solutions that would leave Dolejs ambivalent and sometimes ashamed when he recalled them five decades later.

The history of South Lawndale in the early 1960s, and of the Dallas neighborhood of Oak Cliff in those same years, shows that the urban crisis was more than just a story of black and white. "Persons of Spanish surname" lived right on the racial fault lines of many cities, and their experiences in Chicago and Dallas reveal a longer and more complex history of metropolitan America. In the period before large-scale immigration from Latin America, they occupied a racial borderland. They might be grouped statistically or socially with "Negroes" in a lower racial caste of "nonwhites," or understood as ethnics, "foreign stock" who were mostly akin to "whites." Until sometime after 1965, their racial status remained unclear and, amid the era's tensions between civil rights and massive resistance, that mattered a great deal.[5]

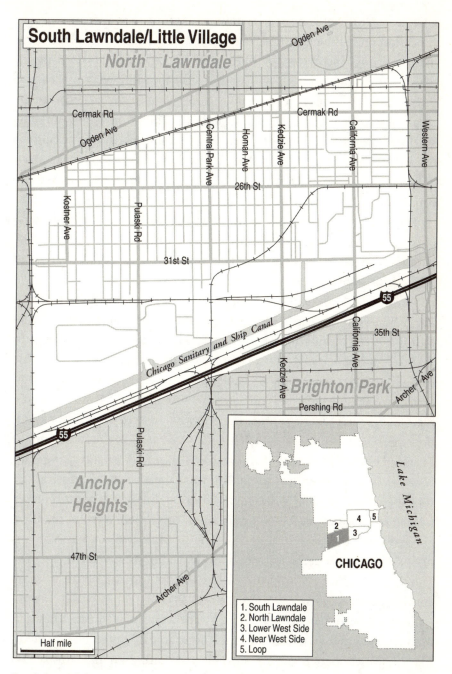

South Lawndale/Little Village

North Lawndale

Ogden Ave

Cermak Rd

Cermak Rd

Ogden Ave

Central Park Ave

Homan Ave

Kedzie Ave

California Ave

Western Ave

Kostner Ave

Pulaski Rd

26th St

31st St

55

Chicago Sanitary and Ship Canal

California Ave

35th St

Kedzie Ave

Brighton Park

Archer Ave

Pershing Rd

55

Pulaski Rd

Anchor
Heights

Lake Michigan

4 5

2 3

1

CHICAGO

47th St

Archer Ave

Half mile

1. South Lawndale
2. North Lawndale
3. Lower West Side
4. Near West Side
5. Loop

South Lawndale, more commonly known as Little Village, was one of several neighborhoods on Chicago's West Side that saw rapid demographic change in the second half of the twentieth century. Map by Philip Schwartzberg, Meridian Mapping, Minneapolis.

CHICAGO HAD LONG been a racially divided city. For decades, African American men, women, and children had been effectively barred from living outside ghettos where they paid outrageously inflated prices for cramped, dilapidated, and unsafe housing. But with the rise of the postwar civil rights movement, African Americans nationwide increasingly took action against housing discrimination as a moral and legal violation of the long-preached but seldom-practiced principle of equality. The courage and determination of civil rights demonstrators inspired Chicago's black citizens to be more insistent in pressing for equal access to housing and in demanding action from their elected representatives. They saw the opportunity to become homeowners, or at least to live in parts of the city that offered larger and better-maintained homes, quieter and cleaner streets, and less overcrowded schools for their sons and daughters.[6]

Clyde and Lillie Ross and their new baby were one such family. Clyde was the son of sharecroppers in small-town northern Mississippi. After serving in the army, in 1947 he moved to Chicago in search of a less racially oppressive environment and a better job. He soon found a position on the assembly line at the Campbell Soup Company. It was "a cheap job," he remembered, "but it was a steady job." Some years later he met and married Lillie, and when she announced she was expecting in 1961, they resolved to find a new place to live. They decided that the apartment they had been sharing with relatives was too cramped a place to raise their child. The first house they looked at was in a white neighborhood, but it was far too pricey for the family budget. A real estate agent took them around the West Side, where they found a two-flat that, while still expensive, was about half the price. They struck a deal and soon moved into the North Lawndale community area, just across Cermak Road from its southern counterpart.[7]

When South Lawndale's white residents looked north, they felt anxious. North Lawndale had once been an all-white neighborhood like theirs, though predominantly Jewish rather than Catholic. As black people had begun to purchase and rent homes over the decade prior, many of its previous residents had left the area. Some tried to create an integrated community, but they mostly failed to persuade their white neighbors to stay. In just a few years the area went from predominantly white to overwhelmingly African American; by 1960 more than 90 percent of North Lawndale's residents were black.[8]

The people of South Lawndale worried that the same could happen in their neighborhood. Like most white Americans they had been raised in a culture in which African Americans were objects of ridicule or personifications of crime. Racist jokes were told constantly on the radio, at the local tavern, and on the playground. Blackface acts were a staple of stage and screen—the 1942 movie *Yankee Doodle Dandy*, for example, had emphasized national unity during wartime but featured a musical number in which its star, James Cagney, and his entire film family danced and sang with black makeup on their faces and huge lips drawn on in greasepaint. Little wonder, then, that the streets of the neighborhood were rife with racial ignorance and suspicion.

These fears would soon be ratcheted up. Over the years that followed, both the Chicago city council and the Illinois state legislature considered whether to enact open housing laws that would prohibit discrimination in the sale and purchase of real estate. The debate became sharpest in 1961, when the state's general assembly drafted, debated, and voted on an antidiscrimination bill, and again leading up to 1963, when Chicago's aldermen did the same in the form of a city ordinance—this even though, at the behest of Mayor Daley, the law applied narrowly and contained minimal means of enforcement.[9]

South Lawndale quickly emerged as a hotbed of resistance to any kind of antidiscrimination law. The area's property brokers had already been fighting "incursions" into the neighborhood through the South Lawndale Real Estate Board (SLREB), which was backed by representatives from twenty-five local firms. The organization's goal, the *Chicago Tribune* gingerly explained in a 1960 article, was "to prevent area dwellings from being sold 'to individuals who are threats to community prosperity.'" The real estate board worked in conjunction with the Home Owners Prevention Enterprise (HOPE), which had been established in the same year and coordinated its activities out of offices on Twenty-Sixth Street.[10]

It was abundantly clear what sort of "individuals" these groups considered to be "threats," but a team of local researchers removed any doubt when they issued a report spelling it out: these organizations, they explained, had been formed "to keep the Negroes out of the area." Within a few years, South Lawndale had given rise to a whole range of groups that vocally opposed antidiscrimination measures. In August 1963, representatives of the South Lawndale Conservation Association and the Property Owners Council of Chicago, which also had headquarters on Twenty-Sixth Street, testified before the Chicago city council's judiciary committee. Officials expected the hearing to be so contentious that the police department reportedly planned to send fifty officers in case the groups tried to pack the room with their supporters. The following month the SLCA's leader, Howard Scaman, presided over a huge meeting at the Chicago Sheraton Hotel at which fifty organizations, including some of the most prominent in South Lawndale, planned a public protest against the proposed antidiscrimination ordinance.[11]

These associations, their spokesmen, and their allies strenuously denied any intent to discriminate and tried to prove it by using racially neutral language. F. L. Majka, a member of the SLREB, testified at a 1961 city council meeting that he was opposed to any open housing statute because "such a law takes away the freedom of man, whatever his color." Others were at pains to emphasize that their opposition had nothing to do with black people but was instead motivated by concern that open-occupancy laws would "lead to socialism" or "take away the property rights of the people of my neighborhood." But it was Scaman who most clearly strained the plausibility of race-neutral usage when he claimed in a 1963 hearing that "the productive people of the City of Chicago would flee" if the law were passed—though admittedly Scaman's statement was less flagrant than that of former White Circle League president Joseph Beauharnais, who at that same hearing declared, "White men will never be mongrelized," before being ruled out of order.[12]

Few people were fooled by these circumlocutions, of course, least of all the city's black journalists. When the *Chicago Defender* published an article about another gathering of protesters from South Lawndale, it ran under the headline "Racists to March on City Hall," and opened with the lede: "The foes of fair housing legislation are marshalling their forces to keep Negroes out of lily-white neighborhoods."[13]

The *Defender* was right. The truth was that, at the grass roots, white people in South Lawndale were fervently opposed to open-occupancy laws, let alone integration. In 1961 local clergy working in the neighborhood reported that as African American families sought to move in from the north, whites were "experiencing something of a 'sense of siege.'" Some of them were so furious that they tried to drag their religious leaders into the argument. At the 1963 judiciary committee meeting, for example, Scaman went so far as to say that "most Catholic clergy he had spoken to were against antidiscrimination laws" but were afraid to speak out for fear of being called racist. Church officials were sufficiently offended by this claim that they specifically rebutted the charge in a public statement. Some South Lawndale residents even expected local clergy to *assist* them in maintaining the color line: one minister later reported that HOPE members had approached a local pastors' group to ask for help in intimidating a biracial couple into leaving the neighborhood. Few in South Lawndale doubted that outright violence might soon come to their neighborhood. After all, most people could remember the massive white riot that had broken out when a black family tried to move into an apartment a few miles to the west.[14]

RICHARD DOLEJS THUS stood on precarious and shifting terrain as he tried to figure out how to manage the tense situation in South Lawndale. He likely shared some of the racial preconceptions of his neighbors—not many whites in Chicago could claim to be true egalitarians, fewer still on the West Side. But he was uncomfortable with local efforts to exclude black families categorically, and he rejected the use of violence as morally wrong—and also because he believed that it would be counterproductive: racist rioting would only prove that local leaders had lost control, leading people to move out even more quickly than before.[15]

His initial effort, which began in 1963, involved an elaborate exercise in public relations. Believing that South Lawndale was easily confused with North Lawndale, Dolejs and other local notables tried to change people's sense of the neighborhood by renaming it. In searching for a new name, he drew on his and the community's roots. Dolejs's grandparents had immigrated from Bohemia, and he remained attached to his ethnic identity. His collection of memorabilia from the era includes an affectionately satirical list, entitled "The Bohemian Creed," that emphasized personal thrift ("Save all brown paper bags, strings, rope, jars and all other valuable and usable articles"), household economy ("Build a 2 flat and live in basement . . . you can get more rent for the first and second floor than for renting the basement"), and especially the importance of picking mushrooms ("Camouflage all houby hunting equipment from neighbors. Proceed to secret place for houby with caution, i.e., drive through alleys, around the block several times, down wide streets to ensure you are not being followed by neighbors").[16]

The name "Little Village" expressed this sense of central European ethnicity by evoking the kind of peasant hamlet that many of Dolejs's Bohemian and Polish immigrant-stock neighbors remembered or imagined as their place of origin in the old country. As he explained in a newspaper interview, the name was inspired by "the idea to kindle a spirit of renewal along the lines of the Old World tradition. . . . If we can influence others to help upgrade the area, we feel we will be able to save the community and develop a feeling of pride in our neighborhood." Dolejs immediately set about publicizing the new name and soon devised an emblem: a patch of houby mushrooms in the foreground, a small European village in the background. He printed a wide variety of materials with the new name and image, from pamphlets to banners to local business directories. He also built a central European identity into the landscape by constructing a new facade on an entire city block in a vernacular Bohemian architectural style, complete with half timbers and gingerbread trim.[17]

This campaign was not racially innocent, of course. The emphasis on European identity drew an implicit contrast with the African American neighborhood to the north. As he strove to establish the new name among longtime residents, Dolejs found himself working alongside the same groups that had been fighting open-occupancy laws—some of which, including SLREB and HOPE, adopted the new name immediately. And not surprisingly, the people whom "Little Village" was intended to exclude did not hesitate to identify its racial implications. "This is to assure the white community that we aren't part of the black community," a local woman later explained in an article in the *Defender*.[18]

Ultimately, the campaign met with mixed success. The plan to renovate the streetscape was short-lived: the second building facade was never finished, and the elaborate cladding was soon removed from the first. The name "Little Village" stuck, however. Within a few years, it became the preferred usage throughout the locality, and when people in the neighborhood refer to it today, they invariably use the newer term. But the underlying purpose of the entire effort—to keep long-time residents committed to staying—remained unfulfilled, as the departure of the old-timers showed no sign of abating. Thankfully for Dolejs and his neighborhood, though, a new group of urban villagers was arriving from elsewhere in the city.

BY THE TIME Guadalupe Lozano was born in 1953, her family had already lived in Chicago for two generations. Her grandfather had come from Mexico to work in the city's railway shops; her grandmother, who arrived some years later, cleaned houses for a living. The family lived on Taylor Street in one of the city's most storied immigrant neighborhoods, a place where a small Mexican *colonia* lived among Greeks, Italians, Jews, and African Americans. Lozano's parents had met while her Tejano father was stationed in Chicago during his army service.[19]

The family moved to South Lawndale in the late 1950s. They settled at the northernmost edge of the neighborhood, just south of the Burlington Railway tracks near the corner of Cermak Road and Sacramento Avenue. Lozano remembered that they were "one of the first Latino families to live in Little Village." And indeed, a few years later the census counted just over one thousand people of "Spanish surname or mother tongue" in the community, with slightly over three-quarters of Mexican ancestry and the others claiming Puerto Rican heritage. Together they accounted for only 1–2 percent of the local population.[20]

The neighborhood was a lonely and sometimes hostile place for these new residents. "Our neighbors were all white," Lozano recalled almost four decades later, "and they accepted you or they didn't accept you." Most did not, and Lozano recalled "a lot of discrimination" in various forms. Oftentimes she and her friends were chased out of public places where they wanted to play. "A lot of older people would call the police on us because we were at the back alley playing ball or if we went to the ballpark to play ball. . . . Families would call police if we played at the kiddie park." Others who lived in Little Village in those years echoed Lozano's memories. One recalled that when her friends would pass one elderly Polish neighbor on the stairs, she would hiss "Mexicans!" at them; another remembered that neighbors would constantly call them "dirty Mexicans." "Racism was awful over there," said Alicia Amador. "People cannot believe what we went through."[21]

Many of the area's white residents were clearly struggling to figure out how ethnic Mexicans and Puerto Ricans fit into a racial order that they understood as either black or white. Amador remembered taking her younger brother to a candy store on Twenty-Sixth Street. The shopkeeper served his white customers but studiously ignored the two Mexican American children waiting patiently at the counter. "Finally, I told the proprietor, 'We've been standing here. My brother wants to buy some candy.' And he said, 'We don't serve niggers here.'" Similarly, several Mexican women who moved into the area in the late 1950s and early 1960s remembered that white children regularly called them "niggers." And longtime resident Cathy Alaniz recalled a woman on her street referring to her niece as "that black Mexican."[22]

As the neighborhood's whites began to figure out where Mexican Americans and Puerto Ricans belonged in their racial picture, there emerged certain limits to how they could be treated. Lozano had lived in South Lawndale for a few years before the police saw fit to protect her. In 1961, when she was only eight years old, a white man who had been shouting at her out his window came and kicked her. An officer grabbed him and warned that he'd be thrown into jail if he went near her again. Although one might expect assault and battery on a little girl to result in immediate arrest rather than a warning, Lozano remembered it as a sign of progress in the context of that time and place: "That was the first time I remember something being done, being treated with respect or anything."[23]

Many more families like hers were moving into the neighborhood, mostly from elsewhere in Chicago. In 1961, city authorities had begun to clear land in the Near West Side for the new campus that became the University of Illinois at Chicago. In the process, they displaced hundreds of Mexican American families, and thousands of others were also driven from their homes. As a result, the Spanish-heritage population of South Lawndale—as well as of the neighborhood to the northeast—burgeoned within the space of just a few years. Perhaps the most important impact of these arrivals was less statistical than experiential: members of a previously small and isolated community could see clearly that their numbers were growing. "I started seeing more Latino faces," remembered Lozano. "There were a lot of Latino families moving into Twenty-Sixth Street."[24]

THESE NEWCOMERS LOOKED to Richard Dolejs like a lifeline for the neighborhood. He tried to make them feel welcome in Little Village by helping organize a local parade in 1964 to celebrate Mexican Independence Day. His real estate firm sponsored a car in the procession: a large Cadillac convertible with a line of Mexican national flags fastened to each side, festooned with bunting in the Mexican national colors, flying an American flag on the radio antenna, and displaying two more Mexican flags attached to the frame of the windshield. Inside the car, passengers wore outfits representing various aspects of Mexican national culture, from a boy in the elaborate and elegant *traje de charro* to women clad in serapes and sombreros. Traveling down Twenty-Sixth Street, the parade drew a crowd of onlookers that included ethnic Mexicans, black people, and whites. In addition to welcoming a new group of people to the neighborhood, the event drew customers to the area's main shopping district and publicly advertised Dolejs's real estate firm to the recent arrivals on whom he had pinned his hopes for the neighborhood.[25]

Dolejs also sought to bring a Mexican presence into the close-knit community life of Little Village. He arranged for a mariachi act to perform at the chamber of commerce's "Nite of Nights," a talent show in which tuxedoed emcees introduced local people performing musical numbers and theatrical skits. The event raised

Mexican Independence Day on Twenty-Sixth Street, 1964. Local leaders organized this parade and other events to attract new Hispanic residents to Little Village. But not everybody was welcome in the neighborhood. Photograph courtesy Richard Dolejs.

funds for local charities and created a sense of camaraderie among local people as it had before, but now it also served to extend a gesture of welcome to Dolejs's sought-after Mexican neighbors. The festivities reinforced the recent renaming of the neighborhood: event signage prominently featuring LITTLE VILLAGE broadened the symbolic content of the term to include Mexican folk traditions in the identity of the community. The idea of a Spanish-American musical performance in an ethnic neighborhood would have been familiar to everyone, since it came just a few years after *West Side Story* won ten Academy Awards in a televised event on which the "Nite of Nights" itself was based.[26]

There were also other clearer, more political precedents on which Dolejs was building. The most recent presidential election—the agonizingly close race between Senator John F. Kennedy and Vice President Richard M. Nixon—had involved the first-ever national mobilization of Hispanic voters. The Viva Kennedy campaign had been coordinated by the same Democratic Party committee that was charged with organizing "white ethnics"—that is, people who were largely the children and grandchildren of European immigrants, like Dolejs and his Czech and Polish neighbors. Mayor Daley himself had lobbied hard for Chicago to be the home of the 1959 Pan American Games and had helped organize Hispanic ethnic celebrations, including parades on Mexican Independence Day and Cinco de Mayo. This had been done with not inconsiderable duplicity, since the mayor was at the same time laying the groundwork to demolish the city's largest ethnic Mexican neighborhood—but that was just a day's work for the Daley machine.[27]

Neither parades nor pageantry, however, would decide the fate of Little Village—the neighborhood would rise or fall depending on the day-to-day work of buying and selling real estate. It would be the seemingly mundane transactions among property owners, aspiring householders, agents, and lenders that would determine who would go and who would stay. And the basic reality of real estate in Little Village in the mid-1960s was the continued exodus of white ethnics. "We had not only spaces in the commercial area, with 105 vacancies, but a lot of housing available," remembered Dolejs. "People were putting up their houses for sale, and very reasonably, very cheaply."[28]

A few prominent figures on the local real estate board, Dolejs among them, tried to persuade their colleagues that while housing demand and property values were indeed in decline, the solution to the problem was staring them all in the face. "We said, 'Well, what about the Mexican community? . . . You know, we should apply to that group and try to bring 'em in.'" Dolejs aggressively courted an ethnic Mexican clientele in a publicity campaign that also positioned his real estate firm as a leader in serving a growing community. His offices on Twenty-Sixth Street in Little Village and Eighteenth Street in the neighboring Lower West Side featured signage in both English and Spanish, and he hired bilingual employees, including two agents, Pedro and Enrique Villa, and a secretary, Josefina Velasco. Dolejs showcased the new agents in a series of formal photographs of his father and him shaking their hands; he also featured the three in the print advertisements for his firm that he placed in local newspapers. And as Hispanic business owners began to open shops in the neighborhood, Dolejs commissioned another series of posed photos: one shows him welcoming the proprietor of a new sporting goods store; in another he is smiling and clasping the hand of the Mexican American owner of the accommodatingly named Little Village Bakery.[29]

These early arrivals were overwhelmingly Mexican American and mostly transacted business in English. Velasco later recalled that few of the buyers she assisted while working at Dolejs & Sons in the early 1960s needed her to speak Spanish; five years later, however, she was working almost entirely in translation. In other words, it was only in the late 1960s that Mexican migrants came to predominate among newcomers to Little Village.[30]

Mexican Americans met Dolejs's appeals with enthusiasm. Paying rent was a low-risk strategy, but in the long run it basically meant pouring money down the drain. Ownership allowed people to turn their labor into property, to build equity and therefore accumulate wealth; indeed, for all Americans of that generation, purchasing a home was the surest path to greater prosperity.

Buying a house or shop was no simple task, however. For these newcomers, as today, real estate purchases were by far the largest transactions of their lifetimes. Primarily working-class people of modest means, they could not become homeowners without the proper financing. If they were to become the next generation of Little Village residents, they needed credit in the form of mortgages. It is here that we can begin to see the double edge of Dolejs's activities in the neighborhood. For beneath the welcoming of ethnic Mexicans to the area was a series of implicit exclusions that, taken as a whole, perfectly fit the definition of "conspiracy."[31]

At that time, lending was extremely discriminatory. Black people almost never received the mortgages for which their credit history and earnings would have qualified them had they been white. One reason was the prejudice of the virtually all-white ranks of mortgage brokers, but the rot went considerably deeper than the attitudes of individuals—it also involved systemic racism in the form of "redlining." According to national standards enshrined in the Federal Housing Administration's *Underwriting Manual*, no loan should be given that would place "inharmonious racial or nationality groups" in a neighborhood. In other words, these rules specified that the mere presence of African Americans in a white neighborhood would devalue the homes there and constitute a reason not to make any more loans in the area. One real estate manual explained the point with a telling comparison:

The prospective buyer might be a bootlegger who would cause considerable annoyance to his neighbors, a madam who had a number of call girls on her string, a gangster who wants a screen for his activities by living in a better neighborhood, a colored man of means who was giving his children a college education and thought they were entitled to live among whites. . . . No matter what the motive or character of the would-be purchaser, if the deal would institute a form of blight, then certainly the well-meaning broker must work against its consummation.

Even an unbiased bank officer would be instructed to avoid lending to black people outside of "their" ghettos—because doing so would threaten all the bank's other loans by devaluing the homes that served as collateral. And even when black families bought in neighborhoods that had become predominantly African American, they were still denied financing: for example, when Clyde Ross had sought a regular mortgage for his home in North Lawndale, the loan officer told him, "We don't finance in that area."[32]

The effect on aspiring black home buyers was horrendous. Unable to get the mortgage credit they deserved, they were forced either to buy into ghettos, where real estate prices were massively inflated, or to seek out alternative forms of credit. The most common of these were home sales "on contract." Contract buyers would have to sign documents requiring a substantial down payment, making them responsible for regular installment payments on a house, but not granting them title. According to such contracts, a buyer who missed a single payment would forfeit all equity and be left with nothing.[33]

Clyde and Lillie Ross had purchased their North Lawndale home under just such a contract. Not long after they moved in, the furnace went out, and they realized that they had no choice but to add 15 percent to their monthly payment to replace it—refusing this arrangement or missing a payment would mean losing the house forever. "I realized then that I was stuck for life," Clyde recalled. To keep up the monthly installments and pay for prenatal care for Lillie and the baby, he took a second job at night. Despite further expenses and surcharges from the contract seller, the Rosses managed to make all their payments over many years and eventually gained title to their home.[34]

Many other buyers, however, were not able to keep up. An exposé of contract sales on Chicago's West Side published by the *Chicago Daily News* in 1963 showed how such schemes worked. A reporter infiltrated the operations of Lou Fushanis, one of the city's most notorious real estate operators. He tried to sell to a black couple seeking a better home. "We have been leasing for so long, we've about paid for the building we're in," they explained when asked why they were willing to buy on contract. "We decided we wanted to own a place." For $19,000, Fushanis offered them a dilapidated tenement on which he promised to make repairs. "That's just something you say to pacify 'em," explained Fushanis's salesman. "Lou fixes some things, but he makes sure the purchaser gets stuck with most of the repairs." Moreover, Fushanis never intended to make them into homeowners. As one office secretary explained, "He loads them up with payments they can't meet, then he takes the property away from them." Even if buyers could keep up, sellers like Fushanis often contrived defaults by refusing to acknowledge receipt of a payment or imposing a surcharge and not informing the buyer of it until the day of the deadline. "He's sold some of these buildings three or four times," Fushanis's secretary admitted. Despite abundant evidence of fraudulent intent, Chicago courts overwhelmingly upheld such contracts. As a result, thousands of contract buyers lost their life savings as contract sellers used the city's real estate market as a means to legally plunder African Americans.[35]

Black people were far and away the primary targets of exploitation by Chicago contract sellers, but the uncertain position of ethnic Mexicans and Puerto Ricans in the city's racial order made them susceptible to victimization in much the same way. Contract buyers began to organize themselves later in the 1960s to collectively renegotiate their purchase agreements and warn others against the kinds of deception and fraud used against them. These groups were mostly run in English by and for African Americans, but a contract buyers' league for Spanish-speaking people was inaugurated on the West Side. In a subsequent federal trial of contract sellers on charges of civil rights violations, the defendants attempted to demonstrate that their corrupt business could not have been racially motivated because they had made some of their sales to people who were not black. If their practices were racially discriminatory, they argued, why were so many of their customers white? As evidence, they submitted lists of people who, they said, were whites to whom they had sold on contract—but the lists offered consisted almost entirely of Spanish-surnamed people. The defendants hoped that the court would ignore their predations against Hispanics by looking only at their census-assigned racial category. And that is exactly what happened: the judge in the case allowed the lists to be entered as evidence. "The court rules out allegations about other minorities," he wrote. "For purposes of this case the world is either black or white."[36]

To repopulate South Lawndale, Dolejs had to ensure that ethnic Mexicans received standard mortgages with fixed rates and terms. But the task still remained of persuading lenders to do so. He began with general entreaties. "I said, 'You know, you gotta make loans to these Mexican people that are coming in . . . if we're going to invite these new people into our community, we've gotta make financing available to them.'" Dolejs followed up by individually lobbying the neighborhood's leading lenders, most of whom he knew personally. This was important because in practice lending had no standardized formulas that determined who got a loan and who did not. Reputation, acquaintance, personal affect, and similar factors weighed heavily in lending decisions. This was especially the case with the kinds of small savings and loan operations that dominated the real estate market in Little Village—the owners of these local institutions had a major stake in preserving the market in the neighborhoods where they made loans. Though neighborhood lenders were not initially interested in Mexican Americans, whom they thought of as undesirable people of color in many ways akin to African Americans, Dolejs recalled that after a year or two of wheedling and cajoling some became convinced: "We finally got John Kuchera from Atlas Federal Savings & Loan, and Stanley Dvorak from Guaranty Savings & Loan, the Vaneck brothers from Civic Savings & Loan . . . eventually the best ones were Western Federal, the Novak brothers, they made loans for Mexican people. That was unheard-of before that."[37]

This did not mean, however, that mortgage credit was given freely in Little Village. The neighborhood's real estate community had a specific plan for where they wanted which people to live, and the means to carry it out—"methods that were totally illegal in today's light," Dolejs admitted. "For instance, we said, 'We'll sell to Mexicans, but we'll only sell to them up to Twenty-Third Street. They can buy anything that's available north of Twenty-Third Street.'" Meanwhile, lenders continued to exclude black people whenever possible by denying them mortgage credit entirely. "That was illegal, that was a violation of civil rights in its finest aspect," confessed Dolejs. "But at that time, we thought it was a good thing to do. We were trying to keep the community strong." Aspiring African American homeowners were left to seek shelter elsewhere, often in North Lawndale and other adjacent parts of the West Side.[38]

DOLEJS AND HIS cohorts were making a specific offer to the new residents of Little Village. They were being invited to join a community of "white ethnics" as ethnics themselves, not as people of color; that status was reserved for black people and was the basis for excluding them. The idea of ethnic Mexicans being defined as white was nothing new: US law had effectively classified them in this way since the Treaty of Guadalupe Hidalgo in 1848. But in practice the great majority of Mexicans were relegated to second-class citizenship, suffering all manner of de facto discrimination and segregation. In Little Village, they were being offered social status and clear economic benefits in exchange for serving as a bulwark against African Americans. This racial bargain was not necessarily explicit, but it was quite clear.[39]

What was not clear, however, was whether Latinos would accept the bargain, or whether they would question its terms and conditions. They had often occupied a racial terrain that, like them, was neither black nor white, and in Little Village their everyday experiences were often those of people of color rather than ethnics. One of the places this played out was in the neighborhood's schools, which, like so many other places, became sites of racial conflict in the middle of the twentieth century.

Guadalupe Lozano remembered having few opportunities for friendship in her virtually all-white elementary school. "I know I did not like school, and I really felt left out." She recalled her confusion and rejection: "You didn't understand why you felt you weren't wanted. Now I can remember, now I know. A lot of the kids were white, and they just didn't accept you if you weren't white." One episode in particular stuck out in her memory: "All the white girls would be inviting our friends to parties and I was never asked. One time I was asked, and I was very happy. I remember I was invited to the project . . . in Twenty-Six and Washtenauw, and I remember going there and I looked at one of the white houses, and I said, 'They [are] beautiful. Why couldn't we live in the project?'" The reason was that this was Lawndale Gardens, an all-white public housing project that had been built in the 1940s. But as a girl she didn't understand that.[40]

Lozano did not find it easier to make friends until she began attending a less segregated middle school on Chicago's rapidly changing West Side. "And then, when I attended John Spry, the majority were African American. They were coming from the other side of Cermak." Given the greater variety of people, she could branch out. "I think those were my best years because I had a lot of African American friends." As early as her preteen years, then, Lozano and other Mexican American and Puerto Rican children found it easier to identify with black youngsters than with white ones.[41]

Indeed, it was only later, in high school, that Lozano found herself amid a critical mass of students of color. At Harrison High, the complex and shifting jurisdictions of the neighborhood temporarily yielded a racially balanced student body: "The high school was half African American and then white and then Latino." Sometimes, she remembered, it seemed easier to just stick with one's own kind. But she had had friends from all three of the West Side's major ethnoracial groups and something impelled her to think more broadly, especially when, as a sophomore, she met the young man who would become her husband. He would not only accompany her into a life of political activism but also become a major player in the effort to change the terms of racial power in Chicago by brokering a political alliance among African Americans, Hispanics, and whites in city politics. For the time being, however, an uneasy alliance between white ethnics and Mexican Americans was taking hold.[42]

A FEW YEARS into Richard Dolejs's plan to "save" South Lawndale, it looked like a losing battle. More Mexican Americans were coming into the neighborhood, to be sure: the dozen or so families moving in every month kept Andrew R. Dolejs & Sons busy. But as encouraging and gratifying as this influx must have been to the young real estate agent, he must have seen that it was not nearly enough to offset the flight of local whites leaving the neighborhood. During the 1960s more than three hundred families were moving away each month. At this rate Dolejs would have renamed Little Village just in time for it to shrink to a very little village indeed.[43]

For Guadalupe Lozano and her newer Spanish-heritage neighbors, the situation was improved, though not ideal. They were indeed making homes in the neighborhood, many of them as first-time owners of their own dwellings. And she and others were finding ways to position themselves in the breach of the worsening racial divisions on Chicago's West Side. But many of the local white ethnics did not see the virtues of their new neighbors. A few years later, a locally produced report found that longtime residents "cannot hide a deep-seated anxiety concerning the changes they may bring in their own style of life and in the cultural and social atmosphere of the whole community." Despite protestations that they did not have anything against the newcomers personally, the authors of the report indicated that local whites saw the influx of "Mexicans, and to some extent the closeness of the blacks . . . as a threat to their very existence in every sense of the word."[44]

IN THESE VERY same years, the Oak Cliff neighborhood in Dallas was also wracked with conflict over race and residence. The area had long been overwhelmingly composed of white Anglos: in 1960 the census found that all but three of its twenty-one tracts were over 95 percent white and non-Hispanic. But Oak Cliff's white majority believed that their neighborhood was threatened because it was located along one of Dallas's racial borderlines. An adjacent black neighborhood ended abruptly at central Oak Cliff's eastern edge, with Ewing Avenue marking the limit of African American settlement. On the other side lived thousands of black families crowded into one of the few parts of Dallas where they were permitted to dwell.[45]

The area's racial complexity did not end there. Mexican Americans were legally classified as white, but this had not protected them

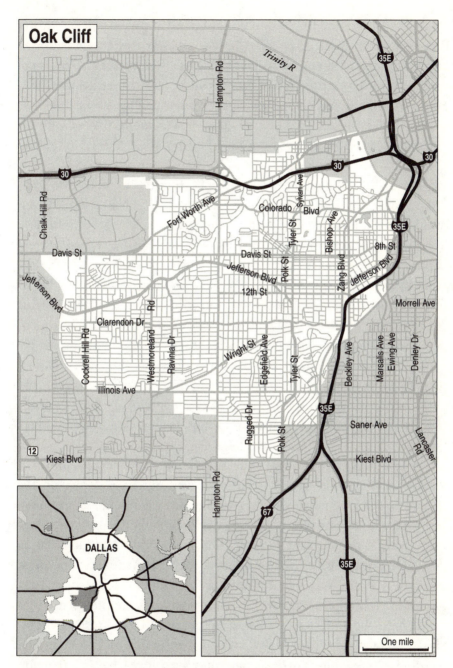

Oak Cliff

Trinity R

Hampton Rd

Chalk Hill Rd

35E

30

30

Fort Worth Ave

Colorado   Blvd

Sylvan Ave

Tyler St

Bishop Ave

8th St

35E

Davis St

Davis St

Polk St

Zang Blvd

Jefferson Blvd

Jefferson Blvd

Jefferson Blvd

12th St

Morrell Ave

Clarendon Dr

Wright St

Edgefield Ave

Tyler St

Beckley Ave

Marsalis Ave

Ewing Ave

Denley Dr

Westmoreland Rd

Ravinia Dr

Cockrell Hill Rd

Illinois Ave

Rugged Dr

Polk St

35E

Saner Ave

Lancaster Rd

12

Kiest Blvd

Kiest Blvd

DALLAS

Hampton Rd

67

35E

One mile

Dallas's Oak Cliff neighborhood prospered because it was located near a defense plant and connected to downtown by bridge and rail. The new interstate highways and state freeways of the 1950s and 1960s, however, made it easier for people to live outside Big D but still get to work in the city. The expressways also cordoned off communities of color to the north and east. Map by Philip Schwartzberg, Meridian Mapping, Minneapolis.

from discrimination in schools, at work, and in public places. During the war, for example, the Dallas-based Lonestar Restaurant Association had produced and distributed placards that read NO DOGS, NO NEGROES, NO MEXICANS, and they could be arbitrarily excluded anytime a boss, storekeeper, or police officer decided he didn't like their looks. But some ethnic Mexicans could live among whites without being subjected to the same kind of racist abuse visited on black householders.[46]

Oak Cliff offered an early example. Future city councilwoman Anita Martínez recalled that after the war all four of her sisters moved to the neighborhood. At that time the oldest and most recognizable Mexican American business in Dallas was El Fénix, whose owners opened their second restaurant in Oak Cliff in 1948. This is not to say that there was no anti-Mexican animosity in the neighborhood: florist Mary Jane Conde remembered that soon after she moved to Oak Cliff in 1952, one of the Anglo clients of the flower shop where she worked made disparaging remarks about how "they" were moving in, not realizing that the fair-complexioned Conde was herself Mexican American. Adding further complexity, in the 1950s Oak Cliff was the site of a Native American relocation center as part of the government's policy of breaking up Indigenous nations and moving their members to urban areas.[47]

As the civil rights struggle gained momentum, a small number of black families had begun to rent and even purchase homes on the white side of Ewing Avenue. They had grown weary of paying exorbitant rents for inferior housing in a city where even the resolutely conservative *Dallas Morning News* had for years run stories highlighting the severe shortage of decent housing for African Americans. Most of these families were members of the city's small black middle class, having managed despite pervasive discrimination to find secure jobs and amass the kind of savings needed to move to a "better" neighborhood. In fact, given that Oak Cliff was seen as one of the city's more working-class white districts, they may have been better off financially than many of their new neighbors. After years of protests during the 1950s, Dallas authorities had recently desegregated the state fairgrounds and city buses; these black families hoped that residential apartheid might be the next barrier to fall, and that they might be accepted as neighbors.[48]

They were soon disabused of any such notion by a campaign of harassment and threats. In the spring of 1960, a black insurance agent named H. L. Fagan moved with his wife into a home in the eastern part of Oak Cliff. One night that summer, at 1:00 a.m., a group of white men built a cross out of wood, carried it into the Fagans' front yard, and stood it up on the lawn. They were about to set it aflame when Mrs. Fagan came outside. The intruders promptly scattered, but she was by no means finished. She ran into the bedroom and woke her husband, who had apparently been expecting trouble, since he had a pistol ready at hand. Fagan ran outside, and seeing the perpetrators packed into a car driving down the block, fired several shots at them as they sped away.[49]

Acts of racial intimidation were by no means unexpected in Oak Cliff. The police department took measures to prepare for the possibility of civil unrest: they instituted a course in anti-riot techniques at the Oak Cliff substation and sent a contingent of officers to Little Rock, Arkansas, to confer with law enforcement officials who had recent experience with racist mobs. The Dallas police also put in orders for spotlights, loudspeakers, tear gas, and other equipment useful in quelling civil disorder.[50]

Oak Cliff was just one of many racial flash points in Dallas at that time. Inspired by the lunch counter sit-ins in Greensboro, North Carolina, the city's African American leadership and young protesters affiliated with the NAACP organized a sit-in at the lunch counter of the H. L. Green drugstore; civil disobedience soon spread to an S. H. Kress lunch counter. Results were mixed, with some black protesters receiving service at the main counter, others being asked to move, and still others being served at first but subsequently ignored. Even so, the campaign of direct action for equality was spreading.[51]

Dallas's white leaders scrambled to coordinate a peaceful desegregation of public places in consultation with civil rights leaders. Together they formed the Committee of 14, evenly divided between black and white representatives. Through the rest of 1960 and into the year that followed, civil rights activists, city leaders, and business owners involved themselves in negotiations, boycott threats, public picketing, and more negotiations in hopes of finding a way forward without violence. The city fathers had worked hard to attract outside investment and federal spending, and they feared that the kinds of assaults and killings that had convulsed communities in Alabama and Mississippi would shatter Dallas's carefully cultivated image of civic peace. Race riots were bad for business.[52]

Meanwhile, school desegregation had created another potential arena for confrontation. After initially stating that they would act in accordance with the *Brown v. Board of Education* decision, Dallas school officials employed a series of delaying tactics. They insisted, for example, that no action was needed in schools with both Hispanic and African American students but no Anglos. Since Mexican Americans were legally classified as white, they claimed, such schools were already in compliance. Faced with a federal court order in 1960, they offered a plan so ploddingly gradual that it would not achieve full desegregation for more than a decade. Meanwhile, officials at city hall continued to negotiate with demonstrators and school parents in an effort to achieve some kind of broadly acceptable solution—by which they meant token desegregation and the maintenance of public order.[53]

Other local officials were less subtle. T. Whitfield Davidson, a Dallas-based US district judge, issued a ruling in the summer of 1960 that shocked not just the city's integrationists and its reluctant gradualists but even many of its passive segregationists. Davidson began his legal opinion with restrained doctrinal language, splitting hairs in an effort to minimize what was required by existing rulings from the federal judiciary. A few pages later, however, he lurched into an outright defense of white supremacy. He offered a "history" of the antebellum South in which slaveholders had been benevolent and enslaved black people responded to the Emancipation Proclamation with tears because they loved their masters and were reluctant to leave them. Davidson went on to explain that during post–Civil War Reconstruction in Texas, black people were kept from the voting booth not mainly by threats of lynching from the Ku Klux Klan and other practitioners of terror, but because local whites had simply "persuaded some of the old-time darkies to stay away from the polls."[54]

Davidson's opinion soon turned from retrograde history to racial incitement as he revealed his absolute conviction that school desegregation was not about education at all, but rather interracial sex. After a lengthy disquisition on the importance of racial purity from ancient Egypt to modern America, Davidson concluded that integrated education was "in all probability the most direct and surest route to amalgamation which in the long run is the most objectionable of all features of integration." He then wondered what might happen "if an overgrown Negro boy in an integrated school should be by premature growth inclined to sex and should write verses on the blackboard of an obscene character designedly for the white girls to read or should make improper approaches to them." This, not the niceties of legal doctrine, was why the judge and many other whites believed that racial integration must be resisted, certainly through bureaucratic obstruction—it took more than a year for the circuit court to overrule Davidson and for him to concede the point—and possibly through large-scale violence. After all, whipping up white fears of black male sexuality had always been a prelude to lynching.[55]

The city's leadership, fearing that Dallas might descend into chaos, took action to ensure an orderly desegregation by launching a massive campaign of public persuasion and reassurance. The highest-profile part of this effort was a twenty-two-minute motion picture entitled *Dallas at the Crossroads*. Ordered by the Dallas Citizens' Council at the urging of the department store magnate Stanley Marcus, the film was produced by Sam Bloom, a leading advertising executive, and narrated by Walter Cronkite, with an appearance by Dallas mayor Earl Cabell. It was shown throughout the city and broadcast on local television, and screenings were coordinated with the distribution of one hundred thousand pamphlets under the same title, including in the pay envelopes of municipal employees.[56]

Dallas at the Crossroads presented the city as a place of prosperity and contentment. Jaunty music played over scenes of well-dressed people strolling downtown, automobiles speeding along expressways, fans cheering at a football game, and young couples getting married and buying homes and raising children. "We call our town Big D," explained the voice-over, "because it is big-hearted, open-handed, both friendly and progressive." This theme of progress was front and center as the scene shifted to an old-timer sharing memories of the city when its main street was a dirt road and horses and mules pulled wagons. "Dallas has never stopped changing between then and now," he offered comfortingly. As the sprightly background music quickly faded out, his tone grew concerned: "Change is not always easy. As we change the face of Dallas, it is our responsibility to see that it is changed for the better. For what we have created, we can also destroy."

The next section of the film amounted to a masterpiece of circumlocution that addressed race and segregation in Dallas so gingerly that those words were not even used, nor were the city's problems mentioned except by implication: "Other cities have faced, and faced recently, the same problems of change which Dallas now faces." The location promptly moved to Little Rock and New Orleans. As federal troops stood guard, children arrived for their first day of desegregated schooling only to face mobs of local whites seething with anger and shouting threats. "They have met these problems with violence," Cronkite said sternly. "The face of violence is the face of hate, unreason, cruelty, personal and civic irresponsibility. Their actions and the results speak in these films for themselves." The narrator then fell silent as the screen filled with scenes of incipient disorder: crowds of white women, many of them holding toddlers in their arms, screamed and jeered at the black children entering the schools; one woman kicked a man in the crowd, another engaged in shoving, and still another raised her arm and struck a cameraman.

Returning to Dallas, the film's setting changed to the city court. A senior judge, wearing his robes of office, explained things matter-of-factly: "Once a decision has been made, it is the law." Now that the federal courts had overruled Judge Davidson and issued their final verdict, desegregation was to begin when schools reopened that fall. He acknowledged that some members of the public might raise objections, but he dismissed them, warning gravely that "the law is the law. Disagreement or dissatisfaction with any law should not and it must not be expressed by citizens in violence." By setting only two alternatives before the public, the judge reiterated the stark choice implied by the film's title.

Leaving no doubt as to which was the proper path, *Dallas at the Crossroads* lined up a series of authority figures to make the point repeatedly. Following the testimony from men in suits and uniforms, Cronkite summed it up for the audience: "On these principles Dallas stands. On these principles the leadership of Dallas is firm. Through the bar association, the medical society, the council of churches, the labor council, from its elected officials and its newspapers, Dallas has found many voices but with a single message." The mayor then delivered the message. "We need all of our citizens to accept their civic and their personal responsibilities and to stand up and be counted for law and order." The film concluded with scenes of babies, schoolchildren, Boy Scouts, parades, and flags as a choir sang "America the Beautiful."

Dallas at the Crossroads was a sincere work of advocacy. Yet it was fundamentally flawed in that actual black people were virtually absent from the film even though their struggle for equality had raised the issue and they were the ones most at risk. Perhaps the film's creators simply knew their audience—white people talking to white people may have been most persuasive at a time when it was whites who were poised to go forth and do harm. And the repeated insistence on rule-following and peace—the word "law" was spoken nineteen times in the film, the term "violence" seventeen times—only highlighted the fears of so many Dallasites that their city might be on the precipice of massive civil disorder and widespread bloodshed.

THE URBAN CRISIS came to the notice of many Americans only when, just a few years later, riots broke out in places like Harlem, Watts, Detroit, and Newark. In the decades since, many more have come to imagine the departure of millions of whites to the suburbs as a response to the breakdown of civil order in the cities. In some variants of this tale, white flight is interpreted as a "backlash" against the emergence of more radical voices within the civil rights movement. These narratives make it seem as if the urban crisis was simply a case of race relations gone wrong.[57]

A closer look at the era reveals a more complicated story, however. The problems of the cities began earlier and were more complex both economically and ethnoracially. The travails of urban America did indeed mostly involve white Anglos and African Americans—not surprisingly, since as of 1960 they accounted for nearly 96 percent of the nation's population; only about 4 percent of Americans were Spanish-surnamed. But in cities where Hispanics lived, certain patterns and proclivities emerged that seemed to foretell how things would play out amid the large-scale Latin American migrations that began toward the end of that decade and swelled the nation's Latino population from fewer than six million to nearly sixty million people. Before we move forward to that story, however, we must examine why South Lawndale, Oak Cliff, and so many other neighborhoods began to fall into such dire straits—we will need to take a more multicultural look at the dawn of the urban crisis.[58]

CHAPTER 2

THE CITY OF YESTERYEAR

AMERICA'S CITY LIGHTS HAD NEVER SHONE SO BRIGHTLY AS they did around 1950. The nation's ten biggest metropolises— New York City, Chicago, Philadelphia, Los Angeles, Detroit, Baltimore, Cleveland, St. Louis, Washington, DC, and Boston—all boasted more inhabitants than at any time in their histories. The same was true of cities of every size, from Buffalo (fifteenth most populous) to Kansas City (twentieth) to Louisville (thirtieth) to Omaha (fortieth) to Worcester, Massachusetts (fiftieth), all the way down to Phoenix, Arizona, and Allentown, Pennsylvania (ninety-ninth and one hundredth). An unprecedented proportion of Americans lived in cities around midcentury: nearly two-thirds of the total population, including almost one-third who lived in urban areas of more than one hundred thousand residents.[1]

Cities were the nation's economic powerhouses. They were where goods were manufactured out of steel and wood and glass and rubber, where livestock and crops were brought to market, and where products of all kinds were loaded onto trucks, trains, and ships that carried them across the country and around the world. So many factory floors, office buildings, warehouses, shops, and other workplaces were concentrated within city limits that most of America's gross national product was produced in a tiny percentage of its inhabited area. And thanks to abundant jobs, the strength of labor unions, and the lack of foreign competition from a globe still shattered by World War II, this prosperity was broadly shared among most American workers—especially those who lived in cities, where incomes were higher, dwellings were newer, and schools, libraries, and hospitals were more plentiful than in rural areas. In the era of the urban industrial economy, the people of the United States had made themselves into the most highly paid workers the world had ever seen.[2]

Even the ways in which people learned about the world were heavily urbanized. Radio and television broadcasting, book publishing, journalism, advertising, and motion picture production were all concentrated in regional metropolises and later, as national networks consolidated, in New York City, Chicago, and Los Angeles. So when people broke news stories, wrote books and articles and advertising copy, or flicked on studio microphones and rolled cameras, they overwhelmingly did so in the heart of the city. The popular imagination of the day regularly hearkened back to farms and small towns, often in a mythical past; these were, after all, the peak years of the Western on both the silver and the small screen. But if you wanted to see where Americans actually went to live and work and play, it was in cities—a fact faithfully reflected in blockbuster films like *Sunset Boulevard* and *On the Waterfront* and in the most-watched television shows of the era, *The Honeymooners* and *I Love Lucy*, all of which were set in urban centers.

As important and indicative as population counts and economic statistics and popular culture remain, there are other ways to discover the history of cities. To understand what they meant to their residents, we need to see both the big picture of American urban history and the street-level view from the kinds of places where people made their homes and lived their daily lives—that is, their neighborhoods. People spent most of their time and money in communities like these—in sidewalk chats with family and friends on playing fields and in schoolyards, at churches and parish halls, or on the way to the grocery store or the bank or the five-and-dime. The neighborhood was where people experienced and understood their place in the city and the nation. It is here that we can most closely observe urban America in its heyday and understand why so many people had chosen to live in big cities.

CHICAGO WAS THE foremost exemplar of the industrial belt that stretched from the East Coast into the Ohio River Valley and the Great Lakes. Other cities shared key elements of Chicago's geography, from its dependence on lake and river navigation to its industrial base of employment, including other Great Lakes cities like Cleveland, Detroit, Milwaukee, Buffalo, Duluth, and Gary and river cities like Pittsburgh, Cincinnati, St. Louis, Kansas City, and Omaha. The Windy City was simply the largest and most economically successful of these.

Manufacturing and transportation supplied the largest share of jobs for urban denizens, with factories, ports, and railroads defining the urban scene. Working people in heavy coveralls, aprons, and tool belts, smelling of smoke or machine oil or slaughterhouse floors slick with blood, were a constant presence on Chicago sidewalks. They made the industrial machinery run, processed the grain and lumber and meat, and loaded the resultant products into boxcars and trailers and ships' holds. The sheer scale of these operations also required elaborate accounting just to keep track of all the things produced and transported—so in addition to mostly male industrial workers there were supervisors who coordinated them, clerks who kept records, and a bevy of men and women who supplied housing, food, clothing, and a wide variety of services.

Chicago's development long predated industrialization, but from an early date the city's growth depended on a large-scale combination of labor and technology. Its location where the river met the lake had made it an important Native American trading point for centuries, a role that it retained as Europeans began to colonize the area. Even before the city was incorporated in 1837, however, entrepreneurs and local legislators proposed an ambitious infrastructure project: a canal system that would join Lake Michigan to the Mississippi River and thereby allow Chicago to dominate the entire region's grain market. Completed in 1848, the canal would fuel urban growth as its volume of waterborne trade grew for more than four decades.[3]

The railroad industry further energized the city's development. As the region's most important rail transportation hub, Chicago became a transfer point and market for a wide variety of commodities in the 1850s. Chicago's railways and waterways allowed the city's grain, lumber, and cattle operations to gather goods from a vast hinterland of fields, forests, and ranches; to process those goods on an industrial scale in enormous grain elevators, lumber mills, and slaughterhouses; and then to ship them to markets hundreds or even thousands of miles away. Chicago's role as an entrepôt and emporium for the West led to explosive growth, and by 1890, little more than fifty years after its incorporation, it had become the nation's second-biggest city.[4]

By then, newer and heavier industries had emerged in Chicago, propelling further urban growth well into the twentieth century. The McCormick Company had made reapers in the city for some time, leading similar manufacturers to build factories there. This led to a concentration of agricultural machinery production that employed tens of thousands of Chicagoans by the early twentieth century. Meanwhile, the city's strategic position astride multiple lines and modes of transportation prompted the fast-growing steel industry to locate production in the Windy City. United States Steel's South Chicago plant was only the best known of various steel mills in and around the city. The makers of rails, machinery, tools, train cars, and countless other products fashioned from steel were likewise drawn to Chicago. The city also boasted a strong light manufacturing sector, with clothing, electrical equipment, and other areas helping to diversify its economy.[5]

All these industries depended on a workforce of migrants and immigrants. The United States had received over twenty million newcomers between 1880 and 1920, about 90 percent of them from Europe, since Asian immigration had been almost totally prohibited by a series of restrictions that began in 1882. Chicago was one of the nation's premier destinations for these migrants, and by 1910 the city had eight hundred thousand foreign-born residents. They made up more than one-third of the city's population; adding in their children raised the immigrant-stock total to a remarkable four out of every five Chicagoans. The biggest groups among them were from Germany, Austria-Hungary, Russia, Ireland, and Italy. (Poland would have figured more prominently had the country not been partitioned at that time.) From 1890 to 1910, the number of Italians in the city increased eightfold and the population of Jews sixteenfold; in these same years African American migrants more than tripled the city's black population. They established a variety of neighborhoods; most of them were a mix of various nationalities, though there were strong concentrations of particular ethnicities in some areas, places that became known as Polonia and Greektown and Jewtown. This was the Chicago of Carl Sandburg's 1914 poem "Chicago":[6]

> *Hog Butcher for the World,*
> *Tool Maker, Stacker of Wheat,*
> *Player with Railroads and the*
>   *Nation's Freight Handler;*
> *Stormy, husky, brawling,*
> *City of the Big Shoulders.*

Among the newcomers were Mexicans who established the city's first small *colonias*. By the mid-1910s, they were making their way to the Midwest by train thanks to the railroad linkages established between Mexico and the United States beginning in the 1880s. American labor recruiters sought out Mexican workers to labor on the railroads and in the steel mills and packinghouses that drove the booming Chicago economy. Many more arrived north after fleeing the violence of the Mexican Revolution of 1910–1920 and, in smaller numbers, the anticlerical Cristero Revolts of 1926–1929. These *mexicanos* gradually brought family members with them and soon established a community among the other immigrants and migrants who lived west and south of downtown, as well as in the foundries further south and east. By the end of the 1920s, the city's Mexicans numbered around twenty thousand. With the coming of the Great Depression, however, many Americans scapegoated ethnic Mexicans for local unemployment. Thousands of Chicagoans, including many US citizens by birth, were arrested and sent to Mexico, driving the city's Mexican-origin population down to about sixteen thousand.[7]

Chicago's growth had been halted by the Great Depression, but it resumed when the city's industrial capacity was harnessed to the exigencies of the Second World War. Military production required a wave of retrofitting and hiring, then factory expansion and still more hiring. If Detroit's automotive and allied industries made it the most important site of war production in what President Franklin Delano Roosevelt called America's "arsenal of democracy," Chicago was a clear second. Its workshops and factories employed hundreds of thousands of people to produce aircraft, munitions, engines, electrical equipment, optics, clothing, and foodstuffs. As the news spread, tens of thousands of men and women from across the nation—as well as fifteen thousand Mexican workers invited by the US government to aid the war effort—migrated to the Windy City seeking jobs. By 1950 they had lifted Chicago's population to over 3.6 million people, its all-time peak.[8]

IF ANY PART OF CHICAGO could represent the city's industrial landscape, South Lawndale was a strong contender. It had been given its name in the 1920s, when researchers at the University of Chicago divided the city into seventy-five named and numbered "community areas." The Local Community Research Committee, which included municipal health officials and leading scholars from the university, defined these areas so they could pursue detailed statistical research on the city. Earlier efforts had foundered because they used the boundaries of aldermanic wards, which changed whenever politicians redistricted the city, making it impossible to maintain comparable findings over time. Instead, they identified "local communities" with "boundaries formed by physical barriers such as railroad embankments, the river, industrial property, or banks and boulevards which mark them off into fixed units." Within such natural boundaries, they explained, there emerge "'natural areas' or homogeneous economic and social units." These scholars, who would become known collectively as the "Chicago School" of sociology, created the most influential approach to American urban studies, one based on the ecological metaphor of cities evolving much like complex organisms.[9]

South Lawndale was Area No. 30. It was bounded by decades-old transportation corridors: the Chicago Sanitary and Ship Canal (the widened and dredged version of the original 1848 canal) to the south, the Burlington Railway to the north, the Pennsylvania Railroad to the east, and the Belt Railroad to the west. These connected the neighborhood to a railway network that stretched across the continent and a system of waterways that extended through the Great Lakes and the

Mississippi River to all the world's oceans. This made the area an ideal location for industry, since it was easy to bring in the raw materials required for manufacturing and then to distribute the finished goods.[10]

Little wonder, then, that dozens of companies built factories in and around South Lawndale. Chief among these was the Western Electric Company's colossal Hawthorne Works, which bordered the neighborhood to the west. Initially opened in 1904 to produce telephone equipment, within little more than a decade it provided jobs for twenty-five thousand people—a level of employment that lasted for more than half a century. The other side of the neighborhood abutted a huge agricultural machinery plant occupied since the 1870s by the McCormick Works, which produced the reapers used by farmers on the prairie lands of the Midwest. Production was dramatically expanded after McCormick's corporate merger with a competitor in 1902 to create the International Harvester Company, and the plant became a source of employment for thousands more people in the area. These and numerous smaller shops—Protectoseal Metal & Plastic Specialties, Champion Screw Company, Royal Knitting Mills, Crawford Pipe Fittings Company, Rinn-Scott Lumber Company, Vittex Metal Stamping Company, Ideal Roller Manufacturing Company, the Celotex asphalt roofing factory, and many others—depended on private and public infrastructure in the form of railroad tracks, switching yards, and the city-operated ship canal, all of which required huge amounts of labor to operate, further adding to the neighborhood's opportunities for employment.[11]

South Lawndale attracted industrial workers and their families looking for inexpensive housing near their jobs, and in the late nineteenth and early twentieth centuries, industry employed immigrants. On the maps drawn by the Chicago school urbanists who named the neighborhood, it is specifically marked as a center of settlement for central and eastern Europeans, who so dominated the area that the 1930 census enumerated more than five out of six residents as either foreign-born (31.5 percent) or native-born of foreign parentage (52.1 percent).[12]

These immigrants and ethnics created a dense urban fabric with a strong sense of local identity. The neighborhood had been laid out before the automobile age, so it was designed for walking, with residential blocks surrounding a central shopping street. The area's residences were mostly small brick houses of one and a half to three stories, their gable ends unfashionably facing the street. They were packed close together on narrow lots with no side yards and only tiny front yards. On corners stood a few small tenement buildings. Many of these structures were already run-down by the 1920s, and there was little new construction; however, that suited local residents, who needed homes to be affordable. Twenty-Sixth Street, the main commercial corridor, was similarly modest. Although it had a few blocks with buildings large enough to accommodate a department store or a five-and-dime, it was mostly lined with small, narrow buildings of two to three stories, typically with an apartment above a shop. Some of these small structures distinguished themselves with stylized facades and rooflines that drew on Italianate, German, and Dutch designs, the details rendered in stone, brick, or terra-cotta. The greatest effort and finest ornamentation were devoted to the neighborhood's churches, parish houses, ethnic associations, and social clubs—the institutions that sustained the community's rich associational life.[13]

The people of South Lawndale also built a formidable political machine that fostered and served a constituency of workers who favored labor-friendly government policy. The area's Democratic club was the home of Anton Cermak, the Bohemian-born alderman who in 1931 challenged the American-born incumbent mayor, Republican "Big Bill" Thompson. After Cermak declared his candidacy, Thompson mocked his opponent's name and heritage in doggerel verse: "I won't take a back seat to that Bohunk, Chairmock, Chermack or whatever his name is. Tony, Tony, where's your pushcart at? Can you picture a World's Fair mayor with a name like that?" In response, Cermak said, "He doesn't like my name. . . . Of course we couldn't all come over on the Mayflower. . . . But I got here as soon as I could, and I never wanted to go back, because to me it is a great privilege to be an American." Cermak went on to win the election, and Chicagoans have not elected a Republican mayor since.[14]

Cermak served for only two years before he was felled by an assassin's bullet while shaking hands with President-Elect Franklin Delano Roosevelt, for whom the bullet was intended. Even so, the labor policies of Roosevelt and Cermak made possible the South Lawndale that existed in the 1950s. The New Deal established workers' rights to join unions, leading to dramatic growth in the ranks of organized labor, which peaked in 1954, when over 28 percent of the nation's workforce held union cards. This created unprecedented prosperity, especially for industrial workers in the cities where organized labor was strongest. It made South Lawndale into a place that was both resolutely working-class and unprecedentedly well paid. The neighborhood's workers were considerably more blue-collar than those in most of Chicago: almost half of them were classified as "operatives and kindred workers" or "craftsmen, foremen, and kindred workers." Among male workers, that proportion was more than half. Accordingly, white-collar occupations were underrepresented in the community area: "professional and technical" workers, as well as "managers" and "officials," were much less common than elsewhere in the city. Notwithstanding their concentration in blue-collar fields, however, South Lawndale workers enjoyed middle-class income levels: in four of the neighborhood's nineteen census tracts, the mean family income in 1960 surpassed the Chicago city average of $6,738; in over half the tracts, it was at least 90 percent of the city average; and in only one did it fall lower than five-sixths of that average.[15]

South Lawndale's well-paid workers offered a strong base of purchasing power for the neighborhood's small-business owners. The *Local Community Fact Book for Chicago 1950* counted slightly under one thousand retail businesses in the community area. More than half of these were restaurants and drinking establishments; the remainder included dozens of clothing shops, furniture and appliance stores, sellers of hardware and building materials, liquor stores, gas stations, and drugstores. In the area's main commercial district, which occupied a twenty-block length of Twenty-Sixth Street, numerous professionals and other providers of services plied their trades. City record-keepers found that the area was very productive; for example, in 1948 it generated a total of $54 million in retail sales. Although some chain stores and other national corporations operated in South Lawndale, small, independently owned businesses were the mainstay of the commercial streetscape; it was these that kept the storefronts filled and the sidewalks lively.[16]

South Lawndale was industrial America at its peak. Men by the millions could graduate from high school and, without further education, walk straight into factory jobs. The work was typically hard, dirty, and repetitive, and it took a toll on people's bodies. But jobs were plentiful, the work was steady, and the paychecks and benefits were sufficient to support a family. Never had things been so good for blue-collar America—for the male half of it at least. Most of the millions of women who had marched into factories to help win the Second World War had been pushed out of the industrial sector and now faced an employment market so divided by gender that jobs for men and women were advertised on separate pages in the newspaper.[17]

THERE WAS MORE to urban America in these years than just industrial cities like Chicago. The nation was also home to a second major type of urban growth in what became known as the Sunbelt. The term "Sunbelt" distinguished these cities dotting the warmer climes of the United States from cities in the country's northern tier, establishing a divide between two different kinds of urban areas. The words "sunshine belt" were first used during World War II in city planning documents and in an armed forces report, though it came to identify a region only later. The cities of the Sunbelt emerged for different reasons than their northern counterparts, and they developed into distinctive urban forms.[18]

Most Sunbelt cities remained small before midcentury. In 1940 only one of them, Los Angeles, was among the nation's twenty largest municipalities. Others were well down the list. Houston was only the twenty-first most populous US city, with just under 385,000 residents, Atlanta was twenty-eighth at 302,000 people, and Charlotte, just over the 100,000 mark, was ninety-first. Phoenix, the future desert giant, did not even make the top one hundred because it had only 65,000 inhabitants. But in the decades that followed, as industrial cities reached their peak populations and began to decline, Sunbelt cities would assume some of the top spots in the nation's metropolitan hierarchy.[19]

Dallas was an exemplary Sunbelt city. It had a long previous history, but its rise from regional to national status only began in the middle of the twentieth century. The area around the city's site on the northern Trinity River had long been the homeland of Native Americans, most notably the Caddo and Comanche. It was later claimed by Spain and then Mexico before being annexed by the United States. Founded in 1841 as an agricultural settlement, Dallas became a county seat nine years later. The arrival of the Houston & Texas Central Railroad in the early 1870s established economic linkages to St. Louis and thence to the Northeast, expanding Dallas's hinterland and attracting additional settlers. Even as it became the nation's largest inland cotton market, however, it remained comparatively small: the city would attain the one-hundred-thousand-inhabitant mark only in the 1910s.[20]

This period also saw the emergence of the Mexican part of Dallas. The city had been home to a few Mexicans since the 1890s, most famously the Florencio Magón brothers, revolutionaries who opposed the Diaz dictatorship from abroad. With the Mexican Revolution, those numbers increased. People fled across the Rio Grande and headed north to escape the violence and deprivation caused by the conflict. A community numbering fewer than one hundred ethnic Mexicans in 1900 grew to more than four thousand by 1920. Mexican workers were drawn to many occupations in the city, especially in cement, paving, and pipe-laying. Many also found employment in agricultural work outside the city. It is worth remembering that they were no more than 2–3 percent of the population in 1920, though they accounted for most of the foreign-born in a city that had drawn only a tiny fraction of the number of immigrants as places like Chicago.[21]

Dallasites took advantage of the city's role as a transportation nexus amid vast tracts of cotton land. They soon dominated trade in North Texas, expanded banking and insurance operations, and courted manufacturers. During the 1920s, the city attracted one hundred thousand new residents, paved most of its streets for the first time, and erected its earliest skyscrapers. Then, just as falling cotton prices threatened prosperity, an underground sea of petroleum was discovered nearby. Dallas became the headquarters of choice, not just for oil companies, but also for oil financiers and oil-field equipment manufacturers, allowing the city to avoid the worst effects of the Great Depression and eke out a gain of just over twenty-five thousand new residents during the 1930s. Still, by 1940 Dallas was only the thirty-first most populous city in the United States, not much larger than Toledo, Ohio, and smaller than Jersey City, New Jersey.[22]

It was the Second World War that set Dallas on the path to its greatest growth and diversification. Like many other Sunbelt cities, Dallas's rapid expansion began as the federal government dramatically increased military spending. War Department officials had decided that much war production needed to be moved away from the coasts for security reasons. Aircraft construction and training were often sited in the inland Southwest, where the dry climate allowed for fewer weather delays and more available flying days. Defense spending around existing military sites also soared, and the increases particularly benefited small cities in the Southeast, the least urbanized part of the country.[23]

Big D's political and business leaders acted quickly to ensure that their city received federal defense dollars. After President Roosevelt announced in May 1940 that the government would seek to produce fifty thousand aircraft per year, the mayor and key business leaders flew to California to persuade officials at the North American Aviation Company to build a plant in Dallas. They emphasized the city's favorable climate and nonunion labor and offered to provide key infrastructure. When construction on the factory began in September, the Dallas Chamber of Commerce called it "the greatest industrial development in the history of Texas" and predicted that it would employ twelve thousand workers—six times the number working in the city's next-largest manufacturing facility. Even this grand claim proved to be too modest: by 1943, there were thirty-nine thousand people producing airplanes at the plant.[24]

Many other wartime manufacturers set up shop in Dallas, with both Lockheed and Southern Aircraft building factories. Military spending also meant contracts for other industries: clothing manufacturers filled orders for uniforms, for example, and producers of electrical equipment supplied components for aircraft and vehicles. The aggregate impact of military spending was astonishing—one estimate held that in the first three years of war production, the government had spent $1.5 billion in the Dallas metropolitan area. The vast majority of these funds went for aircraft manufacturing, creating employment for eighty-five thousand workers in that sector alone. In just a few years Dallas had tripled its industrial payroll.[25]

The economic aftereffects of World War II undergirded further prosperity in Dallas long after the Axis surrendered. Some of the factories built for the war continued production to meet the defense requirements of the Cold War; after all, peacetime lasted barely five years before US forces were directly engaged in the Korean War, and quarter-trillion-dollar defense budgets would continue for decades thereafter. The military bases and commands established in the early 1940s portended a longer-term presence for government facilities and personnel in and around Dallas. By the early 1950s, Washington was contributing more than $22 million a year to the city's economy. Other follow-on benefits to the area similarly outlasted the war. The federal government had invested heavily in training programs for industrial workers, creating a strong base of skilled employees who formed an essential part of Dallas's store of human capital. Similarly, professionals and technicians who had found work in wartime production fostered a strong postwar electronics industry that offered thousands of well-paid jobs in the city at companies like Texas Instruments.[26]

Dallas's business and political leaders had pulled off a remarkable feat common in the Sunbelt: they leveraged massive federal spending while also advocating a small-government business philosophy. The pursuit of government largesse was an essential part of Sunbelt growth strategies, and regional leaders clearly understood the multiplier effects of military expenditures: those dollars not only built bases, harbors, and factories but also generated all kinds of private business opportunities and shaped the way Dallas's leadership attracted private investment. The cities of the industrial North had achieved growth and prosperity in conjunction with a strong labor movement that enjoyed broad support from voters, enabling it to raise wages for working people. In Sunbelt cities, by contrast, civic leaders wooed companies by promising them a union-free environment in which they could pay workers less and management could do whatever it wanted. To this inducement they added all manner of special incentives, from tax abatements to special zoning to free land, all to make their cities more attractive for capital investment.[27]

They also talked a lot about the weather. Dallas and the entire Sunbelt lacked long, cold winters—a fact especially apparent to people living in what was becoming known as the "snowbelt" or "frostbelt." Realizing the appeal of the region's climate, civic boosters promised a sun-kissed, indoor-outdoor lifestyle free of snow shoveling and winter slush. In Phoenix, for example, business leaders launched a publicity campaign in 1949 that repeatedly used the term "Valley of the Sun," coined the phrase "outdoor living," and promised "Golf! Year-Round!" The Sunbelt climate was especially attractive to seniors, who were understandably nervous about slipping on icy sidewalks and suffering serious injury—especially in a world before surgeons could routinely do hip replacements in just over an hour and before Medicare was available to pay for it.[28]

The warm climate of the Sunbelt also meant much hotter summers, of course. But the introduction in the 1950s of affordable home air-conditioning made even the hot summer winds of North Texas, the oppressive humidity of Florida, and the blazing deserts of Arizona bearable—although the chirping of crickets was often drowned out by the low drone of coolant compressors in people's window units.

Another twentieth-century technology, the automobile, had an even greater influence on the form taken by Sunbelt cities like Dallas, which grew into sprawling settlements. Most featured dense downtowns originally built around railroad lines, but then spread outward along roadways. The small cities on Route 66, for example, extended for miles. Business owners learned to mount signs at right angles to their storefronts so that drivers could see them easily as they approached from far away. The new automobile-oriented shopping centers placed parking lots in front, where they could be seen from the roadway. This strong orientation toward the automobile made the Sunbelt into the proving ground of a now-familiar landscape of sprawl: wide roads with narrow or nonexistent sidewalks and scant pedestrian crossings; housing subdivisions accessible only by automobile; and office parks, commercial strips, and shopping malls surrounded by so many parking spaces that people learned what it meant to "lose" one's car.[29]

All these factors—government spending, subservience to business interests, and a more forgiving climate shaped by new technologies—combined to work wonders for Dallas, which grew quickly in the war and postwar years. The city population more than doubled, from 295,000 inhabitants to 680,000, in the 1940s and 1950s. Its geographic expansion was similarly astonishing as aggressive annexation of surrounding land took it from 42 square miles in 1930 to 280 square miles thirty years later. By 1960 it had grown to the fourteenth most populous city in the nation; ten years on, it would be the eighth-largest.[30]

IN MANY RESPECTS the city was typified by Oak Cliff. The neighborhood began as a small agricultural community called Hord's Ridge. It became a municipality in the 1880s, when the first railroad arrived. Land developers quickly purchased several hundred acres of the surrounding prairie, which they renamed in 1887 and incorporated as a town in 1890. After the area drew few new residents, Oak Cliff's voters approved its annexation to Dallas in 1903 so as to tap into the growing city's much-needed infrastructure and services. By 1930 the area had become the city's secondary downtown, with a twelve-block-long shopping district along Jefferson Boulevard surrounded by a few thousand mostly single-family homes.[31]

Federal spending brought rapid growth in Oak Cliff. In 1940, the War Department ordered the construction of the Naval Weapons Industrial Reserve Plant, an 85-building, 153-acre manufacturing site located eight miles west of the neighborhood. It was built and operated throughout World War II by North American Aviation, and then during the Cold War by the Texas Engineering and Manufacturing Company and Chance Vought. The industrial complex produced aircraft, missiles, and other armaments and provided jobs for tens of thousands of local people. In 1957 the *Dallas Times Herald* reported that Oak Cliff's population had grown by more than 75 percent between 1940 and 1950, and the *Dallas Morning News* estimated that fifty families were moving in each month.[32]

The effect on the urban landscape was remarkable. Aerial photographs from 1942 display only seven or eight individual blocks of large retail buildings along Jefferson Boulevard. A walk of less than ten blocks off this main street would lead into undeveloped grassland. The corresponding photographs from 1950 reveal more than twice as many large-scale commercial properties and show numerous roads, house lots, and residences being built on previously open fields.[33]

The employment base provided by federal military spending in turn supported the consumers and proprietors of the Jefferson Boulevard commercial district, which boomed around midcentury. Photographs

Jefferson Boulevard, 1957. Oak Cliff's main shopping street was prosperous around midcentury, lined with scores of small local businesses and a few national chains. The area was already beginning to lose residents, however, and commercial vacancies were on the rise. Courtesy Texas/Dallas History and Archives Division, Dallas Public Library.

from the period show a streetscape crowded with pedestrians, lined with automobiles, and served by a streetcar. Well-maintained storefronts sported elaborate signage, and shops displayed an abundance of consumer goods. Jefferson Boulevard was served by a number of leading national retailers, including Sears Roebuck, J. C. Penney, Woolworth, and S. H. Kress, but the many independent small businesses clustered along the street provided the real backbone of local commerce. In 1950, for example, the boulevard was home to twenty-four restaurants, nineteen beauty parlors and barbershops, sixteen laundries and cleaners, fourteen furniture stores, thirteen physicians, thirteen dentists, twelve used-car dealers, twelve shoe stores, eleven accountants, nine drugstores, and eight lawyers.[34]

The neighborhood's prosperity was also reflected in the occupancy rates of properties on Jefferson. The 1950 city directory recorded only twenty-seven vacancies out of 744 available storefronts and dwellings along the boulevard. The 1960 city directory showed an increase to seventy-eight vacancies, but this was not so many given the recession of 1960–1961. Indeed, the neighborhood's prospects were so strong in the early 1960s that the Oak Cliff Bank & Trust decided to erect an expensive fifteen-story modernist headquarters with a glass-and-steel facade, which stood out dramatically from the almost entirely low-rise masonry buildings on and around Jefferson.[35]

Oak Cliff in 1950 was largely a microcosm of Dallas as a whole. The people who lived there generally worked in the same industries, and in roughly the same proportions, as the citywide average. Industrial jobs ("operatives" and "craftsmen, foremen, and kindred workers") were the most common type, accounting for slightly more than one-third of all male workers; Oak Cliff was slightly above the city average in employment in these jobs. But befitting its location in the economy of a Sunbelt city, Oak Cliff also had a solid base of white-collar professionals and managers, jobs that together accounted for nearly 30 percent of employed men. The neighborhood was somewhat below the city average in the number of residents employed as laborers and service workers; each of these categories totaled just a few percent of employees. Thus, while manufacturing had more workers than other sectors, the area was resolutely middle-class—as reflected in the area's median income, which was somewhat higher than in the rest of Dallas. Of the neighborhood's twenty-one census tracts, only five fell below the citywide average; in all the rest, local households earned more, sometimes considerably more. The local economy was both diverse and robust, supporting area businesses and providing healthy revenues for schools and other public institutions. In other words, Oak Cliff was much like Dallas generally—it was the kind of place where a lot of people wanted to go and live.[36]

AMERICANS OF HISPANIC ancestry joined the move to the cities somewhat later and in smaller numbers than others. In 1950 the nation's Spanish-surnamed population was about 4 million people, between 2 and 3 percent of the national population of 151 million, though it was hard to be precise because census officials did not attempt a full national count of Hispanics until twenty years later. For comparison, in 1950 the United States was home to about 15 million black people, or about 10 percent of all Americans, a proportion that had been fairly steady since 1940 and remained so through 1960.[37]

The place of Hispanics in cities seldom attracted much public attention around midcentury. They lived mostly in the Southwest and remained more rural than the rest of the population. The United

States had become a majority-urban country in 1920, when the census found that the proportion of people living in settlements of 2,500 or fewer had fallen to 50 percent. In the decades that followed, the rural share declined even further as people continued to move to cities. The Spanish-heritage population had also been enumerated as about half rural and half urban in 1920, but those proportions did not change in the succeeding two decades. As a result, at a time when other Americans were increasingly centered in urban areas—along with the publishing and broadcasting industries—Hispanics were more likely to live, and especially to work, in areas far away from the beats of reporters and distant from the environs of most writers and photographers.[38]

The overwhelming majority of Hispanics were Mexican Americans and Mexicans, who were heavily concentrated in Texas, New Mexico, Arizona, and California. Many lived in small settlements within reach of the farmlands where they worked. Prominent among these, especially in New Mexico and South Texas, were old *Hispano* towns that predated the US annexation of northern Mexico by a century or more. Towns like these were typically built around a central plaza that reflected the Indigenous and Spanish settlement history of the region, created a shared community space, and allowed residents to preserve a sense of cultural pride and distinctiveness apart from a frequently hostile Anglo majority. Their residents often maintained public ceremonies that were very old indeed, such as the *moros y cristianos* processions commemorating the clashes between Muslims and Catholics in the reconquest of Spain a half millennium earlier.[39]

In other parts of the Southwest, especially in the fast-growing agricultural economy of California, ethnic Mexicans lived in Anglo-majority communities also located near the farms where they worked. Many of these agricultural towns included a small barrio. The scholar and activist Ernesto Galarza noted: "Hardly a town of any size or pretensions . . . failed to acquire between 1900 and 1940 . . . its Mexican colonia on the weathered side of the railroad tracks." They also dwelled in other kinds of settlements, likewise known as *colonias*; in order to live close to fields or orchards, agricultural workers would choose a place amid unclaimed acreage that was neither being cultivated agriculturally nor developed residentially. They sometimes called such areas *tierra de nadie*, or "nobody's land." There, people would build their own dwellings. Sometimes these were little more than dirt-floored adobes or wooden shanties called *jacales*. Given additional time and resources, families built more formal wooden structures, and they might construct the most important buildings, such as churches and schools, in brick or other masonry. While out of sight of the vast majority of Anglos, this constellation of settlements provided not just shelter but a vital sense of community that helped its members withstand prejudice, exploitation, and violence; it was, as Carey McWilliams called it, "a world of its own."[40]

Barrios also grew in larger cities. There was good reason for this: agricultural labor was the lowest-paid kind of work in the nation, and among the most physically strenuous. So for most people of Spanish heritage—as for black people who had been migrating out of the rural South, European immigrants, and native-born whites—the draw of better-paid, less taxing urban employment in industrial and service jobs proved decisive. Here the Southwest led the trend, but ethnic Mexicans also found their way to the industrial Midwest. As they did so, they created the kinds of social, religious, and commercial institutions that they had established in smaller settlements.[41]

Hispanic urbanization accelerated with the coming of World War II. Mexican Americans joined the war effort in the largest numbers, both through enlisting and, especially among women, through working in defense industries amid a war-driven labor shortage. This was a key point of entry into the better-paid industrial labor force previously off-limits to most of them. It was facilitated by President Roosevelt's Executive Order 8802 mandating equal employment opportunities, which began to weaken racial exclusion in the industrial workplace.[42]

While barrios were growing quickly, it is essential to remember that they did so from a comparatively modest demographic base. Spanish-heritage communities were enormously important to their residents, but to the English-speaking world they still looked small relative to the majority population. This was true even for Los Angeles: in the nation's undisputed ethnic Mexican metropolis, which had for more than half a century been at the forefront of their urbanization, as late as 1960 Hispanics still accounted for only 10.5 percent of the city population.[43]

EVEN AT THE height of its prosperity, urban America was not without problems. The nation's cities had thrived as the engines of an economy that produced great wealth and as the heart of a political system that helped distribute that wealth more equitably than ever before. But some of the conditions that had built American urbanism had begun to change, and others had been changing for some time. This was most visible in the nation's older industrial neighborhoods, but even Sunbelt city districts were affected.

Despite South Lawndale's prosperity and strong community life, more people were moving out than moving in. Indeed, by midcentury this had been the case for decades: the neighborhood's population had peaked in 1920 and then gradually declined in every subsequent decade—falling by nearly 9 percent in the 1920s, over 7 percent in the 1930s, and more than 5 percent in the 1940s; it would lose another 8 percent in the 1950s. In this it was like many industrial neighborhoods: it had a strong local identity and retained the loyalty of long-time residents, but that did not often mean much to their children and grandchildren. There were still plenty of manufacturing jobs in the area, but it remained "a low-rent residential community," as the leading neighborhood guide called it. Its housing stock was old and felt increasingly cramped—family dwellings of six or seven hundred square feet were considered satisfactory in the early twentieth century, but new generations growing up in the prosperity of the postwar years expected to have a lot more room than that. Bigger, better homes were being built elsewhere, some in newer neighborhoods within Chicago and a lot more just outside the city limits in suburban towns.[44]

South Lawndale was not the only Chicago neighborhood that experienced both meaningful prosperity and gradual population loss. The newspaper columnist Mike Royko, himself only a generation removed from eastern European immigrant forebears, said that this was essentially true of "every neighborhood" in the Windy City at midcentury: "For a variety of reasons, ranging from convenience to fear to economics, people stayed in their own neighborhoods, loving it, enjoying the closeness, the friendliness, the familiarity, and trying to save enough money to move out."[45]

Something similar was happening in Oak Cliff. Like almost all its former residents, the journalist Grover Lewis remembered the neighborhood as a place bursting with local pride and opportunity. The street where he had lived was "a leafy tunnel running past tidy bungalows and well-kept Victorian mansions" dating back to before the turn of the century. Along Jefferson Boulevard, the "shopping district had been second only to downtown Dallas in the early '50s" and was anchored by stores like "Skillern's, Sears, J. C. Penney, and all the other blue-chip concerns." The neighborhood's leading entertainment venue, the Texas Theater—where a decade later police would capture John F. Kennedy's assassin—had been "a spit-and-polish place where Daddy took Mama to the show on Sundays." For Lewis, as for the many people who had lived there but mostly moved out in later years, the memory that most stayed with them was of "Oak Cliff, the way it used to be when its housing, roads, and education ranked with Texas's best"—not just a neighborhood, but a concrete manifestation of "a bygone age of discipline and traditional values."[46]

Yet even in those years Oak Cliff was already under pressure. The population gains of the previous decades reversed themselves in the 1950s as local people were drawn to the larger lots and bigger, more modern homes of Dallas's newer subdivisions and its surrounding suburbs. Meanwhile, Oak Cliff faced both internal conflicts and structural problems. For years, local Baptists and other evangelical Protestants had attempted to pass a law prohibiting the sale of alcohol in Oak Cliff. Many neighborhood establishments sold drinks to a loyal clientele of workers and bon vivants who lent the area a racy reputation. The "wet" faction, led by small-business owners and more moderate religious denominations, had managed to hold the line for several years. But in 1956 the "drys" finally called a vote and won. Local clubs, restaurants, and other establishments took a big hit as they lost out on alcohol sales receipts. The tranquility of midcentury Oak Cliff was already fraying.[47]

Meanwhile, the neighborhood's connections to the rest of the city were being weakened. In 1929, municipal authorities had built a viaduct across the Trinity River for a streetcar that ran between Jefferson Boulevard and the city's primary downtown. This line had connected local people to jobs in the city center and brought customers to Oak Cliff's restaurants, theaters, amusement parks, and other attractions. But by the early 1950s, city authorities were questioning whether the expense of the streetcar line was worth it, and in 1955 they canceled service outright, dealing a blow to the local economy by weakening its most important link to downtown.[48]

Nor were South Lawndale and Oak Cliff the only neighborhoods that faced challenges. In city halls across America, planners and other officials worried that their older urban neighborhoods had passed their peak. They were concerned that so many families had begun to move away from the center, whether to peripheral areas that still lay within the city limits or to separately incorporated municipalities. Indeed, they had begun to use the term "urban crisis" as they warned that America's cities were in decline and that without decisive action they might face a future of urban decay.[49]

Some of the problems of midcentury cities were social, having to do with inequality and discrimination. Others were more structural in nature, arising from aging infrastructure that was unsuitable for the emergent postwar economy. In the years to come, these problems would lead to entire neighborhoods being torn apart—both figuratively and literally—as the very people who had most benefited from midcentury prosperity began to destroy them.

CHAPTER 3

"CRACKER EDEN"

THE MIDCENTURY PROSPERITY OF URBAN AMERICA WAS not shared equally among city residents. Grover Lewis might praise the virtues of the old neighborhood, but the Texas journalist was not one to idealize the Oak Cliff of his youth. He had, after all, entitled his essay "Farewell to Cracker Eden" and described his old Dallas neighborhood as "a paradise of the deepest redneck dye" where "the fear of race-mixing was a constant topic because the district's communal identity hinged on being white, conservative, 'saved,' and married with children." He recalled a constant "gabble of bigotry" repeated so regularly that it "became a daily canticle, a sacred text." Looking back across four decades at the Oak Cliff of his youth, he concluded: "The ethos of the place—what it promoted— was absolute white supremacy, reinforced by old-time religion and male chauvinist prickism."[1]

A similar theme echoed through Stuart Dybek's short stories set in and around South Lawndale during the same era. The author lingered on the boundaries between his Chicago neighborhood and the predominantly black areas to the north, and how these dividing lines manifested in everyday conversation. In "Blood Soup," when local boys cross into an adjacent district in search of a special ingredient for a restorative broth, a shopkeeper warns them: "Be careful in that neighborhood . . . the coloreds are moving in." And in "Chopin in Winter," Rudy, a thirteen-year-old aspiring jazz musician, is called away from his first show at a local club when his ailing Polish grandmother is rushed to the hospital. When he arrives to try to lift her spirits, she takes one look at her favorite grandson in his hepcat-inspired outfit, utters the words "Rudesh, you dress like nigger," and immediately dies.[2]

Oak Cliff and South Lawndale were by no means unusual where racism was concerned. Virtually all the nation's cities were segregated, and the patter of casual racial slurs was commonplace throughout histories and memoirs from the "old neighborhood." In the early 1950s the civil rights movement remained relatively cautious and incremental in the face of blatant and defiant segregationism. The sit-ins, freedom rides, and other direct actions to integrate public places were still years away, the push for a federal fair housing law further away still. In daily life, neighborhood segregation was so prevalent that white people could spend almost all their time in all-white surroundings. They could go to work, shop, socialize, worship, and stroll for miles while having scant contact with African Americans, Hispanics, or other people of color, who might easily find themselves in danger if they crossed into the wrong neighborhood.[3]

Few white city-dwellers would have wondered why their neighborhoods were so homogeneous. It seemed as if it had always been that way, as unremarkable as the unbroken ranks of white faces in their high school yearbook photos of sports teams, cheerleading squads, and graduating seniors. This did not mean that they were unaware of race or indifferent to it—they could be very color-conscious indeed, especially if they lived near one of their city's racial dividing lines. But most of the time, undesirable "others" conveniently lived somewhere else, in "bad neighborhoods" that white people knew to avoid—areas they gave nicknames like Darktown and Nigger Hill.

So what was glaringly obvious to others was hard for them to see—that the prosperity of the era came at the expense of people of color, who were excluded from an equal opportunity to produce and enjoy the wealth of the nation. The issue was not just that most urban neighborhoods were virtually all-white. It was that segregation made life extremely hard for people who were forced to dwell and work elsewhere. And the most shocking thing was not that white people often used racial epithets within the boundaries of their neighborhoods, but that so many of them were ready to resort to violence when they thought those boundaries were threatened.

On January 10, 1950, scores of white residents of Oak Cliff and neighboring areas packed into a hearing at city hall to protest against a housing development to be built just southwest of their part of Dallas. The proposed project, sited on six hundred acres of gently rolling land, would include two thousand homes, five parks, three shopping centers, churches, and a school. The Diamond Hill addition, as it was called, was similar to dozens of other new subdivisions springing up around the city, but with one difference: it was intended for black families.

Leading the protesters was George Owens, a local minister and politician who claimed to speak for 29,500 people living in the area. Calling Diamond Hill "an effort to exploit the Negroes for money gain," he proposed that the project be moved elsewhere in the city. Owens sought to portray himself and his supporters as reasonable voices in a volatile situation. "We've been trying to fight this thing on a high plane," he explained, "but there's tremendous bitterness." And lest anybody miss the implicit threat of violence, he added: "There'd be trouble if too many Negroes tried to climb aboard our buses," since their very presence would "produce friction to the flaming point of race riot."[4]

Owens was probably right. For decades the Oak Cliff area had been known as a hotbed of white supremacy. After Dallas enacted a citywide zoning code in 1916 that prohibited African Americans from moving into officially designated white neighborhoods, a man named Roby Williams rented a house in Oak Cliff just a block over the color line. He was promptly sued and lost his case, perhaps because the presiding judge wore the robes of both the judiciary and the Ku Klux Klan. By the early 1920s, the Dallas klavern was among the largest in the nation, Klan-backed candidates were winning numerous citywide elections, and Oak Cliff was known as one of the two most die-hard strongholds of pro-Klan voters. In the other stronghold a few miles to the east, when a handful of black families later moved into the neighborhood so that their children could attend the newly opened Lincoln High School, local whites responded with a months-long campaign of intimidation and violence that included menacing mobs, rock throwing, death threats, and house bombings.[5]

Black Dallasites had spent many years trying to gain access to decent housing in a city where they were unable to live anywhere but the most dilapidated neighborhoods. In 1924 the Civic Federation of Dallas issued a report showing that half of African American households had no gas or electrical service and two-thirds lacked toilets or running water. One-quarter of the city's black residents, the report concluded, lived in dwellings "unfit for human habitation." Following the release of similar reports in the mid-1930s, the *Dallas Express*, the city's leading African American newspaper, published a series of searing editorials on the issue of housing. "Are Negroes to Be Condemned to Filth?" asked one. Another called the city's main black neighborhood "one of the rottenest ghettos in America." When whites questioned why the newspaper was so insistent on the subject of suitable housing for black families, its editors responded, "By all that is decent and Christian, perhaps, Kind Sirs, maybe, as it were, we might need it."[6]

The crisis became even more severe during and after World War II. Tens of thousands of black people came to the city to work in war production and related industries, and many of them stayed when peace returned. Dallas's fast-growing postwar economy offered African Americans better job prospects than anywhere else in the area, but they were nonetheless excluded from many categories of work. In a city that saw itself as thoroughly southern—the two main streets in Oak Cliff were named Jefferson Boulevard and Davis Street—black people were largely relegated to the lower reaches of the labor force. A 1948 report from the Dallas Negro Chamber of Commerce found that though there were dozens of black plumbers, only one black person in the city had been issued a plumber's license; the others were allowed to work only as apprentices at lower pay. The same report noted that of all the people hired with the chamber's help that year, almost all were in unskilled, menial positions. Dallas was also home to a small but growing class of African American entrepreneurs and professionals who managed to carve out a place for themselves in the city's segregated economy.[7]

All black people, however, faced the same infuriating restrictions on where they could make their homes. As an investigative reporter for the *Dallas Morning News* put it, "virtually every Dallas Negro, no matter what his economic or intellectual status, lives under slum conditions or in slum surroundings . . . he has nowhere else to go." The city's black leaders gradually managed to persuade white elites that the housing crisis had to be addressed. Even so, they responded only in the most cautious and incremental fashion. This was characteristic of their broader approach to race relations, which they called "the Dallas way." City leaders avoided the issue of segregation for as long as they could; and when demands for equality made such evasion impossible, they opted for incremental, often token desegregation. In 1953, for example, the mayor promised to desegregate the state fair, but full implementation required eight more years of protests. In 1956 it was only to avoid a Montgomery-style boycott led by black community leaders that city officials finally agreed to establish equal seating on city buses. This strategy was similar to that adopted in the region's other major cities, most notably Atlanta, the self-proclaimed "City Too Busy to Hate." Moderate political and business leaders in the upper and outer South were eager to avoid the kind of racial violence that could jeopardize efforts to attract private capital and government projects.[8]

The Diamond Hill development was a perfect example of "the Dallas way." It offered black families better homes, but only for the middle class and only on a segregated basis. African Americans were still not welcome in white neighborhoods, and indeed, for some backers, that was precisely the virtue of the new development: it would accommodate black families who might otherwise try to desegregate white areas. In addition, the subdivision required no direct public spending: city leaders hoped that a private venture would sidestep the typically furious response of white voters when anybody suggested spending tax dollars to benefit people of color.

Yet even this cautious approach failed to win passage by the city council. The Diamond Hill development had enjoyed the strongest possible institutional support: from the office of the mayor, black civic and economic leaders, white business interests, and the white and African American press. In the end, however, the councilmen were more afraid of white mob violence than they were concerned about the deprivations suffered by black citizens. They blocked the project by denying authorization for Diamond Hill's water lines. They applied the same racial calculus elsewhere in the city, refusing to authorize five more large-scale subdivisions for African American families.[9]

If city leaders thought that decisions like these would be enough to pacify local whites, they were mistaken. Three weeks later, unknown parties began a wave of bombings against black-owned homes and businesses in South Dallas. Of the eleven attacks over the next seventeen months, most involved people throwing sticks of dynamite at homes. In some cases the premises were vacant. In others they were not: Leo Smith, his wife, and their four-year-old son were sleeping in the dwelling behind their store when dynamite blew a hole in the roof, thankfully leaving them physically unharmed. (Dallas authorities managed to secure indictments but never convictions of the alleged bombers.) In this same period, whites threw fireworks at black women to terrorize them as they walked in the street, and mobs of whites menaced real estate agents showing homes to black people.[10]

These would not be the last instances of organized racial terrorism in the city. It was obvious that many whites refused to live, not just among African Americans, but even *near* segregated black neighborhoods. And it was equally clear that city authorities could not protect black people who wanted to live in homes of their own choosing.

DALLAS'S HISPANIC POPULATION was overwhelmingly ethnically Mexican. They occupied a racial status between white and black in a local system that was triracial. The city was part of a Texas cotton culture built on the labor of black, white, and Mexican workers. So Dallas officials segregated the city three ways, maintaining separate public housing projects for what they termed "white," "Negro," and "Latin-American" families. The same triracial thinking was incorporated into city planning, as illustrated by a map drafted by the Department of Public Works in 1945. It presented a color-coded representation of population, with a "Negro Section" demarcated in red and a "Mexican Section" shaded in blue. The map, drawn up after a spate of white bombings, showed in part where populations of color lived and in part where city officials hoped to channel black and Mexican settlement—toward undeveloped areas where there would be as little interracial contact as possible.[11]

The city's Mexican American population was centered in Little Mexico, an area immediately west of downtown where people from across the border settled beginning around 1910. There were other ethnically Mexican neighborhoods in Dallas, but people understood Little Mexico to be the heart of the community—the place they referred to simply as *el barrio*. It contained the most important institutions, including Our Lady of Guadalupe Church, the main Spanish-speaking commercial district, St. Ann's School, Crozier Tech High School, and especially Pike Park, which served as the city's Mexican plaza, its focus of community life. Anita Martínez, who was born in 1925 and went on to become the first Hispanic member of the Dallas city council, remembered the Little Mexico of her childhood as "a very tight, close-knit community . . . everybody was an extended family . . . everybody was *abuelita* or *tía*." It is worth remembering, however, that Hispanics citywide were relatively few in number: in 1960, Spanish-surnamed Dallasites totaled slightly under thirty thousand people—only about 4 percent of the city's population.[12]

Little Mexico was the site of the finest Mexican American homes, but it also included streets that better represented the living standards of most of Dallas's ethnic Mexicans. One of the most widely republished photographs of Little Mexico around midcentury depicted Alamo Street, a lane with a line of dwellings on both sides. The city had left the street unpaved, so it consisted only of packed dirt without sidewalks. In the foreground, four small children clustered on the steps of a simple wood-frame dwelling. The house was rudimentary, but still the nicest home in the image: the others were ramshackle structures, some lacking even windows. The street ran in the direction of downtown, and the modernist steel-frame towers of the emerging Dallas skyline could be seen in the distance. The photograph emphasized how little of the city's prosperity was shared by citizens of Mexican descent.[13]

In truth, many Dallas Mexicans lived in even more desperate conditions. For example, the barrio called El Pozo ("the well" or "the

Alamo Street, Little Mexico, c. 1948–1955. The rising prosperity of postwar Dallas was not shared equally. Many of the city's Mexican Americans lived on dirt roads in dilapidated homes like these, located less than a mile from the gleaming new sky-scrapers downtown. Courtesy Texas/Dallas History and Archives Division, Dallas Public Library.

pit") occupied the floodplain of the Trinity River; the land was so no-toriously flood-prone that no insurance could be issued there. Many in El Pozo lived in wooden shanties with no hard foundation. The resultant conditions took an awful toll on the health of residents and helped explain why ethnic Mexicans suffered some of the highest rates of disease and infant mortality in the city.[14]

Dallas's Mexican Americans, not surprisingly, went searching for better places to live. Because they were legally classified as white, in Dallas as in other cities in the Southwest small numbers of them could sometimes live among white Anglos without being subjected to the same kind of racial terror visited on black householders. The several hundred Spanish-surnamed families who had moved to Oak Cliff in the 1950s were emblematic of this; nevertheless, these early Hispanic arrivals were initially a small population, comprising 2.5 percent of the neighborhood's eighty-eight thousand people by the end of the decade.[15]

Some people of Hispanic origin reacted to their fragile status defensively, by lashing out. They went to great lengths to portray themselves as fully white, including by showing that they could be as racist toward black people as any Anglo. Notably, the ranks of violent whites in Dallas included Spanish-surnamed people. One of the accused bombers was Pete Garcia, who made FOR WHITES ONLY signs that he posted in front of homes whose owners had agreed to uphold the color line by not selling to black people. A neighbor said that Garcia had threatened him with a knife when he refused, and witnesses said that he had chased away black prospective home buyers and real estate agents. Another local man, P. R. Ochoa, published a newspaper called the *Dallas Americano* in which he attacked the NAACP and LULAC (League of United Latin American Citizens) and featured slogans like "*conserve su raza blanca*" ("keep your race white") and "*segregación es libertad*" ("segregation is freedom"). This kind of racial self-classification may seem surprising today, but it was not at all uncommon for Mexican Americans and other Latinos around mid-century to declare themselves white. For some, it was a tactical move to avoid losing legal or social status as a result of being lumped in with African Americans as people of color; for others, it was an extension of Mexican prejudices against Indigenous-looking people and in favor of those who were phenotypically European. This was emblematic of the intermediate position that people who often called themselves "Spanish Americans" occupied both locally and, as the 1950s wore on, nationally as well.[16]

In the 1950s, Anglo Americans were being reintroduced to Latin American cultures through the mass media. In Dallas, for example, the *Morning News* regularly ran stories of Mexican-themed parties, picnics, and other events. These were by no means full appreciations of the depth and variety of Mexican civilization. They were simply dress-up affairs at which Anglos donned sombreros and serapes, ate enchiladas, and sipped margaritas. Actual Mexicans were virtually absent from any of the coverage except as servers or performers, and Mexico was just an interesting source of picturesque visual design and tasty food within a broader context of condescension. A contemporary phenomenon involved Cuban culture as portrayed on the popular TV show *I Love Lucy*, in which Cubanness was synonymous with entertaining tropical rhythms but whose fundamental lack of seriousness was signaled every time Ricky Ricardo's rapid-fire Spanish was played for laughs. The trend was broadened to include Puerto Ricans with the 1957 stage production of *West Side Story* and the subsequent motion picture: here audiences learned to see "Spanish" people as sexually desirable but also potentially dangerous. These were the most widely distributed examples of how US entertainment culture included "Latin numbers" in its productions.[17]

CHICAGO'S HISTORY, DEMOGRAPHICS, and urban form were different from Dallas's, but when it came to racial segregation, the two cities had a great deal in common. Black people in the Windy City had for decades been restricted to a small number of neighborhoods. Bronzeville, by far the most important of these, was already overcrowded by 1940 and became even more so as migrants from the South arrived seeking work in the city's massive wartime manufacturing sector. All Chicagoans were affected by a housing shortage, but for African Americans it was far more severe.[18]

In part this followed from the kinds of jobs available to most black people. Forced to work at the margins of the city's economy, they were excluded almost entirely from the most lucrative professions and relegated to unskilled and menial occupations. They earned their daily bread cleaning work sites or homes, digging ditches, carrying luggage, and washing clothes. A small proportion were skilled operatives, but they got less work and made less pay because they were barred from most craft unions or segregated within them. For example, the Chicago locals of the steamfitters' and plumbers' unions and of the musicians' unions forced black workers to agree not to take jobs outside the Black Belt, even while whites were allowed to work in black neighborhoods. The industrial unions were more inclusive. Some, like the United Auto Workers, actively recruited black members, preached working-class unity over racial division, and offered financial support to civil rights activists to assist in their struggle for equality. But black workers were still the last hired and the first fired—they faced what midcentury sociologists St. Clair Drake and Horace Cayton Jr. called a "job ceiling."[19]

Even during the peak job growth of the immediate postwar years—a time when wages were rising for workers of all races—black people simply did not have equal access to the period's prosperity. In 1961 Drake and Cayton investigated what sort of progress the city's African Americans had made since 1945. They found that black people's job prospects had improved thanks to campaigns for racial equality in employment, a general labor shortage, and increased job vacancies as whites scaled the employment ladder. They also determined that one-third of black women had moved up from the service jobs they previously held, and that African American family income had increased by 50 percent between 1950 and 1956. Yet at the same time, two-thirds of men of color were still doing unskilled labor, while only one-third of white men were; moreover, black median income was still 29 percent lower than that for whites.[20]

Regardless of how hard they worked or how high they rose, black people had little choice but to live in the most overcrowded and extortionately priced housing in the city. In one apartment building on the South Side, one thousand people were crammed into a single seven-story structure. The original apartments had been subdivided, and families of five and six people squeezed into two rooms while having to share bathrooms with other households. In another building nearby, each floor was divided into fourteen rooms, with the only available cooking and washing facilities located in the hallways. And for these spaces black Chicagoans had often paid higher rents than white tenants did for better-quality dwellings in white neighborhoods, just as they had in other American cities.[21]

Dwellings like these put tenants at mortal risk because when fires broke out, the results could be horrific. A single month in 1958 included numerous tragic examples. On January 20, a fire claimed the lives of a baby girl and three adults who lived in an unlawfully subdivided house on the South Side. Three days later and just a few blocks away, an eight-apartment building that had been "cut up" into twenty-seven units went up in flames, killing seven children. Four days after that, two more children suffocated in a nearby basement fire. The *Chicago Sun-Times* criticized "buildings and neighborhoods where families are crammed into unsafe, unhealthy cubicle flats, paying exorbitant rents for the privilege of dying like cattle caught in a barn," and the *Defender* reminded readers that with black people "hemmed into a ghetto by the relentless pressure of residential segregation," it was virtually inevitable that there would be "more fires and more deaths."[22]

Nor was this the sole threat to people's health in a city where only a small percentage of hospitals would admit African American patients, making emergency room waits five times longer than at white facilities. Little wonder that in Chicago black infants died 50 percent more frequently than white ones, and black people were over five times more likely to lose their lives to tuberculosis.[23]

Similar inequalities persisted in many aspects of neighborhood life. One mayor's committee reported that people in the Black Belt suffered from a long list of deprivations and abuses that included "inadequate recreational facilities; lack of building repairs; neglect of garbage disposal and street cleaning; overcrowded schools . . . [and] rough treatment by the police." And indeed, garbage did often overflow trash cans, both because overfull dwellings generated more refuse than they had been designed for and because city workers were negligent about cleaning up a neighborhood they thought of as their last priority. Schools were so desperately over capacity that they ran in shifts: students received inferior education because their school days were shortened and their teachers overworked and undercompensated. And police misconduct was so endemic, legal recourse so nonexistent, and inequality so taken for granted—even traffic tickets were segregated, indicating the race of the driver until 1958—that even middle-class black Chicagoans fully expected to be stopped, harassed, ticketed, or otherwise shaken down whenever they left their homes.[24]

It was no wonder, then, that they sought to move out of segregated neighborhoods faster than ever before in the postwar period. Their efforts embodied one of the basic demands of the civil rights movement: the right to housing on an equal basis with white people was both a statement of principle and an immediate need. One prominent black newspaper wrote that "new areas should be opened to break the iron ring which now restricts most Negro families to intolerable, unsanitary conditions."[25]

Directly in the path of black families hoping to find better homes in better neighborhoods was the West Side, including two Lawndales:

South Lawndale, the area that Richard Dolejs would attempt to re-name and repopulate; and North Lawndale, the community that em-bodied the fears of the people of South Lawndale. The resemblance went well beyond the shared name. North Lawndale was also a long-established neighborhood that abutted the city's western sub-urbs. It shared the kind of worn-down housing stock common in South Lawndale. And it too had been populated by European immi-grants and their "white ethnic" descendants. Like South Lawndale, North Lawndale had been losing population for some time as its upwardly mobile residents sought to leave behind their dilapidated houses and cramped stores for the newer, more spacious environs of the suburbs; many former denizens remembered jokingly calling their neighborhood "Lower Slobovnia."[26]

In the 1950s, however, the two Lawndales diverged sharply as the northern neighborhood became a classic case of "white flight." As thousands of black families tried to escape the appalling conditions of the ghetto, real estate operators made outsize profits by sowing panic among white residents, urging them to accept low-ball offers on their houses before their neighbors sold out and it was too late. In 1959 the president of a white neighborhood association on the South Side explained how this worked. "They have come up to me and said, 'Mr. Gaudette, yours is the only house on this block that is not on our listing. Get out while you can still make a profit.'" These "panic peddlers" would then resell the homes to black people so desperate for housing that they would pay far more than their fleeing predeces-sors had. Lawndale's civil rights community, neighborhood activists, and religious groups did their best to calm homeowners' fears: they founded interracial committees to welcome newcomers, sponsored neighborhood meetings, and launched well-publicized property im-provement drives. But despite the idealism of many area residents, fear won out, and North Lawndale went from 87 percent white to 91 percent African American in a single decade.[27]

In South Lawndale, however, very few black people moved into the neighborhood. So rather than being the result of actual demographic change, the fears of its overwhelmingly white residents existed first and foremost in their imaginings about black people and what their presence in North Lawndale might presage. The question was how the people of South Lawndale might respond—and it was clear from an early date that violence was a real possibility.

In the spring of 1952, civil rights supporters inside and outside the Chicago Housing Authority (CHA) urged the desegregation of four all-white projects across the city, including Lawndale Gardens— the homes little Guadalupe Lozano would later wonder why she could not live in. Lawndale Gardens had been built in South Lawndale in 1942 to house wartime production workers, making it one of the CHA's oldest developments. In its first decade, every one of the 128 two-story houses on its site at Twenty-Sixth Street and California Avenue had been occupied by white people. When a vacancy occurred, the unit was kept open for the next white family who applied to live there. The CHA's commissioners responded to requests to desegregate Lawndale Gardens by promising changes but pleading for caution because they feared that local whites would react violently.[28]

The caution of CHA officials was soon reinforced when they attempted to desegregate the Trumbull Park Homes on the far south side of the city. In August 1953, it became known that a black couple— Betty Howard, who was light-skinned enough to pass for white, and her husband Donald, a veteran—had moved into a house in the development. The next day a crowd of fifty white teenagers attacked the apartment, throwing bricks and stones; within a few days, the mob had grown to as many as two thousand people. Over the following weeks, local whites smashed the Howards' windows, threw firebombs at their home, and set off hundreds of small explosives around the dwelling. The threat of personal violence was so constant that the Howards could not go to the store without a police escort, and Donald felt compelled to carry a pistol when accompanying his wife to church. Acts of racial aggression at the Trumbull Park Homes continued sporadically for more than a decade.[29]

These rioters were of the same working-class central and eastern European immigrant stock as South Lawndale. So while South Lawndale had not immediately become violent, there were signs of brewing trouble: in 1956 and 1957 alone there were several incidents around the boundary with North Lawndale. There could be little doubt that similar violence there was not simply a possibility but very nearly an expectation.[30]

CHICAGO'S HISPANIC POPULATION was small around midcentury, numbering only in the tens of thousands in a city of 3.6 million people. Their racial position was uncertain, though in a different way than in Dallas: in part, Puerto Ricans and especially ethnic Mexicans could be understood as immigrants, analogous to the city's eastern, central, and southern European ethnic communities, but they could also be seen as nonwhite. Whatever their racial status, they were still massively outnumbered: there were about sixty white and ten black Chicagoans for every Hispanic one. African Americans would continue to be the basic reference for nonwhiteness in the Windy City for at least a few decades more.[31]

Mexicans lived in a number of areas in Chicago, but easily the most important barrio was the one on the Near West Side. It had survived the repatriations of the 1930s, in part because Mayor Cermak and other Cook County officials declined to cooperate with Depression-era deportation programs. The area's population surged in the 1940s owing to the *migrantes* who came to the city to work in the war effort, including over fifteen thousand braceros. By 1960 the neighborhood was home to over twenty thousand "Spanish-speaking" people. It was not a purely Mexican barrio, but one in which Mexicans coexisted with other ethnic groups, especially Italians, Greeks, eastern European Jews, and African Americans. That said, it was home to the leading Mexican commercial district, centered on five blocks of South Halsted Street. The area included key institutions—stores, restaurants, churches, bars, nightclubs, tortilla makers and specialty food importers, dance halls, Spanish-language movie houses, baseball teams, settlement houses, and other shared establishments.[32]

The active community life of the neighborhood included various associations: youth groups like the Chi-Mex Club, athletic leagues such as the Ciclistas, and advocacy groups like LULAC and the Illinois Federation of Mexican Americans. There was also a local Spanish-language press; the newspaper *Vida Latina*, for example, was published regularly and featured stories to engage and inspire people in the community. The neighborhood also became home to Mexican *fiestas patrias* that celebrated such key episodes in the national history as independence from Spain on September 16, 1810, and victory over invading French monarchists in the Battle of Puebla on May 5,

1862; events included parades, banquets, dances, and the inevitable beauty pageants.[33]

The city's Puerto Rican community grew through labor recruitment from the island, first by private firms and then through government action when Puerto Rico's Migration Division opened a Chicago office in 1949. All Puerto Ricans were already US citizens as a consequence of the Jones Act of 1917, but this status was complicated: they were racially mixed owing to the island's substantial African-ancestry population and Indigenous roots, so many whites still treated them as aliens despite their legal status. While there were *puertorriqueños* who lived and worked among the Mexicans of the Near West Side, the main Puerto Rican neighborhood was centered on Division Street, which was home to the community's main cultural and commercial institutions.[34]

As racially mixed populations, Mexicans and Puerto Ricans experienced some of the same kinds of discrimination as black people. The authors of *Black Metropolis* had noted in 1945 that "native-born Americans tend to arrange people in a rank-order of desirability as neighbors which places Northern Europeans at the top, and Negroes, Mexicans, and similar colored groups near the bottom." They lived in the same kind of substandard and unsafe housing. One representative of the Mexican Civic Committee of the West Side explained that her coethnics "have to live in the type of house . . . in which thin beaverboard partitions are the only separation between one family and another. People with three or four children live with no privacy, no safety and no protection against delinquency of all types—juvenile and adult." And Mexicans and Puerto Ricans were among the most poorly paid workers in the area. In most cases they were excluded from labor unions in the same way as black workers, though a few progressive unions did work with them to organize their coethnics, as they did with black workers. Puerto Ricans and Mexicans were also segregated in public housing and other places.[35]

As in a number of cities, Puerto Ricans and Mexicans were subject to repeated public defamation in leading newspapers. In 1954, for example, the *Chicago Tribune* ran an array of such articles, including a series of pieces about an air force base south of the city that was allegedly infiltrated by *pachucos*, a well-known term for Mexican

American delinquent youth, under a blaring headline that warned of a "Pachuco Terrorist Gang." The paper demonstrated an inability to differentiate among Hispanics, reporting that among one sweep's arrestees on the West Side "all are Puerto Rican," perhaps confusing *pachucos* with Puerto Rican nationalists. Notably, the articles soon drew a rebuke from a reader who called the reports nonsense and the entire issue a case of scapegoating, accusing city authorities of "publicizing the Pachuco reports to take the heat off themselves for recent gangland slayings." In addition, as labor recruiters were bringing Puerto Ricans to the area in the 1950s, city officials publicized them as a desirable labor force by deriding Mexicans as unreliable workers accustomed to living in squalor.[36]

Mexicans and Puerto Ricans had a complex relationship with the "white ethnics" among whom they lived. Drake and Cayton observed a certain level of coexistence among people of color and immigrants from southern Europe. But there was a key difference: while black people remained segregated in certain neighborhoods, Hispanics typically lived alongside the "white ethnic" descendants of earlier European immigrants. Occasionally able to pass for Italian or Greek, they did so if they could to rent houses that might be off-limits to them if their true backgrounds were known. There were serious disagreements among them, and frequent racial insults and fist-fighting, but also a certain amount of intermingling and intermarriage. Indeed, the stories of Stuart Dybek set on the West Side in the 1950s and 1960s include a number of ethnic Mexican characters, from the new altar boys at St. Ann's, where Father Wojek "could say the service in five languages—Latin, Polish, Ukrainian, English, and Spanish"—to local teenagers whose mixed Mexican and Polish parentage showed how long these groups had shared the neighborhood and how thoroughly they were becoming a part of it. So while Mexicans and Puerto Ricans unmistakably suffered considerable discrimination, the color line drawn against African Americans seemed not to apply to them in the same way.[37]

DALLAS AND CHICAGO were typical of many US cities at that time. A systematic look at the 1950 US census would turn up thousands of enumerated tracts with no or only a handful of people identified as nonwhite (and these were often live-in housekeepers rather than residents in the usual sense). In most cases such tracts were surrounded by dozens of others just like them, which formed extensive areas of overwhelmingly white settlement, comprising the great majority of city neighborhoods. The color lines that divided these neighborhoods were usually quite stark—one could usually find a row of nearly all-white tracts along a similar row of nearly all-black tracts. And these conditions characterized all regions—from the standpoint of racial separation, tract maps reveal little meaningful difference between the de jure segregation common in the South and the de facto segregation practiced in the North and West.[38]

The segregation of urban America was not the result of accident or oversight. It had required decades of deliberate effort by private citizens, elected officials, real estate brokers, mortgage lenders, federal regulators, and, on too many occasions to accurately count, violent mobs. Then as now, a home was by far the most expensive thing virtually any American would ever own, and homeownership was the twentieth century's single most important way to accumulate wealth. For these and other reasons, a home was the possession that most defined people and their families and neighborhoods. So those with power took every available measure to guard home values, in part by making it difficult or impossible for "undesirable" populations to live near them.[39]

In cities across America, virtually every aspect of law, custom, and day-to-day practice supported racial exclusion. Probably the most widespread method was racial steering, the practice of showing buyers only houses in neighborhoods that "matched" their race. Real estate agents almost never took black people to see houses in white neighborhoods (except as a way of "blockbusting," frightening white homeowners into selling at lower prices), and indeed the published standards of their profession defined doing so as malfeasance. Even beyond that, of course, the sheer fact of public pressure in the form of community disapproval or loss of reputation or business dissuaded most real estate operators from challenging this "standard." It was, of course, contested by people who could pass for white, or who used intermediaries to act on their behalf or convey the properties to them—transactions like these had been the origin of both civil rights lawsuits and white riots.[40]

Equally prevalent were racial covenants. Beginning around the turn of the twentieth century, many land deeds specified that as a matter of contract, homeowners could not sell or rent their property to various groups—usually including African Americans but also frequently including people of Asian ancestry, ethnic Mexicans, and Jews. These requirements were legally binding, and if an "undesirable" homeowner slipped through, a transaction could be invalidated retroactively. These racial covenants were valid law for decades, upheld by the nation's highest court in *Corrigan v. Buckley* (1926) on the grounds that they were purely private agreements that, because they involved no "state action" by governing authorities, did not violate the Fourteenth Amendment's requirement of equal protection under law.[41]

Of course, local governments were not shy about taking openly racist state action in the form of zoning ordinances. In the 1910s and 1920s, municipalities were increasingly exercising their authority to shape urban development. Zoning regulations mostly involved situations like separating noxious industries from residential areas, but dozens of cities and towns officially zoned for race. For example, Dallas's 1916 law dictated that each block would be classified as "white," "colored," or "mixed," and that no buyers or renters would be permitted to dwell outside "their" areas. Municipal archives in cities across America contain old racial zoning maps that testify to the longtime popularity of officially sanctioned segregation.[42]

These and other practices were reinforced by lenders and then, in the 1930s, by federal loan guidelines. Banks, savings and loans, and other lenders had long refused to offer mortgages to borrowers of color who wished to move into white neighborhoods—they feared that the mere presence of nonwhites would drive down property values and endanger their existing investments. Beginning in the 1930s, federal loan guidelines nationalized these assumptions by denying federal insurance for loans made in nonwhite areas. The results were the infamous "redlining" maps that showed how both local practice and national policy upheld racial segregation by choking off lending in nonwhite neighborhoods and to people of color hoping to move to white areas.[43]

In the immediate postwar years, these practices had been in effect for long enough that they were taken for granted. Some of them were informal, and others were explicit, but they were invisible to most people in the sense that they did not require publicly posted signs specifying which spaces belonged to which racial group. As a result, white people could live in "their" neighborhoods without seeing the wide range of practices and policies that had created them. Black people and many others of color, meanwhile, understood that there were parts of the city where they could walk or drive or go about their business undisturbed—and many more where simply showing their faces in public would place them in danger.

In that postwar moment, with the state of racial play still uncertain, some long-standing bulwarks of de facto segregation had begun to fall. African Americans and Hispanics, who had helped their country win the war, sought to extend the "Double V"—a victory against fascism abroad and against racism at home. In this they found numerous allies, not least on the nation's highest court; President Roosevelt had named eight of the nine sitting justices, creating a liberal majority willing to facilitate a careful offensive against Jim Crow in all its forms. In 1948 the Supreme Court ruled in *Shelley v. Kraemer* that racial covenants were unconstitutional on the grounds that if a court enforced a racially discriminatory private contract, that itself was "state action" and therefore impermissible. With the rise of the civil rights movement, black people nationwide—and a small but growing number of Mexican Americans in the Southwest—increasingly saw housing discrimination as an unacceptable infringement on their rights. Their readiness to take cases of discrimination to court, and the willingness of the judiciary to recognize their claims, put additional pressure on segregation.

But the response of many whites in urban neighborhoods was not what equality-minded people had hoped for. Instead of accepting the principle of racial equality, white people in many areas decided that if the older methods of enforcing segregation were no longer in effect, they would instead use force to defend the color line. The violence in Dallas and Chicago was hardly exceptional; much the same happened in many other places in the early postwar era. In Atlanta just a year after the war, members of an officially chartered, khaki-uniformed neo-Nazi organization inveighed against "unscrupulous real estate dealers . . . selling white property to Negroes" and perpetrated a wave of beatings, attempted kidnappings, and house bombings against black people in their part of the city. In Detroit in the first two postwar decades, whites committed more than two hundred assaults against black people trying to move into white neighborhoods; these included everything from racial taunts and menacing crowds to effigy burning, window smashing, and arson. In these years, black people faced the constant possibility of attack and could not be sure that the municipal authorities could protect them—or in some cases that they even wanted to.[44]

THE DIFFERENT CIRCUMSTANCES of Hispanics in Dallas and Chicago were emblematic of the general uncertainty that came with Spanish heritage throughout the midcentury United States. In many of the places where they lived, they were routinely denied entry to stores, restaurants, theaters, and other public places, or were segregated within them. Like the second-class citizenship that black Americans suffered under Jim Crow, Juan Crow involved posted NO MEXICANS signs as well as simple refusals of service. In other places, especially larger towns and cities, the brown-white color line could be uneven: depending on their skin tone and the vagaries of local custom, a person of Mexican or Puerto Rican ancestry might be welcome at one establishment and driven out of another. But the possibility of exclusion and humiliation—and the likelihood of police brutality if law enforcement became involved—was present and operated in almost every area of daily life.[45]

The previous history of urban Mexican Americans also hinted at even more dire possibilities. In wartime Los Angeles, many whites resented having to share crowded urban spaces with people of color, and local newspapers and radio hosts stirred up this antipathy by collectively slandering ethnic Mexicans, portraying them as delinquent, diseased, and disloyal. Military personnel in the city took to harassing and accosting ethnic Mexicans and other people of color, especially women, whom they openly deemed theirs for the sexual taking. The victims tried to defend themselves, but what had begun as opportunistic abuse turned into targeted violence in the Zoot Suit Riots of 1943. Over the course of several days, thousands of white soldiers, civilians, and police officers in Los Angeles sought out and attacked mostly Mexican American youth. People were dragged off buses and out of theaters, beaten up, and stripped of their clothes. Rather than trying to quell the violence, onlookers cheered, and instead of condemning the attacks, the Anglo press largely supported them. The chaos abated only when the US Navy prohibited its personnel from going into the city without a specific assignment to do so. But things settled down only locally: publicity around the riots, much of it celebratory, inspired similar racist violence in a number of other cities, including Chicago, Philadelphia, Detroit, Baltimore, and San Diego.[46]

Nationwide, the proportion of Mexican Americans and Puerto Ricans who lived in cities increased over the course of the postwar decades. Because that growth began from a small base, however, their numbers remained limited, whether measured in percentage or in absolute terms. And considering the level of violence against black people moving into white neighborhoods, many people of Spanish-Indigenous descent thought that being mostly overlooked was by no means a bad thing. For many, staying in their barrios and remaining inconspicuous seemed like the best way to cope. Nobody could be sure what might happen as Latino numbers in major cities rose. After all, the proportion of ethnic Mexicans in Los Angeles had been small at the time of the Zoot Suit Riots, and considering the long history of white riots in urban America, Hispanic city-dwellers understood that they faced an uncertain and perilous future.[47]

THE 1950S ALREADY showed signs of an incipient urban crisis—one whose clearest symptom was the refusal of most whites to share the cities fairly with people of color. In Chicago and Dallas, when African Americans sought to live in better homes in safer neighborhoods, they faced campaigns of harassment, intimidation, and violence. Black people faced similar treatment in other cities across the nation. There were some white city-dwellers who tried to create integrated neighborhoods that all might enjoy, and they joined together with their black fellow citizens in campaigns for cooperation and improvement.

But they struggled to keep such neighborhoods together when real estate operators could make so much money scaring white people, buying their houses cheap, and reselling them at a huge markup.

In these years, small communities of city-dwelling Hispanics also became involved in the precarious racial dynamics of urban America. In most cases, their stories were lost among the concerns of the majority and the larger minority, who continued to see black-white race relations as the real issue in urban America; around midcentury, there simply were not enough people of Spanish heritage in most places to change the way people saw the problems of the city. So they just tried to make their way. In so doing, they sowed the seeds of a very different urban order—one that was only beginning to come into view, but whose importance would gradually become clear as their numbers doubled, and then doubled, and then doubled again and again in the decades that followed.

As of the early 1960s, however, much was uncertain. While some neighborhoods had become early examples of white flight to the suburbs, there were many more where white householders showed no intention of leaving. In South Lawndale and Oak Cliff, people remained largely in place—just as they did in many thousands of city neighborhoods nationwide that were still overwhelmingly white and relatively stable throughout the 1950s. The shape of things to come would depend on people's choices within their communities. But even these local decisions would be made against the backdrop of policies that had already been set in motion in national capitals, state legislatures, federal agencies, and corporate boardrooms.

CHAPTER 4

BUILDING
THE URBAN CRISIS

T HE FATE OF PLACES LIKE SOUTH LAWNDALE AND OAK CLIFF
was not preordained or automatic; neither were the fortunes
of the cities of which they were a part. In the early 1960s, people like Guadalupe Lozano, Clyde Ross, and Richard Dolejs sought
to maneuver in the changing terrain of Chicago, just as Dallasites
were trying to do in their own neighborhoods. The most dramatic of
the issues they faced involved race and housing, but there were other
factors in play as well.

Equally important were changes in government policy and industrial management. When families made decisions about where to live
and work and send their children to school, their choices were shaped
by policies established elsewhere—from city halls to corporate headquarters to the corridors of Congress. These public and private policies helped set the highly unequal range of options available—for
example, to African American families hoping to buy homes in previously white city neighborhoods; to white residents deciding whether
to move out to the suburbs; and to Hispanics trying to find their place
in the metropolis.

These policies touched on everything from homeownership to city planning, labor relations to transportation. Their effects could vary greatly from place to place: even neighborhoods located next to each other could develop in very different directions. Indeed, these policies were so complex, and their effects so unclear, that people did not know how to react when they were first implemented. Rather than immediately moving in or clearing out, they waited to see where things were headed.

As the early 1960s gave way to the middle years of the decade, many neighborhoods on the edge of crisis tipped over into the abyss. The intertwined legacies of racial discrimination and rapid disinvestment by both private companies and public authorities stripped neighborhoods of resources, leaving residents with scant means to better their circumstances. Years of deprivation and mistreatment fostered everyday frustration that with the right provocation flared into rebellion and riot. As fires burned and palls of smoke rose over one city after another, a gradual departure to suburbia became one of the biggest migrations in the nation's history.

The sheer magnitude of US deurbanization makes it easy to imagine that this process was somehow natural or necessary. But almost the entire Western Hemisphere was heading in precisely the opposite direction in these decades. As the United States descended into the urban crisis, Latin America experienced the most extraordinary city growth in its history. Over the course of five decades, an astonishing 250 million people would move to the region's urban areas or be born in them. The population of the region's cities exploded, with many of them growing more than tenfold: Mexico City went from 3 million to 18 million people; Lima, Peru, from 645,000 to over 7 million; and Santo Domingo, Dominican Republic, from 180,000 to 1.85 million.[1]

This dramatic divergence in urban fortunes had many causes, but government policy was prominent among them. When presidents, finance ministers, and national legislatures made decisions about taxation, spending, regulations, and subsidies, they strongly influenced their nations' human geography—the patterns of where people lived and worked and played. At the risk of oversimplifying, one might say that in the United States federal officials were paying people to move out of cities, while in Mexico and other nations in Latin America governments were paying people to move into them. These different urban histories would later become intertwined as *migrantes* dramatically expanded the linkages between the metropolitan systems of Latin America and Anglo America.

DURING THE POSTWAR years, urban planners and municipal officials issued regular warnings about the structural challenges facing cities in the United States. Even though populations in urban areas were at an all-time high, these observers pointed out underlying problems that had been left unattended since before the Great Depression.

Urbanists had many concerns. They noted large expanses of old and dilapidated housing in desperate need of repair, observing that vast numbers of city-dwelling Americans were living in homes with failing plumbing, sagging ceilings, and unreliable heat. They worried that many downtown businesses had become run-down and were losing customers to shopping strips at the city's edge. They fretted about congested streets where trucks got stuck in traffic and their drivers struggled to find places to stop and load or unload goods, further clogging roadways. Cities were threatened by obsolescence, they warned, and would be unprepared for the residents and economic uses of the future if they were not upgraded, modernized, or otherwise improved.[2]

Another structural problem facing urban America was deindustrialization. The term itself would not be coined, nor the concept fully understood, until many years later, but by the early 1950s many municipal officials understood that manufacturing and related industries were gradually shifting away from cities. Indeed, this was one of the trends that had alerted city planners to the declining suitability of urban areas as places of employment and spurred them to make improvements to retain existing industries and attract new ones.[3]

Much of the impetus behind deindustrialization stemmed from corporations' desire to pay their workers less—what company executives called "controlling labor costs." US industrial employers had sought out low-wage labor since the nineteenth century, when they welcomed poor rural people and immigrants to their factories as employees. They accelerated this quest in the twentieth century, seeking out unorganized workers by moving away from cities with large and powerful labor unions. At first they did so by siting new plants in suburban and rural areas, then in the South and the West. The clearest example had been the relocation of textile mills from New England to the Southeast in the first half of the twentieth century.[4]

Other developments augmented this decentralizing trend. Manufacturing had been concentrated in cities mainly because factories needed to bring raw materials in and move finished products out. In the pre-automobile era, businesses had to locate around rail hubs and ports. But as trucks gradually came to carry a greater portion of goods, corporate management had a freer hand in relocating factories anywhere good roads could be found.[5]

Changes in the architecture of manufacturing also left cities at a disadvantage. In the postwar period, industrial engineers determined that older multistory plants and warehouses were less efficient than horizontally oriented facilities with long, single-level assembly lines, which sometimes covered millions of square feet. In dense city centers it could be difficult to assemble such large land parcels. So as businesses expanded in the prosperous decades after the war, they mostly built new factories on open land in suburban or rural areas.[6]

South Lawndale exemplified the problems faced by older urban neighborhoods in the industrial North. Its housing stock was old, with most buildings dating to the early part of the century or before. It surprised nobody when a 1940s report from Chicago's main planning agency included a map that showed most of the neighborhood as "blighted," "near blighted," or in need of "conservation." After all, South Lawndale's homes had already been well worn when central European immigrants arrived decades earlier; had they been able to afford better, they would have settled somewhere else.[7]

But it was deindustrialization that was the most pressing problem facing South Lawndale after midcentury. The neighborhood had maintained its industrial employment base throughout the 1940s, holding steady at over sixteen thousand manufacturing jobs that employed more than half the area's workforce. But in the 1950s, South Lawndale lost more than a quarter of those manufacturing jobs over the course of a single decade. The McCormick Works located at the neighborhood's eastern edge was emblematic of the problem. The factory complex had provided thousands of people with employment as Chicago became the nation's leading manufacturer of agricultural machinery. But the plant had been built to nineteenth-century standards, and as the organization of production changed and company managers came to see it as outmoded and inefficient, they began to reduce operations.[8]

In Dallas, though the manufacturing sector operated differently, there was still widespread concern for the city's older neighborhoods. In the 1940s, workers in Oak Cliff had been awash in well-paid employment, thanks in large part to the new naval weapons plant nearby. More than five thousand new industrial jobs had been created for the neighborhood in a single decade. And those positions were durable: through the 1950s and 1960s, the industrial workforce held steady at about eleven thousand—more than one-quarter of Oak Cliff workers.[9]

The problem was that, for fast-growing Big D, flat job growth was not enough. In a northern industrial city during a time of population loss, that kind of employment stability would have been remarkable. But this was Dallas, a Sunbelt metropolis whose population would more than double in the thirty years after 1950. For Oak Cliff to maintain an unchanging population with minimal job growth was in truth not much of an achievement at all; rather, it was a sign of stagnation.

The neighborhood's aging housing stock was also a concern. While Oak Cliff featured some beautiful 1920s Craftsman-style showpieces, most of its streets were lined with smaller wood-frame houses from an earlier era. This was the apogee of midcentury modern design, however, a time when architects and fashion icons alike were inspired by the sleek lines and futuristic silhouettes of the Space Age. Many people were looking for larger houses in a more contemporary style, and those were only being built elsewhere in Dallas.

Planners in both cities had long expressed concern about the condition of older neighborhoods and the central business district and had formulated policies they believed would help. In 1943 the Chicago Plan Commission issued a report stating that twenty-three square miles of the city were "blighted" or "near blighted," with over sixty-seven thousand homes classified as needing major repairs or unfit for use, especially in neighborhoods south and west of the Loop. The report warned that if measures were not taken, this blight would spread, causing city residents and businesses to decamp to the suburbs. Taking their spending power with them, they would deprive the city of property and sales tax revenues.[10]

The commission proposed that the City of Chicago spend public funds to support private investment. It should use the power of eminent domain to take control of land parcels whose structures could be rehabilitated or, when necessary, demolished. Cleared land would be made available to developers for new residential or commercial construction, and the city would offer assistance in relocating the people who would be displaced. At the same time, new expressways linking the city with its periphery also had to be built. Through the 1940s and into the early 1950s, the Illinois state legislature passed a series of statutes granting Chicago city hall extensive powers for coping with its decaying neighborhoods and obsolete transportation infrastructure—enactments that quickly became models for federal urban renewal laws.[11]

In Dallas, city hall came to many of the same conclusions. In the early 1940s, municipal leaders had commissioned a comprehensive planning document from a nationally recognized urbanist, and while the city's rapid growth had rendered it outdated, they remained concerned about two areas it had highlighted. One was an ongoing crisis of slum housing. Decades of shortages had only become worse during the war, and poor people, especially African Americans and Mexican Americans, sometimes lived two or three families to a single-family home. The other major concern was the gradual decentralization of population that threatened the economic primacy of downtown: Dallas planners could see that residents, retailers, large employers, and entertainment venues were gradually migrating to the metropolitan periphery in what an article in *Texas Town and City* later called the "centrifugal movement of people."[12]

Dallas officials and civic associations put together a set of plans that included slum clearance, housing construction, and improved infrastructure for the city center. They proposed using federal funding and the power of eminent domain to clear blighted neighborhoods and construct more and better housing—though always, of course, on a segregated basis. They also sought to build a system of rails and roads that would ease access to downtown and, they hoped, keep economic activity concentrated there. City leaders quickly set about advocating for enabling legislation from the state legislature, and as Congress enacted new urban programs, they moved quickly to apply for funding to carry out their plan.[13]

In their enthusiasm, they were much like leaders in other cities across the United States who filed applications and made ready to spend the available renewal funds. In the face of very real challenges, city planners, elected officials, and many other municipal stakeholders came to the table with goodwill, considerable influence, and substantial resources courtesy of the postwar economic boom. But there were also obstacles to urban improvement, from political corruption to unforeseen consequences, and all concerned were operating within an environment of persistent racial discrimination. Ultimately, even when such plans were successful—and often they were not—they were only a small part of a broader pattern of federal spending that subsidized the suburbs at the expense of the cities.[14]

IN THE POSTWAR YEARS, the US landscape was reshaped by new federal policies that spent the present-day equivalent of trillions of dollars subsidizing migration to the metropolitan periphery. Each of these policies chipped away at the desirability and viability of residential neighborhoods like Little Village and Oak Cliff. These blows had begun to land even before racial integration had moved to the center of community concerns, and they would continue long afterward.[15]

The most important of these policies was federal involvement in mortgage lending. During the Great Depression, millions of people had lost their homes to foreclosure, home financing had collapsed along with small banks and savings and loans, and legions of workers were left jobless. In response, the Roosevelt administration established New Deal agencies to stabilize housing, stimulate lending, and boost hiring by housebuilders. The most important of these agencies was the Federal Housing Administration (FHA). Its primary function was to guarantee home loans: it established standards and collected premiums so that if a lender issued an FHA-approved mortgage and the home buyer failed to make the payments, the lender could collect the insurance and avoid the loss on the loan. By putting the power of the US Treasury behind these loan guarantees, the FHA took most of the risk out of home lending. Also essential was the

Home Owners Loan Corporation, which created mortgages as we understand them today: long-term, self-amortizing home loans with uniform payments.[16]

These federal interventions revolutionized the housing market. Backed by government guarantees, home lenders were largely protected from defaults and could write mortgages freely. Far more people could afford loans thanks to thirty-year terms, low interest rates, and small down payments. They flocked to buy homes, creating strong demand and economies of scale for a booming construction industry.

These policies did not treat all homes or homeowners equally, however: they systematically favored outlying suburbs over city centers. One key reason was that lending guidelines favored single-family detached homes, which were less prevalent inside cities but common outside them. Even more importantly, these guidelines explicitly dictated that lenders should not make loans in racially mixed areas; thus city neighborhoods where people of color lived or were moving in were largely cut off from mortgage credit, while overwhelmingly white suburbs were not. As a result, in the program's first quarter century it made five to seven times more loans to suburban home buyers than to urban ones. More than 98 percent of all its loans were made to white people.[17]

The full suburbanizing effect of these policies was beginning to be felt in the latter 1940s: after a decade and a half of depression and war, the pent-up demand for new homes was unleashed and government incentives flowed freely. In practical terms, this meant that, for those who qualified, out-of-pocket costs would be much lower for a larger suburban home than for a smaller city dwelling. One former New Yorker explained his move to New Jersey: "We had been paying $50 per month rent, and here we come up and live for $29 a month. That paid everything—taxes, principal, insurance on your mortgage, and interest." Millions of people came to understand precisely this kind of cost comparison, fostering a nationwide trend of urban depopulation and suburban growth. Hence the rapid proliferation of places like the three Levittowns: outlying housing tracts with small, affordable single-family homes that were essentially off-limits to African American families and most other people of color. The sheer scale of this suburban subsidy was astounding. For example, the mortgage interest deduction—allowing homeowners to subtract the interest on their home loans from their taxable income—cost the government almost five times more than all its direct spending on housing programs combined; it became one of the most expensive categories of deduction in the entire federal tax code.[18]

A second major component of the federal government's suburban subsidies came in the form of the very programs that had been intended to save center cities. Planners and other municipal officials focused their energies on preventing the spread of "blight," which they defined as down-at-heel neighborhoods with dilapidated housing and decaying streetscapes. Talk of blight returned compulsively to the metaphor of disease, especially cancer, and to prevent it from spreading, they created programs to cure the condition. First among these was the Housing Act of 1949, under which municipal authorities could obtain federal funding to clear areas deemed "blighted" and "renew" them. The idea was that by demolishing these obsolete parts of the city and rebuilding them in a more rational way—as high-rise housing complexes (including public housing) that would shelter more people on less land, and with room for large-scale projects like new civic centers and hospitals and university campuses—the city could recover its health, retain residents and businesses, and find new economic uses.[19]

But because of these officials' preconceptions about poverty and race, their projects disproportionately affected poor neighborhoods, especially ones where people of color lived. They promised relocation housing but seldom delivered anywhere near enough of it to those they displaced. The results were summed up by an alderman on Chicago's West Side: "Every time that iron ball bats down one of those slum buildings on the South Side, twenty Negro families move west." It was for good reason that African Americans punned with bitter humor that "urban renewal"—the name given to this approach—was more accurately termed "Negro removal."[20]

Black people were most likely to be displaced by urban renewal, but large numbers of working-class white ethnics, like Italians, Jews, Greeks, and others from southern Europe, were similarly pushed out. Hispanics were also affected. The roll call of demolished neighborhoods included the ethnic Mexican community of Chávez Ravine, displaced for the building of Dodger Stadium in Los Angeles; the substantially Puerto Rican neighborhood (the location for the movie *West Side Story*) that was demolished to create New York's Lincoln Center; and many other lesser-known examples in smaller cities. While these kinds of clearance strategies had fallen out of favor by the late 1960s, the damage had been done: dozens of districts were cleared, their homeowners forced out, their businesspeople deprived of stores and offices and clienteles, and entire communities divided or scattered.[21]

The road to suburbia was literally paved with federal dollars in the form of the most massive public works project the world had ever seen: the interstate highway system. Planners, politicians, and industrialists had long dreamed of a national network of roadways, but it was simply too expensive. It was the support of a wide range of groups with a strong interest in automobility—including carmakers and the steel, glass, rubber, and petroleum industries, as well as the labor unions that represented their workers—that made the Highway Act of 1956 possible. The law funded a continent-wide network totaling forty thousand miles of roadway. Constructing it was the work of a generation, with a huge labor force paid out of the federal treasury. The total cost was in the tens of billions of dollars—the present equivalent of over a trillion dollars.[22]

Interstate highways were meant to help cities. Mayors, city councils, and planners had largely favored the new freeways. Postwar urban planning doctrine held that older downtowns had become too crowded and congested, making it hard to get around. (And indeed, upon reaching the city limits, motorists often confronted a maze of small, pre-automobile-era streets that seemed to jam with traffic as soon as anyone stopped to make a delivery.) The political coalition behind the highway act was in large part urban, representing a wide variety of businesspeople and employees whose homes, jobs, and investments were centered in cities.

Rather than simply improving access to urban centers, however, freeways made it easy for people to commute: a suburbanite could often drive to and from work more quickly than a resident of an outlying city neighborhood could get downtown on public transportation.

The harm done to cities by freeways had begun, however, well before the first cars drove up the on-ramps. To "open up" cities, the new expressways had to run directly through densely built urban neighborhoods. Some families saw their homes and entire blocks demolished, and even areas that escaped the bulldozers were still cut off from adjacent neighborhoods. Few people who had any choice wanted to live next to an expressway, with its honking horns and exhaust fumes. As highway construction joined urban renewal in the destruction of vast tracts of housing, many city residents decamped to the suburbs, where, at least for white people, federal subsidies waited like a warm embrace.[23]

There was one more federal subsidy for suburbia, a seemingly minor modification of the tax code in 1954. Completely unknown to the great majority of Americans, it went by the unexciting name of "accelerated depreciation." To developers and accountants, however, it was very important indeed—it transformed any new commercial real estate project into a tremendous tax shelter. Simply put, accelerated depreciation allowed real estate developers to take big tax deductions on new building projects; they could quickly claim on-paper losses and write them off against profits they made elsewhere. This financial strategy was not a secret: publications from *Architectural Forum* to the *New York Times* to the *Wall Street Journal* ran articles on the subject.[24]

Developers dramatically stepped up the construction of shopping centers: within a few years the number being built annually tripled, and average total square footage increased fivefold. The great majority went up outside city limits because the tax law made it much more lucrative to build anew, and on inexpensive land. The idea of putting retail space and offices near people was not new. But most companies had left their main branches downtown, assuming that shoppers and employees would go into the city for work and to make major purchases. Accelerated depreciation made new suburban shops and offices much cheaper to build than the old flagship store or headquarters. This one instance of tax leniency thus helped guarantee that businesses would follow people out of the city.

The era of massive federal subsidies to suburbia coincided with the end of more than a century and a half of urban growth. The nation's cities had confronted decentralizing pressures before: railways and streetcars had made it possible to live far from one's workplace, and mass-produced automobiles allowed settlement to sprawl even where there were no train tracks. But the cities had not yet lost population—that is, not until these factors intensified, reinforced each other, combined with white racial fears, and were amplified by a federal government that focused the power of public spending beyond the city limits. Only then would the vital center of urban America truly begin to hollow out.

ELSEWHERE, ANTI-URBAN GOVERNMENT POLICY was not the norm in these years. The United States was the exception around midcentury and after, a period that saw dramatic urban growth throughout most of the world. Across mid-twentieth-century Latin America, for example, government policies favored the growth of cities. Urbanization was not necessarily the official objective: what these countries enacted was less a set of coordinated and consistent policies than an improvisational and sometimes haphazard group of initiatives that failed as often as they succeeded. These initiatives were also not the only reason for city growth, which was determined by everything from macroeconomic trends to international development agencies to Cold War geopolitics. Nevertheless, government decision-making played a major role in determining not just where people would live but how they would make a living. After all, as of the 1940s Latin America had been predominantly rural: two-thirds of its people lived in small towns and villages, mostly doing agricultural work. Fifty years later, three-quarters of Latin Americans lived in urban areas, and specialists could discuss the region's "mega-cities," including several metropolitan areas of over five million inhabitants.[25]

The civilizations that created Latin America boasted a long tradition of urbanism. Spain had been an urban culture since the Roman period, and Indigenous America boasted a number of substantial cities and other population centers with large and elaborate buildings that required extraordinary technical ability in stone construction and exceptional creativity in ornamentation. After 1492, the urban orientation of the region was further reinforced. In 1573 the Spanish crown established ordinances for constructing colonial settlements.

These rules, which were codified in the Recopilación de Leyes de Indias (Compilation of the Laws of the Indies), mandated numerous details of city form and rewarded town founders with heritable titles of nobility as hidalgos. In the wake of Latin American independence, the region's leading intellectuals likewise counterposed the culture and sociability of the city against the isolation and backwardness of rural life. And as the region's cities grew in the late nineteenth century and into the early twentieth, elite society found it desirable to live in the center of cities; concentrating key functions like trade, governance, and culture in metropolitan areas reinforced urban dominance.[26]

Yet despite this cultural orientation toward urbanity, the era of the mega-city in Latin America did not begin until the middle of the twentieth century. In those years, governments across the region—especially in what would become major immigrant-sending nations—began to use the power of the state to foster urban growth. Their programs emerged from the two most influential economic theories of the era: modernization and dependency. Modernization theory held that different societies would follow the same general path of economic development—from domestic exchange to international trade, from agriculture to industry, from subsistence to prosperity. Developing nations should therefore try to move briskly along that path, just as had wealthy nations in Europe and North America. By contrast, dependency theory, which emerged in opposition to modernization theory, proposed that an internationalized economy allowed developed nations to prosper at the expense of the so-called Third World, and that the conventional path of development would lead poorer countries not to national wealth, but to exploitation and subordination. Despite the two theories' different assumptions and politics, both prescribed urban industrialization: modernizers believed that city growth was part of the natural sequence of economic development; dependency theorists counseled governments to expand industrial centers to establish economic independence by producing basic goods instead of importing them.[27]

Mexico instituted the largest-scale set of government policies that promoted industrialization and thereby channeled resources to cities. Beginning in the 1940s, successive Mexican governments spent decades using the power of the state to foster industrial growth. Federal officials devoted huge amounts of government resources to the task in a wide variety of forms. With government ownership or management of major sectors of the economy—most notably petroleum, steel, and electricity—policymakers could decide where facilities and infrastructure would be built or expanded. When officials approved spending on factories, power stations, railroads, bridges, water supplies, and the like, funds flowed overwhelmingly to cities. Even in sectors not controlled by the Mexican government, it helped finance the establishment of new companies, clustering them in Mexico City, Monterrey, and other major municipalities. And given the location of most industries, other state policies directed government spending to cities: when Mexico imposed tariffs and import quotas on manufactured goods, it was city-based concerns that were protected, and when it subsidized energy costs, the benefits went to industrialized, electrified cities.[28]

These policies helped usher in the era of the so-called Mexican miracle of the 1940s, 1950s, and early 1960s. These years saw extraordinarily rapid economic expansion, with average growth rates of more than 6 percent annually. The most numerous beneficiary of this expansion was the fast-growing urban working class, who took home strong earnings, in part because the Mexican government had instituted wage supports in the industrial sector. At the same time, the work of administering and coordinating this burgeoning economy was taken up by a rising middle class of white-collar workers. Mexico's gross domestic product more than tripled between 1940 and 1960. People could afford more consumer goods than ever before, generating in turn demand for many of the commodities that Mexican workers were producing. The nation's improving situation was also reflected in dramatic increases in the average Mexican's life span, which went from only forty years around 1940 to over sixty-one years in 1970.[29]

The very government policies that fed the cities, however, were bleeding the countryside dry. Domestically, the Mexican state imposed price controls on basic agricultural products to keep food prices low for industrial workers in urban areas. As a result, farmers could expect to earn little for the products they produced. Externally, federal officials spent foreign exchange gained from agricultural exports to fund their various subsidies to urban industry, further exacerbating disinvestment in rural Mexico. The countryside was impoverished and increasingly abandoned as millions of Mexican peasants reacted in the only reasonable way: by seeking work in the growing cities. Between 1940 and 1970, the population of Mexico City rose from 1.76 million to 6.87 million; Guadalajara grew from about 250,000 to 1.19 million, and Monterrey from 190,000 to 858,000. The proportion of Mexico's economy and of its workers in the industrial sector grew while the agricultural sector contracted. As a result, the urbanized population grew from 20 to 59 percent over these same decades, making a predominantly urban society out of traditionally rural Mexico.[30]

In these same years, Caribbean governments put analogous pro-urban policies into effect, with similar results. In Puerto Rico, officials sought to compensate for the decline of the island's agricultural economy by fostering industrialization. Beginning in 1942, the government organized and financed new companies, constructed factory space for them, and provided other forms of subsidy. This policy gave way within several years to using tax abatements and offers of low-cost labor to encourage foreign investors to industrialize the island. In both cases, however, the great majority of the industrial employment created was located in and around the island's largest cities, particularly San Juan, whose 450,000 people accounted for almost one-fifth of Puerto Rico's population by 1960. The neglect of rural areas was so clear that the Puerto Rican development agency tried to refocus its efforts on the countryside, but rural people continued to leave, and the populations of metropolitan San Juan, Bayamón, and Carolina soared—as did the size of Puerto Rican communities in cities like New York, Chicago, and Philadelphia.[31]

Urban development was also official policy in the Dominican Republic. From the 1930s through the 1950s, the Trujillo regime reconstructed and expanded the capital city of Santo Domingo, constructing monuments, buildings, street grids, and entirely new residential neighborhoods. These and many other urban projects were offered as evidence that the nation was achieving progress under the watchful eye of the dictator. This urbanizing effort was accelerated under Joaquín Balaguer, who directed public funds to finance the further modernization of the city, constructing everything from boulevards and parks to housing and hotels to museums and theaters—all symbols of an increasingly urbane nation. This pattern of development was bought at the expense of rural areas, since government transfers were designed to feed urban workers and fund city development. Little wonder, then, that the national capital's population grew from over 70,000 people in 1936 to almost 170,000 by 1960 to more than a million twenty years later, by which time it dominated a predominantly urban nation.[32]

Policies like these helped transform the human geography of the entire region. Cities grew at different rates in different parts of Latin America, but within a few decades the largest cities had become demographically dominant: metropolises like Mexico City, Santo Domingo, Buenos Aires, and many others accounted for as much as one-quarter to one-third of the total national population. If such a level of urban dominance had characterized Anglo America, the results would have been astonishing—it would have been as if the present population of New York City were more than 100 million people instead of its actual 8 million, or as if Toronto were home to 11 million people rather than just over 2.5 million. The urban divergence between Spanish America and Anglo America was extraordinary, and it highlighted how important government action could be in shaping a nation's cities.[33]

IN THE UNITED STATES, meanwhile, even though the federal government was mostly subsidizing suburbia, there were still monies available for use in rehabilitating urban areas. Municipal governments, some of which were already feeling the pinch of falling tax receipts, moved quickly to claim federal funding and remake their cities.

In Dallas, the leadership began with plans to renew the areas most in need of improvement. These varied from the small-scale renovation of some of the most underserved streets in Little Mexico to a grand plan to redevelop large sections of West Dallas—a project that would displace thousands of its predominantly African American, Mexican American, and poor white residents. City officials set about preparing applications for federal aid, by some accounts moving faster than almost any other municipality in the nation. Their enthusiasm for urban renewal did not translate quickly, however, into federal funding for clearance and redevelopment. Municipal leaders encountered a series of roadblocks and bottlenecks. A Texas appeals court ruled that the city could not acquire and clear land without a specific enabling law from the state legislature. Texas lawmakers failed to pass such a law for several years, introducing bills that failed to advance. Only in 1957 did legislators in Austin finally enact the needed statute.[34]

By then, however, the city's planning agenda had roused a determined political opposition. Many Dallasites not unreasonably suspected that urban renewal was being co-opted by downtown interests intent on helping the central business district while ignoring the city's neighborhoods. At a 1958 public meeting, an Oak Cliff resident argued that the city council could "clear the air" only by pledging not to undertake any clearance projects in the downtown core. Urban redevelopment became a key issue in that fall's congressional race for Dallas's only seat in the US House of Representatives. The source of the opposition combined concern over property rights with racism and suspicion of the federal government: as one candidate, incumbent Republican Bruce Alger, put it, "Federal regulation follows use of federal funds, which means acceptance of forced integration in public housing, and wage rates on urban renewal land clearance set by the Secretary of Labor, not by the local people or the economy." Alger received the endorsement of the *Oak Cliff Tribune*, which cheered his opposition to urban renewal and disdain for downtown business elites. He narrowly won reelection even though his opponent was supported by the city's business community, the *Dallas Morning News*, the *Dallas Herald-Tribune*, and organized labor.[35]

These legal and legislative delays and electoral defeats broke the momentum of urban renewal, along with expansions of housing programs and other government efforts to address the city's common problems. While a number of public housing projects had been completed and a few rehabilitation programs undertaken, large-scale urban renewal ground to a halt in Dallas—just as it did in many Sunbelt cities that similarly declined to participate in federal clearance and redevelopment.[36]

That did not mean, however, that bulldozers would never roll. Dallas officials were still persuaded of the need for automobile access, and there was still a great deal of public money available for the purpose. Municipal authorities constructed mile after mile of roadway in and around the city, not just Interstates 20, 30, 35, and 45 but also the Central Expressway, the Dallas North Tollway, and the Woodall Rogers Freeway. The city's new expressways put Oak Cliff at a clear disadvantage because they helped orient future development northward. Previously, the neighborhood had offered affordable residences fairly near downtown: it was just a short streetcar or bus ride across the bridge over the Trinity River. But the new highways brought a huge expanse of open land to the north of the city into commuting range of downtown, and residential and commercial development followed. The city was initially able to incorporate new areas, but it was suburban municipalities that grew most quickly—places like Richardson and Denton and Plano. The new highways had become convenient routes of departure for those who wanted to flee neighborhoods like Oak Cliff.

Dallas's highway projects were hardest on Mexican Americans. Freeway construction required municipal leaders to decide which areas would be torn down to accommodate the big interstates. Like decision-makers in so many cities, they decided to sacrifice the barrio. In the late 1950s and early 1960s, Dallas officials ran three different highway projects through Little Mexico, bulldozing or disrupting dozens of blocks at its very center. The result was the gradual dismantling of the neighborhood and the scattering of its households. The city's Mexican Americans remember clearly what happened and why. Longtime resident Ronnie Villareal recalled, "They cut right through the heart of the barrio with the Dallas North Tollway. When you cut right through the heart of it, what are you going to do?" He added: "We were young at that time. . . . We didn't participate in politics, you know, and they just went through. . . . People were, they were good people." At this point his wife Leonor broke in: "*No se sabían defender. Eramos tan inocentes y tan buenos.*" ("We didn't know how to defend ourselves. We were so innocent and so good.") Little Mexico regular Jesse Tafalla echoed these sentiments: "Back then we didn't have any recourse," he remembered. "We had no representation, we didn't understand the politics. They just kept us in the barrio."[37]

When the destruction of Little Mexico forced thousands of people to find somewhere else to settle, many of them made new homes in a neighborhood that had been losing population for more than a decade: Oak Cliff. This was in part because Oak Cliff had joined many other Dallas neighborhoods in resisting school integration; as late as 1964 the *Dallas Times Herald* reported that a segregated school, "a 12-grade, $1.2 million facility for Negroes," was being completed in the neighborhood, and the following year the newspaper explained that local people were "trying to stem the flood of white residents from Oak Cliff." After ten years of evasion and delay, William M. Taylor, a federal judge appointed in 1965 by President Johnson, issued an order declaring that Dallas schools would be integrated through a program of busing. No school could have less than one-quarter of its students be "minorities," defined as African American or Mexican American.[38]

The prospect of having their children bused to faraway schools with racially mixed populations generated fierce opposition in Oak Cliff, where local whites quickly rose up in protest. One Dallas newspaper reported a 1965 demonstration by Oak Cliff parents, children, and businessmen outside the offices of the Dallas Independent School District. The photograph showed a crowd of white people, with one woman holding signs reading, WHY OAK CLIFF? and DON'T BUS US! It soon became clear, however, that Oak Cliff's schools could not remain strictly segregated. In response, many white families decamped for North Dallas or the new suburban municipalities that had grown up beyond the city limits and therefore beyond the reach of the judge's order. The response was less pronounced in other parts of the city, but the trend was clear. The veteran Dallas journalist Jim Schutze later looked back and concisely described the response: "The whites yanked their kids, took off for the educational hills, and they haven't come back yet."[39]

IN CHICAGO, PEOPLE on the West Side hoped that new state and federal urban programs would be used to improve their neighborhoods, where the housing stock and infrastructure were among those most in need of renewal and rehabilitation. They too were concerned that the city's focus would be on the central business district inside the Loop, and downtown interests were indeed the first to secure funding for improvement; nevertheless, people in the neighborhoods still held out hope that their needs would be met next. The Daley administration made it increasingly clear, however, that their strategy was to use federal funding first and foremost to shore up the Loop.

The Daley agenda's effect on South Lawndale and other working-class neighborhoods on the West Side would involve at best neglect, at worst disruption. As West Siders came to understand that funds would not be spent to remove or rehabilitate dilapidated properties in their neighborhoods, residents who were sufficiently well paid and white were increasingly attracted to the newer suburbs. Meanwhile, the urban renewal and other federal projects favored by the mayor often involved the demolition of African American neighborhoods. With relocation housing slow or insufficient, thousands of black families were forced to go in search of new places to live—and the most affordable housing was on the West Side. This in turn made that part of Chicago into a "racially changing" area—the kind of place where guidelines made it difficult to get loans either for home improvements or purchases, further depressing local home values. Even those West Siders who wished to stay and make a go at creating a harmonious interracial neighborhood—and there were a number of community groups who dedicated themselves to precisely that—were faced with sinking property values.[40]

Even when they escaped direct disruption from urban renewal, West Side neighborhoods like South Lawndale were indirectly harmed by suburban subsidies from the federal government. The Chicago area's new expressways, which had been intended to "open the city up" to those eager to come downtown, often accomplished the opposite. The Eisenhower Expressway, sections of which began to operate in 1955, ran directly west from the Loop, allowing quick access to the growing western suburbs, and other highways running between the city center and the suburban periphery followed. South Lawndale had appealed to residents because it was close to both downtown and nearby industrial jobs. But these advantages meant much less when a worker could drive to the suburbs on a new expressway and live in a home that was newer, more spacious, and, thanks to federally backed mortgages, very affordable.

At the same time, the impact of large-scale renewal projects was often demolition and displacement rather than neighborhood rehabilitation. One of the most notable examples occurred around the new

Chicago campus of the University of Illinois. The Daley administration had for years been seeking a site for a new university branch. Some West Side communities welcomed the project, which Daley thought would wall off the growing minority populations from the Loop. During these years, the persistent uncertainty as to the location of the project produced confusion among homeowners, real estate operators, and others unsure of whether and how to respond. That confusion was relieved in 1961 when a site in the Near West Side community area was selected, but then even greater problems arose. The demolition of working-class housing displaced many thousands of people and scores of businesses. The effect was unmistakable. South Lawndale's residents continued to depart, closing businesses and leaving their homes behind. By the end of the 1960s, home values continued to decline, and the vacancy rate in the area was half again as high as it had been ten years earlier.[41]

As with Oak Cliff, the only people moving into South Lawndale in substantial numbers were Mexican Americans displaced by federally financed urban renewal. Among the various working-class communities that lay in the path of Mayor Daley's bulldozers was the Near West Side, still the city's largest barrio. The people displaced by the new University of Illinois campus streamed southwest into the Lower West Side and South Lawndale, both of which were gradually being abandoned by their longtime central European immigrant-stock residents. Although there were not nearly enough of those moving in from the Near West Side to compensate for the departure of the neighborhoods' previous residents, they at least made a start in stabilizing the population of the area. But that was before the departures quickened in Chicago and nationwide amid accelerating civil unrest.[42]

THE RIOTS OF the mid- to late 1960s were not the beginning of the urban crisis. They were not even the first instances of civil disorder. Whites had staged race riots and smaller-scale acts of intimidation and assault against black schoolchildren, civil rights protesters, and aspiring black homeowners hundreds or thousands of times in the preceding twenty years alone. But the scale of the disturbances was taken by many people, especially whites, as a signal that the time had come to leave the city. As the racial violence that preceded the riots was forgotten, the original meaning of the phrase "there goes the neighborhood"—white people's belief that black people moving into an area meant that it would be ruined—became a better description of whites' readiness to move away.

The large-scale urban violence of the 1960s began in fits and starts, often with law enforcement using excessive force in black neighborhoods where a combination of disinvestment, discrimination, exploitation, opportunism, and police brutality created extremely tense relations with the community. In the fall of 1963, police in North Philadelphia shot and killed a twenty-four-year-old man named Willy Philyaw, who had been accused of shoplifting a wristwatch. A gathering crowd responded by smashing store windows in protest. "This community is like a lighted stick of dynamite," said one resident to reporters. "It could blow at any moment." In New York City the following summer, after a scuffle between neighborhood teenagers and a building superintendent, a police officer shot a fifteen-year-old black boy in full view of a crowd of his friends. The ensuing Harlem Riot of 1964 resulted in hundreds of injuries and one death. The pace picked up in 1965. That August, police assaulted a black motorist while arresting him in the Watts neighborhood of Los Angeles. This drew a crowd of protesters, including a young woman whom police violently arrested. Residents responded with outrage, leading to six days of civil disorder in which thirty-four people died and $35 million in damage was done.[43]

Incidences of civil disorder soon became commonplace: in 1966, there were thirty-eight riots in the United States, resulting in a total of seven deaths, four hundred injuries, and $5 million in damage. The situation got even worse in 1967, which saw civil disturbances in more than 160 cities and towns. Among them were two of the most high-profile uprisings of all. The Newark riot began in mid-July after two policemen arrested and beat up a black cab driver. A crowd gathered, and the National Guard was brought in; then the situation escalated when one guardsman discharged his rifle. He was promptly reprimanded by a superior, who said, "Do you know what you just did? You have now created a state of hysteria. Every guardsman up and down this street and every state policeman and every city policeman that is present thinks that somebody just fired a shot and that it is probably a sniper." Rioting and looting began and lasted for four days, during which twenty-six people lost their lives. The Detroit riot began after police raided an after-hours bar and decided to arrest all its predominantly black patrons rather than the usual practice of simply dispersing them. Five days of disorder followed in which over seven thousand people were arrested and forty-three individuals were killed, almost three-quarters of them by the police.[44]

In response to the 1967 riots, President Johnson appointed the National Advisory Commission on Civil Disorders. Its report, released in March 1968, found that the disturbances were the result of pervasive racial discrimination in employment, housing, education, and other areas of life, ignited by misconduct and incompetence on the part of law enforcement and National Guard troops. In the nation's cities, the report observed in its opening section, "Segregation and poverty have created in the racial ghetto a destructive environment totally unknown to most white Americans. What white Americans have never fully understood—but what the Negro can never forget—is that white society is deeply implicated in the ghetto." In explaining the recent urban disorder, the report was clear: "This is our basic conclusion: Our nation is moving toward two societies, one black, one white— separate and unequal." Only five weeks later it became clearer just where things were moving.[45]

On April 4, 1968, the Rev. Dr. Martin Luther King Jr. was assassinated, struck in the head by an avid white supremacist's rifle bullet as he stood on the balcony of a Memphis motel. That night on the West Side of Chicago, people reacted with grief and rage that led to two days of rebellion. By the time some semblance of order was restored, eleven people lay dead and thousands had been arrested. Along a two-mile stretch of the main thoroughfare, more than two hundred buildings were destroyed by fires that left a pall of smoke floating over the neighborhood. The Windy City was not alone in the outpouring of despair and rage that followed King's assassination: similar uprisings broke out in more than one hundred American cities, resulting in forty-six deaths, twenty thousand arrests, and $100 million in property damage. The darkest days of the urban crisis had clearly not ended.[46]

The scale and intensity of these years of rebellion and riot marked a watershed for urban America. In the areas directly affected, many small-business owners decided to redouble their efforts and stay in business, some to train more local people in entrepreneurship. But many more took the insurance money and moved their operations to the suburbs, leaving behind long stretches of urban business arteries with shuttered stores or only occasional shops. These departures, in conjunction with the simultaneous loss of faith in urban redevelopment as a solution to the crisis of cities, seemed to leave many of the people most interested in fixing the nation's urban areas at a loss. And with a new presidential administration taking power after the election of 1968, the federal government would soon begin to cut aid to and spending in cities, depriving them of resources at the very time they were most needed.[47]

Within a few years, key indicators of big-city pathology were flashing red. Millions of people left their city neighborhoods and relocated to suburbia. In Dallas, a 1973 report found, 100,000 people had departed, most of them since 1968; the city would never again be home to as many white Anglos as it had been in 1970 as population growth slumped to its slowest pace in more than a century. Chicago was even harder hit: the 1970s saw the worst losses ever recorded for the city, with more than 360,000 people moving away on top of the quarter million who had left previously. In that decade alone, the city lost one-third of its white residents.[48]

Nationwide, urban population loss accelerated in the 1970s. By decade's end, many municipalities had lost one-third or more of their residents since midcentury, with the effect most severely felt in the industrial Midwest and Northeast: Detroit shed 36 percent of its denizens, Cleveland 37 percent, Pittsburgh 38 percent. Many smaller cities in the region, like Scranton, Youngstown, and Camden, suffered similar losses. Nationally, the proportion of Americans living in cities was falling for the first time in the nation's history.[49]

The everyday implications of population loss were devastating to local communities in a way that statistics could not express. As friends, neighbors, and even family members moved away, houses went empty. Unoccupied dwellings were a constant detriment because they easily became havens for criminals, drug users, and the dispossessed. It eventually fell to city officials to deal with these vacancies, and the least harmful option was often demolition, which was both expensive and wasteful.

For local property owners, the problem of empty buildings was especially alarming. Vacant premises produced no income, yet mortgages on those properties still had to be paid. It became increasingly common for owners to hire professional arsonists, known as "torches," to burn down their properties so that they could collect insurance payments and avoid taxes and maintenance. The legendary sports announcer Howard Cosell saw buildings near Yankee Stadium in flames while announcing the World Series in 1977, and millions of Americans remember him exclaiming, "Ladies and gentlemen, the Bronx is burning." That year the borough's district attorney, a World War II aircraft navigator, observed, "The destruction is reminiscent of the bombed-out cities in Europe." Nationwide, hundreds of thousands of burned-out structures dotted scores of distressed neighborhoods. At a time of rising homelessness, people were destroying dwellings that could have sheltered vast numbers of families and individuals.[50]

People leaving the cities carried away a great deal of economic activity. Through the 1960s cities were still identified with key industries; sports teams reflected this, as with the Detroit Pistons (1957), the Houston Oilers and Astros (1960 and 1964), the Seattle Supersonics (1966), and the Milwaukee Brewers (1969). But big industries were increasingly slipping away. Over the course of the 1970s Chicago lost about 1,900 factories; between 1972 and 1978 alone, it shed 118,000 jobs. Some of these workplaces simply closed, while others relocated to the suburbs or small towns in the region. In Dallas, business growth was positive throughout the metropolitan area, but more and more companies were moving out of the city or were founded in surrounding municipalities. In 1970, for example, the Ford Motors assembly plant that had opened in 1925 on East Grand Avenue shut its gates forever, taking with it a $17.5 million payroll. In 1971 the Cowboys moved out of the storied Cotton Bowl in Dallas's Fair Park to the new Texas Stadium in suburban Irving. And when Big D got a new airport in 1974, it too was located well outside the city. Nationwide, the result was the gradual loss of more than thirty-two million jobs—many of them the kind of industrial jobs that had allowed workers with a high school diploma (and sometimes less) to support families on a single wage.[51]

Retail sales were even more directly influenced by accelerating urban population loss. Countless small service establishments—restaurants, laundries, barbers and beauty parlors, repair shops, and the like—had once clustered around employment centers downtown, but now they followed their customer base to the urban periphery. In Chicago, many of the shops on the West Side were damaged or destroyed during the 1968 uprising. Most never returned, and it did not help that the leaders of their trade associations were discouraging them from doing so: by the late 1960s, retail journals were openly describing city customers as less desirable than suburban ones. Mostly, though not always, such admonitions were phrased in race-neutral language that conveniently obscured the fact that the urban clientele they were derogating was predominantly African American. Over the course of the 1970s the Windy City lost over seventeen thousand small businesses, an average of more than thirty-four each week, as nearly one-sixth of proprietors decided to call it quits. This rate of entrepreneurial flight was also common in other cities where there had been urban disturbances, but it was not limited to them: throughout urban America, small-business disinvestment quickly became endemic.[52]

Other workplaces were also leaving the city, including the white-collar variety. The offices filled with professionals and secretaries and clerks that had long been located downtown were now following their overwhelmingly white workforce and clientele elsewhere. Employers were encouraged in this by architects who explained that their employees would be more productive and contented in more bucolic settings. Thousands of corporate headquarters and small businesses moved outward to office parks and research campuses set within verdant landscaping and approached by winding drives. This was perhaps understandable at a time when Brutalist buildings, with their raw concrete facades, minimal ornamentation, and tiny windows, had become so common in redeveloped city centers. The 1960s buildings of the University of Illinois at Chicago exemplified the style: University Hall rose 338 feet, making it the tallest building on the West Side, while the surrounding cityscape was dotted with ornate churches, rowhouses, and parks. But because its fenestration consisted of vertical-slit windows only a few inches wide, to look out on what should have been a grand panorama, one literally had to close one eye and move one's head from side to side. Suburban offices, typically low-slung with ample windows, might have seemed like an appealing alternative to concrete fortresses that looked out at the city in fear.[53]

The decentralization of both population and economic activity brought on municipal fiscal emergencies. City budgets were dependent on a certain level of property taxes, sales taxes, and similar sources of revenue from residents and businesses. Suburbanization hit the first of these because families who moved out of a city now paid taxes in their new location, even when they still worked downtown and used city services during the day. This problem was compounded because home values went down as neighborhoods emptied out. When the assessed value of property dropped, city revenues based on taxes on those assessments fell as well. Municipal governments had little choice but to balance their budgets by raising taxes. This created a vicious cycle because higher city taxes drove more residents to move to outlying towns with lower tax rates.[54]

Meanwhile, the departure of manufacturing and retailing from the city dealt a double blow in much the same way. The sales, licensing, and other business taxes paid by firms and stores depended on their being located within the city limits. But when they moved away to outlying shopping centers in suburbs or adjacent municipalities, their taxable receipts followed them. And as cities tried to court new businesses to replace those lost, their bargaining power was so reduced that they were effectively forced to woo employers by offering massive tax breaks that, even when employers did move in, often deferred any effective payout for many years.[55]

Even apart from these essential factors, the increasing influence of fiscal conservatism made the position of cities more precarious than ever. "Tax revolts"—homeowners and other taxpayers voting to slash rates and reduce revenue—were accompanied by cuts to federal funding to cities. (The *New York Daily News* created the most direct and evocative image of this dilemma for cities when, in the wake of a presidential demurral on helping the city in its fiscal crisis of 1975, it ran the headline "Ford to City: Drop Dead.") Big-city mayors realized this and regularly reminded the voters and city councils of the fact, but in the climate of 1970s retrenchment and a political culture of slashing many kinds of government spending, beyond making clear the political reasons for budget shortfalls, they had limited room for maneuver.[56]

Crime was the frightened human face of the urban crisis. While population loss, economic devitalization, and fiscal crisis were over-all indicators, violence was something that people could be scared of in individual, everyday life. In part this was because crime received so much media attention—especially with the highly publicized serial killers of the 1970s, among them New York City's Son of Sam, Los Angeles's Hillside Strangler, and San Francisco's Zodiac Killer.

Popular fear of crime was not just a superficial impression, nor a product of overactive media: offenses of all kinds were indeed be-coming more common. The rise began in the early 1960s and in little more than a decade had reached very high levels that would persist for twenty years. Nationwide, property crimes doubled from 1960 to 1970 and soon climbed to triple the previous rate; homicide rates also doubled over the 1960s and 1970s. It was in urban America that the crime wave reached its most awful heights. Homicides, considered the most reliable indicator of the actual level of crime because the discovery of a dead body is not subject to reporting error like other offenses, offers a sense of the plight of the cities. In Chicago killings soared from 331 homicides in 1959 to 970 in 1974; and because these years saw the city lose more than one-fifth of its population, the murder rate more than tripled. In Dallas these figures likewise rose throughout the 1960s and 1970s; adjusted for population, the rate rose 150 percent between 1960 and 1979. In the nation's largest city, New York, killings soared over the course of the 1960s and 1970s to more than four times the previous rate.[57]

Here, then, were the material origins of a popular imagination in which muggers and killers lurked in the shadows along trash-strewn streets and in graffiti-covered subway cars, as well as an entertain-ment culture that produced and sustained more than a decade of vigilante revenge films like the *Dirty Harry* (1971) and *Death Wish* (1974) franchises, in which the suffering of crime victims served as the pretext for the main characters' killing sprees. These in turn fostered a public culture in which a decade later a Queens-born man named

Bernhard Goetz could become a strange sort of folk hero for pulling a .38-caliber revolver and shooting four teenagers whom he said had ordered him to give them five dollars; they said that they had simply been panhandling when they asked for the money. Afterward one jury acquitted Goetz on all counts except carrying an unlicensed handgun; in a civil trial, another jury found him guilty and awarded one of his victims a $43 million judgment.[58]

The fact that Goetz was white and his victims were black highlighted a basic fact of the urban crisis. As dire as all the symptoms of the crisis were, they were rendered all the more volatile for being increasingly racialized in the imaginations of fearful whites, many of whom continued to see the decline of cities as primarily the fault of black people. (Notably, these notions had originated with the "culture of poverty" theory first elaborated in the anthropologist Oscar Lewis's observations of poor Mexicans and reprised in a subsequent work on Puerto Ricans; Lewis's theory was widely criticized because it largely blamed poor people for their own impoverished condition.) Virtually every aspect of the urban crisis was inflected by this way of thinking, from the notion that blacks and other people of color ruined healthy neighborhoods to the insistence of many white people that the fiscal crisis was evidence of taxpayer money being wasted on supporting and policing "welfare queens" and shiftless young men who didn't want to work. And the rise in crime drove whites to imagine criminality as a black phenomenon and the city as a racialized danger zone or "jungle." Despite the findings of official and scholarly inquiries into the urban riots and rebellions, much of white America understood these events in terms of a racial folklore that cast black people as inherently prone to irresponsibility and violence.[59]

IF THE YEARS of rebellions and riots signaled the start of the severest period of crisis in the rest of urban America, Dallas's distress had begun several months prior, on November 22, 1963. The assassination of President Kennedy was a different kind of urban violence, but it tarnished the image of the entire city, and not without reason. In the weeks before the president's fateful visit, Dallas's leading voices had ratcheted up the rhetoric: the *Dallas Morning News* had run a column under the title "Why Do So Many Hate the Kennedys?" and people circulated a "Wanted for Treason" flyer with simulated mug shots of the president. Little wonder, then, that "Dallas killed Kennedy" was a phrase so often heard afterward; one journalist observed that Big D had become "perhaps the most mistrusted city in the Western world, an object of scorn, comedy, and myth."[60]

Dallas leaders spent years struggling to rehabilitate the city's image. They recruited a new mayor, moved to construct a new airport, and pursued or publicized various sports franchises, most notably the Dallas Cowboys. There was a massive, concerted effort to make the city's recently acquired football team, rather than the tragedy at Dealey Plaza, the first thing that people thought of when they heard the name "Dallas." And by the end of the 1960s, Dallasites could tell themselves that the effort was working: the city was gaining population, registering a third decade of double-digit growth rates; it had avoided the kind of highly public racial violence that was afflicting so many other municipalities; and as a result its reputation was beginning to climb out of the figurative basement.[61]

But in the summer of 1973, the relative racial peace of the city came completely undone. Dallas's police force was overwhelmingly white and had mostly been able to cover up decades of endemic racial abuse. That became impossible shortly after two officers pulled Santos and David Rodríguez out of their home in the middle of the night. Somebody had stolen eight dollars from a gas station vending machine, and the patrolmen thought the boys, just twelve and thirteen years old, were responsible. One of the policemen decided to frighten the already-handcuffed youths into confessing by improvising a game of Russian roulette in their squad car. After the "click" of one empty chamber, the officer put the gun to Santos's head and pulled the trigger, but the second chamber was loaded, and the bullet crashed into the boy's skull. Santos died in the back seat in full view of David, both brothers covered in blood. When the city's Mexican American community learned of the horrifying police murder of a child, they organized a protest downtown; understandably, the march soon turned to anger, leading to multiple injuries and more than two dozen arrests. Big D's prosperity had not made it immune to racial violence and rebellion after all.[62]

In the summer of 1973, a Dallas police officer handcuffed twelve-year-old Santos Rodríguez in his patrol car and shot him in the head while attempting to force a false confession. The Mexican American community organized this protest at city hall. Courtesy Texas/Dallas History and Archives Division, Dallas Public Library.

The Windy City fared even less well in this period. Several years later the *Chicago Tribune* published "City on the Brink," a five-part feature that looked back at how Chicago had changed in the 1960s and 1970s. The series was almost unremittingly bleak as it described mutually reinforcing problems—"the loss of people, factories, and jobs; the shrinking tax base, growing debt, and looming expenses; the creation of an economic wasteland between the booming Loop and the suburbs." The series concluded that this was not a temporary problem, noting that the losses had been going on for at least two decades. And it warned of worse to come: "According to available evidence and many experts, there is no reason to think it will ever turn around." It dolefully quoted a local urban specialist to the same effect: "Chicago is not going to disappear," he predicted. "But all the trends I see are against it. I see very little hope for locating economic activities here again."[63]

By way of consolation, the article gamely pointed out that the Windy City still compared well with other cities: it had not "collapsed spectacularly, as New York City did," it noted. "Nor is it yet as bad off as Detroit or Cleveland." But it certainly was a sign of the times that a city's largest newspaper could call it "an economic invalid" in a "condition that may be permanent," and then offer that—on the bright side, as it were—many of the nation's other big cities were doing even worse.[64]

PART TWO

HERE COMES
THE NEIGHBORHOOD

CHAPTER 5

NINETEEN SIXTY-FIVE

O N A CLEAR AUTUMN DAY TWO YEARS AFTER HE ASSUMED office, President Lyndon Baines Johnson sat at an antique desk for the formal signing of the Hart-Celler Immigration and Nationality Act of 1965. As he applied his signature to the bill, he was surrounded by its leading sponsors and supporters, who looked on with satisfaction. It was a fairly ordinary signing ceremony except for the location: on Liberty Island in New York Harbor, with the Statue of Liberty towering over the assembled political figures. Johnson had gone to considerable effort to achieve the greatest possible effect, dictating every detail regarding whom to invite and how his aides should set the scene.[1]

With the sunlit Manhattan skyline behind him, Johnson called the law "one of the most important acts of this Congress and of this administration" because "it corrects a cruel and enduring wrong in the conduct of the American nation." For the previous forty years, he explained, the United States had unfairly limited immigration by granting entry to people from a small number of nations while denying it to people from most of the rest of the world. These restrictions, he affirmed, "violated the basic principle of American democracy—the principle that values and rewards each man on the basis of his merit as a man," not the country of his birth.[2]

But that old regime was now at an end. "Today, with my signature, this system is abolished." Johnson vowed that discriminatory laws would "never again shadow the gate to the American nation with the twin barriers of prejudice and privilege." Extolling the nation's return to its proper place as the refuge of newcomers, the president waxed sentimental: "Our beautiful America was built by a nation of strangers," he affirmed. "The land flourished because it was fed from so many sources—because it was nourished by so many cultures and traditions and peoples." The new law would therefore "make us truer to ourselves both as a country and as a people."

In many respects the president was right. The new law was indeed the culmination of a long struggle over the meaning of America and the question of who would be eligible to become a citizen: some of the act's principal supporters had been fighting for more than forty years to enshrine the basic principle of equality in the nation's immigration policy. The law was also a product of the idealistic politics of the 1960s, of a readiness to use the power of government in new ways to end discrimination, care for the needy, and apply the nation's highest ideals to the task of governing. And it was a transformative law, one that helped usher in a new era of immigration to a United States that would be more populous and more diverse than ever before—and just as quarrelsome.[3]

In other ways, however, Johnson was just smoothing over unpleasant facts—the fundamental flaw in the law, and the contentious and tragic circumstances that had led to its passage. For despite its many virtues, the Hart-Celler Act imposed unprecedented limits on Latin American immigration in a way that would place the stigma and the burden of illegality on millions of Hispanics in the decades to come. Though this had not been the intention of the bill's authors, it was an unintended consequence of the cultural turmoil and blood-soaked politics of the era. After all, the Hart-Celler Act had been shaped by some of the most momentous events in the history of the twentieth-century United States: its greatest social movement, its closest presidential election, its most perilous Cold War confrontation, its most infamous assassination, and its second-biggest political landslide.

It was not the immigration act alone, however, that changed America. When people speak of "post-1965 immigration," they are usually referring to the Hart-Celler Act. But the nation was transformed at least as much by who wanted to come as by who was allowed to. Events that took place beyond the nation's borders were ultimately more important than domestic legislation. The year 1965 marked a turning point in US demographic history because it was the culmination of long-term trends in Mexican migration and urbanization. Any understanding of the transformation of Little Village and Oak Cliff, and the Latinization of urban America more generally, must begin with one basic observation: the millions of Mexicans and other Latin Americans who migrated to the United States showed up just when the nation's cities needed them most.

FOR NEARLY HALF the twentieth century, the rules of immigration to the United States were set by a series of laws that culminated in the National Origins Act of 1924. Congress enacted the law in response to the massive wave of newcomers that began around 1880 and within three decades raised the proportion of the foreign-born in America to about one in seven. The act was in essence a panicked and prejudiced response by a large Anglo-Protestant majority to the arrival of so many Catholics and Jews from southern and eastern Europe. The purpose of the law was to severely limit immigration and prevent further changes to the nation's ethnoracial profile.[4]

The bigotry behind the law was clear. "The trouble," explained one congressman, "grows out of a country composed of intermingled and mongrelized people." Another said the law would keep the United States "the home of a great people. English-speaking—a white race with great ideals, the Christian religion, one race, one country, and one destiny." After the applause from his fellow congressmen died down, he added: "The African, the Orientals, the Mongolians, and all the yellow races of Europe, Asia, and Africa should never have been allowed to people this great land." The law's senior supporter in the Senate, Henry Cabot Lodge, had for decades proclaimed the racial inferiority of continental Europeans and had authored a statistical "analysis" that purported to show how intelligence was distributed among US ethnic groups, with the English on top and recent immigrants near the bottom. Newcomers to the country, he had asserted, were causing "a great and perilous change in the very fabric of our race." Supporters outside Congress were similarly clear about their intentions: the Daughters of the American Revolution and the Ku Klux Klan were in agreement that the law was just what was needed to make America as white, Anglo-Saxon, and Protestant as possible. "I would build a wall of steel, a wall as high as Heaven," declared the governor of Georgia at a Klan convention in 1924, "against the admission of a single one of those Southern Europeans who never thought the thoughts or spoke the language of a democracy in their lives."[5]

Sentiments like these were neither shocking nor surprising at a time when open expressions of prejudice were common at all levels of society. White supremacist books with titles like *The Passing of the Great Race* (1916), *The Rising Tide of Color against White World Supremacy* (1920), and *The Revolt against Civilization: The Menace of the Under Man* (1922) found a ready audience. Their authors claimed that the United States was threatened by inferior breeds of humanity. Speaking of people from northwestern Europe as a master race with natural leadership and intellectual qualities, the books dismissed most other Europeans and all non-Europeans as biologically unfit for citizenship. They received support from adherents of the pseudoscientific eugenics movement, who believed that genetically inferior groups should be discouraged or prohibited from bearing children to improve the human race. Advocates of eugenics held prominent positions in leading universities and operated well-funded research labs where they refined and popularized scientific racism. These ideas found favor among influential politicians and other prominent Americans: the aviation hero Charles Lindbergh was an avid eugenicist; the automobile manufacturer Henry Ford regularly published anti-Semitic articles, tracts, and books; and the filmmaker D. W. Griffith enjoyed a huge hit with *The Birth of a Nation* (1915), which glorified the Ku Klux Klan and was screened at the White House. The late 1910s and early 1920s also saw the reemergence of the Klan, which added militant xenophobia to its virulent racism on the way to electing several governors and hundreds of state-level officials nationwide.[6]

The National Origins Act put an end to more than a century of largely unregulated immigration from Europe, limiting each country's annual arrivals to a mere 2 percent of its ethnic population in the United States as of 1890. In this way the law was an attempt to return the nation's demographics to where they had been a third of a century earlier, before the mass migration of the preceding decades. The law also severely limited immigration from Africa, and another 1924 enactment virtually prohibited arrivals from Asia, extending earlier restrictions and barring nearly half of humanity from ever becoming American citizens.

The politics of the US-Mexico border were more complex. There had been little official interest in limiting crossings before 1900. Immigration officials were largely uninterested in the Mexicans and Americans who crossed the border tens of thousands of times a day, instead focusing the earliest restrictions on Chinese migrants. Anti-immigrant agitation led to the first laws officially limiting Mexicans' access to the United States in 1917 and 1921, but employers widely evaded them and officials often overruled them because the economy of the US West, especially the rapidly expanding agricultural sector, simply could not function without Mexican workers. The authors of the 1924 immigration act wanted to impose the same limits on the Western Hemisphere as on the rest of the world, and for the same reasons: one leading restrictionist called Mexicans "illiterate, unclean, peonized masses," nothing more than "a mixture of Mediterranean-blooded Spanish peasants with low-grade Indians." But the nation's thirst for Mexican labor dictated that the National Origins Act ultimately did not restrict immigration across the Americas. Still, the US-Mexico boundary did not escape official scrutiny. When Congress passed the 1924 act, it simultaneously established the United States Border Patrol, under which hundreds of men were hired to police the nation's boundaries and report to a director who had previously worked on the southern border as a "Chinese inspector."[7]

The era's nativist crackdown entailed far more than just border control. These same years saw the passage of an Oregon statute prohibiting the teaching of foreign languages to young children, a Nebraska enactment effectively outlawing Catholic schools, and a California law mandating the forced sterilization of women judged "unfit" or "feeble-minded," to take just a few among dozens of similar examples. It was no coincidence that 1924 also saw Virginia enact a law outlawing marriages between black people and whites (the same one famously struck down by the Supreme Court forty-three years later in *Loving v. Virginia*). In the decade that followed, Nazi officials would cite statutes like these as inspiration for their Nuremberg Laws; after the war, they would use them again to defend themselves when they were put on trial for crimes against humanity.[8]

The effects of the National Origins Act were dramatic. Immigration fell off sharply, with virtually all nations seeing a decline. But there was a huge discrepancy between the few countries favored by the law and those targeted for the most severe restrictions. Arrivals from the United Kingdom fell by about one-sixth, but those from Italy plunged to about one-tenth of their previous level. As US officials worked out the formulas specified by the law and put them into effect, the overall rate of immigration fell by 80 percent.[9]

The most horrific effects of the law, however, would not emerge until the late 1930s and early 1940s. With the rise of fascism in Europe, hundreds of thousands of people tried to flee the expanding Third Reich. European nations had also placed limits on immigration, but in the moment of international crisis, many accepted a far higher proportion of refugees. The restrictive immigration laws of the United States, however, severely limited how many could leave, and numerous would-be emigrants instead joined the ranks of the war's fifty million dead. As the particular atrocities of Hitler's regime became undeniable, some US officials tried to convince lawmakers to pass a bill making an exception to the National Origins Act for twenty thousand mostly Jewish children to escape the Nazis, but the bill never even made it to Congress.[10]

AMERICAN IMMIGRATION LAW would remain mostly unaltered until the postwar period, when a combination of factors opened up the possibility for reform. Beginning in the 1930s, "white ethnics" of southern and eastern European immigrant stock who had gained influence as part of the New Deal political coalition sought to abolish the national origins system. During World War II, the nation had struggled against the Nazis and other enemies who were convinced of their own racial superiority, thereby discrediting the open bigotry of the early twentieth century. Beginning in the 1940s, movie audiences could see these factors combine as Hollywood produced dozens of "platoon movies" that featured clearly labeled ethnic soldiers—usually Irish, Italian, Jewish, Polish, and sometimes African American—fighting side by side. The exigencies of geopolitics were also important. During World War II, the United States put an end to six decades of Chinese exclusion because the obvious racism behind the policy gave imperial Japan a propagandistic advantage in the Pacific. The Cold War broadened such considerations even further: as ideology became the main theater of conflict, in the words of one official, the unfair quotas "needlessly provide grist for the propaganda mills of Moscow and Pe[k]ing."[11]

Cold War presidents of both parties were thus eager to put an end to the National Origins Act quota system. In 1948 President Truman ordered an official inquiry into the administration and effects of the system and used the resultant findings that it violated national ideals and harmed US prestige abroad as the principal rationale for urging Congress to repeal it. As one of his allies in the Senate put it: "Let those who defend the National Origins Quota System . . . recite the daily casualty lists coming out of Korea—and then let them dare to say that those of one national origin are less fit to be Americans, less fit to live and die for America, than those of another national origin." President Eisenhower was quieter in his opposition. He spent years privately lobbying legislators to do away with the quotas. His efforts became more vocal as international diplomacy became more fervent and racially fraught; by the time he left office he was openly chastising senators and congressmen over the issue.[12]

Congress thought differently, however. For many legislators, the possibility of foreign influence or subversion was a potent reason for excluding newcomers. In an atmosphere of fervent anticommunism, and at the height of Wisconsin senator Joseph McCarthy's red-baiting, members of Congress drafted and passed the McCarran-Walter Act in 1952. The law was designed to maintain in place the discriminatory quotas of the 1924 act and was supported by restrictionist legislators and ultraconservative organizations like the Veterans of Foreign Wars and the American Legion. Senate sponsor Pat McCarran of Nevada accused its opponents of being communist sympathizers, and his supporters insisted that detractors were part of a Jewish conspiracy to "weaken the procedures designed to exclude and deport Communists and other subversives, and overrun the United States with a flood of aliens." The McCarran-Walter Act passed over Truman's veto, with a congressional override.[13]

Further action on immigration reform awaited the outcome of the 1960 presidential election, which pitted incumbent vice president Richard M. Nixon against Senator John F. Kennedy. The charismatic young Democrat from Massachusetts was the scion of a famously Irish immigrant family, and in 1958 he had put his name to *A Nation of Immigrants*, a celebratory account of America's ethnic ancestry. He had voted against the McCarran-Walter Act as a congressman, and once in the Senate he proposed bills to replace it. Kennedy's campaign platform pledged to end the national origins system.[14]

The Democratic ticket that Kennedy shared with Lyndon Johnson could not win without strong turnout from the core constituencies of the New Deal coalition. Prominent among these were urban immigrant-stock voters. Americans of Italian, Jewish, Polish, Bohemian, Greek, and other southern and eastern European origins, understanding that the national origins system had targeted their co-ethnics, led the charge to replace it. That year also saw the first nationwide mobilization of Hispanic voters in the Viva Kennedy campaign, in which mostly Mexican American and Puerto Rican activists made their bid for a greater share of power in national politics. All these groups, along with African Americans, had been targets of nativist contempt and mass violence in the 1910s and 1920s, most notably by the reborn Ku Klux Klan, which had extended the bounds of their hatred to focus additionally on Catholics; in 1924, Klansmen had fought a pitched battle in the streets of South Bend, Indiana, against students at the University of Notre Dame. Kennedy was the first Catholic presidential candidate since Al Smith, whose 1928 campaign had gone down to a punishing defeat amid the xenophobic frenzy of the period. Indeed, in his speech accepting the nomination, Kennedy had said, "I am fully aware of the fact that the Democratic Party, by nominating someone of my faith, has taken on what many regard as a new and hazardous risk—new, at least since 1928." His candidacy was both practically and symbolically important for the nation's urban and ethnic constituencies.[15]

These constituencies came together under the aegis of the Nationalities Division of the Democratic National Committee. The purpose of the division, initially formed by President Truman as part of his 1948 campaign against Thomas E. Dewey, was summed up in a 1960 letter from its chairman, Michigan governor G. Mennen Williams, to Senator Kennedy. "Our Division," he wrote, was intended "to reach the about 36 million Americans who are immigrants or are the children of immigrants. Twenty-three million of these habitually use languages other than English."[16]

Notwithstanding the mythology of a time before "identity politics," the Nationalities Division organized its appeal explicitly on the basis of nationality, ethnicity, and language. Mennen advised Kennedy to court Americans of German, Polish, and Italian extraction by attending celebrations of Von Steuben Day, Pulaski Day, and Columbus Day in New York and Detroit, and he suggested that Mrs. Kennedy deliver speeches in Spanish and Italian. For one August press conference, the division invited reporters from newspapers published in Arabic, Chinese, German, Greek, French, Hebrew, Hungarian, Italian, Japanese, Latvian, Lithuanian, Polish, Russian, Spanish, Slovak, Swedish, and Ukrainian.[17]

Hispanic politicos had good reason to organize through the Nationalities Division. It allowed them to classify themselves as immigrants, their identities defined by nationality and language rather than race. Following their preference in many areas of political and civic life, they mostly wanted to be considered white because they saw this as the way to secure rights that were routinely denied to people of color—especially African Americans, but also darker-skinned Hispanics. They could avoid equivalency with "minorities" if they were just another "white ethnic" group, and indeed throughout this period Mexican American and Puerto Rican political operators often consciously designated their clubs and caucuses as "Spanish American" or "Spanish Speaking." The Viva Kennedy effort allowed them to present themselves as a single group whose collective numbers would make their voting power more relevant. Their campaign materials reflected this wish in repeatedly invoking a united pan-ethnicity with shared interests: "Kennedy is the first man who, in running for the Presidency, speaks clearly of the problems of the Hispanic population in the United States. Kennedy is the first presidential candidate who considers our traditions—which we or our parents have brought from Puerto Rico, Mexico, or South America—and our language as integral parts of the culture of the United States. . . . Kennedy, the protector of the dignity and pride of all Hispanics."[18]

All these ethnic constituencies proved essential to the Democratic ticket. In what turned out to be the closest presidential election of the century, Kennedy and Johnson—who won the popular vote by only one-fifth of 1 percent—depended on both Texas and Illinois for the electoral votes needed to claim the presidency. In Texas, Johnson worked hard to turn out the Mexican American electorate. Years before, he had worked as a teacher in the "Mexican school" in the town of Cotulla. "I had my first lessons in the high price we pay for poverty and prejudice right here," he later recalled, remembering "Mexican children going through a garbage pile, shaking the coffee grounds from the grapefruit rinds and sucking the rinds for the juice that was left." Mexican Americans turned out strongly for him, their votes an essential part of the Democratic ticket's total in the Lone Star State.[19]

European ethnics were even more numerous and represented a huge pool of voters in big cities, as one could see clearly in South Lawndale. The neighborhood was populated overwhelmingly by Roman Catholics, people whose Polish and Bohemian ethnicities had been among those excluded under the national origins system. Mayor Daley knew this better than anybody; his regular visits to the area were part of the machine's method of running up huge margins in the city to counteract the votes in the suburbs and downstate. After all, in an election where the Democratic ticket won Illinois by only 8,858 votes, South Lawndale alone was home to nearly thirty-nine thousand people old enough to cast a ballot.[20]

The Kennedy-Johnson ticket's path to the White House also implicated Oak Cliff, but for a different reason. Bruce Alger, the congressman who represented the neighborhood and had been endorsed by the *Oak Cliff Tribune*, orchestrated a protest against Johnson on the day he and his wife visited Dallas, four days before the election. A crowd of well-dressed women, later dubbed the "Mink Coat Mob," surrounded the senator and Lady Bird, spat at them, and seized her gloves and threw them on the floor. Standing nearby holding a sign reading LBJ SOLD OUT TO YANKEE SOCIALISTS, Alger revealed himself as a conspiracy-minded provocateur. The stunt backfired completely, generating sympathy and good press for the Democratic ticket. Kennedy had been running behind Nixon in recent Texas polling, but on election day he and Johnson carried the state by 2 percent. Nixon himself later complained, "We lost Texas in 1960 because of that asshole congressman in Dallas."[21]

The Democratic Party knew that it had to reward its ethnic constituencies for turning out to vote. As president, Kennedy declared the 1924 National Origins Act "an anachronism" that was "inconsistent with our traditions of welcome" and again proposed legislation to replace it. The bill was introduced in the Senate by Philip Hart of Michigan and in the House by Emanuel Celler of New York—both of whom sat on the executive committee of the Nationalities Division. The initial draft would eliminate the restrictive quotas of the National Origins Act and replace them with fair proportions allowing immigration from anywhere in the world. The Western Hemisphere would still be exempt, however, from all numerical quotas. Preference would be given on the basis of a prospective immigrant's skills, though family ties were also given some priority. But Kennedy's immigration bill had yet to come to a vote when he was assassinated in Dallas on November 22, 1963.[22]

Upon assuming the presidency, Lyndon Johnson worried that immigration reform would complicate other parts of his agenda, particularly civil rights legislation. Kennedy's former aides and his own advisers soon persuaded him that the bill was politically advantageous. In his State of the Union speech of January 1965, Johnson declared that America "must open opportunity to all our people. . . . Let a just nation throw open to them the city of promise." He spoke of hospital care for the elderly, a war on poverty to aid the poor, civil rights laws to protect African Americans and others, and for "those in other lands that are seeking the promise of America . . . an immigration law based on the work a man can do and not where he was born or how he spells his name."[23]

"Speaking Of National Origins —"

"Speaking of National Origins—." A 1965 political cartoon clarified the stakes of the campaign to abolish the discriminatory quotas of the National Origins Act of 1924. President Johnson and the authors of the Hart-Celler Immigration and Nationality Act of 1965 saw it as essential to advancing equality regardless of nationality or race and making good on the unfulfilled promise of democracy in America. A 1965 Herblock Cartoon, © The Herb Block Foundation.

The Democratic Party had highlighted these promises in the 1964 presidential and congressional elections. Once again the party's campaigns reached out to voters along ethnic lines, with specific appeals to the nationality and language groups most concerned with changing immigration policy. These appeals were significant but less decisive than previously, since for various reasons involving both policy and temperament, Johnson defeated conservative Republican senator Barry Goldwater of Arizona in one of the biggest landslides in the nation's history. The president piled up the century's highest popular vote share, just over 61 percent, and won forty-four states to six, 486 electoral votes to 52. And after that year's legislative elections, the president's agenda would go forward with the support of the most powerful Democratic presence in Congress since the New Deal itself.

The immigration bill was backed by key constituencies. White ethnic and Catholic voters continued to provide the core support for the repeal of the national origins system. Other major religious groups lined up to rally support, as did advocates for refugees. The bill also had the backing of organized labor. AFL-CIO president James B. Carrey testified before the Senate's immigration subcommittee in early 1965, assuaging workers' fears by affirming that the bill would "do little or nothing to add to unemployment" because new immigrants "would amount to only a small fraction of the American labor force" and would bring "badly needed skills to this country." It was the already-existing discriminatory system, Carey explained, that was "offensive to the American labor movement."[24]

The bill also had opponents, however, and key choke points in the legislative process remained under restrictionist control. In the Senate, there was James Eastland of Mississippi, who had already used his position as chair of the immigration subcommittee to block any measure that would remove the national origin quotas. He was joined by Everett Dirksen of Illinois and Sam Ervin of North Carolina, who threatened to bottle the bill up in committee. In the House of Representatives, the restrictionists were led by Michael Feighan of Ohio, who had become chair of the immigration subcommittee after the death of Congressman Francis Walter, coauthor of the 1952 act that bore his name.[25]

The senators in particular were already well known in Washington for their fervent opposition to equal rights for African Americans. Eastland had long resorted to racial demagoguery and red-baiting to uphold segregation: President Johnson himself had once said, "Jim Eastland could be standing right in the middle of the worst Mississippi flood ever known, and he'd say the niggers caused it, helped out by the Communists." For more than twenty years, Eastland used his position as chairman of the Senate Judiciary Committee to oppose every civil rights measure that came before Congress. Ervin, for his part, opposed all civil rights legislation throughout the 1950s and 1960s because he believed that it unfairly deprived white people of their right to discriminate and segregate.[26]

Immigration restrictionists made it clear that they supported the ethnic and racial quotas of the National Origins Act because they did not want the nation's demographics to change. Most elected officials were able to restrain themselves rhetorically from making outright racist statements. In floor debates and hearings in Congress, they mostly used euphemisms like "tradition" and "heritage" to mask their white supremacist politics. By contrast, some of the concerned citizens who came to offer testimony were less artful in their language. One representative from what was described as a states' rights–oriented organization said that he and his associates opposed the Hart-Celler bill because "immigrants from Mexico, Asia, and Africa would enter in great hordes, lowering our standard of culture and a finer civilization."[27]

As political opinion shifted against their defense of the national origins system, restrictionists fought on other fronts, most notably the status of immigration from the Western Hemisphere. Senator Ervin played to the religious prejudices of his constituents, pointedly observing that "virtually all of those people, all the people of Mexico, Central America, or Latin America and the West Indies are Catholics by faith . . . as one who believes in the national origins system, I think that I should point these things out . . . even at the risk of being called some kind of a bigot." Others sought to inflame the fears that many Americans felt about being overrun by people different from themselves. Congressman Feighan welcomed Mark M. Jones of the National Economic Council to testify before the House of Representatives. "What character of an American society do we desire to maintain?" Jones asked. He spoke at length about "the big city situation," emphasizing crime, corruption, communism, and welfare dependency. He then pivoted quickly to "the avalanche of Puerto Ricans and other Caribbeans which have inundated the Atlantic seaboard," "the Cuban revolution and the way an immigration crisis has been imposed upon Florida," and his concerns about ethnic Mexicans: "With 6 million people in the United States of Mexican origin, the number of aliens is said to have doubled in the last 20 years. What about assimilation? To what extent are they contributing to the sound development of our country?"[28]

But restrictionists repeatedly raised another, much more specific objection: the possibility of large-scale migration from newly independent Caribbean nations with overwhelmingly African-ancestry populations. When places like Jamaica and Trinidad and Tobago had been colonies of European countries, they had been subject to the quotas placed on the Eastern Hemisphere. But with the advent of decolonization, they were now independent nations. If there were no numerical quotas on the Western Hemisphere, their citizens could migrate fairly freely to the United States. White supremacists, it seemed, feared the prospect of migrants from a place populated by black people educated in the British system, heirs to a two-hundred-year freedom struggle. This was a key reason why southern senators openly held the entire bill hostage.[29]

Foes of immigration reform also tried to change the bill's priorities to maintain the nation's existing ethnoracial profile. The initial draft of the bill granted first preference to immigrants with needed job skills. Restrictionists instead proposed that first preference should be for family reunification, reasoning that this would at least give priority to the relatives of people who were already US citizens and therefore overwhelmingly of European ancestry. Virtually all observers saw it the same way. The Japanese American Civic League objected: "Inasmuch as the total Asian population of the United States is only about one half of 1 percent . . . in actual operation immigration will still be controlled by the now discredited national origins system and the general pattern of immigration which exists today will continue for many years to come." When congressional negotiators met with traditionally anti-immigration groups like the American Legion and the Daughters of the American Revolution, they emphasized the family reunification provision to persuade them not to oppose the bill.[30]

Johnson initially rejected the restrictionists' demands, especially the Western Hemisphere limits. But after spending twelve years in the Senate, he could see that there was enough procedural opposition to jeopardize the entire bill. His legislative allies, meanwhile, were hearing mainly from their European ethnic constituents, who were focused on the restrictions as applied to the Eastern Hemisphere. In the end, they agreed to privilege family ties and to apply numerical limits to the Americas to ensure the abolition of the 1920s-era quotas in the Eastern Hemisphere. "Listen," explained Johnson's congressional liaison, "we're not going to walk away from this because we didn't get a whole loaf. We'll take half a loaf or three-quarters of a loaf." The revised bill passed the House by an overwhelming 320 to 40, the Senate by 76 to 18.[31]

The final version of the Hart-Celler Act clearly displayed its mixed parentage: both the high ideals of equality that had inspired it, and the problems created by that final concession to white supremacists. The law did indeed abolish the discriminatory system of ethnoracial quotas—it declared that no person would have "any preference or priority or be discriminated against in the issue of an immigrant visa because of his race, sex, nationality, place of birth, or place of residence." In their place the act established hemispheric and national limits. The United States would accept 170,000 legal immigrants each year, with the nations in Europe, Asia, and Africa each assigned a maximum of 20,000 spots. Within these allocations there would be seven categories of preferences, including 74 percent for family reunification, 20 percent on the basis of professional skills or other labor needs, and 6 percent for refugees. The nation would also welcome 120,000 people annually from the Americas—imposing the first limitation on such migration in the nation's 189-year history. The Western Hemisphere would have no schedule of preferences, and no country-specific limits were imposed because Mexico and Canada accounted for the majority of immigrants from the region. Reflecting the intentions of its main authors, the law created formal equality among the nations of the world for the first time in the history of the United States—a remarkable and important achievement.[32]

In practice, however, the Hart-Celler Act was a poor match for actual patterns of international migration. The equal division of immigrant visas among the countries of the world was a tremendous improvement over the national origins system, especially for people from Asian nations, who had long been banned from citizenship. But equalization did not account for the fact that some nations had long histories of immigration and others did not; it put Mexico, with its forty-five million people, decades-long tradition of migration to the United States, and two-thousand-mile shared border on the same footing as countries thousands of miles away with tiny populations and scant histories as immigrant-sending nations.[33]

The result was that labor migration across the Rio Grande, largely taken for granted for many years, was increasingly redefined as unlawful—especially after the subsequent introduction of a cap of 20,000 per country in the Americas. Migration from Mexico in particular was thus transformed from a widely accepted stream of seasonal workers into a problem. Meanwhile, European immigration declined as most of the continent's economies became increasingly prosperous or were ruled by communist governments that strictly limited emigration.

So when the Hart-Celler Act took full effect in 1968, proportional country quotas made immigration from Europe small-scale and legal; while immigration across the Americas, especially from Mexico, was growing and increasingly forced into unauthorized channels. Even if there had been no change in conditions in Mexico and other parts of the Americas, the Hart-Celler Act would have produced a crisis of undocumented immigration. As it turned out, though, tremendous shifts were already underway.

THE GREATER INFLUENCE on immigration to the United States came from south of the Rio Grande. As much as the new law changed the status of people arriving from the Western Hemisphere, the number and origin of migrants would be determined mainly by conditions in Mexico and the Caribbean. A series of shifts in policy, demography, and economy would ensure that departures to the United States would rise beginning in the mid-1960s and accelerate into the 1970s and thereafter.

Labor migration between Mexico and the United States had been an everyday occurrence since the late nineteenth century. US employers offered wages several times higher than were available south of the Rio Grande, and Mexicans were ready to work. These migrations tended to be relatively limited in scale, however, and circular in nature. The fields and factories and railways of El Norte absorbed many workers, to be sure, but their number was likely in the range of hundreds of thousands of people rather than millions. Equally important, most of these migrants returned home when seasonal work became less available, preferring the low living costs, cultural familiarity, and the company of their families and communities. This was not specific to Mexicans, of course—among the European migrants of previous decades, between one-third and one-half chose to return to their homelands rather than stay in the United States.[34]

Mexican government policy in the early decades of the twentieth century sought to limit emigration. The Mexican state, intent upon economic development, feared that too much emigration or seasonal migration into the United States would mean the loss of essential population and labor power needed to modernize the country. These efforts were largely ineffective in controlling migration from rural areas, but in some circumstances they could moderate the volume of expatriates heading across the Rio Grande. Culturally, both government officials and nationalist writers and artists accused Mexicans who went north of abandoning their homeland to selfishly chase gringo dollars. Terms like *malinchista* (one who prefers foreign things to one's own nation, a word derived from La Malinche, the Nahua woman who became the mistress and adviser of the conquistador Hernán Cortés) and *fuereño* (outsider or foreigner) were deployed to dissuade people from migrating.[35]

This became especially important as the Mexican government, like others in Latin America, saw that it needed a large labor force to achieve industrialization. As the region urbanized, prosperity increased overall, but agriculturalists often found themselves on the losing end of the transformation. Rural areas were left behind both because of their place in the global economy and because governments favored cities. Yet even in urban areas, old problems persisted and new ones arose. Many of those who migrated to cities were unable to find work in the mainstream economy and had to scrape by in an informal sector characterized by minimal wages and irregular work. Cities as a whole were far better off than rural areas, but many urban-ites nonetheless struggled to get by. As they did so, they also had to contend with a severe housing shortage. Amid the arrival of millions of new people, informal housing—everything from shanties made out of scrap materials to sturdy cement-block structures—became the fastest-growing category of shelter, and Mexican officialdom actively encouraged *autoconstrucción*, or self-building, as a solution to the housing crunch.[36]

In the Mexican countryside, people had another means of sub-sistence besides moving to the nation's cities: they could work in the United States. Indeed, beginning in 1942, there was a binational agreement to facilitate precisely that. The Bracero Program originated shortly after the entry of US forces into World War II. The need to send men abroad to fight in both the European and Pacific theaters seriously drained the nation's workforce and threatened the Allied ef-fort to prosecute the war against Nazi Germany, imperial Japan, and their allies. Modern warfare depended on the ability to supply not just weapons but also food—"an army marches on its stomach," the old saying went—and without these workers, the nation's soldiers, sail-ors, and marines would have gone hungry and been unable to fight.[37]

The Bracero Program made it possible for Mexican men to work in a variety of areas—agriculture, animal husbandry, and railway trans-portation, to name the three most important—in support of the war effort. It resulted in 4.6 million labor contracts authorizing people to cross the border to work in the United States. The program continued after the war, as American agricultural interests benefited from the mi-grants' work at controlled, low wages, and it continued for more than two decades before a variety of factors led to its cancellation in 1964.

With the end of the Bracero Program just a year before the Hart-Celler Act, there were suddenly far fewer legal ways for Mexicans to work in the United States. Despite the consistent exploitation and mistreatment of Mexican braceros, many of them had fond memories of their participation in the program and of the economic opportunities that it afforded, and the official foreclosure of this option hit families hard in much of the country. Strong demand for agricultural labor continued in the rapidly growing US economy. So from both sides of the employment equation, people wanted to work, and to hire, across the Rio Grande. And now nearly the only option to do so was without documentation.

Then things got worse. In 1965, Mexico's agricultural economy entered a period of crisis that would soon plunge the country's rural population into years of intense and widespread suffering. Over the previous two decades, the introduction of immunization, antibiotics, and other essential medical services had helped Mexico recover from the demographic catastrophe of the Revolution, and the nation's population had nearly tripled since 1920. The country's condition of underpopulation had become one of overpopulation. But the *campesinos* who farmed in the half of the country that was still rural and agricultural were untouched by many of these benefits. As the price of agricultural products declined into the early 1960s, many people in rural areas depended on a massive government program of basic food supplementation to have enough to eat. Within a few years, the entire Mexican economy, including even the once-booming industrial sector, began to falter.[38]

In rural Mexico, even as crop yields had increased, a rapidly growing number of farmers were effectively idled. The new methods of cultivation depended on technologies that replaced workers with machines and fertilizer. With ever-larger harvests produced by early forms of agribusiness, the small farms that had predominated among the rural population saw their markets dwindle. In an attempt to respond to the distress in the countryside, the Mexican government imported foodstuffs, further undercutting the rural economy that had sustained the *campesinos*. Farmers in rural areas had virtually no recourse against these policies. Local officials were most often compromised politically because of their dependence on higher-ups in the party system; others were straightforwardly bought off. And outright resistance was dangerous, since it could bring violent repression from the security forces. Just a few years before, in 1962, when Rubén Jaramillo, a former lieutenant of Emiliano Zapata and supporter of former president Lázaro Cárdenas, had agreed to lay down arms after nearly two decades of resistance, he was promptly arrested by federal forces, who murdered him alongside his wife and their three sons.[39]

By the early 1970s, Mexico faced a national catastrophe. Nearly a third of the country's people were suffering severe malnutrition. Things were worst in the countryside, where a shocking nine out of every ten people did not have enough to eat. Children were most at risk because going hungry left them especially vulnerable to disease: across Mexico, these devastating conditions condemned more than 350,000 to death annually—a horrifying rate of nearly a thousand children dying every single day, year after year.[40]

Faced with these conditions, rural people had begun to migrate to Mexico's largest cities even during the years of the most rapid economic growth. Now, as the entire economy slowed and employment growth in the cities stumbled, many of them, especially those in the country's central and northern regions, turned their steps to El Norte, preferring the uncertainties of a foreign land to the certainty of hunger in their rural homelands. (The suffering of those in southern Mexico was often more severe, but they mostly lacked the information and the means to emigrate.) Indeed, in 1974 the Mexican government revised its earlier migration policy: instead of discouraging emigration, they permitted and even encouraged it.[41]

Mexico was by far the most important source of migration to the United States after 1965. But that same year was also pivotal in other important sending nations, for other reasons. In Cuba, Fidel Castro suddenly announced in late September 1965 that those who wished to leave the country had permission to do so via the port of Camarioca. This set off a boatlift and the subsequent "Freedom Flights," jointly organized by the United States and Cuba, in which more than a quarter-million people fled the island and, thanks to special legislation passed through Congress, quickly became US citizens. Also in 1965, the US Army occupied part of the Dominican Republic in the aftermath of an attempted coup and resultant civil conflict in the Caribbean nation, which US officials feared would lead to a revolution like the one in Cuba. This intervention brought in its wake a substantial diaspora of Dominicans. Although Dominicans had begun to migrate in large numbers a few years earlier at the end of the brutal dictatorship of Rafael Leonidas Trujillo, many remembered 1965 as the point when they resolved to emigrate to the United States.

The year 1965 was not only transformative for migration within the Western Hemisphere; that year also marked the dramatic escalation of US involvement in Vietnam, including the first large-scale deployment of ground troops and the beginning of a multiyear campaign of strategic bombing that reduced substantial tracts of the agricultural nation to crater-pocked, uninhabitable wasteland. Within several years, this involvement gave rise to another flow of refugees to US shores, not just from Vietnam itself but also from neighboring countries where governments had been destabilized or overthrown in the wake of the US intervention. In sum, the post-1965 diversification of the national population came from many places where the United States involved itself in the affairs of other nations.[42]

WHEN WE SPEAK of the "post-1965" immigration to the United States and the Latin Americans who made up by far the greatest proportion of newcomers, we should recognize that this transnational process began south of the Rio Grande and only later came to involve US cities. The urban growth that had exploded in Latin America earlier in the twentieth century expanded to El Norte because rural people extended the range of their migration to include urban areas in the United States.

In this respect, the new Latino immigrants were simply following earlier migrants to US cities. After all, native-born whites had been moving to the cities since the late eighteenth century in the earliest part of the rural-to-urban trend in the United States. Immigrants, mostly from Europe, had followed them in the nineteenth and early twentieth centuries, further filling up the cities. And beginning in the late 1910s, African Americans had arrived in US cities in the Great Migration.

What was different now, however, was that Latin Americans were arriving at a time when other net migrations had ground to a halt and even reversed. As we learned in Part One, white people had been leaving cities since the 1950s. The Great Migration of black people had come to a close by the end of the 1960s, and new civil rights laws had enabled some to depart for the suburbs or move to other locations. In other words, we can speak of Latinos saving the nation's cities in part because they began to arrive when cities were in demographic distress—they turned up at the point when they were most needed.

Meanwhile, US-born Hispanics had been seeking entry into the corridors of power by presenting themselves as an immigrant group defined by nationality and language rather than race. They sought to position themselves in the same way as Italians, Jews, Poles, and other groups who were European ethnics and thus definitely not black. This was in some respects a corollary of the offer Richard Dolejs made to ethnic Mexicans in Chicago. And it seemed promising at the level of neighborhoods like Little Village and Oak Cliff. But the road to the Immigration and Nationality Act of 1965 revealed some of the limitations of this strategy. The racial politics of the immigration bill showed that identity was not just a local or national phenomenon—Latinos' status would also be determined at the hemispheric level. The Nationalities Division of the Democratic National Committee was strong enough to get the Hart-Celler Act passed, but not in its original form. By the historical accident of hemispheric policy, the door was slammed on the immigrant relatives of Mexican Americans. In part this was just prejudice against them of a kind that they had seen before. But the hemispheric restrictions were also forced into the 1965 immigration law because of segregationists' fear of immigrants of African ancestry. This was an early sign that Latinos might have to fight against more than just anti-Hispanic prejudice, and that in so doing they might need allies where their leadership least expected to find them.

The passage of the Hart-Celler Act dismantled a grotesquely unjust immigration system after more than forty years, opening the nation to people from around the world and setting the stage for remarkable demographic change. Yet the limitations on Western Hemisphere immigration imposed by segregationists in Congress transformed an unequivocally superb bill into a law that created a crisis of legality in immigration. It was Hispanics who bore the burden when large-scale border crossings that had been legal for decades were suddenly criminalized. And it was ethnic Mexicans especially who would be seen as presumptive illegal aliens.

The year 1965 thus marked the culmination of a number of changes that had begun many years before—with the struggle against the immigration act of 1924, the hopes of US Hispanics to participate fully in their democracy, and especially the out-migration of rural Mexicans into cities. The Hart-Celler Act opened the door for many immigrants, to be sure. But it was Latin Americans who surged toward that door in the greatest numbers—this even though it was in truth less open to them than ever before.

CHAPTER 6

BIENVENIDOS A OAK CLIFF

O N APRIL 2, 1978, TELEVISION VIEWERS TUNED IN TO THE first episode of *Dallas*. The show's opening sequence was filmed from a helicopter that approached from the south, flying low over the bridges that spanned the Trinity River, the camera tracking across the city center with its row of gleaming skyscrapers. The subsequent shots, all similarly filmed from the air, alternated between older sources of wealth—cattle being driven across the prairie, tractors tilling farmland, nodding donkeys pumping oil—and newer landmarks of metropolitan prosperity, from downtown corporate office towers to the suburban stadium where the Dallas Cowboys played football. As the show's musical theme pounded out its heavy thumping rhythm, with more emphasis each time the four-bar motif was repeated, the montage and soundtrack together drove home the idea of a dynamic, forward-looking metropolitan area.

The Sunday evening soap opera revolved around the Ewings, a clan grown fabulously wealthy in the oil business. It followed the romantic travails of heirs Bobby and Lucy, the feud between the Ewing and Barnes families, and especially the corporate machinations of the dastardly J. R. Ewing. The program all but ignored the city's working class, though in all fairness it was probably challenge enough coaching the cast on the finer points of North Texas accents. At any rate, the show was a smash hit. Its season three finale, the "A House Divided" cliff-hanger, generated such intense curiosity that the episode revealing the perpetrator drew more than three hundred million viewers in fifty-seven countries, one of the largest prime-time audiences in television history.[1]

Dallas premiered at a pivotal moment for the city. At the beginning of the decade, Dallas had for the first time entered the ranks of the nation's ten most populous cities, jumping from number twenty-two in 1950 to number fourteen in 1960 to number eight in 1970—and it was closing in on the symbolically important million-resident mark. *Dallas* the television show seemed to validate the idea that Dallas the city had somehow transcended the disorder and violence of the 1960s and definitively arrived as a leading American metropolis.[2]

But in real-life Big D, there was cause for deep concern. The city's population growth had slowed dramatically in the 1970s: it would draw only 7 percent more residents over the course of the decade, a sharp falloff after remarkable increases of 47 percent in the 1940s, 56 percent in the 1950s, and 24 percent in the 1960s. Dallas had not grown so slowly since before the Civil War, when it was just a dusty town of fewer than one thousand people.[3]

Meanwhile, the city's public image, so painstakingly rehabilitated after the Kennedy assassination, was by the early 1970s coming apart again. The persistence of racism and inequality in Dallas was made clear by the sheer speed of white flight to the suburbs in response to desegregation efforts in the city. And the routine brutality meted out by law enforcement against citizens of color was exemplified by the shocking 1973 police killing of twelve-year-old Santos Rodríguez and the subsequent public revolt by so many of the city's infuriated Hispanics.

Even the most heavily promoted of Dallas's municipal symbols could not escape exposure. In 1973, former Cowboys wide receiver Peter Gent published *North Dallas Forty*, a roman à clef about his years with the team. The book depicted the dark underside of what local boosters had worked so hard to brand as "America's team," belying its heroic image with insider accounts of rampant drug and alcohol abuse, physical cruelty, and sexual misconduct and assault.

For anyone willing to look squarely at the city's condition in these years, it was difficult to avoid the conclusion that "the Dallas way" had not provided an easy path around the urban crisis after all. But then, just as Big D found itself in need of a new factor to change the equation, tens of thousands of immigrants arrived in the nick of time. Their arrival was fortuitous not just because *migrantes* could help with sluggish growth and deserted streets, but also because the region's financial community was already, to use the regional vernacular, fixin' to wreck things across the city and beyond.

TERESO ORTIZ WAS born in 1949 in Ocampo, a village in the far northeast corner of the Mexican state of Guanajuato. The fifth of sixteen children, he lived on the family's farm and grazing land. The surrounding region was mountainous and semi-arid, not an easy place to wrest a living from the soil. In part for this reason, Guanajuato and its adjacent states became the country's leading source of migrants to the United States.[4]

When he was ten years old, Tereso told his father that he would finish fourth grade, but did not want to go back to school after that. "Can you give me a reason?" his father asked. "No, I just don't like school," he responded, though the truth was that other boys at school were bullying him. Much as he enjoyed his studies, they would not leave him alone. "I have many children, and I will never demand that they study or force them to," his father replied. "But I do have to ask why, and I also have to tell you what you're giving up." The elder Ortiz could see that Mexico was changing, and he hoped his son would work in its growing cities rather than its declining countryside. He mentioned some of the leading stores in town and spoke of the many private offices and government departments. "You'd be a good clerk," he said to his son. "Doesn't that sound nice? Wouldn't you like that?"

"No, no," answered Tereso.

"Would you like to tend cows?"

"Yes, that."

"All right," his father concluded, "then tomorrow you'll go and tend cows."

Tereso spent the next eleven years looking after livestock and raising crops. "We harvested a lot of tomatoes, corn, beans, chile . . . the
usual things in the village."

When he was twenty-one, he recalled, "I got married and decided
to take another path in life." It had not been easy as the fifth sib-
ling in an increasingly crowded household. "Everybody looked for
work wherever they could find it," he said, but there simply was not
enough. And because he labored on the farm with his father, very few
opportunities beyond agriculture came his way.

Tereso knew about one opportunity, however: the possibility of
going to El Norte. Many men of his father's and grandfather's generations had been braceros, and their example had opened the eyes of
their fellow townspeople to the wider world. "The first braceros were
simply the spark that lit the fire," he remembered, "because when we
were young it was exciting to go in the afternoon to the center of
town or to a bracero's house and watch a television or hear a radio,
because there hadn't been any before . . . nor any way to get them."
But the braceros, he remembered, worked in the United States for several months and then "came back with interesting things."

His older brother Guadalupe had sojourned in El Norte, but when
Tereso told him that he hoped to go as well, his brother waved him
off. "Forget it, it's not for you," he had said. Tereso was not discouraged, however, and another opportunity soon arrived. He had been
giving music lessons to a friend whose father worked in the United
States, and hearing about Tereso's interest, the father sent a letter offering to bring him over. "I spoke with my wife," he remembered,
"and we decided to go." They crossed for the first time in 1971.

As fate would have it, Ortiz arrived in Oak Cliff just as its urban
crisis intensified: a period of gradual depopulation was giving way to
rapid white flight. Dallas's growth slowed in the 1970s, to be sure, but
by that time Oak Cliff had already been losing residents for more than
twenty years. This was by no means a rush for the neighborhood's
exits, but it certainly was a worrisome trend.

Mexican-origin migrants had been drawn to the neighborhood by
the falling rents and low home prices occasioned by the departure
of longtime residents. Among the first to take advantage were those
displaced from Little Mexico after the city's leadership decided to

bulldoze Dallas's main barrio to build a series of expressways. As a result, during the 1960s Oak Cliff's Spanish-surnamed population rose more than fivefold, to eleven thousand people, while remaining overwhelmingly American-born. The neighborhood became a new center of Hispanic population even before people began to arrive directly from Mexico. Indeed, these intracity migrants had prevented more serious population loss in Oak Cliff. Notwithstanding the growing Hispanic community, however, the neighborhood remained overwhelmingly white and Anglo, with an African American population of only about 2 percent.[5]

Things changed dramatically in 1971 when a federal judge ruled that Dallas schools had to be integrated immediately. City officials had managed to forestall desegregation for more than a decade, in part through simple administrative foot-dragging and in part by putting African American and Hispanic students in the same schools and declaring that since the latter were technically white, no further action was needed. The newer ruling, however, made it clear that white Anglo residents would no longer be able to keep their children in segregated schools. Many white families in Oak Cliff, as in other white neighborhoods in Dallas, decided to move out. In the 1970s alone, nearly 40 percent of white Anglos, about thirty thousand of them, left the neighborhood. The racially driven population loss of the urban crisis had unquestionably reached Oak Cliff.[6]

As soon as Tereso Ortiz arrived, he immediately began looking for a job. There was plenty of work available in the city. The previous year's census had found that only 3.1 percent of Dallasites were unemployed, a rate low enough that economists deemed it full employment—a condition in which most of the people not working were simply switching jobs. The jobless rate in Oak Cliff was even lower, about 2 percent. The kinds of positions Ortiz found were decidedly humble. "When I arrived, just for a month I worked in a restaurant and then at a plant where we packed produce." Other 1970s migrants to Dallas shared similar accounts. One of Ortiz's fellow *guanajua-tenses* said that he first worked in a restaurant, then at a hotel washing dishes. A migrant from rural Jalisco remembered, "I washed dishes at first . . . then I started learning other things." He studied cooking and English and found employment as a chef. A woman from Michoacán explained, "I came on an airplane on a tourist visa, so it wasn't a rough trip. . . . I had a job, working as a secretary."[7]

Underlying these and many other migrants' accounts was a dramatic transformation in the kinds of work available to new arrivals. For the first time in the history of Mexican labor in the United States, most migrant workers were finding their first jobs outside agriculture. Previously, the overwhelming majority had come to do farm labor—without the Mexican workers who planted, tended, and harvested crops, the rapid expansion of the US West's agricultural sector in the early twentieth century would have been impossible. In the twenty years before 1965, no fewer than eight out of ten people who made their initial journey from Mexico to the United States found their first job in agriculture. In the twenty years that followed, however, that share dropped sharply: between 1966 and 1986, it plunged to just over one-third.[8]

So in precisely the same era when mass migration from Latin America to the United States began, newcomers increasingly worked and lived in cities and metropolitan areas. This trend toward urban employment was not limited to Mexicans. It had begun earlier with Puerto Ricans. Starting in the 1940s, officials and employers in the United States and Puerto Rico made agreements to bring agricultural workers to the mainland, primarily to do farm labor. Many participants were cheated of their wages and otherwise mistreated, however, and had no real recourse in isolated rural areas. Many quit and sought work in cities, where wages were higher in industrial and other occupations; they were also attracted by the social life and support available in large Spanish-speaking communities. The urban-bound trend continued with the post-1959 arrival of immigrant Cubans, then the third most numerous group of Latinos. Most had held jobs in the better-paid sectors of the economy during the Batista regime, and they continued to work in urban-based trades and professions in the United States rather than in agriculture.[9]

There was a good reason why Latinos, whether American-born or immigrants, would opt for jobs in an urban rather than a rural setting. Farm labor was among the lowest-paid kinds of work in the nation. It was performed outdoors, often in high heat or damp cold depending on the crop and the season, and it involved stooping, working on one's knees, or up in trees, all of which produced high rates of physical strain and injury. Farm laborers were ill housed; they often lived in shacks, basements, boxcars, or trailers, or simply out in the open, under a lean-to or riverbank. Because farmwork was seldom unionized, it was extremely difficult to bargain for higher wages or even to ask for better conditions. And the remote location of so much agricultural work left all such laborers, especially migrants, with few local allies, if any, to defend them against wage theft and the threat of violence from employers. Indeed, whatever their background or legal status, people in rural areas faced some of the poorest working and living standards in America. Little wonder, then, that as other alternatives became available, most headed for the cities.[10]

Although the jobs available to migrants in cities were certainly better than those on farms, they were still poorly paid. "I think I started work at seventy cents an hour in 1971," remembered Ortiz, "but that was only for a month." Then, he explained, "I switched to another job where I made a little more, about eighty cents, and then to another where I got to ninety cents." The reports of other *migrantes* suggest that this was fairly typical for newcomers at the time, and it was very low pay indeed. The minimum wage in 1970 was $1.65 per hour, but many migrants were undocumented and thus in no position to call for enforcement of fair pay laws.[11]

Thankfully, the cost of living in Oak Cliff was still quite low. Most people were paying less than one-quarter of their income in rent, and one could get a place to live for under sixty dollars a month in some parts of the neighborhood. So if *migrantes* worked long hours and shared a place with others and were frugal in every way—as most did and were—they might put away as much as a hundred dollars a month.[12]

Even at less than a dollar an hour, wage rates in the United States were still three to ten times higher than what the *migrantes* could earn back home. And so even those who initially planned to do seasonal work or intended to stay in the country for only a limited time were often drawn back to El Norte. This was certainly the case with Tereso Ortiz. After a year and a half in Dallas, he had managed to save up the equivalent of 20,000 pesos—"that was a fortune in '72!" he exclaimed—and he and his wife returned to Ocampo, where they used their earnings to start a business buying and selling shoes. Sales were steady, but he soon grew tired of hauling loads of footwear from the city of León, fifty miles away over rough roads, for only modest profits. He knew from experience that his labor would be worth far more in the United States, and he soon decided to return, alone this time.[13]

Ortiz found work in a distribution facility that sent goods out to grocery stores. "We were loading thirty trucks a day," he remembered. "It was really an enormous plant." After a few months working there, he was called over by the director. "He said to me, 'Tereso, I need a lead man.' A lead man is like an assistant. And I told him, 'No.' 'Why not?' 'Because I like my job, and I don't want to get fired if I do something wrong.'" The director insisted that he had been watching Ortiz closely for three months. "You're the right guy," he assured him. Ortiz accepted the offer and the higher pay that came with it.[14]

As pleased as he was with being promoted, he felt the great loneliness of being without his loved ones. This sentiment was common among *migrantes*, so much so that absence and devotion were the most frequent themes of ballads by Mexican recording artists on both sides of the border; not far behind in popularity were songs about the pain of relationships broken by the strain of distance. "I saw that I couldn't do it alone," Ortiz remembered, "that I needed the support of my family." He called his wife, asking her, "Are you willing? I've got steady work and I feel like I'm ready." She arrived in Dallas within a week and a half. "We can say," he recalled, "that this was the beginning of our decision to stay here."[15]

That decision was based on Ortiz's judgment that his new position was the kind of job that would allow him to support a family in the United States. Over the many years that followed, he would continue to work at the plant as he and his wife became the parents of their second, third, fourth, fifth, and sixth children. Over time he was repeatedly promoted, moving up the job ladder until he was working directly for the owner. In addition, his employer became the source of more than just a paycheck. He was so amiable and impressed with Ortiz that he served as a sponsor for him to regularize his legal status and that of his wife and their eldest daughter, the only one of their children who had not been born a United States citizen.[16]

In the spring of 1984, however, the owner called him into his office. "Tereso," he explained sadly, "you're my right-hand man, and it really hurts me to tell you . . . I have to sell the business." After ten years of hard, steady work, this was difficult news, but Ortiz was understanding. In part this was out of affection for the man he called *"mi patrón"* and in part because he was confident about finding another job. "Don't worry," Ortiz reassured him, "there are plenty of places to find work." The owner offered him his support by way of a personal recommendation: "I'm going to write a letter," he said. "Just tell me what you need, so that anywhere you go, they're going to know who you are."[17]

Ortiz had heard from a friend that there was an opening at the Gifford Hill Company, a manufacturer of cement pipes. Letter in hand, he went to the plant office and asked for the job. But reading over the recommendation from his previous employer, the hiring officer told him that they didn't have any such position. Seeing that Ortiz had been a supervisor, he assumed that he was looking for something more advanced; what they had was an entry-level job. Ortiz agreed to sign on nonetheless. "And so they gave me that opportunity on the nineteenth of March," he recalled. "It was St. Joseph's Day, which is my father's saint's day, so I never forget the date."[18]

A few months later, Ortiz's supervisor had seen what he could do on the job. "You know what," he said, "I need a lead man and it seems to me that you could put together a whole team." He asked Ortiz to train the new employees as they were hired. Ortiz was certainly willing, but as he explained to his new employer, there was something he wanted to do first. "I've been here for so many years without going back to Mexico, and we just got our legal residency last year," he explained. "I'd like to know if you could give me a week to take my kids to visit," especially since his village of Ocampo would soon be celebrating the festival of their patron, St. John the Baptist. "'You know what,' the boss told me, 'I'm not even going to ask anyone, I'm going to give you two weeks, paid.' So now I had the opportunity to travel to Mexico legally for the first time with my kids, with my wife." And so, "after two weeks of enjoying the traditions of my village, we returned to our home"—in Dallas.[19]

TERESO ORTIZ WAS one of the lucky ones. He and his family had been able to cross the border undetected and unharmed. He had worked extraordinarily hard, to be sure, like virtually all his fellow migrants. But Ortiz was able to move quickly from the entry-level work that so many newcomers described as their first jobs—dishwashing, housecleaning, carrying loads, and clearing grounds—to more consistent employment in the production and transportation sectors. This kind of gradual progression, from temporary work below the minimum wage to more regular, better-paid positions, is common in accounts from this cohort of Mexican migrants. The leading study from this period showed that among nonagricultural workers arriving in the latter 1960s and the 1970s, newcomers could expect to see their annual earnings increase by almost 40 percent within the first few years of work, more than double in less than ten years, and more than triple with fifteen years of migratory work experience. Notably, he was eventually able to regularize his immigration status, gaining security of residence, greater confidence in public, and more bargaining power in the workplace.[20]

For every migrant like Ortiz, however, there was another with a story that was not quite so rosy. The overwhelming majority were indeed able to get to the United States safely, but the border could still be a dangerous place. Every year during this period, there were *migrantes* who died on the journey. Some lost their way in the desert and succumbed to severe dehydration. Others drowned while crossing the Rio Grande at high water. It is difficult to know how many, since some people's bodies were never found or could not be identified. There were also a few widely publicized cases in which smugglers, pursued by the authorities, abandoned their clients in locked cargo containers, leaving them to slowly asphyxiate.[21]

Once in the United States, migrants faced other risks, including at work. Most newcomers were able to find jobs with little difficulty through family and friends who had arrived earlier. The quality of those jobs varied considerably, however. The most systematic surveys indicated that the average Mexican migrant could expect to earn from $4.90 to $5.30 per hour in 1982, the 2018 equivalent of about $12.80 to $13.80. But there were many, especially the undocumented, who got considerably less: those same surveys showed that one out of three newly arrived *migrantes* from Mexico were paid less than the legal minimum wage of $3.35 ($8.72 in 2018). Of course, that assumes that they were actually paid, which was by no means guaranteed. Virtually all migrant workers could tell stories of wage theft: of the employer who paid less than promised, the one who threatened to telephone *la migra* and have people arrested, and of course the one who suddenly disappeared when payday rolled around.[22]

Even worse was the possibility of being injured on the job. Bosses typically chose undocumented workers for the most dangerous tasks—the ones that American-born or permanent resident employees would simply refuse to do. As a result, many *migrantes* were injured in falls after reluctantly agreeing to climb unsteady or defective ladders; others lost fingers or limbs to machinery that employers had installed without the required safety equipment. For the many who suffered permanent damage to their bodies, their working life was subsequently restricted to the even lower-paid tasks assigned to disabled people. Such injury could also lead to a return to their homeland, since workers who could not find employment at good enough wages to afford the expense of living in the United States would soon be compelled to leave the country. Injured migrants might leave behind little or no trace of their presence; only their families and coworkers would know they had even been in the United States.[23]

Meanwhile, beginning in the 1970s, many Americans began to portray Mexicans and other Latin American migrants as a danger to the nation. The Latino threat narrative came from many different sources. It was certainly a central obsession among superpatriotic groups and with dedicated racists. Under the headline "Our Illegal Alien Problem," the December 1974 cover of *American Legion* magazine depicted brown-skinned people charging, sailing, and flying into the country from Mexico and the Caribbean. Four years later, a longtime neo-Nazi who had moved to Dallas as a boy published *The Turner Diaries*, a novel that fantasized the violent overthrow of the United States government and a worldwide extermination of nonwhites. The narrator raged against the day "when the government granted automatic citizenship to everyone who had managed to sneak across the Mexican border" and recounted how he saved "a red-headed girl" named "Elsa" from sexual assault by "two young thugs" who "looked like Puerto Ricans or Mexicans." Anti-Hispanic attitudes were not limited to the fringes of American culture. They gained more purchase as economic conditions worsened in the wake of the 1973 oil crisis and during the recession and stagflation that followed. Elected officials and mainstream newsmagazines alike described migrants using words like "flood" and "invasion" and worried that they and their descendants would damage the economy and threaten national unity by not assimilating. The invasion narrative was so pervasive that it could be played for laughs, as in the 1976 *Saturday Night Live* skit involving "swarms of South American killer bees . . . crossing the border into California." But whether they were presented as an invading horde or just as a punchline for comedians, it was *migrantes* and their families who bore the weight of contempt and ridicule.[24]

No single migrant can stand in for all who came to the United States; even beyond the variation in individual fortunes, there were important differences among Mexican states and regions. At the same time, Ortiz's story highlights aspects of migration in the 1970s and early 1980s that we know about from other sources, most notably the many years' worth of systematic surveys that researchers have done with *migrantes*, both in the United States and in their home countries.[25]

The first of these features is the regularity of movement back and forth across the US-Mexico border. Notably, Ortiz's first journey was relatively brief, and he went back home and started a business with the proceeds. His initial foray was for the purpose of supplementing his family's income in Mexico; at that time, he hoped to find a way to make a living back home. This was not unusual for Mexican *migrantes*—nor, it should be noted, for earlier migrants from Europe. Despite the popular myth that the immigrants of a century ago came to the United States to stay, more than one-third of European immigrants were in fact sojourners—people who crossed the Atlantic for just long enough to pay off old debts, or perhaps buy the land on which their ancestors had toiled as peasants, before returning home.[26]

Ortiz did return to El Norte, however, which raises a crucial aspect of Mexican border crossing in this period: though not exactly easy, it was fairly routine. Those with documentation had to wait on line and put up with the standard bureaucratic inconveniences, but crossing was a predictable chore that many thousands of people undertook every day. For those without authorization, the border was patrolled, but never effectively because there was too much terrain to watch. As a result, people could reliably cross over, with most succeeding on their first attempt and others getting in sooner or later. In fact, over the years, Ortiz crossed the border less often than many of his compatriots: other oral histories and survey data from the 1970s and early 1980s indicate that many migrants went back and forth regularly, sometimes more than once a year. The border had not yet been heavily militarized, as it would be beginning in the late 1980s, so migrants' decisions to come or go were fairly reversible. Those who wanted to return home and then go back to the United States could do so fairly routinely.[27]

The second major factor shaping the fortunes of migrants to Dallas and other cities was their legal status. Those without documents could be easily exploited because they had little prospect of legal relief for underpayment or mistreatment on the job. It is important to recognize, however, that their legal status was by no means the only reason for their vulnerability: Mexican Americans had also long been forced to the bottom of the labor market through discrimination, threats of violence, and lynching. But being undocumented added another layer of disadvantage and exploitation; by contrast, gaining legal residency, as Ortiz did in 1983, dramatically improved a person's chances of finding work and being paid a reasonable wage.[28]

Oak Cliff was the leading edge of labor-force Latinization in the city because it was the destination of choice for so many migrants and immigrants. In the most general terms, Latinos were arriving just as Anglos were departing (or retiring, since on average they were substantially older than their new neighbors). In one sense, the neighborhood was quite stable—there were almost exactly the same number of workers in Oak Cliff in 1980 as there had been in 1960. But looking more closely at the demographics, it becomes clear that the neighborhood was dependent on a large Hispanic influx just to replenish the labor force. In 1960, only 1.3 percent of the neighborhood's workers had Spanish surnames. That grew ten years later to slightly over 9 percent, and by 1980 to fully 29 percent. The foreign-born, the vast majority of whom were Mexican, made up an increasingly important part of this total: while the population of Spanish heritage was under 9 percent foreign-born in 1960, twenty years later that figure had risen to almost 30 percent.[29]

In most cases, Hispanics were taking on the same categories of jobs that the departing Anglos had done. The newcomers arrived just in time to power an Oak Cliff economy that had changed in previous years. In the 1950s and 1960s, the neighborhood had lost nearly four thousand jobs in key categories, including managers and sales workers, while gaining only half that many in service and clerical work. With the arrival of more ethnic Mexican immigrants and migrants, the allocation of work in Oak Cliff stabilized: during the 1970s, most sectors and job types maintained roughly the same share of the labor market. One exception was the construction industry, which expanded noticeably in Oak Cliff: there were 35 percent more jobs in this sector by 1980. This, not surprisingly, was an area in which immigrant labor would continue to grow in the years to come as construction work became a mainstay among newcomers from Latin America, especially Mexico.[30]

That immigrants did the same kind of work did not mean, however, that they were paid the same wages as their Anglo predecessors. In 1970, the median income of Spanish-surnamed families was 86.5 percent of the median for all families; by 1980, it remained steady at 86.9 percent of the median. In other parts of urban America, such discrepancies had to do with both discrimination and differences in union density, but the Dallas establishment had always been an implacable foe of organized labor, so these disparities were more likely due to the relatively low pay of people who faced prejudice and were new to the job market, some of whom were also undocumented.[31]

The citywide demographics of the workforce were also changing. The 1960s and 1970s were a time when Big D was very much in need of a boost in its labor force. Dallas proper was showing a net gain of only about nine thousand new workers a year in these decades—a period when the metropolitan area's suburban workforce was expanding more than three times that fast. The growing Spanish-heritage population, including the rising share of residents born in Mexico, was an indispensable part of the solution to that problem. From 1960 to 1970, the number of Latinos in the city's workforce more than doubled, and from 1970 to 1980 it doubled again, to almost fifty-two thousand men and women. They remained a relatively modest proportion of the total—rising from about one out of thirty workers in 1960 to approximately one out of fifteen in 1970—but their already-rapid growth accelerated, and they accounted for one out of nine in 1980. Across the city, the percentage of foreign-born Latinos was not dissimilar from what it was in Oak Cliff: in 1960 they had been only 13 percent of all Hispanics in the city, but by 1980 they totaled nearly 30 percent.[32]

Their place in the citywide labor force was clear: at the end of the 1970s, Latinos were heavily concentrated in industrial occupations in Dallas. One-third were classified as "operators, fabricators, and laborers," a category that included such occupations as machinist, driver, and equipment cleaner. Another one in six were in "precision production, craft, and repair," bringing the industrial total to more than 50 percent. About 22 percent of working Latinos were in technical, sales, and support occupations, while fewer than one in six were listed in service occupations. Latino managers and professionals made up 9 percent. Overall their incomes were slightly lower than for others in the city, coming in at 89 percent of that of the median household.[33]

In sum, white workers moved out of the city center to North Dallas and the suburban periphery in the wake of new desegregation plans. As that happened, a Latino migrant and immigrant working population moved within the city or into it, taking up the jobs that the departing population had left behind and, as we shall see shortly, providing new sources of job creation in the area. This first generation of predominantly urban Mexican Americans and Mexicans in the United States was essential to creating the prosperity of the Dallas area. Their ancestors and predecessors had provided the labor essential to the modern US agricultural economy, which became the biggest producer in the world. Many Mexicans continued to work on farms. But after 1965, the majority of *migrantes*—and before long the overwhelming majority of them—would help stabilize and build metropolitan economies rather than rural or agricultural ones.

IN ADDITION TO replenishing the workforce, Latino newcomers stabilized their neighborhoods through the housing market. Asked about how the arrival of his fellow Mexicans changed Oak Cliff, Tereso Ortiz immediately answered, "The first thing is this change: migrants come and buy houses, so migrants, even undocumented ones, soon have their own homes."[34]

As Ortiz and thousands of other *migrantes* began to arrive in Dallas, they saw in Oak Cliff a neighborhood with at least two potential advantages. The presence of a substantial and growing population of ethnic Mexicans, some of whom still listed Spanish as their mother tongue, was doubtless reassuring. But the even greater draw was the same one that had already attracted so many of the city's working-class Mexican Americans: affordable housing.

As many of the earlier residents of Oak Cliff gradually moved to other parts of the city and the suburbs, their departure left numerous properties unoccupied. Housing was getting more affordable in Oak Cliff even as it was becoming more expensive in Dallas as a whole. In the 1970s the neighborhood's median gross rents—the average amount that tenants paid to landlords plus the cost of utilities—were declining in seventeen out of Oak Cliff's twenty-one census tracts while rising citywide and across the metropolitan area.[35]

This is why it was important that as renters, ethnic Mexican migrants and immigrants propped up the value of housing in the area. As any landlord could have told you, to have a rental property vacant was nearly the worst-case scenario. Even beyond the prospect of foreclosure for unpaid notes, there were other dangers with vacant properties. When they were left unattended, roof leaks and plumbing problems could go unnoticed, leading to water damage and mold—and this was especially prevalent in the warm, moist climate of Dallas. Worse still, an unoccupied property would be quickly noticed, perhaps by scavengers, who would simply strip fixtures and wiring to sell them off, and perhaps by criminals, who might take it over as a base of operations.

The specter of abandoned properties in the neighborhood was especially ominous during the urban crisis: this was, after all, an era that would witness a systematic campaign of arson in many depopulating areas. As inner-city landlords saw the neighborhoods where they owned property emptying out, they were under increasing pressure to make their rental units profitable. If they could not find tenants, they could neither keep up the payments on their properties nor afford the taxes. At that point it was tempting to just have the property burned down.

So it was hugely important to maintaining the housing stock in Oak Cliff to see a new wave of arrivals at a time when the neighborhood was so much in need of new tenants. And indeed, it was noticeable that after stagnating or declining for two decades—the period when the gradual departure of whites had given way to a scramble to move away to avoid school integration—rents began to rise again in Oak Cliff: in the 1980s, as twenty-six thousand new Latino residents moved in, rental rates not only rose but did so more quickly than in Dallas generally, reflecting not simply a local iteration of a citywide trend, but an improvement despite that trend.[36]

As important as they were as renters, it was as home buyers that Hispanic newcomers were most effective in preserving Oak Cliff's viability. The neighborhood's tens of thousands of new residents collectively devoted hundreds of millions of dollars and hundreds of thousands of hours of labor to the purchase and upkeep of houses and grounds. This is a conservative estimate, since the 1980s saw the aggregate income of Hispanic households in the neighborhood rise from over $100 million to more than $300 million per year. Ortiz's own residential history offers a useful example—one that suggests both the migrants' desire for homeownership and the apparent readiness of local property owners to sell to them. While there was no apparent racial real estate conspiracy as there had been on Chicago's West Side a decade earlier, Ortiz's own story and the experience of other migrants suggest a convergence of interests between the people leaving the neighborhood and the people moving in.[37]

Homeowners who were thinking of moving away could seldom do so without first selling their houses and thereby getting their money out. In a neighborhood like Oak Cliff with more people leaving than arriving, it could be difficult to sell at all, let alone at a good price. For the neighborhood's overwhelmingly white longtime residents, the arrival of acceptable buyers—that is, those who were clearly not African American and whom city authorities in the desegregation era were insisting were legally white—represented a much-needed opportunity. As in Chicago, Dallas

Hispanics who bought into declining neighborhoods in effect financed white flight, or to put it differently, they counteracted the residential dis-investment that would otherwise have drained Oak Cliff of capital.[38]

Describing his fellow Mexican migrants as they were in the 1970s, Ortiz noted, "Most of us were country folk, from provincial areas, with dreams of a house and land." For the first few years, he and his family rented a smaller structure behind the home of a longtime Anglo resident of Oak Cliff. Before long, however, he began to aspire to homeownership: "The landlord got along so well with my family, because he and his wife were elderly and had never had children, that it occurred to me to ask him, 'When one of the main houses becomes available, I would prefer to live in front, so if it's open I'd like to move in.' A little later, I said to him—this was in 1979, when we were still undocumented—'When you sell the house, I think I'd like to buy it from you.' 'Sure, I'll let you know.' And a little later, he suddenly comes up and says, 'Tereso, I'm already very old, and I can't look after houses, and I remember what you told me, and I'm going to sell it, and you're first in line.' It was a gift from God, because he really loved my kids as if they were his grandchildren, and he was like a father to me. He said, 'Go find somebody to advise you about the price, so that nobody thinks I want to take advantage of you.'"[39]

The building was said to be worth more than $20,000, but when Ortiz consulted his friends, they evidently believed it was overvalued and suggested that he offer considerably less. He proposed $10,000, and the owner agreed. Three days later, a man telephoned Ortiz and asked him to come to his office. "Before we begin," he said, "I want to tell you that my uncle really cares about you, and he'll sell you the house. He said ten thousand. Is that correct?" At this juncture, Ortiz thought that the owner's nephew was going to call off the deal, but in-stead he asked how much Ortiz had saved up for a down payment and offered to arrange the financing. Ortiz had been paying a hundred dol-lars a month in rent, so he proposed a payment a few dollars less than that, and the deal was done. Ortiz was elated: "Undocumented, with a house for my family and my brothers and sisters, who then started coming . . . there were about twelve of us. Blessed be God, no?"[40]

That initial purchase of a home was for his family, but before long Ortiz got more involved in real estate. After he bought the first house, the same owner offered to sell him another for even less than he had paid for the first, just $7,500, and he accepted. "I was keeping an eye out for opportunities," he explained, "and before I knew it I owned seven houses." What had begun as a bid for homeownership became a regular sideline, one that helped provide for members of his extended family. "These were not all from the same person, but since I liked to work and people were selling them off cheap, I fixed them up and relatives would move into them."[41]

Ortiz was hardly alone in his enthusiasm for real estate. Many of the *migrantes* interviewed for this book spoke at length about buying and selling houses and remembered renting them out to family members and others. These immigrants often emphasized their eagerness to buy houses as a method of investment rather than continuing to pay rent. Susana Hernández, who moved to Dallas from San Luis Potosí, recalled telling her father-in-law, "Every time I pay rent, it's like I'm throwing money into the trash." Seeing FOR SALE signs like one that read SIXTEEN THOUSAND CASH, HOUSE FOR SALE, SIXTEEN THOUSAND CASH, she immediately sought out the seller, arranged for a mortgage, and she and her husband were soon homeowners. Many other *migrantes* also emphasized the low prices they could get— largely in the range of $7,500 to $15,000, or $23,000 to $46,000 in 2018 dollars. These were rates at which one could pay around $100 a month on a mortgage, the equivalent of about $310 in 2018. Migrants buying homes was becoming common enough that people outside the Latino community began to take notice. Among them was Arnold McKee, an experienced real estate agent who recognized the trend a few years later. McKee, then seventy-five years old, told the *Dallas Morning News* that he had seen "a number of Hispanics buying quite a few houses," including some who had turned them into rental units to be let out to mostly Latino tenants.[42]

This pattern of buying houses to rent out highlights one of the reasons that these new Latino homeowners were able to do so much to preserve and improve the housing stock in their neighborhood: many of them knew how to renovate homes because of their experience in the construction industry. McKee said that homes had been available for between $25,000 and $40,000, probably because, as an agent, he handled dwellings that were in "reasonably good condition." But migrants often found much cheaper dilapidated houses to buy, then used their skills and labor to renovate them. Construction was, after all, one of the fastest-growing sectors of the neighborhood economy in the early years of Oak Cliff's Latinization, and for a growing number of locals, home improvement was not just an enthusiasm but a trade. They could work on their own houses and advise others on what to do with theirs. This knowledge became an important form of social capital for Oak Cliff and other immigrant-heavy Hispanic neighborhoods, and a key factor in their revitalization. As Tereso Ortiz remembered, "I learned electrics, I learned how to build homes, all kinds of things, so I never had problems with any of that."[43]

The aggregate effect of these efforts was remarkable. In the 1960s the median value of owner-occupied property had fallen in seventeen of Oak Cliff's twenty-one census tracts, and in the 1970s it also fell in seventeen of them—this at a time when property values in Dallas as a whole were rising. But beginning in the 1980s, the median value of property in Oak Cliff increased in every single tract, climbing far faster than in the city as a whole. Median gross rents in the neighborhood had remained fairly stable in the 1960s but then fallen in seventeen out of the twenty-one tracts during the 1970s; starting in the 1980s, they rose in all tracts but one, far outstripping the citywide rate of increase. The neighborhood's new residents had in effect reinvested in their community, slowing the process of devaluation and gradually putting Oak Cliff back on the road to recovery.[44]

A GROWING LATINO workforce in an expanding barrio should have set the stage for rapid commercial growth, but new shopkeepers came to Oak Cliff relatively slowly. Along Jefferson Boulevard, Spanish-surnamed proprietors operated only a single identifiable business in 1970, and there were still only a handful in 1980. Municipal officials thought that the neighborhood had real commercial potential: in 1981, city planners conducted a study of the area and proposed a major Hispanic-serving retail development project along Jefferson Boulevard, but it went unbuilt in the deep recession that began that year. City officials also directed spending to the area in the form of a municipal office building big enough to accommodate seven hundred employees.[45]

Consistent business creation picked up a few years later, driven by both Mexican American and immigrant Latino entrepreneurs. Some of the last remnants of Hispanic-serving businesses in Little Mexico were among those that relocated. "There has been a sort of Hispanic flight from this area," explained Sergio Murillo, who planned to open an office on Jefferson Boulevard. One Anglo-owned but Latino-serving supermarket moved to Oak Cliff in 1983 and was later followed by the grocery store owned by Jesse Mongaras, who cited a drop in demand at his old location in what remained of Dallas's previous main barrio.[46]

But it was Oak Cliff's immigrants who predominated. Raúl Rodríguez opened a popsicle shop named Frutitas Paletería on Jefferson Boulevard in 1983 because, he said, "The Latino traffic [was] picking up." He would see customers "from all the states of Mexico" in addition to a growing contingent of newcomers from Central America. Around the same time Laura and Oscar Sánchez, a husband-and-wife team from Monterrey, Mexico, opened two restaurants in the area that served predominantly immigrants. "We wanted to cater specifically to the [native] Mexican clientele . . . so we made our menu very Mexican, not so much Tex-Mex," explained Laura Sánchez.[47]

Three years later, the *Dallas Morning News* ran a story entitled "Rebirth in Oak Cliff." It was written by Mercedes Olivera, a ten-year veteran of the newspaper and one of Dallas's most knowledgeable commentators on Hispanic affairs in the city. The article detailed the Latinization of the neighborhood and the revitalization that had come with it. It also showed how much attention this demographic shift was garnering from the city's largest and most influential newspaper.

The article was in part an account of changes that had already taken place. Noting that Oak Cliff had become the largest barrio in the city, home to nearly one in four Dallas Hispanics, Olivera described the proliferation of new businesses in the area: the growing profusion of brightly colored signs in both Spanish and English, she wrote, created a "kaleidoscopic display" along Jefferson Boulevard. She also emphasized the predominance of Mexican immigrants along the neighborhood's main shopping street, which they had taken to calling La Calzada, or the Road. "It's just like Laredo on a Saturday," a local store owner told her. "The men walk around with their straw hats, and all you hear is Spanish. It's changed a lot, all right."[48]

In other respects, Olivera's article underscored the changes as uneven and incomplete. Even though Oak Cliff had become the city's leading barrio, its Hispanic residents were still a local minority, only slightly more than one-third of the neighborhood's population. Many of the Spanish-speaking shopkeepers had opened their doors only recently, and other proprietors had just begun to cater to the changing clientele. "We've put a lot of money in here because we think it'll pay off in the long run," said an Anglo drugstore owner who had recently remodeled his premises. "The merchants are taking more pride in the area, and we've gone mostly to Hispanic employees to service that group." He still emphasized the street's prospects rather than its present: "The area is on its way back," he explained.[49]

Local business growth was constrained, however, by a lack of interest from lenders. Al González, the owner of a local construction company, explained the nature of the problem. "Oak Cliff is a community whose time has come," he said. Then he predicted, "People will come down from New York, and they won't care what the myths are about Oak Cliff. It's the biggest thing going." Yet banks had been reluctant to make loans in the community, slowing development and leaving many Hispanic entrepreneurs starved for capital. González himself had been trying to redevelop an unoccupied Sears Roebuck store into a mini-mall called Plaza del Sol. Despite backing from Dallas's mayor and numerous community organizations, he explained, "I've been turned down by twenty-five lending institutions . . . and most of the people making those decisions have never been to Oak Cliff or seen the changes that have occurred there in the past few years." He was not alone in seeing this as the problem: Dallas mayor Starke Taylor went on the record agreeing with his assessment, as did a member of the Economic Development Department: "The city staff agrees it's a good project worth pursuing, but there hasn't been that much interest on the part of borrowers or lenders."[50]

Ironically, the very people who were so reluctant to invest in a quickly Latinizing Oak Cliff were the same ones who had been hard at work crashing the Dallas economy. The city's financiers, bankers,

and other lenders—the ones who were supposed to be good at deciding who could make productive use of capital and who could not—
turned out to be catastrophically bad at their jobs. The deregulation of
savings and loans in the early 1980s had enabled local lending practices that ranged from the merely unsound to the positively ludicrous.
Dallas-based banks loaned vast sums of money for investment in real
estate and other assets. The value of that real estate had often been
deliberately inflated through fraudulent bidding-up practices that were
so clearly criminal that numerous practitioners were later sentenced to
decade-long jail terms. And the "other assets" had included things like
a fleet of eighty-four hand-painted Rolls-Royce automobiles owned by
the self-proclaimed Oregon guru Baghwan Shree Rajneesh and purchased with a loan from Dallas's Sunbelt Savings Bank.[51]

As the extraordinary level of financial malfeasance became apparent, regulators began to close banks. Beginning in 1983, they shuttered more than five hundred commercial banks, including most of
the largest ones in Texas. Financial institutions in the city continued
to collapse in a cascade that not only wiped away tens of billions of
dollars in wealth but stuck the public with the bill for billions of dollars in red ink that had to be covered by federal insurance payments.
The financial cataclysm lasted for an entire decade, with high-profile
bank failures and prosecutions for financial crimes persisting into
the 1990s. The accompanying real estate crash left downtown Dallas
with one of the highest vacancy rates in the nation. Even twenty years
later, a Dallas banker and financial writer averred in *D Magazine* that
the city had still not fully recovered from the catastrophe.[52]

The contrast between the upward trajectory of Oak Cliff and the
citywide banking debacle was a serviceable metaphor for Dallas in
the early decades of mass migration from Latin America. In precisely
the years when the city's mainstream banking community snubbed
or ignored potential borrowers hoping to build Spanish-serving businesses in Oak Cliff, and when they were recklessly lending to borrowers everywhere else in the city, migrant and immigrant Hispanics were
building an important new commercial district along Jefferson Boulevard. At a time when white Anglos were departing the neighborhood
and the city en masse, Latinos were renting and buying homes there.

WHAT WOULD BECOME clear in the years to come was that Oak Cliff was the leading edge of Dallas's new urban majority. By the early 1980s, the neighborhood had finally turned the corner after thirty years of declining or stagnant population and vanishing business activity. Oak Cliff's urban crisis was not over, but its leading symptoms had begun to abate. These demographic changes emerged more slowly in the city as a whole, but they could be seen with increasing clarity over time. Between 1970 and 1980, Dallas's Latino population—still overwhelmingly Mexican-origin but with small contingents of Cubans and Puerto Ricans—rose from under 8 percent to more than 12 percent of all residents.[53]

The main citywide trend was still white flight. In 1970, Dallas had reached its all-time peak population of white Anglos, about 565,000 people. There would never again be as many whites in Dallas: the overall population would continue to grow, but the number and share of non-Hispanic whites would keep declining. Big D would not face the same kind of urban crisis as Chicago and older industrial cities in the sense that it would never actually lose population, but only because enough Hispanics and, in smaller but still significant numbers, African Americans moved to the city.[54]

In the years to come, the Latino proportion of Dallas's population would grow much more quickly, in substantial part because of an important new driver of change: the first major immigration reform in more than two decades. The Immigration Reform and Control Act (IRCA) of 1986 would take virtually everybody by surprise, not least the immigrants it most directly affected. But in the urban crisis years, perhaps the biggest surprise was the difference it made in further revitalizing cities.

The reason for this takes us back to Tereso Ortiz, the Mexican migrant whose story is woven throughout this chapter. He arrived in the United States undocumented but was later able to gain legal status, which allowed him to participate more fully in the life and economy of the city. One key result of the 1986 immigration act was essentially to multiply Ortiz's story by tens of thousands in Dallas—and by millions nationwide.

CHAPTER 7

THE WINDY CITY
PITCHES THE WOO

*L*A REINA, THE QUEEN OF THE MEXICAN INDEPENDENCE DAY celebration, stood smiling, her hands holding an elaborately embroidered *sombrero charro*. Also holding the archetypal Mexican hat, and looking awkwardly past the young woman, who did not meet his gaze, was the most powerful mayor in the United States. The photographer assigned to capture the moment carefully arranged the shot so that *la reina* was flanked by an American flag—and so that the official seal of the City of Chicago that hung on the wall encompassed the mayor's head like a halo in a Renaissance painting.

Richard J. Daley was no saint, though. The photograph would serve as the frontispiece for *Chicago's Spanish-Speaking Population*, the 1973 report that was the first official study of the city's Hispanics. Prepared by the consulting firm founded by the son of the city's top lawyer, a close associate of the mayor, the report described its subjects as underprivileged but hardworking and family-oriented people and noted that Chicagoans of Spanish heritage had more than doubled their population over the previous decade—an increase that it called "very substantial."[1]

But at the same time Mayor Daley was showing up for photo opportunities with the city's ethnic Mexicans, he was also at work on other plans. Indeed, at *exactly* the same time: in the same month of the same year that city hall released *Chicago's Spanish-Speaking Population*, it also unveiled *Chicago 21*, the official city plan. With a title that gestured to the century to come, it was the latest edition of the official city planning document, following previous versions from 1958 and 1966. It specified which parts of Chicago should be redeveloped, which rehabilitated, and which simply left alone.[2]

The two documents were released amid a deepening urban crisis. The recently released results of the 1970 census made clear that Chicago's decline, which had begun twenty years before, was actually accelerating: the city had lost population more than twice as fast in the 1960s as it had in the 1950s. Both reports thus had to contend with the immediate reality of a city being abandoned by hundreds of thousands of its residents.[3]

But *Chicago's Spanish-Speaking Population* and *Chicago 21* set forth different visions of the place of Latinas and Latinos in the Windy City. One report described a demographic process already underway that could continue at no additional cost to the municipal coffers beyond the usual expenditures required by new residents. The other proposed to spend millions of dollars of municipal and private funds in hopes of reversing migration out of the city center. The question, then, was which set of moves would bring more new people to Chicago, and on what terms.

IN MOST RESPECTS *Chicago's Spanish-Speaking Population* was fairly ho-hum. Its authors described it as "the first in a series of projected publications on the Spanish-speaking population." Its forty pages included sections on employment, education, housing, and related subjects. Based almost entirely on statistics from the most recent census, it limited itself to compiling and commenting on the resultant numbers. The report noted that while Hispanics made up a modest proportion of the city's population, a bit over 7 percent, they were particularly numerous in specific neighborhoods. It highlighted the strongly Puerto Rican area on the city's Northwest Side and what it called the mainly Mexican areas on the West Side. The city's Mexican-origin population was the largest group of Latinos at that time, and the report correctly identified the barrio centered in Little Village and Pilsen as the principal Mexican neighborhood. "Most of the Spanish-speaking concentrations in Chicago," it observed, "are expanding in area as well as in population."[4]

This focus on the growing population of Latinas and Latinos allowed the report's authors to position the city in a particular way. On the very first page of its analysis, the report conspicuously noted that Chicago boasted the fourth-largest Hispanic population of any city in America. In a brief table, it listed New York first, followed by Los Angeles, San Antonio, Chicago, Miami, and Houston. In every other respect, however, these cities—which were used as points of reference throughout the report—were different from Chicago: none was in the same geographic region, none was nearly so industrial, most had populations that were either larger or far smaller, and all had substantially higher proportions of Hispanic residents.[5]

This was a telling choice. Every one of the other cities on the list had been gaining population in the previous decade while Chicago had been losing residents. So when the report's authors listed cities by absolute numbers of Hispanics, they were aspirationally putting Chicago in the company of municipalities that were growing and that had much higher percentages of Latinos. They knew, in other words, that ethnic Mexicans, Puerto Ricans, and other Spanish-heritage people were becoming essential to the Windy City's future. This was the most intriguing aspect of the report. It was something that its authors never explicitly stated, even though it undergirded the entire document from the first chart to the final section: the demographic transformation that Hispanics had wrought in Little Village was something they thought might take hold in the entire city.[6]

Chicago 21 was a far better indicator of the Daley administration's priorities. It was the city's foundational planning document, with a lineage that stretched all the way back to the legendary Burnham Plan of 1909. As such, it showed where the leadership in city hall intended to concentrate its efforts and expend its resources. The 128-page plan included directives in areas like public housing, transportation, and parks. But by far its most important element was a proposal to convert the empty rail yards located in the South Loop into a new residential area. The plan projected that as many as 120,000 people would live in and around the six-hundred-acre parcel once it was acquired by the city and redeveloped.[7]

Chicago 21 was a straightforward attempt to revitalize downtown, an extension of earlier efforts by Daley's city hall to shore up a city center threatened by "blight" and abandonment. The new development was intended to appeal to the middle-class families who had been fleeing Chicago, enticing them back to the city by creating an attractive neighborhood that would feature what so many others lacked: quality housing, stable schools, and easy access to good jobs and shopping.

The plan had its critics, particularly on the subject of its racial politics. They saw it as an effort to use municipal resources to wall off populations of color from downtown to create a neighborhood in which white people would feel comfortable. The placement of *Chicago 21*'s development zones reminded many observers of earlier projects that had been sited between poor minority and prosperous white populations. The Carl Sandburg Village redevelopment, which in the 1960s had displaced thousands of Puerto Rican families to build a half-mile-long, three-hundred-foot-wide strip of middle-class residences between the Cabrini-Green housing projects and the ultra-wealthy Gold Coast, underscored a clear pattern of spending public funds to effectively build walls within the city. Indeed, it was hard to see it any other way after a leading backer of *Chicago 21*, who had also been the principal developer of Sandburg Village, told the *Chicago Daily News*, "I'll tell you what's wrong with the Loop. It's people's perception of it. And the perception they have about it is one word—black. B-L-A-C-K. Black. . . . The ghetto areas have nothing but rotten slum buildings, nothing at all, and businessmen are afraid to move in, so the blacks come downtown for stores and restaurants."[8]

Chicago's Mexican and Puerto Rican communities certainly saw red when they examined the new plan. "So when we finally got down to the Department of Planning," recalled a prominent neighborhood activist, people "went in and looked at these plans, and they said, 'Hey, here's the plan for Pilsen, and we're not in it!' You know, 'Here's Little Village, and we're not going to be there!'" Community resistance soon emerged and consolidated: one poster showed a visage with a bandit mask labeled CHICAGO 21 glowering over the cityscape. Underneath were the words, "*¡Atención, familias de Pilsen!* 'Big business' wants to move in on our neighborhood!!!" while small figures in the foreground cried, "*¡Ay ay!*" And "*¿Qué vamos a hacer?* [What are we going to do?]" Indeed, the plan became one of the rallying points in a new era of political activism among Chicago Hispanics.[9]

Both *Chicago's Spanish-Speaking Population* and *Chicago 21* focused on new populations moving into the city proper. The main difference was what city hall intended to do about the prospect. The answer could hardly be clearer: it expected the Hispanic population to continue growing, but it did not plan to offer these new Chicagoans any resources. By contrast, it proposed to spend many millions of dollars to encourage predominantly white middle- and professional-class people to come back to the city, by both developing industrial sites and renewing areas around the Loop. And if those areas were populated by black people or Latinos, it was expected that they would simply depart to other parts of the city. What city officials could not yet see was that the West Side would not be stabilized by clearance and redevelopment; it would be redeemed by immigrants.

THE TENS OF THOUSANDS of Mexicans and other Latin Americans who repopulated Chicago's West Side and other parts of the city came by a variety of routes. One way to get a sense of their markedly different experiences in coming to the area in this era is through oral histories of those who made the journey.

José Luis Loera was twenty-seven years old when he left Mexico in the summer of 1978. He had spent a difficult childhood and adolescence in a Mexico City shantytown filled with people who had migrated from the countryside. "I did not live in poverty, but instead in misery," he recalled. "I am one of many people in Mexico who does not even know what childhood means . . . my activity was work, work in order to survive." He eventually managed to find employment as a policeman but was disturbed by the level of corruption and violence around him; he was especially haunted by the 1968 Tlatelolco Massacre, in which Mexican security forces opened fire on student demonstrators, killing hundreds. His police identification made it easy for him to board a US-bound flight, and on July 30 he stepped out onto the tarmac in Chicago.[10]

He knew just where to go. "The first thing I decided to do was to go to a Mexican neighborhood," he remembered. "The neighborhood was Little Village . . . around me there were only Mexicans." His first response was elation: "I felt I had arrived at a palace, in fact the place seemed to be magnificent," especially "compared to where I lived" in Mexico. But Loera had limited time for reveries: more urgent matters presented themselves. "The first thing I did right away, like any Hispanic would do, when he has no documents or anything, was to look for a job." He started out washing dishes and sweeping floors, a humble position to be sure. But even before he worked his way up to better-paid employment, as a just-arrived migrant he was already far better compensated than he had been in Mexico. "And right away, when I first began earning my first salary, that was twenty dollars," he explained. "For me it was a lot because I think that was what I earned in the police force per week. And here I earned it in one day."

The most important task for any migrant was to find employment, and Loera's example was hardly atypical. A Mexican worker in the United States could expect to make five to ten times as much as back home, sometimes even more. A few years later, survey data showed that the average Mexican worker in the United States could save up between $4,000 and $5,000 per year, the equivalent of $10,400 to $13,000 in 2018. But agricultural work in Mexico was so poorly paid and irregular, and the *peso* so devalued by inflation, that this translated into 300,000 pesos. This was a level of income that, the researchers noted, "can appear astronomical to poor jornaleros with limited prospects for work in Mexico," who at that time were paid an average of 200 pesos per day.[11]

But even when they were provided for materially, many newcomers still found it difficult to adjust to American life. Women faced particular challenges in this respect. Margarita Arredondo had left her native state of Guanajuato in 1974, along with her children and husband. He had relatives in Chicago, and like many migrants with such connections, he had a job waiting for him upon arrival. Arredondo was thankful for this, and she admired her husband's ability to provide. "Your dad did everything," she told her daughter years later. But other aspects of her life as a newly arrived, undocumented mother in Chicago were harder for her. She didn't like their living arrangements and felt isolated and idle. "No landlord wanted to rent to a numerous family," she explained. "We were six altogether. . . . In one living room, your dad and I slept on the floor along with the children lying next to us. You had your own room along with your sister. It was a very small apartment." Their basement accommodations flooded frequently, and there were rats. Moreover, she often felt like a prisoner. The other undocumented people who lived in her building didn't want her to answer the door or the phone or otherwise attract any attention, and they preferred that she not go outside. "I felt very lonely and my only consolation was having to wait for the mailman in hopes that my family would write to me soon. . . . I always kept to myself. All I did was keep track of the clock while I prepared some soup for your dad." Arredondo's husband insisted that she not work, and so she was never able to achieve any real measure of economic independence. "Is that the American dream?" her daughter asked. "Sí, m'hija. To make money of some sort. To have extra money, but those illusions were gone. One's dreams don't always come true. Some are able to triumph, others don't. El Norte is not for everyone."[12]

Not all Mexicans left home to escape economic privation; some were motivated more by curiosity and family history. Miguel Ramírez was born in 1952 in El Teúl, a rural village in the state of Zacatecas. He enjoyed a happy childhood among a large extended family, spending days keeping up the ranch, tending to livestock, and attending school. But he and his siblings were curious about life in the city, and at the age of thirteen they asked their father for permission to seek work in Guadalajara, the capital of the neighboring state of Jalisco, about seventy-five miles to the south. Their father reluctantly assented, and off they went. They spent the next several years working in, and eventually taking charge of, a variety of businesses, including a mechanic's shop, a fruit truck, a photographic studio, and a tortilla bakery. Ramírez was making good money and soon married and started a family. But he also thought about even more promising opportunities, and one day, as he remembered it, "I decided in a determined moment to try my luck and come to the United States."[13]

The road north was a familiar one for his family. His father had been a bracero working in the United States during World War II, and Ramírez had been inspired by his success: "Working hard and knowing how to administer his money," he explained, "he was able to buy some properties in Mexico, which went very well for him. Therefore, there was always that curiosity." In coming to the United States, Ramírez wanted "to see if in fact by working hard, I could accomplish what a lot of people had achieved . . . it was a challenge for me." For Ramírez, as for many other ambitious migrants, it was not economic privation that set him into motion; indeed, he was getting by quite well economically in Mexico. Instead, it was knowledge and experience that gave him the confidence to make the journey. It was not the poorest who were most likely to emigrate; rather, it was those whose parents and grandparents had already made the crossing.

Two decades after his journey, Ramírez could still convey every detail with a sense of excitement. He described the precise route from Laredo, Mexico, to Nuevo Laredo, Texas, the hotel at which he stayed on the Mexican side, the ruses used to avoid the authorities there, the mad dash across the border. He even found something worth telling about being captured by the Border Patrol on his first unsuccessful attempt on July 27, 1977: "I remember that the immigration agent, when he did the interview, he told me, 'And today it's your birthday!'" To which Ramírez gamely answered, "Well, yes, and this is the way that you are celebrating it for me." In describing his second attempt, his successful crossing and arrival in the United States that September, he maintained his sense of wonder. "The adventure," he enthused, was "something unforgettable!"

As the now primarily Mexican-origin community in Little Village continued to grow and develop, it became more accommodating to migrants who were just arriving. Rosina Magaña left her home city of Sahuayo in Michoacán and came to Chicago as a girl in 1979. Her father had come to the United States several years earlier, succeeded in gaining legal residency, and found a secure job at the Zenith electronics plant just west of the city. He rented a basement apartment big enough for the entire family of two parents and six children and then immediately sent for them. While their basement apartment was hardly luxurious—Magaña remembered it as "too dark, too secluded . . . so cold"—the surrounding neighborhood left her with an altogether different impression:

> I remember coming out the first day. I guess we got to Chicago in the night. I went outside and I was just amazed because in Mexico the houses are—you know, in Mexico it is very poor, we all know that—and just the streets and seeing pavement and cars and really nice houses, it just looked like I had moved into a mansion or something. That's how I felt. Not that we were living in bad standards in Mexico, but . . . the housing is just terrible. I remember walking out of the apartment on the first day and looking out and it must have been sometime in autumn or something because I remember the trees, that the leaves were turning colors and I remember the leaves were falling and the wind was blowing. I was just amazed because in Mexico it was so hot. And that felt good. It really did.[14]

Notwithstanding her delight over her new neighborhood, Magaña was still apprehensive. But she soon learned that Little Village was in many respects an extension of Latin America. Having arrived after almost fifteen years of a large-scale Latino migration to Chicago, she had the benefit of living in what she called a "Spanish neighborhood." This started with school. Asked whether there were other Spanish-speaking children in her class, she responded, "Oh yes, definitely. Because where we lived was populated mainly by Mexicans." She became habituated to the local shops, and also the local clubs, which she remembered as featuring a combination of various musical styles, not just from Mexico but also from Colombia and Puerto Rico. Indeed, there were so many Latinos in her neighborhood that she remembered them being able to help protect her against the stresses of acculturation in a city with plenty of racism. Asked about mistreatment as a Hispanic, she responded, "I don't really think there was . . . discrimination because it was a Spanish community. We pretty much kept to ourselves, you know."

Magaña's description of Latino Little Village reveals a major transition in how the neighborhood worked. By the late 1970s, Hispanics were no longer the junior partners in the area; they had become the dominant population. Although the plan had been merely to make them a buffer between black North Lawndale and the white sections of the erstwhile South Lawndale, Hispanics had instead fashioned a neighborhood that worked for their own purposes. Its new residents looked to each other for everything from services to support, and with good reason: the neighborhood had become easily the most important barrio in the entire city.

IN THE 1970s, Little Village's overall population showed its first significant growth in a half century, climbing from 59,478 people to 70,441. Non-Hispanic whites had continued to leave, their numbers plunging as nearly two-thirds departed the neighborhood, leaving only about 11,500 still living there. The number of African Americans also fell slightly, from about 4,000 to just over 3,000. Thus, all the decade's population increase consisted of what the census counted as "persons of Spanish/Hispanic origin or descent," who rose from just under 20,000 in 1970 to about 55,000 in 1980, for a gain of over 35,000 people. In percentage terms, Hispanics—the great majority of them ethnic Mexican, with 7.7 percent of Puerto Rican or other Latin American heritage—had risen from about one-third of the Little Village population to nearly four-fifths of all residents by 1980. Whites fell from three-fifths to one in six, and blacks from under 7 percent to slightly over 4 percent. The foreign-born accounted for 45 percent of all neighborhood residents, double their share ten years earlier. By 1980, the Latinos of Little Village had become the largest Hispanic population in any community area in the city.[15]

Many newcomers came, and fewer departed; notably, those who moved to Little Village and other parts of Chicago tended to cross between nations more than once. The US-Mexico border was not yet so heavily militarized as it would be starting in the late 1980s, and much of the circular migration of the bracero era continued. Many of these newcomers had long family and community histories of migration back and forth: some, like Jesús Serrato and Rosalio Torres, had been braceros themselves; other *chicagoenses* traced their family histories in the United States back to fathers or grandfathers who had participated in the Bracero Program or had otherwise worked in the United States decades earlier. Little Village resident Bertha Martínez, who followed her aunt to Texas and then to Chicago, recalled "various times of coming, going back and forth from Mexico to Texas." Many others had worked in a number of places on both sides of the border before settling in Chicago. Miguel Ramírez moved from a small rural town to Guadalajara, and from there to Mexico City, before arriving in Little Village in 1977. Eustolia Martínez was born in Texas to Mexican parents. As a young woman, she met a bracero and moved to Mexico to marry him; they had two children born in Mexico and two in Texas before he moved to Chicago and she joined him two years later. José Pérez left the Mexican border town of Piedras Negras, following "one of my wife's sisters" to go work in Fort Worth, Texas. He then became an asparagus and pea picker in Walla Walla, Washington, before returning to Piedras Negras. Pérez then met a group of Mexicans in Eagle Pass, Texas, and decided to go with them to work in a Chicago cannery. Many of these Chicago Mexicans had come to the United States and returned to Mexico to dwell for years at a time.[16]

As the neighborhood's population was replenished, so was its labor force. There had been over twenty-six thousand workers in 1960, when the area was still named South Lawndale. That figure fell by about 8 percent over the decade that followed. In the 1970s, however, Little Village's population of workers recovered and rose past its earlier level as the newcomers succeeded the departing population. The neighborhood's occupational profile remained remarkably stable, however. In one employment sector after another, from the larger blue-collar categories ("operatives," which included all the manufacturing jobs, and "craftsmen, foremen, and kindred workers") to the smaller, largely white-collar categories ("professional, technical, and kindred workers," "clerical and kindred workers," and "sales workers"), there was minimal change during the 1970s. Over half of all the neighborhood's residents were in manufacturing, crafts, and transportation jobs, one-fifth did clerical work, about 6 percent were professionals and technicians, and under 5 percent were in sales. In other words, as Little Village made the transition from neighborhood to barrio, it was still a place where the proportion of people working in manufacturing was almost twice as high as it was citywide—the barrio remained part and parcel of industrial America.[17]

Although people were still working the same kinds of jobs, the pay was not as good. Between 1970 and 1980, the average income of both individuals and families in the neighborhood fell by 14 percent. One of the many causes of this drop in earnings was deindustrialization. Little Village had been hit by the same losses as the rest of the Chicago area, which by 1980 had less than half as many industrial jobs as it did at its manufacturing peak in 1948. Much of the city's industry had been relocated to the suburbs and then further out into more rural areas as employers sought out low-wage workers. Indeed, some of the Latinos in metropolitan Chicago had moved out of the city in pursuit of these jobs or continued to live in the city and commute out. But this worked for only a short period of time: beginning in 1967, industrial employment began to fall in the suburbs too as manufacturers decamped once again to rural towns in search of even cheaper labor.[18]

Meanwhile, the profile of industrial labor had changed, with high-value heavy manufacturing replaced by smaller shops that operated with thinner margins and paid lower wages. Many of these companies remained in the area only because they could pay Latina and Latino workers lower wages than had been offered to their white Anglo predecessors. Without the newcomers, falling profitability would have prompted them to move overseas, as so many others had done. As one West Side employer explained, "I don't need to move to Mexico to get cheap labor. We have plenty of them here. By staying in Chicago I have the best of both worlds." Indeed, subsequent research would show that at the national level, when immigrants arrived in a particular county, employment, including manufacturing jobs, usually expanded there.[19]

Another reason for falling wages was the lower rate of unionization among the neighborhood's new residents. There was nothing about manufacturing work that made it intrinsically lucrative, but in decades past South Lawndale's industrial jobs had been well paid thanks to organized labor. Most Latino workers in Little Village did not enjoy these benefits because Hispanics had been excluded from many unions. By the 1970s, a strong Latino labor movement had emerged in Chicago's West Side, with Hispanics finding a home in the garment workers, food service, and typographical unions, among others. But Mexican American and Puerto Rican unionists remained fewer in number than white Anglo unionists, and because they were on average much younger, they had less seniority than their predecessors in the neighborhood.[20]

There were also outright racial disparities in pay. Wages were largely stagnant for all workers, but Mexican-origin and Puerto Rican people—the overwhelming majority of Chicago Latinos—were paid even less than average. Overall, in 1980 Latinos earned one-third less than non-Hispanic white men; Latinas faced a smaller differential, their incomes running about one-seventh lower than white women's incomes. Adding to the burden of these low wages was their real value, which was declining in these years for low-income workers regardless of race.[21]

Then, of course, there was the question of legal status. The city's growing population of undocumented migrants could be easily exploited by employers. In 1981, the *Chicago Tribune* ran a four-part series on immigration that detailed the situation faced by three immigrant workers in the Windy City, people whom they called Linda, Joe, and Luis. All had been born in Mexico; two were undocumented, and the third had obtained a work authorization but doubted it was still valid. "Three apparently typical Chicagoans," the article read. "They live and work in the Chicago area. They pay taxes here and contribute to Social Security. None has ever been arrested in Chicago or been on welfare. . . . All grumble about inflation and bus fare increases, but they feel at home here." But because they were or might have been unauthorized, they had to worry about being cheated by their employers or arrested and deported by immigration enforcement. "It's a worry that is with you 24 hours a day," explained a local labor organizer who was born in Argentina and had legalized his status nearly a decade before. They were also prime targets for wage theft. "They are vulnerable when an employer decides to take them for a ride," noted an official from the International Ladies' Garment Workers' Union.[22]

The three Chicago Mexicans earned a range of incomes. Linda was a master seamstress at a garment factory and earned $150 a week, about three times what she had earned in Mexico doing the same kind of work; Joe, who loaded goods at a toy factory, took home just under $200 a week, which he said was twice his pay in the country of his birth; and Luis, a welder, earned just over $285 per week. This was at a time when the minimum wage was $3.35 an hour, or $135 a week. (The real value of the minimum wage was much higher in 1981; $3.35 an hour was the equivalent of $9.25 an hour, or $370 a week, in 2018 dollars.) And indeed, the *Tribune* series cited a federal immigration official who said that the majority of undocumented people earned around or above the minimum wage. This certainly described the circumstances of Miguel Ramírez, whom we met earlier in the chapter. When he had arrived in Chicago a few years earlier, he found a position washing cars, then another applying undercoatings. He started at $3.00 per hour, slightly over the minimum wage, and then gradually negotiated his way up to $4.75.[23]

Undocumented immigrants and the employers who underpaid them both fixated on the disparity between wages in Chicago and the wages available in their home country, which for most meant Mexico. As we have seen, *migrantes* themselves often commented on how much more they could make in the United States—and systematic surveys found that after accounting for expenses, migrants took home at least six to seven times what they had earned in Mexico. This helped justify the expense of the journey and the separation from their families. Exploitative employers who pushed their immigrant employees' wages down as low as they could also used this comparison, defending their minimal pay with the observation that it was justifiable, since after all it was still much more than these migrants could earn at home.[24]

For migrants, working in Chicago was a trade-off: they accepted the possibility of being cheated and abused by employers in return for a far higher income than they could expect to earn at home. The migration to the area reflected the ongoing economic crises in Latin America, especially just south of the Rio Grande. "Poverty," explained a local Catholic priest to a newspaper reporter in 1981, "has become institutionalized in Mexico." Conditions south of the border at this time explain why one of the city's immigrant services lawyers could say that he had seen migrants to Chicago "stacked up like pancakes in the back of U-Haul trucks or trailers."[25]

DESPITE THE DISADVANTAGES and discrimination they faced, Latina and Latino workers found ways to house themselves in Little Village. Many of them became homeowners. As white ethnics rushed out of the neighborhood during the 1970s, its new residents eagerly bought up their homes. The process that began with Richard Dolejs's help in the 1960s accelerated in the decade that followed. As ethnic Poles and Bohemians had initially been succeeded by Hispanics, there had been a slight drop in the percentage of people in the community who owned their own homes, from 41.3 percent in 1960 to 37.4 percent in 1970. But as the process of ethnic succession picked up speed and Little Village went from one-third to more than four-fifths Latino, the rate of homeownership held steady for two decades, never varying more than one-half of 1 percent through 1990. Monthly mortgage and owner costs averaged $333 across the entire neighborhood in 1980, but there were tracts where the median mortgage payment and costs added up to less than $200 ($610 in 2018 dollars)—not unaffordable for a household with multiple wage earners sharing expenses.[26]

Less than ten years after the city's first official report on Spanish-speaking Chicagoans, another city document looked closely at Little Village, noting the extent and meaning of Hispanic migration to the neighborhood. The report cited a doubling of property values between 1975 and 1979 and two thousand examples of home repairs and improvements, attributing both to the "deep-seated commitment of the community to upgrade South Lawndale." It also stated that the community area boasted "the highest rate of homeownership among Hispanics in the nation."[27]

Still, the majority of Little Village residents were renters. In 1980, 45 percent of the neighborhood's tenants paid less than 20 percent of their income as rent, and about 63 percent laid out under 30 percent, which was the threshold for being defined as rent-burdened. This did mean that around one-third of households struggled to pay the rent. But the majority did not: for example, the pseudonymous Mexican migrant "Joe" described in the 1981 article in the *Tribune* lived in Little Village with a compatriot, and the two shared the monthly rent of $155. That was on the thrifty end of the housing market: at the time the median rent in the neighborhood was $215. So Joe's housing costs consumed a relatively small proportion of his wages, perhaps as little as 12 percent.[28]

One apparent result of the Hispanic-driven stabilization of the housing market was that Little Village landlords generally did not resort to arson to rid themselves of properties that they could neither rent nor sell. Although there was very little new construction in the community area and virtually all its structures had been built before 1940, the number of dwellings barely moved at all, hovering around twenty thousand housing units for decades after midcentury.[29]

In other parts of the West Side, landlords with decrepit properties they could no longer rent profitably—or who simply preferred the quicker payout—sometimes had them burned down so that they could collect the insurance payment. In one much-publicized case elsewhere in the Lawndale area, two landlords named Al Berland and Lou Wolf were found to have deliberately spread flammable liquids in building basements and set them alight. Berland alone had owned no fewer than forty-seven buildings where fires had broken out. By the time their machinations were discovered, they had collected $800,000 in insurance payments; they were arrested, found guilty, and sent to prison. It soon became clear that they had run their scam in collusion with local officials. And they were not alone in a time and place where landlords' "torches" often set their fires with no regard to the families in the building. One Chicago operator soaked a room with accelerant, packed a toaster with paper, and put the appliance on a timer so that he could be far away when the blaze started.[30]

The differences between neighborhoods could be incredibly stark. In North Lawndale, for example, there had been just over twenty-eight thousand housing units in 1950. But thirty years of arson, abandonment, and decay had claimed an astonishing one-third of all dwellings—almost ten thousand housing units had been lost in just one of Chicago's seventy-seven community areas. As North Lawndale lost nearly four in ten residents and deteriorated into a terrain dotted with burned-out apartment buildings, abandoned houses, and lots left empty by teardowns, the South Lawndale neighborhood's housing stock remained intact as it became the Little Village barrio.[31]

THE MOST VISIBLE manifestation of the Latinization of Little Village was its commercial district along Twenty-Sixth Street. Although businesses there served a generally low-income community, it included enough people to generate a great deal of aggregate spending power. Spanish-speaking entrepreneurs and professionals saw the growing demand for goods and services and set up shop. As the neighborhood's population made the transition to a Hispanic plurality and then a majority, Twenty-Sixth Street grew into the preeminent shopping street for the community, especially its Mexican immigrants. It was where they went to find the things that helped them feel more at home in the city, from special dresses for their daughters' *quinceañera* celebrations to prayer candles and home remedies sold at the nearest *botánica*—but especially the ingredients they needed to cook their *comidas típicas*, the special recipes that distinguished their towns or states within Mexico's astonishing variety of local and regional dishes. "You have to understand," recalled Isidro Arroyo, who arrived in Chicago in 1973, "in order to find Mexican foods, well, there just wasn't anything other than Twenty-Sixth Street and Eighteenth Street, Little Village and Pilsen."[32]

The changes registered clearly on the neighborhood's streetscape by the 1970s. The small English-speaking mom-and-pop stores that had been disappearing for more than a decade were succeeded by shops and offices doing business in Spanish. Establishments like *taquerías*, *carnicerías*, *botánicas*, and *quinceañera* shops became the nucleus of a fast-developing enclave economy. By 1980, according to the city directory, the twenty-one-block stretch of Twenty-Sixth Street was home to at least eighty-four Hispanic businesses. Mirroring the kinds of small, family-owned establishments with local clienteles that had been the backbone of shopping districts across Anglo America, the street's Spanish-designated businesses included restaurants, groceries, clothiers, bakeries, jewelers, shoe stores, photo studios, bridal boutiques, nightclubs, hairstylists, doctors, attorneys, real estate agents, auto parts stores, a butcher, a florist, a pet shop, a record store, an insurance agency, an upholsterer, a liquor store, and the inevitable funeral home.[33]

People from outside the neighborhood were quick to take note. A 1982 study prepared by the same consulting firm that had produced the earlier report on Hispanic Chicago noted, "Many of the businesses in South Lawndale specialize in Hispanic goods and services.... Business in the area is reportedly very good, and merchants have been working together to improve the area and develop its distinctive Hispanic character." This, the report added, made the area "unusual in that its retail sales volume is increasing."[34]

Little Village was just the most prominent example of what was becoming a citywide phenomenon. The number of self-employed

Latinas and Latinos in Chicago grew by almost half during the 1970s, a time when non-Hispanic self-employment dropped by 20 percent, though many of their businesses were small operations with few employees. By 1984, an official report by the city counted as many as 5,200 Hispanic-owned businesses in Chicago.[35]

Journalists increasingly saw Little Village in a different light. Their new understanding of what was happening became evident in the late 1970s in a series of articles in the *Chicago Tribune*. A 1977 feature piece entitled "La Villa Chiquita: An Oasis of Harmony in the Inner City" exemplified this new view of the neighborhood. The writer described Little Village as "a bright spot of ethnic color in an otherwise gray area." It then provided vignettes of ethnic Mexican businesspeople who spoke of their own investment in the community and its prospects. Pat Villareal, for example, "started a small bridal shop four years ago," and it had since grown into a business with annual sales in the six-figure range. Similarly, Guadalupe Martínez, who opened a small grocery store on Twenty-Sixth Street in 1962, was described as owning La Justicia Food Market and the Cañada Shoe Store, with combined sales of over $1 million per year. The article also noted that people had bought houses: "Homeownership is high in the village, and a dozen financial institutions and as many real estate agencies flourish." By way of explanation, Villareal said of his coethnics: "These people want to help themselves and each other. They want to buy their own homes and fix them up." The article did allow that the neighborhood had its problems: overcrowded schools, buildings in need of renovation, gang activity. But the overall tone here and elsewhere was clearly optimistic. In another article published two years later, the president of the local chamber of commerce said, "This is a very stable, viable community. . . . You never see a vacant storefront, and property values are rising." A local shopkeeper—identified as "one of a sizable number of Hispanic businessmen in the area who have benefited from the boom"—averred: "This store has been a great investment for me. . . . There's no question that the Mexicans have upgraded the neighborhood. I can't see it getting anything but better." And in the years that followed, the same sorts of images were deployed in articles with titles like "Enterprising

Immigrants Converge on Little Village" and "Old Mexico Is a Hit in Old Chicago."[36]

These celebratory accounts were, of course, not without their particular racialized context. Written as they were about a decade after the civil disturbances of 1968 and the subsequent depletion of businesses in the predominantly African American neighborhoods to the north of Little Village, the surprised tone of the articles suggested their larger rhetorical strategy: to contrast entrepreneurial growth in this Hispanic neighborhood with the relative lack of commerce on the black West Side. But these articles did not account for the mortgages and commercial loans that had been made available to ethnic Mexicans, allowing them to build equity and a measure of wealth at a critical point in the neighborhood's development. Such opportunities had been withheld from their African American neighbors to the north. Hispanic shopkeepers and professionals had worked hard to build their local businesses, but so had many others on the West Side. As much as city hall was segregating Chicago by race, many Mexican Americans and other Latinos still occupied a racial middle ground that afforded them at least a few advantages.

BY THE MID-1980S, the two reports issued by the city in September 1973—*Chicago 21* and *Chicago's Spanish-Speaking Population*—had each found a material manifestation on the landscape as the city attempted to address the depopulation that was the leading symptom of the urban crisis.

The *Chicago 21* plan had for nearly a decade enjoyed the backing of the city council and a phalanx of business leaders and top architects, and so its main proposal leapt from the planning to the construction phase very quickly indeed. The result was Dearborn Park, a development filled with a combination of townhomes and tower dwellings, all located in a redeveloped South Loop neighborhood of smaller-scale streets and carefully manicured plantings. The residences in the completed northern half were all sold by 1986. The developers, anticipating criticism of the racial politics behind the project, had carefully managed the home sales and assembled a racially diverse though not entirely representative neighborhood population:

the initial residents were 67 percent white, 28 percent African American, and 5 percent Asian or Hispanic. After this first round of sales, developers were ready to purchase lots further south and ordered designs for more residential construction.[37]

The completion of Dearborn Park was greeted with a chorus of plaudits. The mayor hailed it as an example of how people who had left the city could be drawn back in. Local columnists lovingly described its neighborhood charm and approvingly cited its diverse demographics. Political figures led tours through the development, framing it as a lasting legacy of Mayor Daley's efforts to make good on the grand plans of Daniel Burnham himself. Nor did the praise quickly die down: more than a decade later, the project was the subject of an entire book by a Pulitzer Prize–winning journalist; its jacket copy enthusiastically described it as the story of "how a small group of Chicago business leaders created a thriving and viable neighborhood on the carcass of old rail yards and, in the process, managed to reinvigorate the central city."[38]

In fairness, the project had accomplished something significant. Dearborn Park was indeed an economically successful and architecturally distinguished development. With one-third of its residents having lived in the suburbs before moving in, it served to demonstrate how upper-middle and professional-class families could be attracted back into the central city. Even the demographics improved over time: fifteen years later, the distribution had shifted to 58 percent white, 30 percent black, and 12 percent Asian or Hispanic (though in truth mostly the former). At fifty-one acres, it was considerably smaller than initially conceived; the area became home to only 14,500 residents, about one-eighth as many as the *Chicago 21* plan had projected. But it was still an exemplar of how idle land in the middle of a major industrial city could be developed into a functional residential neighborhood.[39]

It looked much less impressive, however, compared with a new landmark rising over another of the city's old industrial districts. Beginning in 1983, the Little Village Chamber of Commerce and a group called the United Latin American Businessmen held a series of meetings with municipal officials to plan a public monument. They envisioned a Spanish Colonial–style arch over Twenty-Sixth Street bearing the words BIENVENIDOS A LITTLE VILLAGE. One of

The Little Village Arch, Twenty-Sixth Street. A project envisioned in 1983 and completed four years later by the Little Village Chamber of Commerce, the United Latin American Businessmen, and the City of Chicago, the Spanish Colonial–style structure symbolized the role of Little Village as the city's leading gateway for newcomers from across the Americas. Photograph by the author.

the project's directors called it "an ethnic symbol of our community," and indeed it was an aesthetically fitting gesture—this entryway to Chicago's preeminent concentration of Latinas and Latinos would be the neighborhood's single most distinctive architectural feature. The Little Village Arch was completed four years later.[40]

What was most remarkable about the Little Village Arch was less the structure itself than the demographic changes it symbolized. Within its own neighborhood, it was emblematic of the new Latino Chicagoans Little Village had welcomed: the 35,000 new residents in the 1970s, followed by 13,000 more in the 1980s. Citywide, by the beginning of the 1980s, the number of Latinos had grown dramatically over the previous decade. The proportion of Latinos in Chicago nearly doubled in the 1970s, from just over 7 percent to about 14 percent citywide, and in absolute terms from 247,000 to 422,000; in the Chicago metropolitan area, the increase was from 324,000 to 581,000 people.[41]

Overall, though they still represented a relatively modest proportion of the city and metropolitan populations, Latinas and Latinos were essential to keeping Chicago from slumping more severely in its most difficult decade of the urban crisis. After all, the 1970s were the years in which the city lost residents more quickly than it has before or since: by 1980, Chicago had shed over 360,000 denizens over just ten years. But that population loss would have been even greater had the city not gained 175,000 new Latino residents over the same period. Their rate of increase slowed somewhat in the 1980s, but the Latino city population still rose by 123,000, and by just over a quarter million in the metro area.[42]

Both Dearborn Park and the Little Village Arch highlighted processes that countered the population losses and deindustrialization of the urban crisis. But the multimillion-dollar public-private undertaking, backed by the most powerful leaders in the city and supported by substantial government subsidies, was ultimately far less effective than the initiative that proceeded at no additional cost to taxpayers and that reflected the collective strivings of hundreds of thousands of people working unheralded in their barrios and throughout the city.

While Latinos successfully revitalized their neighborhoods and repopulated the city, Chicago's elected officials did not welcome them into the corridors of power. Those who held power in city hall had made note of the fast-rising numbers of Mexican, Puerto Rican, and other Hispanic denizens of the city and welcomed their votes, but mostly avoided setting them up as aldermen or letting them share in municipal patronage appointments. As the 1970s gave way to the 1980s, Latino voters and activists were growing restive. They would soon begin to challenge the political status quo, with some running independent candidacies against the Chicago Democratic machine. And a few years later, they would join politically with African Americans to revolutionize the city's establishment and inaugurate a new era of politics in Chicago—as their counterparts were doing in Dallas and other key cities across the nation.

CHAPTER 8

LA POLÍTICA

I T IS THE MOST FAMOUS POLITICAL ANECDOTE IN CHICAGO
history. In 1948, an idealistic young man moved to the city to
attend law school. Inspired to volunteer in that fall's campaigns,
he ventured into the headquarters of the Eighth Ward Regular Democratic Organization.

"Who sent you?" asked the ward committeeman.

"Nobody sent me," answered the young man.

Speaking around the cigar in his mouth, the committeeman responded, "We don't want nobody nobody sent!"[1]

Decades later, Latino political hopefuls knew exactly how the
young man felt. This was how things worked in the big city—and
not just in Chicago by any means; Dallas had its own version of a
self-dealing political class.

In both cities, Hispanics had established themselves as the inher-
itors of neighborhoods that had been mostly abandoned by white
Anglos. What remained to be seen, however, was whether they could
gain access to the power that had been vested in these neighborhoods
and exercised in the name of the people who lived there. To do so, they
would have to campaign within political systems designed or manip-
ulated to marginalize or exclude them. They would come up against

political operatives who would go to great lengths to disenfranchise, divide, or sabotage them. And they would confront the reality that while some Anglos had accepted Hispanics as neighbors, many others would race-bait, bloc-vote, or switch parties rather than allow them to occupy positions of authority. Beating these odds would require that Latinos build and sustain alliances with another major group of underserved and exploited urbanites: African Americans.

LATINOS IN CHICAGO and Dallas sought representation within two very different systems of governance. In Chicago, they had to reckon with the ward system. The city was divided up into territories, each with its own alderman elected to sit on the common council. This framework had been in place since the city's incorporation in 1837, when there were only six wards. As the population increased, wards were steadily added until 1923, when municipal officials decided to fix the number of wards at fifty, redrawing the boundary lines every ten years based on new census counts. The common council, together with a mayor popularly elected by the voters, ran the affairs of the city.[2]

The political machine that would govern Chicago for half a century was established in 1931 with Anton Cermak's victory in that year's municipal elections. City politics had previously been dominated by ethnic English, Irish, and Germans, but after building a power base among his Bohemian coethnics in South Lawndale, Cermak was able to outmaneuver his rivals. The new mayor consolidated his authority by allying with President Roosevelt's New Deal and inviting Germans, Poles, Jews, and other white ethnics into the corridors of power. Cermak's campaign motto had called for city hall to become a "house for all peoples," though it was a house from which African Americans in particular would continue to be excluded for years to come.[3]

Chicago's political machine worked by distributing patronage among the wards in return for votes. Each ward's alderman and his precinct workers were responsible for getting out the vote in municipal, state, and federal elections. They and other local political operators were keenly aware that the mayor and his advisers would be scrutinizing the number of votes cast in each ward and precinct as a measure of local support. In return, local leaders would be owed all manner of favors large and small. High-turnout areas could expect prompt trash collection, street sweeping, snow shoveling, and even new parks or playgrounds, and their residents would be chosen for city employment as meter readers, sanitation workers, clerks, cops, and the like. The amount of patronage doled out was considerable: not long after mid-century, city hall controlled tens of millions of dollars in spending and a startling total of thirty-five thousand jobs in the municipal workforce.[4]

Chicago was the last major US city to sustain such a powerful machine. One reason it had survived was that the road to the White House ran through Chicago. The Windy City was electorally pivotal because Illinois was a swing state and the Chicago machine was essential to getting out the vote. Since most of the rest of the state was solidly Republican, its largest city typically accounted for the margin in the state between victory and defeat for the Democrats, as Mayor Daley demonstrated in the Kennedy-Nixon contest of 1960.

Dallas, governed through an at-large system of representation, was a different story entirely. Rather than distributing political authority geographically throughout the city by allowing neighborhoods to elect their own locally serving representatives, the entire city voted for all the council members in an at-large system, and each member was expected to consider the needs of the city as a whole. This had a certain logic to it, but in practice it tended to sideline city subcultures: immigrants and ethnics, African Americans, Catholics, and working-class communities. Instead, it concentrated decision-making power among older, wealthier Anglo-Protestant elites.[5]

This system had not been implemented accidentally. Across the country, just as southern, eastern, and central European immigrants were gaining political influence in the ward- or district-based systems that had been by far the most common form of city government, the at-large system became a popular "reform." Old Protestant elites became frightened and tried to disenfranchise the ethnic voters who sustained urban political machines. The at-large system was designed to forestall the kinds of power that had long been wielded by Irish Americans and then, after a period of rapid demographic change, by figures like Chicago's Cermak or New York's Fiorello LaGuardia, the son of Italian and Jewish immigrants to the city.[6]

At its founding in 1856, Dallas had a district-based system similar to the one in Chicago. But as the city industrialized and a new class politics came into play, municipal leaders believed that a new mode of governance was necessary, and so a plebiscite was called in 1906 to replace the previous ward system with an at-large one. It was not coincidental that this came just a few years after the imposition of a poll tax and a party-controlled primary—both effectively disfranchising black people and some poor whites. As one opponent of the at-large system put it, it would let "banks and the *Dallas News* . . . dominate all the wards." Notably, Oak Cliff had been one of those wards for some time; its working-class white residents were perennially suspicious, and with good reason, that the downtown interests had been underfunding their area while lavishing disproportionate spending on the area north of the Trinity River. The at-large system ensured that there was little that the residents of Oak Cliff could do about it.[7]

In Chicago, the ward system offered new arrivals a path to power. Chicago had long been a "city of neighborhoods" in which ethnic groups established locally based political clubs. So as Hispanics grew from a tiny minority in South Lawndale into the majority population of Little Village, they naturally expected access to political power commensurate with their numbers. After all, Anton Cermak had achieved just that in the same neighborhood. At least a few of the ruling Democrats in city hall seemed to understand that they should bring Mexican Americans and Puerto Ricans into the ranks of the ethnics who had been among the party's core constituencies for more than a century. But it proved harder to persuade local leaders on the West Side that the time had come.

The Twenty-Second Ward, which covered most of Little Village and part of North Lawndale, was a case in point. Alderman Otto Janousek had maintained good relations with constituents in his ward and representatives from neighboring ones, but the tone seemed to change after he passed away in 1969. A group of dissenting activists told the *Chicago Defender* that the ward had been taken over by "racists who do not represent the best interests of the community or the Democratic party." In response, they sought to create an "underground coalition" that would remain loyal to Mayor Daley and the regular party organization but would also work "to put control of our community into the hands of the community. This would include all our residents, black, Spanish-speaking, and—believe it or not—the white membership of this community." This effort was stymied when Frank Stemberk became the ward's new alderman. Stemberk showed scant interest in representing his Latino constituents; focusing spending on the ward's shrinking white ethnic population, he refused to hire any bilingual staff to help Spanish-speaking residents.[8]

This was not the first time machine officials had ignored the city's growing Latino constituencies. Barely a year before, a labor union–backed political club, the Tenth Ward Spanish Speaking Democratic Organization, had been founded to give voice to the Mexican Americans who lived and worked around the steel plants at the city's edge in South Chicago. A machine functionary named Edward Vrdolyak then joined the ward committee and promptly took away their patronage positions. When party leaders told him that they should instead be incorporated into the ward organization, Vrdolyak responded by promising to put one prominent Hispanic laborite into the leadership circle—but on the condition that the appointee disband the Spanish-speaking club and take orders from the machine. "There was no way we could go for that deal," recalled Vrdolyak's intended designee. "Here he fires our guys, a few lousy jobs, nothing like Ward superintendent or stationary engineer, you know, and he expects us to turn around and join his organization like that. We couldn't have looked our people in the eye." When they refused, Vrdolyak arranged with city hall to divide the Mexican American community up between wards, using the 1970 redistricting to gerrymander it into irrelevance.[9]

Hispanic voters in districts with fast-diversifying populations like the Twenty-Second and Tenth Wards were dismayed that their European ethnic aldermen were doing so little for newer constituents. The lion's share of resources devoted to Chicago wards—everything from priority for trash collection to new parks and other recreational facilities to city employment—went disproportionately to wards with non-Hispanic white residents. Black and Latino neighborhoods were systematically shortchanged on spending and jobs.[10]

The neighborhood's schools were a particular point of contention. South Lawndale had already been short on public schools, in part because the heavily Roman Catholic population often elected to send

their children to the parochial schools in the nearby parishes. As ethnic Mexican families succeeded the European ethnics, their children
were the perfect fit for the Catholic educational system. But parish
schools were becoming fewer in number and more expensive as the
ranks of Catholic sisters and brothers, who had for decades staffed
urban parish schools, began to thin out. At the same time, city hall
routinely underfunded public schools on the West Side, where the
student body was increasingly black and brown. As a result, by the
1970s Hispanic children were increasingly crowded into an inadequate number of schools. The situation in the schools—where there
was also conflict between black and Hispanic students—soon led
Mexican American parents and students to launch a grassroots campaign for a new school in their neighborhood. Faced in 1973 with an
extraordinary mobilization of residents in Pilsen and Little Village—
what the school superintendent called "a community that would not
take 'no' for an answer"—the school board authorized the construction of Benito Juárez High School, which opened four years later.[11]

The Chicago machine was increasingly dogged by scandal, but
it kept grinding along until five days before Christmas 1976, when
Mayor Daley suffered a massive heart attack. His funeral and memorial were grand and solemn events, and he was eulogized by many of
the city's and nation's leading political, journalistic, and literary figures. Then, Chicago politics being what it was, everyone started jock-
eying for position—that is, if they hadn't begun doing so the instant
they'd found out that Daley was dead.[12]

Latino politicos surely hoped that in the shuffle to come they might
be in line for the committee assignments, precinct captainships, judge-
ships, and even aldermanic seats they had been seeking for years. And
at first there seemed to be some promise of rewards to come: when
Jane Byrne ran for mayor in 1979, she portrayed herself as a reformer
in opposition to the drab placeholder the machine had put up to finish Daley's term. She even campaigned in Puerto Rican and Mexican
American neighborhoods, where she suggested that Hispanics would
enjoy patronage appointments and other rewards if she won.[13]

Disappointment set in quickly. A year after Byrne took office, Chicago was still almost entirely without Hispanic appointees. There was
only a single Latina county commissioner, two Latino county court

Latina and Latino students and their families launched public demonstrations in response to crumbling facilities, exclusionary curricula, and arbitrary closings at schools serving Pilsen and Little Village, including this march downtown to the Chicago Board of Education in 1973, the same year the board authorized the construction of Benito Juárez High School. Photograph by Bob Black for the *Chicago Sun-Times*.

judges, and a Latino state university trustee. Even worse, in 1981 the mayor's officials used the recent census to redraw ward boundaries to divide up Latino and black populations among new wards that continued to favor the existing, nearly all-white aldermen. She had made a few new Hispanic appointments in the meantime, but they did little to make amends for the shocking and systematic effort to gerrymander communities of color out of power for the rest of the decade. Black and Latino constituencies were furious. Three groups went so far as to file lawsuits alleging that the new boundaries amounted to violations of the Voting Rights Act of 1965.[14]

Tired of systematic neglect and frequent hostility from city hall, many Mexican Americans and Puerto Ricans concluded that they had to find a way around the regular political machine. They founded a series of independent political organizations (IPOs) in key Hispanic wards around the city. The most prominent of the local leaders behind this effort was Rudy Lozano. Born in Texas, he was the son of a Mexican worker who was himself a tireless labor organizer. After moving with his family to Chicago as a boy, he attended Harrison High School on the West Side, where he met his future wife, Guadalupe, who featured in the first chapter of this book. In 1970, in the wake of the "blowouts" in East Los Angeles schools in 1968 and school demonstrations like those in Denver and Crystal City, Texas, they helped organize a school walkout to protest the lack of Latino teachers and the absence of Mexican American subjects in the curriculum. "Mexicans were not in the books," remembered Lozano's sister Emma, "unless we were sitting under a tree, taking a siesta, with our big sombreros and our donkey on the side."[15]

Lozano went on to become a labor and political organizer, building on his neighborhood ties, union experience, and strong relations with African Americans. In the 1970s, he worked with legal aid organizations to assist undocumented workers in the city, most of them Mexican; he was convinced that organizing these workers was an essential part of the labor movement's strategy. Like his father, he was a lifelong labor activist, working in the needle trades and later becoming the head regional organizer for the International Ladies' Garment Workers' Union in the Midwest. At the same time, Lozano and his family sought ways to forge alliances with black leaders in the area. In the 1970s, Lozano established partnerships with black activists around educational as well as labor issues. The Lozanos' deep roots in the immigrant, labor, and racial justice movements shaped their entire approach to political organizing.[16]

Awakening to the emerging challenge, the Daley machine responded by appointing a few obedient Hispanic officeholders. City officials had also begun to make a few gestures toward granting Hispanics some of the privileges traditionally reserved for white Anglos. The mortgages made available to Mexican-origin people in Little Village had been emblematic of this move. The IPOs therefore had to contend with some Latino voters' belief that continued loyalty to the machine would bring political influence, and that an alliance with reformers, black activists, or both would spoil the small gains they had won thus far. Nevertheless, there were significant African American populations around the northern boundaries of Little Village and Pilsen, and Lozano, local activist Jesús "Chuy" García, and their allies calculated that a multiracial reform coalition would offer their best hope for challenging the machine. It would not be long before circumstances handed them a golden opportunity to do just that.[17]

THE OPPORTUNITY CAME in the form of Harold Washington. Born in Chicago, Washington went to high school on the city's South Side and served in the Pacific during the Second World War. He attended college and law school before embarking on his political career, beginning as a city prosecutor and serving as a precinct captain in the Third Ward. Washington was elected to the state legislature in 1965. He had run for the Democratic nomination for mayor in 1979 but was unable to gain enough traction to defeat Jane Byrne. He continued to serve as a state representative until 1980, when he parlayed his popularity in his ward into a successful run for the US House of Representatives. After working hard to ensure the reauthorization of the Voting Rights Act of 1965, he was persuaded by his supporters to run for mayor, encouraged by the rising unpopularity of Mayor Byrne.[18]

The IPOs wasted no time in putting their theory of multiracial coalition governance into effect. They endorsed Washington for mayor within a few weeks, in preparation for the February 1983 Democratic primary election, which usually determined the winner of the mayoral election. At the same time, they readied their own slate of candidates for that spring's aldermanic elections. Lozano ran for city council in the Twenty-Second Ward, and Juan Velásquez ran in the Twenty-Fifth Ward. They also fielded candidates in the heavily Puerto Rican Twenty-Sixth and Thirty-First Wards. Central to these efforts was José "Cha Cha" Jiménez, the Young Lords founder who labored unceasingly to build Puerto Rican political power and maintain connections with black community organizations. The response from established white ethnic political figures was sadly predictable. For example, when Twenty-Fifth Ward alderman Vito Marzullo was notified about his primary opponent, he sneered, "These people better learn something about America or go back to Mexico where they belong."[19]

In the actual balloting, Washington won the primary, but the IPO candidates fell just short of the mark. The margins were tight enough, and the ballot challenges aggressive enough, that even though IPO leaders believed that there had been fraud, they chose to focus on supporting Washington in the general election two months later. They understood that with Hispanic candidates loyal to the machine also in the running, they would have to forge a coalition of the wards' black and Hispanic residents, alongside some white residents. Rudy Lozano's sister Emma remembered a day when she found Rudy in his basement making a banner that read BLACK-LATINO UNITY.

"Does that exist?" she asked, explaining later, "I was just, you know, young, and I didn't see it."

"It's gonna exist now," he answered. "Sometimes you just have to write it down!"[20]

The general election campaign exposed the city's ugly racial fault lines. In previous elections, the outcome was a foregone conclusion after the primary: Chicago was so lopsidedly Democratic that once the party's candidate was chosen, he or she would coast to victory with the support of the majority of white Anglo, black, and Hispanic voters. But when Washington became the first African American mayoral candidate, a majority of whites switched their support to his opponent, giving a Republican a chance at the mayoralty for the first time in decades. Black voters swung strongly behind the Washington campaign; Latinos, interestingly, were more divided but seemed to lean toward him. Washington's opponent sought to exploit this racial tension. The Chicago-area artist Carlos Cortez later recalled: "I remember a few years back, the Latino and black coalition that put Harold Washington in the mayor's seat . . . well, during the campaign the establishment was doing its damndest to sow dissension between the two." Their tactics were familiar to him, as he'd seen employers doing the same thing: "I knew as a construction stiff working on the job, they'd come to the black workers and say, 'You don't want that greaser having as good breaks as you do.' They'd come to the greaser and say, 'You don't want that nigger having as good of a job as you do.' And of course they would use the both of us against the white workers. Or if it were all white workers they'd be playing off the Poles against the Italians and vice versa."[21]

Seeing that the African American vote would not be enough to win the general election, as it had been in the primary, Washington recognized that Latino voters would be essential. Jiménez arranged the first official Latino endorsement of Washington, and Lozano guided him as campaign manager for Hispanic outreach. Washington expressed interest in restoring spending to neighborhoods like those on the West Side and Northwest Side that had been so severely short-changed by the machine's focus on downtown. He emphasized that Mexican Americans and Puerto Ricans should have their fair share of city employment and vowed to enforce laws against racial discrimination in labor unions. Washington also highlighted his support for immigrant rights and the sanctuary movement for Central American refugees from US-backed civil conflicts. It did not hurt that Washington had fought to include protections against language discrimination while working on the 1975 reauthorization of the Voting Rights Act of 1965.[22]

Multiracial coalition politics won the day. Although Washington unmistakably depended on an African American electoral base, his 51–49 percent victory would have been impossible without the support of large numbers of Latinas and Latinos and a pivotal segment of liberal whites. Washington claimed an extraordinary 99 percent of African Americans, who were clustered on the South Side and in parts of the West Side. The "lakefront liberals" were essential as well: Washington won only 12 percent of the non-Hispanic white vote, but in such a close election liberal white support was indispensable. The Latino vote was crucial in a different way: while the city's overwhelmingly Mexican American and Puerto Rican Hispanic voters had divided their votes among the Democratic candidates in the February primary, in the April general election they favored Washington, supplying a crucial segment of his margin of victory of 46,250 votes. According to one estimate, Latinos provided him with a net total of 51,000 votes, with 75 percent supporting his candidacy; another count found almost 28,000 votes for Washington coming just from the city's four most Hispanic wards. After his primary victory, he promised to thwart the Chicago machine with the support of "a working people's coalition of blacks, whites, and Hispanics who could force them to yield this city." These constituencies had now put him in a position to do so.[23]

Washington's mayoral powers were blocked, however, because key Democratic aldermen chose to ally themselves with Republicans. The balance of power was held by the "Vrdolyak 29," a virtually all-white bloc led by "Fast Eddie" Vrdolyak, the same race-baiting alderman from the far southeastern boundary of the city who had attempted to disband the Tenth Ward Spanish Speaking Democratic Organization a decade and a half earlier. Mayor Washington's support, by contrast, was concentrated among aldermen from the South Side of the city, joined by those from predominantly Mexican American and Puerto Rican areas of the West Side and the Northwest Side, as well as representatives of white voters among the professional classes of the city living along the long eastern lakefront. The preponderance of white aldermen backing Vrdolyak kept the city council from acting on any of the new mayor's initiatives.[24]

It would take key rulings in the federal courts to end the "Council Wars," as they became known. At a time when Chicago was roughly 40 percent white, 40 percent black, and 14 percent Latino, the city council was hugely disproportionate, its fifty seats occupied by thirty-three whites, sixteen blacks, and just one Latino—a Daley loyalist widely derided as a *vendido*, or sellout, because he had gone along with a severe slashing of city funding for dozens of Latino organizations that had for years enjoyed municipal support. In the last week of 1985, a federal judge ruled that seven of the city's wards had to be redrawn, and furthermore that early elections would be held in those wards the following year.[25]

In the resulting aldermanic elections, the mayor needed a total of four more council seats to create a 25–25 tie that would give him the tie-breaking vote and allow legislation to move forward. There were seven wards where the new electoral map had made black and Latino populations more preponderant, threatening white Anglo incumbents. This could be seen clearly on the West Side: Stemberk, looking at the new demographics of the Twenty-Second Ward, decided not to run again; in the Twenty-Fifth Ward, Marzullo was mapped entirely out. These changes led the way for runs by Jesús García and Juan Velásquez in the Twenty-Second and Twenty-Fifth Wards and by Puerto Rican candidates on the Northwest Side. In the first round of elections that followed, pro-Washington candidates picked up three new seats, including García in Little Village. Control of the city council thus depended on a runoff election in Humboldt Park, the city's biggest and most important Puerto Rican neighborhood. Luis Gutiérrez, who had run as the anti-machine candidate in the primary, managed to defeat his Vrdolyak-friendly opponent (who was also Puerto Rican) in a race with a highly mobilized local electorate.[26]

Mayor Washington finally had a working majority on the city council, and he understood that he would have to reward the key constituencies who had made that possible. He redirected spending from the Loop to the neighborhoods, canceling costly programs that mainly benefited the business community at the expense of working-class Chicagoans. He also took up measures of specific interest to Latinas and Latinos, dramatically increasing their presence in city government. His administration's new hires had been 11 percent Hispanic—still less than their proportion of the city's population but a much better record than his predecessor, whose new employees had been only 7 percent Latino. Washington's record was even better on administrative positions, with one-fifth of his appointments being Hispanic, including twenty-seven people with supervisory responsibilities—nine times more than in the Byrne years. The dollar total assigned to Latinos in city contracts was fully ten times higher in 1985 than the year before Washington took office. Washington also issued an executive order that removed questions about citizenship from City of Chicago application materials (except where specifically required by federal law) and barred city workers from turning information over to federal immigration officials without a court order. The mayor had not done all that his Latina and Latino supporters hoped for: it was only under pressure that he established the Mayor's Advisory Council for Latino Affairs, and some of his city agencies hired few or no Hispanics. But these were exceptions to the rule of greatly improved access for Chicago's Latinas and Latinos.[27]

There were still fault lines in Washington's coalition, such as disagreements among black and Latino officials and leaders about the allocation of important posts in the city: African Americans noted that their votes had been by far the largest factor in the mayor's victory; Hispanics looked for proportionate inclusion in governance. Among Mexican American and Puerto Rican officeholders, a trial balloon had been floated (but soon deflated) about creating a Latino bloc independent of the mayor. Vrdolyak himself was sufficiently convinced of the possibility of undermining the mayor's coalition that he became Washington's main opponent when he ran for reelection in 1987.[28]

With the help of the self-declared Rainbow Coalition, the mayor won reelection with 54 percent of the vote. He repeated his extraordinarily strong performance in the city's predominantly African American wards and improved on his performance in the four wards with large populations of Latinas and Latinos. He had hoped to get a greater proportion of the white vote the second time around and spent a great deal of time courting this demographic, but to his disappointment, there was no improvement in those numbers. Even so, on the city council he managed to expand his margin by two seats, including in the strongly Puerto Rican Thirty-First Ward, which tossed out a Hispanic Vrdolyak loyalist in favor of the mayor's ally Raymond Figueroa.[29]

Washington's victories had confirmed the political importance of Mexican American and Puerto Rican voters in the Windy City. By the time of the Council Wars, Latinos could see that while European ethnics like Richard Dolejs had offered them a provisional sort of whiteness as acceptable neighbors, Mayor Daley's city hall would not make the same offer when it came to political power. They responded by rejecting a subordinate role within the city's political machine, instead forming alliances with African Americans and a smaller population of progressive whites and exercising authority on their own behalf as part of a new Democratic coalition. The turnabout was especially noted in the Little Village council district. "At one time a machine bastion," wrote Chicago's leading authority on ward politics the year after the election, "the 22nd now hosts perhaps the most efficient independent political organization in the city."[30]

The gains that Latinas and Latinos won through multiracial politics were substantial, but the coalition turned out to be fragile and ultimately short-lived. Only months after Mayor Washington took office, Rudy Lozano was shot to death in his home in what many community members believed was an assassination orchestrated by his foes among politicos or anti-union employers. And less than seven months after his second inauguration, Washington suffered a heart attack in his city hall office and was pronounced dead two hours later. The late mayor's political coalition soon began to break apart. An era of reform had ended, but the role of Mexican Americans and Puerto Ricans in Chicago politics had changed forever.

IN DALLAS, EFFORTS to build a multiracial political coalition faced even greater obstacles and took longer to come to fruition. Mexican American political influence in Big D was limited by the same means that had long operated to exclude African Americans from the levers of power in the city. The at-large system, together with the all-white Citizens Charter Association (CCA) having effective control of city council nominations, endorsements, and funding, had kept blacks and Hispanics off the council during the first one hundred years of city history, even though there had been black Dallasites since the nineteenth century and a significant ethnic Mexican colony since the 1910s. One might have expected these shared circumstances to lead to durable political alliances between African Americans and Mexican Americans, but sustained cooperation was elusive. Black and Hispanic Dallasites wrestled with these divisions at the same time they were fighting against a recalcitrant white Anglo majority backed by a system designed to be undemocratic.

It was African Americans who first tested the impermeability of Dallas's political system. The first black candidates for city council ran in the 1959 municipal elections and then again in each election through 1965. In every case, despite overwhelming support among African

American voters, all lost to white opponents. Whites dominated the electorate, and the great majority refused to vote for black candidates. This simply overwhelmed the smaller population of African American voters, leaving them without representation.[31]

Black Dallasites largely fought these battles alone. Throughout Texas, Mexican Americans had long claimed rights by insisting that they were legally white and therefore entitled to the same treatment as Anglos. After the successful Viva Kennedy campaign of 1960, it made a kind of sense that Mexican Americans would continue to cast themselves as white ethnics, since this would prevent their being grouped with blacks as people of color. This stance often led Hispanic leaders to deny that they were making the same kinds of claims as African Americans; they also frequently felt compelled to disavow the public demonstrations that were a key strategy of the black civil rights movement. One Mexican American activist from Dallas remembered that, among leading Hispanic advocacy groups, "when you tried to say, 'Start demanding or picketing or marching,' they say, 'No. We are above that. . . . We have more pride or education than that. You leave this to the Negroes.'" Shocking as it may seem now, the Texas-based League of United Latin American Citizens reflected the sentiments of many Hispanic politicos when it officially denounced Martin Luther King's 1963 March on Washington, at which he would deliver his "I Have a Dream" speech.[32]

The mid-1960s saw rising efforts among Mexican Americans to join forces with African Americans, especially after passage of the Civil Rights Act of 1964 and the Voting Rights Act of 1965 rendered the whiteness strategy increasingly untenable. Essential to this shift was the work of Francisco "Pancho" Medrano. Born in Dallas to immigrants from Guanajuato, Medrano was a lifelong organizer for the United Auto Workers and a regular participant in campaigns for the civil rights of both blacks and Hispanics. His career in the labor movement taught him to emphasize the importance of bringing people together on the basis of class regardless of their ethnoracial background. He was a member of the Dallas branch of the NAACP, and when Hispanic activists finally embraced the direct-action strategy of the black civil rights movement, he welcomed black participants into the predominantly Mexican American farmworker strikes and demonstrations in South Texas in 1966 and 1967.[33]

Dallas's white leaders were growing concerned about the prospect of demonstrations and lawsuits under the recently enacted Voting Rights Act, and by 1967 they were ready to modify the city's political structure. As they had done with other issues of racial discrimination, however, they chose the path of minimal action. In a negotiation with civil rights activists, they agreed to expand the city council from nine seats to eleven with the understanding that the new places would go to members who were not white Anglos. In the elections held two years later, the CCA, under the leadership of the relatively racially progressive Mayor J. Erik Jonsson, endorsed and helped fund one African American candidate, George Allen, and one Mexican American candidate, Anita Martínez, both of whom won election in a field cleared of significant opposition. It was the first time the city's shadow government had ever endorsed candidates of color. Still, as some pointed out, since one-third of Dallasites in 1970 were black or Hispanic, two out of eleven council seats was still a considerable underrepresentation. And when Councilman Allen proposed that the at-large structure of the council be phased out, his motion found no support.[34]

Meanwhile, black-brown discord continued to flare up. Black activists and elected leaders were suspicious of Mexican American and other Hispanic leaders when they took to claiming equal rights not as whites, but as discriminated-against people of color—thereby adopting a language and a logic of minority rights that had been created by the black freedom movement. Black activists worried that this strategy would cut into the gains they had won through decades of struggle. Hispanic politicos, for their part, felt mistrust when state and federal officials met with delegations of overwhelmingly or exclusively African American leaders. They saw this as an effort to exclude them from political discussions in which they, as another large minority population, had a real stake. In some cases the distribution of resources became a sticking point. As funding from the War on Poverty became available, rivalries emerged as to how this money should be divided between programs in predominantly black and primarily Mexican American communities. Should the VISTA worker hired be black or Hispanic, for example? These disagreements sometimes overshadowed the fact that both black and Hispanic people in Dallas and elsewhere created innovative programs with federal funding that greatly benefited public health, welfare, and education.[35]

Dissension could also arise from the grass roots in Dallas, especially from the city's schools. In part this reflected the complex triracial politics of school integration. African Americans seeking better educational opportunities through school integration were often at loggerheads with Mexican Americans looking for curricula that better addressed their culture and language. But the sheer fact of group conflict among immature youths was also an issue. In 1969, black-brown relations nearly boiled over after Mexican American leaders alleged that a group of black high schoolers were extorting "protection money" from Chicano students. A year later, tensions escalated again after a group of Mexican American youngsters said that African American boys had thrown rocks at them at a community center. As young people traded in stereotypes about each other, black and Hispanic leaders in Dallas found it difficult to mediate these conflicts effectively.[36]

All these points of division led most black and Hispanic Dallasites to undertake political action on separate tracks. For example, in 1971 Al Lipscomb, an African American community organizer and army veteran who had worked on civil rights causes, filed a lawsuit in federal court on behalf of eighteen black plaintiffs alleging that the city's at-large system of representation unconstitutionally diluted the votes of racial minorities. The filing initially involved Mexican Americans as plaintiffs, but they were not included in the case as it moved forward. Apparently, the representatives of the Hispanic parties had to be removed because they did not respond to queries about whether they wanted to be party to the suit.[37]

Nonetheless, in early 1975 the US District Court ruled in the plaintiffs' favor. Judge Eldon Mahon afforded the City of Dallas the opportunity to create a new plan that would pass constitutional muster, a ruling that was subsequently affirmed by the US Supreme Court. Yet city officials remained unwilling to move to fully district-based voting and instead proposed a mixed plan known as "eight-three." The city council would now have eleven seats, of which eight would be held by members elected from geographically defined districts and three would continue to be elected at-large. During the court proceedings, Latino representatives testified that they preferred a district system, but it was noted that given their relatively small population in the city, a much larger number of districts would be needed to create a Hispanic-majority council seat.[38]

Hispanic candidates still trusted that the eight-three plan would offer them a real opportunity to select their own council members and expand their representation in municipal affairs beyond a single seat approved by the city's Anglo leadership. They accordingly launched campaigns in at-large districts in the 1975 elections. Every single one of their candidates went down to defeat, their concentrated support for Hispanic candidates overwhelmed by white Anglos voting for their opponents. Among Mexican Americans, this outcome was widely seen as proof that they would not be allowed to wield real power in the city in proportion to their numbers. As a result, no Hispanic candidate ran for an at-large seat for more than a decade thereafter. Hispanic voters did, however, continue to support black candidates as they attempted to create a more racially equitable city council.[39]

The problem of at-large districts in a city where white Anglos represented the largest group and heavily supported "their" candidates would be a recurrent theme. The 1983 city council election offered a case in point. Black leaders in Dallas resolved to run an African American candidate for one of the at-large seats, having been assured on many occasions that the right contender could win citywide. They chose Marvin Robinson, a respected businessman and military veteran with a long record of public service. Yet Robinson still ran at a distinct disadvantage: his fund-raising efforts drew limited support outside the black community, while his main opponent was a white North Dallas man wealthy enough to fund his own campaign. In the general election, even though Robinson drew the overwhelming support of African American voters, his citywide vote came to less than one-third of the total ballots cast because nearly 90 percent of white Dallasites supported his opponent, who won with a nearly 70 percent majority. After that, no substantial black political figure thought it worthwhile to embark on the fool's errand of running in an at-large city council race.[40]

The problem of minority voting dilution was compounded by ongoing discord between black and Latino political figures. During the 1980s, for example, council members Ricardo Medrano and Elsie Faye Heggins—the former the son of Pancho Medrano, elected from a heavily Hispanic Oak Cliff district; the latter elected from a predominantly African American part of South Dallas—often clashed over redistricting. Heggins and her political allies hoped to create a new district that would likely put three African American members on the council, but their plan would add numerous white voters to Medrano's district, potentially jeopardizing his council seat. Indeed, these tensions led to the dismaying spectacle of Medrano and Heggins raising their voices at one another in what the *Dallas Morning News* described as "a redistricting workshop punctuated by sharp exchanges between minority council members." The frayed relationship between the two endangered the effort to expand minority voting strength just as nonwhites were approaching an absolute majority of the city's population.[41]

GREATER COORDINATION IN confronting the thorny issues of race and representation seemed to emerge in 1988, when a group of black and Latino citizens jointly launched a new voting rights lawsuit. They contended that the eight-three system violated federal law because it continued to dilute the voting power of minority communities, preventing their preferred candidates from holding more than a small share of seats on the city council. That same year recently elected mayor Annette Strauss created Dallas Together, an eighty-eight-member committee charged with addressing the city's racial tensions amid rising crime and police violence against people of color. Notably, when the committee issued its formal report the following January, it officially concurred with the lawsuit's basic contention that the eight-three system of governance had not allowed the city's minorities—now fully half the city's population—to exercise real political authority.[42]

The good intentions of the city's leadership were difficult to translate into a policy consensus, however. In the summer of 1989, a meeting called to decide what system of representation should be proposed to the city council—an entirely district-based plan or a ten-four-one plan (ten geographic districts plus four members elected from the quadrants of the city plus the mayor)—descended into recriminations and racial hostility as participants selected the ten-four-one plan even though it did not expand black representation and would most likely keep Hispanics off the council entirely.[43]

That year's citywide referendum was even worse. Voters were asked to either ratify or reject the new ten-four-one mixed system that had come out of the city council. After a campaign characterized by consistent racial hostility, Dallas voters approved the plan with a two-thirds majority. But underlying that figure was an extremely racially polarized electorate. Black and Hispanic voters overwhelmingly rejected the new plan by 95 percent and over 70 percent, respectively, demonstrating their view that it would not allow them to exercise power commensurate with their population. But white Anglo voters signaled their approval of the new plan, which got 85 percent of their votes. They, it seemed, would not part with the old system that had favored them for so long. The political leader Domingo García remembered that the deadlock seemed so hopeless—"the city polarized and a majority of the council dug in to keep the status quo"—that he and other political figures of color met at a South Dallas church and resolved that they must embark upon a campaign of civil disobedience.[44]

A federal ruling on voting rights intervened. Judge Jerry Buchmeyer of the Northern District of Texas struck down the city's continued use of at-large council districts. In an extensively documented opinion, the judge summarized the record behind the ruling: "The history of minority participation in the political process of Dallas is not one of choice; it is a record of what blacks and Hispanics have been permitted to do by the white majority." The court found that the eight-three system violated the Voting Rights Act of 1965 and directed the city to hold the next elections under a fourteen-one plan, with all council members elected from geographically defined districts and only the mayor elected through a citywide vote. The plaintiffs and their allies were jubilant. "We called all the people who had struggled for so long," recalled García, "and went to El Ranchito Restaurant in the heart of North Oak Cliff to celebrate."[45]

But since the city could still appeal the ruling, the fight was not quite over, and Oak Cliff would once again be the site of a decisive deal. The city council representative from northern Oak Cliff agreed to block any appeal and thereby ensure that the fourteen-one plan would be adopted as Dallas's official system. But there was a price: he wanted to see a districting that would ensure that the neighborhood's representative would continue to be Anglo. Fearing a long, drawn-out process to be decided by courts that a decade of Republican presidents had tilted conservative, the plaintiffs agreed.

Domingo García, who the following year would be elected to the city council, remembered thinking "of the residents of the Ledbetter neighborhood in far West Dallas, who still had few paved streets and, of course, no curbs or gutters. Could we change their lives? I thought of how the neighborhood I grew up in, once called Little Mexico, had been destroyed with little thought to the community who had lived there for decades. They had no voice at city hall." In the first election following the end of at-large voting, the people of Dallas put four African American and two Latino representatives on the fourteen-member city council.[46]

Four years later, they took up an even greater challenge: trying to elect the city's first mayor of color. The candidate was Ron Kirk. Born in the state capital of Austin in 1954, he graduated from college in 1976 and earned his law degree from the University of Texas in 1979. Following a family tradition of political participation, he had served as an intern in the state legislature and upon graduating became an aide to Senator Lloyd Bentsen. Based on years of work for the state's Democratic Party and his legal expertise, Kirk was later appointed secretary of state by Texas governor Ann Richards.

Kirk's path to mayoral candidate was not unlike Harold Washington's. His base was unmistakably among African American voters, whose rate of voter participation was the highest in the city: they were 30 percent of Dallasites, but fully 38 percent of registered voters. Hispanic voters were in the opposite position: more than one in five city residents were Hispanic, but only 9 percent of them were registered voters. Even though Kirk was opposed by Domingo García, he was expected to perform strongly among Latino voters. Summarizing his situation, *D Magazine* commented that Kirk had "put together an alliance of minority support that appears to unite people who literally have been unable to speak to each other for years."[47]

Kirk still needed white people's votes to become mayor. Even though Dallas had become a minority-majority city, white Anglos were still 53 percent of registered voters. Understanding this, Kirk maneuvered his way through the political thickets and emerged as the preferred candidate of both the city's voters of color and its civic and business establishments. To demonstrate his moderation and pragmatism, he recruited a Republican campaign manager and was so successful at courting voters in both parties that he won endorsements from the downtown business community and a number of high-profile conservatives.[48]

The candidate had positioned himself so adeptly across both racial and party lines that a few months in advance of election day, one political observer published an article titled "Is Ron Kirk Inevitable?" And indeed, he was declared the winner of the election not long after the polls closed. Kirk had won 62 percent of the vote, and when he ran for reelection four years later, he retained his position as mayor with a crushing majority of 74 percent.[49]

The triumph of a multiracial, coalition-backed mayoral campaign in Dallas had been a long time coming, both in the sense that it was the culmination of a long struggle and that it took more than a decade longer than in Chicago. Various factors accounted for the difference, including Big D's long-standing at-large political structure, its far smaller labor movement, and a political establishment that was more Republican than Democratic. But the key difference was that it simply took longer for Dallas's black and Latino leaders to find enough common ground to work together effectively rather than continue competing against each other for influence and resources. The mayor they elected was fairly conventional politically and made relatively modest changes in the city; he had, after all, been agreeable to many of the city's whites. But Kirk's election did finally bring political power in Dallas more in line with the city's fast-changing demographics.

As THEY SOUGHT political power commensurate with their growing numbers, Mexican American, Puerto Rican, and other Latino voters became an indispensable part of new urban political coalitions that challenged the entrenched and frequently racist politics that had kept them out of power. In so doing, they moved away from whiteness as a political identity and instead turned to allies of color who would help them exercise authority in municipal affairs.

Their efforts in Chicago and Dallas were part of a broader pattern in other big cities with substantial Hispanic communities. In San Antonio in 1981, a triracial coalition succeeded in electing Henry G. Cisneros as mayor, making him the first Hispanic and first person of color to hold that office. In 1983, a similar Latino-black-white alliance came together to put Federico Peña in the mayor's office in Denver.[50]

By the time these political mobilizations had come to fruition, migrant and immigrant Latinos had spent two decades stabilizing the neighborhoods and cities that were being abandoned en masse by white Anglos. These newcomers had repopulated declining neighborhoods, reoccupied housing, and begun to restore local economies devastated by disinvestment and deindustrialization—even as the hollowing out of these economies had made it difficult for Latinos to approach the kind of earning power enjoyed by their predecessors.

As transformative as these years had been, however, they were only the beginning of the Latino-led revitalization of urban America. The years to come would see dramatic changes in the sources of Latin American migration, the basic rules of US immigration law, and the economic conditions under which immigrants would work. They would see immigrants transforming urban space through the way they interacted in public places and the way they earned a living in their shops and barrio streets. In the three decades that followed, the electoral coalitions that they had built up in the cities would undergird new political possibilities at the national level. All these factors and more would soon reshape the world of *el migrante*—and of one hundred million other urban Americans.

PART THREE

THE SEEDS OF
THE FUTURE CITY

CHAPTER 9

TRANSNATIONAL CITIES

G LORIA RUBIO FLED EL SALVADOR WHEN SHE WAS TWENTY
years old. She had lived in El Sauce, a small river town named
for the willow trees that grew nearby. The surrounding
countryside, hilly and verdant, had long nourished indigo plants and
livestock, the leading products of the local economy. The town itself
had been built in accordance with Spanish planning ordinances, with
a central plaza flanked by the parish church and lined with smaller
buildings. Situated in the eastern reaches of the country only about
two miles from the boundary marking the frontier with Honduras, El
Sauce occupied a borderland of sorts. It was relatively quiet before the
coming of the civil war. But like the rest of the country, it would soon
be convulsed with killing.

For a brief period after the 1979 coup that brought a military junta
to power, there was only scattered violence. But in 1980 the horror escalated rapidly. In March, Oscar Romero, the Roman Catholic arch-
bishop of San Salvador, was murdered while celebrating mass shortly
after a sermon pleading for the armed forces not to participate in
repressing the people. His earlier preaching on the country's startling
poverty and inequality—the stark divide between "some who were
born to have everything and leave others with nothing, and a majority

227

that has nothing and can't enjoy the happiness that God has created for all"—had attracted the attention of the military, and a leading general had ordered his assassination. Later that year, members of the Salvadoran national guard raped and murdered four American missionaries—three Maryknoll nuns and a lay worker who had all served among the rural peasantry—and buried their bodies in a shallow grave near the capital airport. Large-scale killings erupted and continued for more than a decade. Nationwide, the civil war would claim the lives of more than seventy-five thousand people, most of them civilians shot to death by the armed forces. For almost the war's entire duration, the Salvadoran government was receiving hundreds of millions of dollars in military aid from the United States.[1]

Like hundreds of thousands of Salvadorans in those years, Rubio decided to leave the country. After she departed, the area around her hometown would see the war up close: military personnel and rebel fighters would clash nearby, and a few years later it was the site of a mass murder by government forces. Rubio first made her way to Houston, where she held down two jobs to support herself. A year and a half later, in 1983, she moved to Dallas, where her older sister had found steady employment at a restaurant in Oak Cliff. Rubio spent most of her time working. During the day, she kept house for a wealthy family in the area. In the evening, she sold food from a small stand at a nightclub, the tastes of the changing local population reflected in her offerings: American hamburgers, Mexican tacos, Salvadoran *pupusas*.[2]

Gloria Rubio's journey highlights a series of changes in immigration that began in the 1980s—changes that linked US cities ever more closely with Latin America. A larger number of people were arriving from a greater variety of countries in the Americas. They came for different reasons and from different backgrounds than before, and they helped establish stronger and more durable connections between the United States and the rest of the hemisphere. Throughout the decade and beyond, government policies—some made in Washington and others in Mexico City, Santiago de Chile, San Salvador, Havana, Bogotá, and other capitals across the hemisphere—were a fundamental cause of this new, more transnational era in the history of American cities. Some of these policies gave greater impetus to immigrant urban revitalization in the United States, while others extended the reach of *migrantes*, who in turn began to reshape the landscapes of their home communities.

A MAJOR SOURCE of the transformations that began in the 1980s was a hemispheric sea change in economic policy. In a number of Latin American countries, governments shifted toward neoliberalism. The underlying doctrine had been fostered in economics departments in the United States, most notably at the University of Chicago, which educated a generation of elites who became known collectively as *los Chicago boys*. Their policy prescriptions were first practiced in Chile under the murderous dictatorship of Augusto Pinochet. They became more influential across the region in the wake of the debt crisis that began in 1982. Under pressure from their creditors, many governments turned away from efforts to gain economic autonomy through import-substitution industrialization, instead engaging in more international trade, which in turn exposed their economies to direct foreign competition. At the same time, they began to slash social welfare spending and other government programs.[3]

These policies altered the character of emigration from the region, especially by reshaping its cities. The previous practice of import substitution had directed resources and investment to urban areas; now the newer policies denied cities such sustenance, with effects felt by people from various backgrounds. The rural poor who had poured into Latin American cities found it harder to survive there, and many simply extended their range of rural-to-urban migration internationally by moving to cities in the United States. The region's urban industrial workers, especially in Mexico, increasingly chose to emigrate as their formerly protected and subsidized sector confronted heavy competition from foreign companies. This pushed down their wages and forced many city-dwellers to send family members abroad to work, often in US industry. And the urban middle and professional classes faced dramatic reductions in public-sector jobs as the people who had administered government agencies were laid off. These jobs had "constituted the backbone of the urban middle class in many countries," as one scholar put it, and as they were cut back, even many of those who had lived well in the city began to emigrate. They were joined a decade later by a new group of rural Mexicans who had been impoverished by the flood of cheap, subsidized corn unleashed by the North American Free Trade Agreement (NAFTA).[4]

Another cause of heightened migration to US cities was the outbreak of civil conflict in Central America. The Salvadoran civil war that drove Gloria Rubio to Texas had much in common with another fought at the same time in Nicaragua, where the overthrow of the Somoza dictatorship was followed by the Contra insurgency, which, with US backing, battled the Sandinista government until a cease-fire in 1988. Nearly thirty thousand people were killed in the conflict, and hundreds of thousands fled abroad to escape the war's violence. Meanwhile, Guatemala had already suffered nearly three decades of dictatorships after the US-backed coup against the country's democratically elected government in 1954. After another coup in 1982, the Guatemalan military conducted a murderous campaign against political opponents, insurgents, and much of the rural Indigenous population. By the time of the 1996 peace accords, as many as two hundred thousand people had been killed, mostly civilians at the hands of the army, whose systematic massacres were widely deemed acts of genocide. The United States became the destination for more than one million refugees from communities shattered by these and other conflicts in the region.[5]

Starting in the 1980s, immigrant Latino populations in the United States grew even more quickly than in previous decades. This influx not only augmented the Latino populations of each city's leading barrio but spread into new neighborhoods that became Latinized along with the population overall. In Little Village in the 1980s, the Latino population grew by almost 13,000 people, pushing their proportion of the neighborhood from 78 percent Hispanic to 90 percent, and in the 1990s they increased further, by another 6,000 to 92 percent. But the changes were far more noticeable across the city and its metropolitan area: from 1980 to 1990, the Latino population of Chicago grew by 124,000 and its metro area by more than 250,000; by 2000, those figures had risen even higher, with 208,000 more Latinos in the city and an amazing 568,000 more in the metropolitan area. In the city proper, Hispanics climbed from 14 percent of the population to almost 20 percent in the ten years to 1990, then to 26 percent by 2000. In Dallas, meanwhile, the Oak Cliff Latino population grew by 25,000 people during the 1980s, totaling 56 percent of the neighborhood, then by almost 32,000 during the 1990s to reach 76 percent; across Big D, Hispanics totaled 21 percent of all residents by 1990, and over 35 percent by 2000.[6]

In both cities, people of Mexican ancestry remained the predominant group, but by 1990 other nationalities, especially those from Central America, had grown considerably. In that year, more than three thousand Latinas and Latinos not of Mexican ethnicity lived in Oak Cliff, and at millennium's end that number had nearly tripled; in both counts, Salvadorans were the single largest national group. Little Village in 1990 was home to about 1,800 non-Mexican-origin Hispanics of whom Guatemalans and Salvadorans were the largest subgroups; by 2000, this total had more than doubled. Both the Dallas and Chicago metropolitan areas became home to around 200,000 Hispanics not of Mexican or Puerto Rican origin at the end of the millennium, including about 30,000 Central Americans in each city's largest county.[7]

THE FACTORS THAT DROVE refugees and other newcomers to the United States also created renewed pressure for legislation—what eventually became the Immigration Reform and Control Act (IRCA) of 1986, also known as the Simpson-Mazzoli Act. The combination of the first-ever numerical limitations on migration and the crisis in Mexican agriculture had already made a mess of immigration policy. The changes of the mid-1960s had propelled people across the border to perform the enormous amount of available farmwork, but also suddenly redefined a vast number of crossings as unauthorized and counted them as such. Subsequent changes in immigration law reduced opportunities for legal migration even further, especially the per-country numerical limits that were imposed in 1977, cutting the number of visas available to Mexicans to the smallest number since the years of the Bracero Program. As a result, more migration than ever before was reclassified as illegal: there were fewer than sixty thousand apprehensions in the late 1960s, but that number had increased by more than an order of magnitude by 1977, when around one million people were intercepted as they tried to enter the United States. Notably, however, in this era more than five-sixths of Mexican migrants returned home after working for a time in El Norte.[8]

Over these years lawmakers in the United States repeatedly attempted to fashion some kind of legislative solution. In 1971, the House of Representatives held hearings and readied a bill to address the issue, but were unable to come to agreement with their counterparts in the Senate. They made a second attempt two years later, but it failed as well. In 1976, it was the Senate that took up the issue; they too held hearings but could not come up with the votes to pass a bill. The following year President Carter proposed his own plan, but the bill again went nowhere on Capitol Hill. In 1978, the White House and leaders in Congress cooperated on the creation of the Select Commission on Immigration and Refugee Policy in an effort to find a way forward, but it too made little headway.[9]

As Ronald Reagan took office in 1981, issues touching on immigrants and refugees had once again been pushed to the fore. Undocumented migration was continuing at high levels, and a series of refugee crises involving people from Haiti and Cuba kept the issue in the news. The new president's inclinations were very different from those of his predecessor: Reagan consistently favored business interests over organized labor, and his administration's immigration proposals prioritized helping employers through deregulation and supplying their demand for agricultural labor with a new guest worker program.[10]

In Congress, however, the balance of power was shared between a Democratic House of Representatives and a Republican-controlled Senate. Any viable bill would therefore have to be bipartisan, with provisions that would satisfy constituencies in both parties. There were therefore three parts to the general outline: an employer sanction to penalize those who hired unauthorized workers; a legalization program to give well-established but undocumented people a chance to come out of the shadows; and increased border enforcement to reduce new illegal crossings.

The complex politics of the issue cut across both parties' constituencies, making consensus difficult even on the same side of the aisle. Among Democrats, for example, organized labor and Hispanic groups were united by their opposition to guest worker proposals that they feared would be as exploitative as the bracero system. But organized labor wanted an employer sanction, which Latinos worried would lead to discrimination against people who looked racially "different." Among Republicans, meanwhile, the party's business-friendly wing sought a reliable and generous supply of low-wage workers. But this alarmed the xenophobes and racists within the GOP, who were especially angered by the proposed legalization provision.[11]

The restrictionists and segregationists who had fought so hard against the Hart-Celler Act had reorganized in the 1970s, seeking to use that decade's stagflation as a pretext for reducing all immigration. The Federation for American Immigration Reform (FAIR) had been formed in 1979 and soon became the center of opposition to the immigration bill. Although the organization's representatives often couched their views in terms of concern over labor or the environment, the racism underlying their lobbying became clear during the debates over the new bill. The group's founder, John Tanton, circulated a memorandum in which he fretted about what he called "the Latin onslaught," characterizing Hispanics as inherently prone to corruption, academic underperformance, Catholicism, and high birth rates. He brooded about the rising proportion of nonwhites in the United States. "As Whites see their power and control over their lives declining, will they simply go quietly into the night?" he asked suggestively. "Or will there be an explosion?" In later years, Tanton and his associates openly consorted with white supremacists, anti-Semites, eugenicists, and Ku Klux Klan associates.[12]

But in 1986, FAIR recognized the unpopularity of its own ideas. The unmistakable subtext of its leader's secret communiqué was that they could not speak openly about their racial beliefs and should therefore try to convince people through misdirection. FAIR's efforts failed to generate effective opposition to the immigrant-friendly provisions of the bill. President Reagan had regularly used the racially charged rhetoric of immigration panic, but ultimately he supported legalization for undocumented people, saying in a televised debate during his 1984 reelection campaign, "I believe in the idea of amnesty for those who have put down roots and lived here, even though sometime back they may have entered illegally." Even the ultraconservative Strom Thurmond of South Carolina, who had spent most of his career as an avowed segregationist, was persuaded of the need for the amnesty.[13]

By late 1986, the tangle of conflicting political interests had stymied progress for a decade and a half, and despite bipartisan negotiations, it once again seemed that an immigration bill was dead. But at that juncture Congressman Charles Schumer of New York proposed an amendment in an effort to shake loose holdouts on both sides of the aisle. It would add to the bill's legalization clause a new provision under which undocumented agricultural workers who had arrived too late could nonetheless apply for residency; a few years later, they would have the opportunity to become US citizens. It was paired with a provision allowing additional immigration of farmworkers in the event of an agricultural labor shortage. The move met with the approval of Schumer's constituents—his Brooklyn district was home to many people of Jewish and Italian immigrant stock largely sympathetic to newcomers to the country—as well as farm-state politicians concerned with ensuring orderly crop harvests.[14]

Schumer's gambit brought the bill back to life. One California congressman later joked that it had been "a corpse going to the morgue, and on the way to the morgue a toe began to twitch and we started CPR again." Lawmakers who had been reluctant to vote for the bill came back around. Democratic congressman Bill Richardson of New Mexico, descended from Hispanos like nearly half his state's population, declared: "This is the final hour for immigration reform. . . . This is the final hour for millions of people who have no lobbyists, but deserve some status in this country . . . I don't want my legacy as a Hispanic to be that I obstructed immigration reform." The move also garnered key votes from members of the Congressional Black Caucus and from a number of Republicans who continued to oppose the employer sanction but signaled that they wanted to get a bill passed nonetheless. As the bill's senate sponsor, Alan Simpson, put it, "Every one of us gave up something painful as hell, but we stayed at the table." The bill passed not long after the centennial of the Statue of Liberty and may well have benefited from the swell of immigrant-friendly patriotism that accompanied the event.[15]

In its final version, the IRCA had three main provisions. The first was the employer sanction section, which made it unlawful to knowingly hire a person not eligible to work in the United States. It stipulated the establishment of an employment verification system, specified penalties for violations of the law, and prohibited discrimination against legal employees based on their actual or perceived national origin or citizenship status. The second section boosted funding for border security, including immediate increases for the Border Patrol and the Immigration and Naturalization Service, and established a $35 million fund to reimburse states and localities for enforcement costs. The third section offered permanent-resident status to those who had entered or remained in the country without authorization before 1982, maintained continuous residence since then, and had no criminal record; they could then apply for citizenship five years later. This section also included the provision for temporary agricultural laborers to become legal residents and then citizens, and it gave assurances that growers would have access to a reliable source of agricultural workers.[16]

Several supporters of the law admitted that they were taking a chance. "I don't know what the impact will be," said Simpson. Representative Leon Panetta of California conceded that he was unsure how it would operate in practice, and California congressman Brian Donnelly said that he had supported it even though he thought it little better than the status quo. Even Schumer himself said as much, candidly calling the law he had worked so hard to enact "a gamble, a riverboat gamble. There is no guarantee that employer sanctions will work or that amnesty will work. We are headed into uncharted waters."[17]

THOSE MOST IMMEDIATELY affected by the passage of IRCA were undocumented people eligible to gain legal status through the law's amnesty provisions. They had to move quickly, since the deadline to apply was only twelve months away. The application required elaborate paperwork and documentation of residence, work history, and family members; moreover, it was expected that the number of applicants would run into the millions. Indeed, the complexity of the process and the challenge of reaching so many intended beneficiaries were acknowledged in the law itself, which provided funding to help immigrants register.[18]

Undocumented people found allies among local community organizations. In Chicago, a number of nonprofits were formed specifically to help people normalize their status. The city's Mexican Americans took the lead with help from Puerto Rican activists who, though they were all US citizens from birth, saw the importance of aiding fellow members of the city's broader Hispanic community. Both also had the support of the Roman Catholic Archdiocese of Chicago. In Dallas, Catholic agencies worked with Dallas Area Interfaith to bring together a wide variety of religious and civic groups, most notably the Industrial Areas Foundation, to aid in the legalization campaign.[19]

These community efforts required month after month of long days at work. Vanna Slaughter, a longtime worker with Catholic Charities of Dallas, remembered some of the busiest of the sixty-five sites set up around the diocese. "We were organized," she recalled. "If we had not been, it would have been absolute chaos." Their efforts were focused particularly on Oak Cliff, where Catholic Charities' immigration services headquarters subsequently relocated. They labored every evening after people had come home from work, starting at six and continuing until at least ten. "We would be at tables like this," she recalled, indicating the folding table at which we sat during the interview, "flipping through to find the right sheets—the green sheet especially, since it had their work history, residential history, children born, and the like, so that they had what they needed to make the jump from resident to citizen." At one parish, applicants formed lines that went down the front stairs, around the corner of the building, and along the street. "It was a carnival atmosphere," she remembered, "with people going home dead beat tired but exhilarated at what we were doing."[20]

Nationwide, nearly three million people were able to regularize their status under the legalization and special farmworker provisions. In the Chicago area, about 155,000 people gained legal residency through IRCA, including 124,000 from Mexico. In Dallas, the corresponding figures almost certainly ran into the tens of thousands.[21]

IRCA's amnesty provision had an immediate effect on the everyday lives of many millions of people—not just those who had been undocumented, but also their families, friends, and coworkers. In Chicago, Frank De Avila recalled being struck by how viscerally and immediately the difference was felt: "Number one, the fear of being deported was completely eliminated. That was an emotional relief for the individual and for the community. Not to have that worry anymore that at midnight they'll knock on your door and off you go." As they progressed from temporary to legal permanent status, and as many continued forward to apply for citizenship, that sense of relief developed into a deeper sense of security and belonging. Frank Trejo worked the immigration beat in those years as a reporter for the *Dallas Morning News*. He recalled that people living in Oak Cliff behaved differently after they were legalized, and especially after they became citizens. "It took a while to get legal after 1986, so after their temporary little red cards, after a certain period of time people gained a new status," he remembered. "It was gradual, but especially after 1990 people started being less afraid once they started getting their documents." Vanna Slaughter similarly recalled that the regularization allowed immigrants in Dallas to participate more broadly in a range of areas: "After they became legal, people could come out of the shadows. They could speak up, go to meetings at school with teachers, register to vote, become confident."[22]

But IRCA turned a different face to those who were not eligible for legalization. This was a very large group, since the five-year residency requirement—unusually long for legislation of this kind—excluded much of the nation's undocumented population, leaving more than a million people with no way to regularize their status. For them, the most relevant part of the law would be its militarization of the US-Mexico border, with dramatic increases in the presence of patrols, fences, and other enforcement mechanisms.[23]

The reinforcement of the border did not, however, have the expected effect. Mexican and other Latin American migrants were confronted with a more binding decision about whether to remain in the United States or to return home. They quickly understood that it would soon be much more difficult, expensive, and dangerous to cross the border without authorization. So they responded logically: those without legal status became much more likely to remain in the United States, since the kinds of temporary departures that had been commonplace before might now leave them unable to reenter the country.[24]

Under these circumstances, family considerations came to the fore. In earlier years when enforcement was easier to evade, migrants would return home periodically to see their families. With much harsher enforcement, however, many thought it better to keep their spouses and children with them, or if they were still back home, to pay for them to come to the United States. After all, enduring the loneliness of being away from family was one of the most difficult aspects of working in El Norte—whenever they turned on Spanish-language radio they would hear songs about longing for loved ones and the sorrow of separation.[25]

There were many other reasons why *migrantes* decided to stay. Undocumented people with US-born children unsurprisingly wanted to stay and raise them so that they could enjoy the opportunities of their native land. Agricultural workers who had crossed back and forth across the border saw that they would do better to find year-round work in the United States and settled down to do so. In truth, migrants often had their own personal reasons to stay. In 1987, just a year after the passage of IRCA, an anthropologist interviewed undocumented Mexicans in Little Village. They offered a wide variety of explanations for their decision to stay permanently in the United States. A woman named Caridad from a rural part of Mexico enjoyed having running water and a lavatory inside her home. Another was happy to see her children learning English, a skill she considered very valuable. A man named Chano, an engineer originally from Mexico City, admitted that he admired how well run things were in the United States. And Rosario, the mother of two American children with physical disabilities, emphasized the quality of health care and special services for her family.[26]

These and millions of other accounts confirmed the unintended consequences of a harder border. The undocumented population of the United States continued to grow because strict border enforcement had not kept migrants out—it had shut them in, turning them into immigrants who were here to stay.

As northward migration to the United States became more permanent, it also became more evenly balanced between men and women. In the decades before IRCA, the flow of people across the Rio Grande had been predominantly male. The most common practice was for men to cross into the United States to work and thereby support their families. Women also migrated, but in smaller numbers. In emigrant-sending parts of Mexico, for example, once a family had children who needed care, it became much more likely that only the father would head north. The crossing was risky enough without children coming along, so sons and daughters would stay in Mexico, and their mother would stay to look after them. Absent fathers could console themselves with the thought that it would not be long before they would return for a visit to see their families and friends and celebrate holidays. As the border became more militarized, however, women were more likely to cross into the United States and stay there. Husbands and wives (and *novios* and *novias* not yet married) who lived apart because one had migrated missed each other enough already without the prospect of fewer or no visits, and the likelihood of long-term separation led many women to migrate north to join their men. If they already had children, the little ones mostly came along. Once reunited, they usually had (or continued to have) children, and since half the new births were girls, the community's gender ratio was further equalized. Before IRCA, fewer than half of documented migrants from Mexico were women; afterward, that proportion gradually climbed to nearly three in five; among the undocumented, the proportion rose from about one in five to roughly one in four.[27]

The last main provision of IRCA, the employer sanction, reinforced the different opportunities available to the newly documented and the still undocumented. Unburdened of their legal vulnerability as unauthorized workers, the newly documented were now free to ask for raises, participate fully in labor unions, and pursue other methods of bargaining for better wages. Researchers would later report that these migrants' wages rose by about 15 percent within five years, and that over the longer term those gains continued, eventually reaching 20 percent. These earnings were also much more secure thanks to the guarantees of legal residence. De Avila remembered that in Little Village "on the day when they could receive the amnesty, people were still keeping their savings under the mattress for fear that they could be repatriated at any moment and lose their money. But once they could be here more securely, they took this money and invested it." One of the places they invested it was in training and education.

Those who had hesitated to improve their skills because they might be deported and never get to use them now signed up for classes of various kinds, significantly raising their years of education and degrees completed; indeed, increasing education levels was the driver of some of their wage gains over time. Those who came to be called *amnistiados* or *rodinos* (because the Simpson-Mazzoli Act was better known in Spanish as *la ley Simpson-Rodino*, owing to New Jersey Congressman Peter Rodino's role in passing it) made great strides thanks to their new legal status.[28]

But for those not documented, the challenges were very different. The law's employer sanction had been written so that only those who "knowingly" hired unauthorized workers could be fined. This word proved pivotal because it allowed employers to escape the penalty for such infractions by claiming that they believed they had been shown valid documents. Just as counterfeiters across the nation had long provided underage drinkers with hard-to-detect fake IDs, they soon learned to produce realistic counterfeit working papers. In other instances, employers adopted a different method of evading enforcement: hiring workers through subcontractors. This allowed employers to offload the legal liability of undocumented hiring onto the subcontractor. Either way, the result was that employers were free to continue their practice of hiring undocumented people.[29]

Even so, under IRCA working conditions for the undocumented worsened. Employers began to reduce the pay of their immigrant Latino workers by claiming that they had to spend money to guard against the potential legal costs of hiring them, whether directly or through subcontractors. Thus real wages began to fall for the undocumented within a few years after the implementation of the employer sanction. Whereas before IRCA the undocumented had suffered relatively limited wage discrimination, by the 1990s their pay was regularly one-quarter less than the pay of those with papers. Chicago immigrant rights leader Carlos Arango opined, "This is a kind of slavery—that's a joke, but a grim joke still." He was not alone in using the language of human bondage to describe labor conditions. An anthropologist who worked with migrants in Chicago from 1993 to 1995 reported similar hyperbole among Mexican machine-shop workers angered by low wages and mandatory overtime that the company used to squeeze double shifts out of already-exhausted employees. And these were relatively good industrial jobs. In other workplaces, subcontractors had learned that they could push migrants' wages down to five or six dollars an hour by interposing themselves as labor brokers. Women workers, who were concentrated in garment piecework and childcare, also found themselves laboring for long hours at little more than subsistence wages.[30]

Moreover, it soon became apparent that this effect was not limited to undocumented people. Quite clearly, many employers were cutting the pay of anyone who *seemed* like they might be undocumented, and in practice this usually meant people who looked Hispanic. This was, it should be noted, precisely the outcome that the advocates for US Latinos had feared, and the reason why they had strongly resisted including the employer sanction in the Simpson-Mazzoli Act. This was also the source of real tension between different groups of Hispanics, especially Puerto Ricans and Mexicans. Puerto Ricans, all of whom were born US citizens, sometimes faulted Mexicans for the low wages on offer in places like Chicago. In response, undocumented Mexicans sometimes pointedly asked why Puerto Ricans were not doing better, since they had the advantage of citizenship. The mutual recriminations that followed sometimes partook of the ugly stereotypes used against each group. Similar divisions often emerged when African American and ethnic Mexican workers found themselves competing for the same jobs, a conflict that turned into an international incident some years later when Mexican president Vicente Fox ventured that Mexicans abroad were "doing jobs that not even the blacks want to do there in the United States."[31]

Another of the major effects of IRCA was the way it led *migrantes* to concentrate themselves in urban areas. The wages paid to migrants in cities had long exceeded those available in the countryside, driving an ongoing shift away from farmwork. And even those who performed agricultural labor seemingly preferred the comforts of a larger community: nearly five out of six applicants to IRCA's legalization program for agricultural workers gave addresses that were within metropolitan areas. In the aftermath of the law's passage, the existing gradual decline of the proportion of migrants working in agriculture accelerated from 33.1 percent to 19.5 percent among the undocumented, and even more sharply, from 7.4 percent to 2.6 percent, among the documented.[32]

Driving this was IRCA's interaction with the nature of agricultural labor. Farmwork had always been heavily seasonal: the need for workers was greatest from spring to fall, especially in the planting season and even more in the harvesting season. Although there was some work available in maintaining facilities over the winter months, far fewer laborers were needed then, so many simply returned home across the border. But as crossings became more difficult and dangerous, agricultural workers increasingly sought jobs in cities during the off-season. For some, this led to finding work that was higher-paid and less physically taxing, but if a nonagricultural job in the city or suburbs offered year-round rather than seasonal pay, it might be more appealing even without better remuneration.[33]

For this reason, the effects of IRCA were concentrated in cities, and it is there that we can see the law's influence most clearly. It shaped the circumstances and status of some immigrants and allowed them to prosper. But it also meant that they could live in the same neighborhoods as still-undocumented people who saw their wages fall and had to take up second or third jobs, including the kind of informal work so common in the nation's barrios. The difference between a person who became a successful immigrant entrepreneur and one who worked for years at poverty-level wages may have had something to do with their respective abilities, but it was also *definitely* linked to the blind luck of whether they were eligible for legal status in the United States.

In broad terms, real income growth in both Little Village and Oak Cliff was better in the 1990s, after the effects of IRCA had become well established, than it had been in the 1980s. In Little Village, as the proportion of Latinos, especially the foreign-born, had increased in the 1970s and 1980s, wages dropped noticeably. Real household income there fell a dismaying 5 percent during the 1980s. This was a decade when deindustrialization led to massive layoffs in older industries, and even those who kept their jobs worked with substantially less labor union representation than their white ethnic predecessors (and often without the protections of citizenship). This decline turned around in the 1990s, when a combination of the consistent economic growth of that decade and the legalization of thousands of people in Little Village drove up real household income by about 10 percent, with Latino wages rising almost 16 percent—a significant increase in purchasing power. In Oak Cliff, the general trend was similar. The 1980s saw a gain of 9 percent in real household income; then, in the 1990s, households saw a 10 percent gain. Notably, for Hispanics income rose 15 percent. As of 2000, median household income was nearly the same in both neighborhoods: $32,324 in Little Village and $33,096 in Oak Cliff.[34]

One of the ways in which Latinos sought to maintain a manageable economic position was through the same method that had in previous decades been the most important way for working people to build wealth—through homeownership. Without the security of legal status, many people had chosen to rent because of the threat of deportation. Frank De Avila noted the change that followed amnesty in Chicago: "I know cases in which people were renting, but once they could stay here, they took out their money and bought the houses they had been living in." And indeed, available data show that beginning a year after the passage of IRCA, residential lending in Little Village more than doubled over the course of only five years.[35]

The newly documented achieved a significant degree of success, if statistics reflecting homeownership are anything to go by. As the number of Latinos and immigrants in these neighborhoods rose, the percentage of homeowners held steady or even increased. In Little Village, the proportion of people who owned their own homes had barely budged, varying by little more than 1 percent over the three decades leading up to 2000, when the figure was 36 percent. This was by no means a high rate of homeownership, but this had always been an industrial working-class neighborhood. Notably, the statistic in 2000 was not much different from what it had been when the neighborhood was still called South Lawndale and the labor market and the labor unions were at their peak: the homeownership rate had been 39.6 percent in 1950 and 41.3 percent in 1960. In Oak Cliff, the numbers were even better, exceeding the citywide average: its percentage of homeowners rose slowly but steadily in the 1980s and 1990s, reaching 53.5 percent in 2000. This figure was higher than it had been in 1970 just before the large-scale arrival of immigrants from Mexico, El Salvador, and other parts of Latin America. And remarkably, the ownership rate was exactly the same in 2000 as it had been fifty years earlier when the neighborhood was at its previous population peak.[36]

The value of homes in these neighborhoods also tended to increase over the years, sometimes even in excess of the corresponding figures citywide. The median value of a home in the South Lawndale community area more than doubled between 1980 and 2000, with the bulk of the increase occurring over the course of the 1990s. In Oak Cliff, median home values rose as well, though considerably more gradually, increasing 13 percent from 1980 to 2000; notably, this included a 25 percent rise during the 1980s, a decade when the median price of a home fell slightly across Dallas as a whole. These increasing values enabled homeowners in these neighborhoods to accumulate a key form of wealth by building equity in their residences.[37]

In both neighborhoods, most of those who did not purchase homes could afford to pay their rent without excessive strain on their income. In large part this was because incomes were rising about twice as fast as rents in these areas. In Little Village in 1990, the average tenant paid 23 percent of their income for rent, a proportion that was virtually identical ten years later. In Oak Cliff, the corresponding figures were slightly higher, at 26 percent in 1990 and 25 percent in 2000, but showed the same improved trend as the century came to a close. There were some, however, who were finding it harder to pay the rent. They fit the definition of "rent-burdened" because they had to lay out more than 30 percent of their income for shelter. This was the point at which a household faced economic hardship because so much of its earnings went to housing costs. In Oak Cliff in 1980, about one-third of households were rent-burdened; ten years later that figure had risen to close to four in ten before the wage gains of the 1990s drove it down to about 36 percent in 2000. In Little Village, those figures were roughly 32 percent in 1980 and just under one-third in 1990, a number that was unchanged in 2000. As much as that was, it compared fairly well with the rest of the Windy City, since in 2000 38 percent of the city's renters were cost-burdened. Little Village still worked as a relatively affordable neighborhood in an increasingly expensive city.[38]

The upshot was that the improving economic situation of people in Little Village was accompanied by substantial inequality—a familiar story from big cities in the late twentieth and early twenty-first centuries, where Latino barrios remained on average substantially poorer than, for example, white Anglo neighborhoods. Some of the neighborhood's overwhelming Latino majority had managed to buy into the housing market. These tended to be documented people and longer-term residents. For them, things were relatively good: for the most part they managed to keep their mortgage payments down to a reasonable share of their income. In addition, because they were able to build up equity in their homes at a time of falling mortgage rates, they were in a strong financial position: thirty-year mortgage rates had peaked at the end of 1982 and then began a sustained decline that lasted for about thirty years. At the time IRCA was passed, standard mortgage rates were about 10 percent, but in the subsequent quarter century they fell as low as 3.5 percent. Thus a homeowner with equity could refinance and thereby draw on the value of the dwelling to make living costs more affordable.[39]

Many barrio residents, however, were not able to take advantage of such benefits of homeownership. Undocumented workers faced increasing hardship as real wages fell at the same time that rents were going up. The housing data show that a rising proportion were paying more and more of their income to their landlords, putting stress on their family budgets and subjecting them to economic precarity. Indeed, one local observer suggested that the rising cost of housing was one of the reasons why many Hispanic residents moved out of Little Village and relocated to more affordable neighborhoods. Real estate may therefore have augmented inequality: there was enough opportunity for some, even a majority, to purchase homes, but many others were faced with rising housing costs and no real income growth. "The bad thing about the inflated prices," explained Frank De Avila, "was that many people could not buy a house."[40]

THE EFFECTS OF IRCA could also be seen in other kinds of ownership, particularly of small businesses, in both Little Village and Oak Cliff. In the former, De Avila remembered, "The economy got an unexpected boost . . . the result was that for this reason Little Village is one of the most successful commercial areas in the whole city. Because people stayed there, bought houses, invested. And they started buying in their neighborhood, and the stores grew, and all that." Gloria Rubio expressed this in nearly the same way: "The key was when they passed the amnesty for so many people," she remembers, "and the people who were here, we started investing, started buying homes, started opening second businesses, third businesses, and so all those people, just like us, that's what they did, and that's what made Oak Cliff improve."[41]

Rubio was in a position to know. When she arrived in Dallas, there were no Salvadoran restaurants at all, so she and her sister and her husband opened the first one. When her sister moved on to other kinds of work, the building's leaseholder proposed that Rubio start her own business in the space. She did so in 1985 with the grand opening of the original Gloria's Restaurant on Davis Street in Oak Cliff. In a small space with only ten tables, she served basic Salvadoran fare: *pupusas*, yuca, plantains, and beer. She did much of the work herself, both waiting the tables and preparing the food.[42]

Through IRCA, Rubio herself gained legal residency, which allowed her to strengthen the position of her first restaurant before expanding to new locations. Even with her immigration status regularized, it was an uphill climb, especially with regard to securing investment capital. When she decided to open her second restaurant, nobody wanted to lend her the needed funds. "When I went to the bank to ask for a loan, they laughed at me," she remembered. "Seriously. I swear to you, they laughed." Even though she had had an account with the bank for a long time, she explained, "They just didn't believe in Hispanic people at that time . . . so they thought it was funny, you know?"[43]

Unable to find a regular source of capital, she financed her second restaurant by carrying small balances on a handful of credit cards. It opened just north of downtown in 1992. Her third restaurant opened for business five years later in the Lower Greenville neighborhood, which was down at the heel at the time but would later become Dallas's leading dining and bar district. By 2007, there were ten Gloria's locations at which she employed six hundred people, with Salvadorans,

Mexicans, Central and South Americans, and Anglo Americans among them.[44]

Not all Hispanic enterprises blossomed into multimillion-dollar companies, of course. Much more common were smaller businesses of the kind familiar in Latino neighborhoods: *bodegas*, *panaderías*, *taquerías* and other restaurants, insurance agencies, *botánicas*, jewelers, travel agencies, *quinceañera* and bridal shops, and international money transfer agencies. Establishments like these became mainstays of local retailing.

The new conditions of the 1980s fostered strong growth in the small-business-driven economies of neighborhoods like Little Village and Oak Cliff. The new legal residents created by IRCA, the great majority of them immigrant Latinos, enjoyed increased earnings that enabled them to spend more on goods and services; some of them also became business owners. A rise in migration among Latin America's middle and professional classes brought people with new skills and more education to barrio business districts. And the increased urbanization of all immigrants concentrated more of that spending power in cities.

Abundant evidence from census returns, neighborhood surveys, and other sources confirmed people's impressions of increased business activity. In 1987, there were slightly fewer than eight thousand Hispanic-owned firms in Chicago; ten years later, that number had more than tripled, to twenty-seven thousand such businesses. That growth rate far outstripped the overall pace of business creation citywide. Moreover, the number of firms with paid employees rose even faster. Total sales by these firms went from $411,000 to $5.2 million. Two-thirds of the immigrant Hispanic business owners were first-time entrepreneurs. And 27 percent of these Latino businesspeople had previously worked in the informal sector (60 percent in home-based concerns and 40 percent in public spaces), suggesting that this was a key method for building up capital to open their own shops.[45]

As important as this entrepreneurial growth was, the businesses involved were often small and precarious. A large proportion of Hispanic-owned businesses had no employees, indicating that they were family operations in which spouses, siblings, and children did the needed work. They were also more likely to bring only a modest income to their owners, and they were more prone to closing and being replaced by other, similar firms. As citywide studies showed in Chicago, for example, it was harder for these businesses to grow because, as Gloria Rubio discovered in Dallas, they found it more difficult to get access to capital when they wanted to expand. Nonetheless, small firms like these were good at populating empty storefronts and bringing dynamism and variety to the streetscape.[46]

Some of the new business opportunities created by IRCA involved cross-border travel. People who gained legal status or citizenship could serve many others who were now free to travel back and forth between the United States and their home countries. Among the best examples was the transit network established between Dallas and many communities in Mexico. As late as the mid-1980s, the city's Mexican *migrantes* still relied on an unlicensed fleet of large vans called *camionetas* to carry them to and from their homeland. After IRCA, however, immigrant entrepreneurs built larger, more durable, and more professional transport businesses; seven firms were established between 1986 and 1989, another thirteen in the 1990s, and fourteen more after 2000. These newer companies, none of which had existed on any official level before *la amnistía*, added full-size motor coaches, used computerized ticketing, and offered passengers continuous carriage without having to transfer to Mexican-registered buses. They provided direct service to scores of cities, and even smaller *municipios* like Ocampo had Dallas-based bus lines of their own. Oak Cliff emerged as the network's most important travel hub, boasting, as one of the city's leading immigration researchers put it, "the greatest number and highest concentration of Hispanic transportation firms" in the metropolitan area. Travel between parts of Mexico and Dallas even spawned its own transnational television program. *Me voy pa'l Norte* (*I'm Off to the North*), a weekly show about small communities in Guanajuato state and the lives of migrant *guanajuatenses* there and in the United States, was produced in Guanajuato and broadcast there and in Dallas.[47]

In these migrants' wake there followed other connections between Dallas and larger cities. For example, when the US-based, Hispanic-serving supermarket chain Fiesta Mart opened a huge store on Jefferson Boulevard in 1993, its parking lot became the liveliest marketplace in the neighborhood; in the following decade, the Mexican furniture retailer Grupo Famsa also crossed the border, opening thirty-seven US stores, including an Oak Cliff affiliate. More broadly, these years saw a 75 percent increase in metropolitan Dallas's total volume of exports as Mexico became by far its largest trading partner.[48]

The influx of new immigrants from Latin America also created opportunities for non-Hispanic entrepreneurs. In Oak Cliff, the clearest example is the Charco Broilers restaurant, the most noticeable business on the entire length of Jefferson Boulevard. Its signature symbol, Sonny the Steer, is a gigantic fiberglass animal mounted atop the premises, its horns pointing out at a height of nearly twenty feet above the pavement below. Its owner, Nick Cordova—his name sounds Hispanic but he described himself as an "Anglo Texan good ol' boy"—explained that his family opened the restaurant in 1963. He started working there as a teenager in 1977, and he remembered that it still served an almost entirely white clientele. As the neighborhood emptied out, however, they considered closing or moving it somewhere else. He described "a down phase in the mid-'80s when you were lucky to do three, four hundred dollars for dinner, which was nothing for a restaurant." Instead, they decided to adapt: "When the Hispanic era came through this area, you know, what we did here is just tried to start catering to Hispanics, you know, doing more Hispanic dishes, offering jalapeños, offering stuff that we didn't do before, stuff that we just thought might work for them." Ultimately, explained Cordova, "it kinda came back around, I think the Hispanic crowd is what saved us. And so I've become very loyal to them because I've seen them come in, large families, big groups, bringing our dinner crowd back up." The same dynamic applied to many other Anglo-owned businesses: for example, the Oak Cliff Bank and Trust tower became home to a Bank of America branch that began to offer services in Spanish in the 1980s and prospered by catering to a mostly Latino clientele.[49]

Barrios were home to a great deal of cross-cultural business investment. In Little Village eight years after IRCA, the business community was strongly but not uniformly Hispanic. Spanish-speakers accounted for three-quarters of all business owners, but Koreans, whose population presence in the neighborhood was negligible, accounted for one out of seven. The remaining 12 percent were Middle Eastern, South

Asian, and non-Hispanic white. Immigrant Latinos, whether documented or not, had become an essential part of the overall demand for goods and services.[50]

Although these changes began in urban neighborhoods like Little Village and Oak Cliff, the transformation extended outward to entire cities and the nation as well. Hispanic entrepreneurship was a major part of the economy nationwide: the Kauffman Index, an established measure of entrepreneurial activity, showed that in almost every year from 1996 through 2008, Latinos were more likely than any other demographic group to open their own businesses.[51]

LATINO-LED REVITALIZATION has not been limited to the United States. The rapid growth of Spanish-language households and businesses in US cities has been the most visible sign of the growing connections across the Americas, but there are other aspects of Latino landscapes that, while relatively inconspicuous, also reveal a great deal about the ways in which US metropolitan areas have become closely tied to cities and towns in Latin America. A process that started with small groups of Zacatecans in the United States eventually gave rise to a broad-based economic strategy that would be copied across the hemisphere and become a development policy enthusiastically endorsed by economists and development officials around the globe.

The 1980s saw the origins of what became known as *clubes de oriundos*, or hometown associations (HTAs). These groups resembled older immigrant organizations and followed some of the same practices, but the new conditions that emerged in that decade led them to transform the older ways of helping people in the homeland. In the process, they attracted the cooperation of officials at the highest level of government in their home countries.[52]

Among Mexican migrants' most common and important practices has been *remitting*—sending money, information, and other important resources back to their places of origin. Remitting has a long history in the United States: in the 1780s and 1790s, French expatriates exchanged radical new ideas about equality with thinkers in the newborn American republic; in the mid-1800s, Irish emigrants who had fled the potato famine sent money back home to sustain their families in a time of widespread starvation; and in the late nineteenth century,

Chinese and Italian immigrants sent wages earned in the United States back home to buy land and build homes. In recent decades, Mexicans have been by far the most active remitters; today the average Mexican migrant sends $100 to $200 per month to help with the needs of family back home. The great majority of these remittances have been used to purchase food and basic goods, serving for decades as an indispensable part of community economic survival in rural Mexico. The second-largest category of expenditure, as the architecture scholar Sarah Lynn López shows, has been in construction. Some families have rebuilt old, dilapidated dwellings; others have elected to expand their homes or build entirely new structures, often much larger houses that incorporate American-style building techniques and amenities.[53]

New conditions in the 1980s led many migrants to change their pattern of remittances. In addition to direct aid to their families, they began to send collective remittances to benefit the home community as a whole. As Mexican immigrant populations grew in cities like Chicago and Dallas, each hometown had a larger contingent of *oriundos*, or fellow townspeople. And with rural Mexico gaining telephone lines, the families of migrants were able to stay in closer touch to explain the needs of the town. In part for this reason, and in part because they were now living in a place with a much more developed infrastructure, migrants gained a new perspective on their home communities. At a time when Mexican officials were cutting funding for rural municipalities, *migrantes* in the United States realized that, without their help, their hometowns would simply not have basic services. When the sociologist Xóchitl Bada conducted interviews with Mexicans migrants, they expressed concern for women who had to walk for miles to get water because wells or pumps were lacking, for children who arrived at school with mud-soaked shoes due to poor drainage and unpaved roads, and for families who had to complete their daily activities early because after nightfall it was pitch-dark and they had only candles for illumination. "Each return trip from the United States," explained Bada, "meant facing the shocking reality that many of the comforts of modernity such as running water and electricity that they enjoyed on a daily basis were lacking in many of their communities." In *The Other Side of the Border*, a 1987 Dallas

Public Television documentary on migration from rural Mexico, some of the most memorable images were of dirt-floored homes and storehouses, and of marketplaces with meat and other perishable foodstuffs displayed on open tables without refrigeration.[54]

To gather collective remittances and undertake community projects, *migrantes* developed associations. For migrants and immigrants to create their own organizations was nothing new, of course. In Chicago, for example, Italian migrants around the turn of the twentieth century established associations to maintain cultural traditions, arrange for religious worship, provide social insurance, handle burial expenses, and generally help create and maintain community. Similar associations were common among migrants and immigrants from central and eastern Europe, with *sokols* just the best-known instantiation. The first generation of Mexicans in Chicago in the 1910s also established organizations to help their members and the community survive in an often-hostile host society. After the repatriations of the Great Depression era, these organizations saw sharp drops in membership, but a new generation of Mexican associations emerged in the late 1960s and early 1970s. Initially, their purposes were not primarily charitable. For example, in Chicago, migrants from Michoacán formed the Club Deportivo Taximaroa, a sports club; the Club San Luis Potosí, to maintain cultural identity among *potosinos*; and the Club San Miguel Epejan, a devotional group dedicated to the veneration of the Virgin of Guadalupe. Whatever their initial function, in the 1980s the members of these Chicago clubs devoted an increasing share of their efforts to providing assistance to their communities of origin.[55]

A similar process unfolded in Dallas. As the president of the city's association of migrants from the state of Durango explained, "As soon as we established ourselves in Dallas and managed to get steady jobs . . . we set about finding ways to build or renovate our homes in Mexico." They also began to work on shared projects: "We started inviting friends, neighbors, and relatives," said the association president, and in this way the city's *duranguenses* "organized migrant clubs and neighborhood associations . . . and started pooling our money to pave the streets of our towns, fix up the schools, provide electricity, and paint our churches."[56]

The resources that began flowing into rural Mexico through the efforts of hometown associations soon drew the attention of government officials, who sought ways to establish more cooperative relations with Mexicans abroad. It was not a search for a rural development strategy, however, that initially inspired this effort—instead, it began with politics. Carlos Salinas de Gortari won the Mexican presidency in the 1988 election amid suspicious voting irregularities and subsequent protests by his main rivals. Afterward, as he struggled to establish his legitimacy in the face of accusations of vote rigging, Salinas learned that his political opposition was gaining adherents among the millions of Mexican expatriates in the United States. He established a government fund to persuade *migrantes* to see the benefit of cooperation with the ruling party in Mexico City. He also followed up with personal gestures: in 1991, he made an elaborate official visit to Chicago—the first visit to the city by a Mexican head of state in more than ten years. (Notably, his defeated opponent Cuauhtémoc Cárdenas also visited to strengthen connections with members of the Mexican diaspora in the city.) Little Village, by then widely known as the Mexican capital of the Midwest, played a key role in the visit. Recognizing the Twenty-Sixth Street Arch as the symbol of both migration and pan-American connectedness that it was, Salinas presented Little Village leaders with a clock to be installed in the arch, which had been completed just four years earlier; it was given as a gift on behalf of the governors of six Mexican states.[57]

Salinas wasn't alone in seeking transnational connections with the nation's émigrés: the same political impulse soon found its way to hometown associations. In 1992, the governor of Zacatecas state initiated a program that he thought would both engage the diaspora and bring their earnings to bear on the problems of rural areas. He established the Dos por Uno (Two for One) program, under which the state provided double matching funds for hometown infrastructure and development projects: for every dollar the *migrantes* sent home, the state government would put up two dollars for approved public projects.[58]

Zacatecanos in America were quick to respond, since their state was home to scores of small, underdeveloped, and mostly impoverished communities in rural areas, all the more so after NAFTA disrupted the corn economy. The Federación de Clubes Zacatecanos del Norte de Téxas (FCZNT, Federation of Zacatecan Clubs of North Texas)—whose headquarters we visited in this book's introduction—was established in 1997 as a US nonprofit specifically to participate in Dos por Uno. The founding president of the federation, Manuel Rodela Rodríguez, maintains an archive of correspondence, official paperwork, photographs, newspaper clippings, posters, and reports that document the organization's twenty years of coordinating the activities of its many constituent clubs. Hometown-based clubs had financed projects in the years before Dos por Uno—an era that some migrants jokingly refer to as "Cero por Uno" ("Zero for One")—but with the support of state and municipal authorities, they multiplied their initiatives: these included a medical clinic, a church, and a rodeo ring.[59]

The Mexican government dramatically expanded its program of engagement with Mexicans abroad by following Zacatecas's lead and adopting Dos por Uno at the national level in 2002 as Tres por Uno, adding a federal matching program to the county and state levels. This greatly extended the efforts of Mexican HTAs by providing an additional source of funding for their efforts. The FCZNT's archive contains numerous examples of the Mexican government's official "Toma de Nota" forms certifying each new club that joined the organization to qualify for matching funds, and its collection of photographs displays a wide variety of activities in the years that followed. Hundreds of images show the FCZNT's officers attending national conferences that brought together Zacatecan clubs and federations from across the United States, as well as Mexican state and federal delegations making official visits to Dallas. The photographs also depict many trips home to Zacatecas to unveil Tres por Uno projects: in one, Rodela stands in front of a poster announcing the construction of new classrooms in the tiny town of El Fuerte; in another, FCZNT members are cutting the ribbon and opening the main valve of a new water well they have financed in the *municipio* of Tepechitlán.[60]

But perhaps the clearest evidence of what these projects meant to the *zacatecanos* comes from the *anuarios*, the federation's yearly publications. In addition to letters of greeting from state officials and advertisements for Zacatecan-owned local businesses, the *anuarios* contain numerous announcements of the projects completed that year

A 2010 *anuario* from a Zacatecan hometown association. In publications like these, association members celebrate achievements in both their home country and their adopted country. They publicize their meetings and banquets, advertise their US businesses, and showcase their building and renovation projects in Mexican towns. After transnational associations like these originated in Mexico, the idea of government-assisted collective remitting was adopted by other nations across the hemisphere and beyond. Courtesy Manuel Rodela Rodríguez/ Federación de Clubes Zacatecanos del Norte de Texas.

by Dallas clubs. These public notices demonstrate the migrants' pride in their contributions to improving infrastructure and institutions in the small towns and cities of Zacatecas.[61]

Dallas-based migrants from many other Mexican states and hometowns also registered clubs and federations and began to undertake projects as part of Tres por Uno. The records of the Secretaría de Desarrollo Social (SEDESOL), the federal agency responsible for coordinating these initiatives, display the tremendous variety of projects initiated from Dallas, including the construction, extension, or renovation of roads, housing, drainage systems, electrical grids, street paving, potable water pipes, lecture halls, community centers, streetlights, schoolyards, shelters, chapels, athletic fields, public resorts, a town cemetery, and a water park. By decade's end, Dallas's Mexican migrants were initiating dozens of projects every year, setting into motion tens of millions of pesos in construction funding annually.[62]

Chicago Mexicans also participated. By the early 2000s, they had established a multitude of connections with their places of origin, extending the revitalization effect that they had created in Little Village and other neighborhoods. In 2004 alone, Chicago hometown associations were involved in a huge number of building projects that improved, and in many cases established for the first time, basic elements of local infrastructure, important public spaces, and community institutions. These projects included paving roads in the Mexican state of Hidalgo, building community centers in Guanajuato and Oaxaca, constructing potable water plants and a bullring in Guerrero state, and improving an electrical grid and building a child welfare office in San Luis Potosí; in the state of Michoacán alone, the associations helped build or improve roads, children's parks, agricultural facilities, egg incubators, playing fields along with their stands and bathrooms, and a public library. Five years later, Chicago's Mexican consulate counted 275 HTAs in the metropolitan area, more than twice as many as there had been ten years before.[63]

Moreover, their compatriots in numerous other US cities were doing the same. Within two years of the introduction of Tres por Uno, the Secretaría had registered projects by migrant clubs in dozens of cities ranging in size from Watsonville, California, to Racine, Wisconsin; Portland, Oregon; Los Angeles; and New York City. In its first ten years of operation, the program grew from 20 clubs and just over 100,000 pesos in annual spending to 795 clubs and more than 546 million pesos. In that first decade, 12 billion pesos were invested in Mexico through Tres por Uno.[64]

Other governments across Latin America followed Mexico's lead, establishing closer cooperation with their citizens abroad and instituting migrant building programs of their own. In Dallas, for example, Salvadorans, the second-largest group of *migrantes* in the city, formed the Asociación Salvadoreña Americana in 1991 and began to sponsor public projects in their hometowns. The association started channeling remittances through the government as part of the relief efforts after the 1998 hurricane and the 2001 earthquake, and in 2004 the government of El Salvador established Unidos por la Solidaridad, a program modeled directly on Tres por Uno in Mexico. Similar programs were launched by other governments, including Colombia, Ecuador, and Guatemala; Honduras and Nicaragua also made initial efforts in this direction. Indeed, the use of remittances and the matching programs that augmented them soon became popular among international development workers and economists.[65]

In the broadest sense, then, Latino migrants initiated a sustained exchange of people, money, and construction that linked communities and reshaped built environments throughout the hemisphere. Collective remitting extended the benefits of revitalization to include the home communities of the migrants and immigrants who had already transformed US urban neighborhoods. And hometown associations revealed *migrantes* as people who were active agents in a globalizing world—people who had, to be sure, often been set into motion by decisions made beyond their control, but who had nonetheless found ways to render aid to the families and communities still living in their pueblos of origin. Their decades of hard work made it possible for their townspeople to remain in place if they wished rather than be compelled by circumstances to leave—a familiar sentiment for millions of Americans who were raised in small rural communities and moved to the city but never lost a special fondness for their hometowns.[66]

By around the turn of the millennium, Latino migrants and immigrants had transformed Little Village and Oak Cliff twice over.

Having stabilized the population and economy from the 1960s to the early 1980s, in the latter 1980s and 1990s they achieved a remarkable degree of economic revitalization. It had been a particularly difficult task, and it was achieved amid growing economic inequality among neighborhood residents, attributable in part to the broader characteristics of the US economy, especially its stagnant growth in real wages for working-class people. Indeed, native-born white Anglos had also experienced skyrocketing inequality in the mainstream economy. But in these neighborhoods those inequalities were exacerbated by the persistence of undocumentedness. The fact was that many people had been excluded from legalization, and the overall population was swelled by additional undocumented migration and the elimination of circular migration caused by the hardened borders that IRCA created.

One of the basic features underlying these changes was the involvement of Little Village and Oak Cliff in a pan-American urban system in which faraway municipalities were increasingly bound to one another. The rest of Chicago and Dallas were also clearly being incorporated into this system as migrants established and intensified personal, economic, and infrastructural connections with towns and cities across the Americas. The most easily recognizable signs of this system were immigrant populations themselves, and indeed Latin American newcomers had accomplished much of the work of creating this emergent hemispheric network through the simple fact that more of them were arriving, and from a greater variety of countries. They were important not only as new workers and consumers in their cities' metropolitan economies but also as the creators of the growing number of cross-border businesses there; notably, big-city political and business leaders had already begun to highlight the economic importance of their various immigrant communities as they touted the improved condition of their municipalities.

Even in the years after 2007, when the national economy entered its worst crisis in more than seven decades, key indices of municipal well-being were continuing to improve. A leading reason why was that Latino neighborhoods functioned differently from before. Everywhere from sidewalks to playing fields, from front yards to commercial districts, immigrant newcomers and their families had transformed urban places in durable ways. Some of these transformations could be clearly described in words and statistically measured. Others were more difficult to capture through observation and quantification because migrant- and immigrant-led urban revitalization involved more than reoccupying housing and reviving commerce.

To fully understand the Latinization of urban America, it must also be explained spatially. We must attend closely to the changing expectations for urban space, dwellings, and places of business—and especially the way in which, as cities were drawn into a hemispheric urban system, Latino migrants were importing cultural landscapes from their home countries and adapting them to their urban neighborhoods in the United States.

CHAPTER 10

BUILDING
LATINO URBANISM

"WHEN I ARRIVED IN CHICAGO, ONE OF THE FIRST things that caught my attention was the absence of life out on the streets," observed the author José Angel N., who came to the city from Mexico in the 1990s. "Life in the United States, I would soon learn, is lived indoors." Frank Trejo, a longtime Dallas journalist covering Spanish-speaking immigrants in the city, agreed. "One of the things that people say to me is that there's a real absence of public life. That they miss having everybody hanging out in front of their houses, walking down the street, hanging out in the plaza." Latin American immigrants have often expressed variations on this same basic theme: compared to how people live in their home countries, people in the United States make much less use of sidewalks, yards, parks, plazas, and similar gathering places, preferring to spend more of their time at home in private.[1]

The people of Anglo America had been saying much the same thing for decades. Books like *The Fall of Public Man* (1967), *The Lost City: The Forgotten Virtue of Community in America* (1995), and *Bowling Alone: The Collapse and Revival of American Community* (2000) offered well-grounded critiques of the decline of a public-spirited populace going out into their communities and spending time with their fellow citizens. These and other studies showed that middle-class Americans were gradually moving away from activities that they had enjoyed together in public places and instead pursuing them in private: movie palaces lost out to home theaters, municipal pools gave way to backyard pools.[2]

In some respects this rising anxiety about the loss of the public sphere in America was prefigured by concern about the fate of the built environment. In the late 1950s and early 1960s, groups of citizens, activists, urbanists, and architects criticized midcentury city planning as a key cause of the abandonment of public places—and hoped that better planning ideas could help restore them. Most prominent among them was Jane Jacobs, who in her enormously influential 1961 masterpiece *The Death and Life of Great American Cities* decried mainstream city planning—which emphasized demolishing older areas and systematically rebuilding them in modernist styles, with their large-scale and often severe geometry—and instead advocated for traditional, small-scale neighborhoods designed to accommodate pedestrians and foster daily contact among their residents. Rather than tearing down old neighborhoods, Jacobs proposed, city planning practice should look to preserve them. In the years that followed, these ideas reemerged as another group of architectural professionals, who eventually dubbed themselves the New Urbanists, organized around a manifesto that called for reinvestment in city and town centers, the construction of neighborhoods built around walking and public transportation, and an end to public policies that subsidized suburbanization and sprawl. These and other changes, they maintained, would help revitalize public life and encourage shared efforts and consensual solutions for metropolitan problems. These and allied people and organizations dedicated themselves to restoring a strong public sphere.[3]

Even as people in the United States worried about the abandonment of the public realm, however, help was already on the way. Latinas and Latinos were, in a less programmatic but much more efficacious way, creating a new kind of urbanism of their own. It was becoming apparent in barrios across the country. You could see it in the sheer number of people in public: the throngs of excited children frolicking in once-empty playgrounds, the women and men sharing family news and stories, playing dominoes or cards, arguing about homeland politics, or listening to sports announcers so distinctive that English speakers far outside the barrio learned to recognize and eventually adopt the term "*Gooooool!*"

It was also visible on every barrio shopping street—for instance, in the many *ambulantes*, or itinerant vendors, selling drinks like *horchata* and *aguas frescas*, desserts like *paletas* and *helados*, snacks like *chicharrones* and *elotes* and tacos. You could see it in the supermarkets and other large stores whose owners volunteered their parking lots to be periodically transformed into open-air public markets where vendors sold clothing, phone cards, and toys to delight and distract little children brought along on shopping trips by their parents. And you could see it on barrio walls in the murals of figures ranging from La Virgen to more recent heroes like Padre Hidalgo, Simón Bolívar, Benito Juárez, Emiliano Zapata, Frida Kahlo, Che Guevara, and Subcomandante Marcos.

Truth be told, you could have figured out where you were even with your eyes closed. Everywhere there was the sound of Spanish being spoken, shouted, and sung. You might be able to determine the dominant nationality in the neighborhood by the distinctive accents—from Mexican Spanish, with its rising and falling pitch that other Latin Americans say sounds like songbirds, to the staccato delivery and dropped *s* so common in the islands of the Caribbean. Even without these cues, there was always the music: the *norteño* or *ranchera* styles beloved by millions of Mexicans, the mambo and salsa that Cubans and Puerto Ricans created and refined in the United States, the *punta* rhythms common in Honduras and other parts of Central America, and the *cumbia* so popular and so emulated in Peru, Bolivia, and especially Mexico that if you informed some people that it was invented in Colombia, you could easily find yourself in a friendly argument.

These Latinos, along with immigrants from other regions, helped revitalize street life and public space in numerous US cities, making the sidewalks not just more vibrant but also safer. They ameliorated key symptoms of the urban crisis, most notably by helping reduce crime rates but also by improving other measures of public health. It would be years before specialists would start using the term "Latino urbanism," but its key elements emerged with the arrival of the first *migrantes*.[4]

The Latinization of US cities involved much more than simply the arrival of tens of millions of people in metropolitan areas. Equally important was the distinctive urban culture of the newcomers—the way they gathered, walked, dwelled, shopped, and socialized. It was the combination of these quantitative and qualitative factors that made their arrival in American cities so transformative.

Latino urbanism—the everyday modes of city-dwelling that Latin American immigrants and their descendants created in the United States—was a hybrid form with origins in their homelands. They imported key elements of Hispanic-Indigenous spatial culture, adapting them in the United States to create a new mode of city life that combined key features from across the hemisphere. This was the case whether they were freshly arrived from Latin America or their ancestors had lived on what is now US territory for centuries or millennia. They were by no means the only group of people to leave their stamp on the cityscape, but because Latin American immigration involved so many people from a culturally coherent region of nineteen different countries in the hemisphere, it was Latino urbanism that became the most expansive version of immigrant space in American cities.

THE SPACES AND PRACTICES that underlay Latino urbanism originated in the encounter between Indigenous America and imperial Spain. In both areas, people built settlements around dominant central places. From the ancestral Puebloan communities in what is now called New Mexico to the principal cities of the Aztec and Inca empires, architecture was focused on a shared open space surrounded by the most important ceremonial structures and dwellings. The Spanish colonizers carried with them a city planning tradition based on plazas. Their efforts to remake other civilizations in their own image resulted in a hybrid form that overlay the Spanish city atop Indigenous urban settlements. This pattern was repeated in thousands of plaza-centered cities, towns, and villages, from the Cuzco area in Peru to Mexico City to the region that became the US Southwest.[5]

The plazas of Spanish-Indigenous America were the most important sites of both high ritual and everyday sociability. In many Native settlements in the Southwest, for example, annual feast days were celebrated with shared observances around kivas and other ceremonial spaces that marked the community's location at the center of their sacred world. Scores of small *Hispano* towns across Texas, New Mexico, and Arizona celebrated Catholic saints' days with processions in which holy objects were taken out of the church and paraded along the streets before being venerated in the plaza and returned to the altar. And indeed, many of the region's people held both Indigenous and Christian observances, sometimes simultaneously. Just as important were people's day-to-day habits of public gathering. Plazas were places for conversation, buying and selling, debate, demonstrations, courtship, and many other aspects of civic life. This combination of the sacred and the mundane created what the landscape scholar Chris Wilson has called the plaza's "web of memory and myth, of celebrations and everyday interactions that combine with the physical setting to create and sustain a community's identity."[6]

As millions of people migrated to the United States from Latin America and settled outside the US Southwest, they faced a quandary of sorts: How would they organize their communities in a landscape without plazas? The cities into which they increasingly moved had already been laid out on nineteenth-century grid plans, and the homes, stores, and other structures that they occupied had mostly been built several decades earlier. Their solution was to create an even more hybrid landscape that was defined by Latin American urban practices adapted to Anglo-American city spaces.

The most fundamental way in which migrants and immigrants began transforming the urban scene was by using their feet. The single most important element of Latino urbanism was the tendency to walk from place to place more than most people in the United States did, especially the native-born. The growth of Latin American immigrant communities less dependent on cars was a decisive development in urban America as a counter against the tendency toward sprawl—the automobile-oriented, low-density, often bland and repetitive landscape that had gradually become the fastest-growing part of the built environment in the United States. Latinas and Latinos repopulated parts of the city that had been abandoned for car-centric places at the periphery.

Asked why he and so many of his fellow *migrantes* chose to settle in Oak Cliff, Tereso Ortiz almost immediately mentioned how it
worked as urban space. "You could play in the street, in the parks,"
he noted. "Not like North Dallas, where you never got out of your
car." A similar note was sounded by the bank officer Rosario Gaytán,
who was born in the United States and moved to Oak Cliff in 1974.
Thinking back on how the neighborhood had changed since then, she
contrasted the customs of Mexican and Mexican American residents
with what she saw when her family first moved in. "Walking, I mean,
it's a culture thing to me," she remarked. "Around here, everybody,
they'll walk to the bank, they'll walk down the street. And growing
up, Anglos didn't." A similar transformation took place as thousands
of Mexican Americans resettled in Little Village and tens of thousands
of Latin American migrants came to the neighborhood.[7]

The data substantiate these observations. For example, by 1990,
when Oak Cliff was 57 percent Latino, including about 36 percent
foreign-born, Hispanic households owned substantially fewer automobiles per person than white Anglo households. The tract-by-tract
disparity ranged from a low of Anglos having 46 percent more cars
available to a high of 101 percent more, with most tracts showing
Anglos driving about 70 percent more cars. The ratios in and around
Chicago's Little Village were comparable.[8]

In a very real sense, Latin American immigrants were importing a
different understanding of the urban landscape, one that arose from
the simple fact that they had not grown up in a US-style car culture.
Across Latin America, far fewer people owned or used automobiles
than in the United States. Even in Mexico, the nation with the most
contact with the United States, cars were relatively uncommon. The
Organization for Economic Cooperation and Development found that
nationally there was only one automobile for every forty-five Mexicans
in 1960, a time when the US rate of ownership was eighteen times
higher, at one car for every two to three Americans. Remarkably, even
half a century later in 2010, the US figure was still far higher: one car
per six Mexicans and approaching one car per American.[9]

Even these figures considerably underplayed how unaccustomed
most Mexican migrants were to driving, since automobiles were least
common in the rural areas in which most of them had grown up. For

example, in 1945 the village of Tzintzuntzán, Michoacán, had 246 inhabitants, none of whom owned a car. Fifteen years later, the town population had grown to 320, but had added only one driver. And even as late as 1970, around when the mass migration of rural Mexicans began, only 11 out of the town's 360 residents owned a car. While affluent urban Mexicans in the early 1950s organized the annual Carrera Panamericana auto races to show off the roads that had been completed in 1950, the country's rural majority remained largely untouched by automobility.[10]

Hispanic newcomers used American cities in distinctive ways, but this was not without precedent. After all, before the coming of the automobile, Anglo-American urbanism had been based on walking just like every other urban culture. The cities of early America had been "walking cities"—settlements no more than a mile or two across, their size limited by people's need to get from place to place on foot. (Animals were used to draw carts and carriages, but in the city they moved at a pace not much faster than walking.) The major cities of the early nineteenth century consisted of no more than a few tens of thousands of inhabitants living on just a few square miles. When lithographers printed bird's-eye views of cities—a popular genre throughout the century—they were typically small enough to fit on a single broadsheet, the entire built-up area visible in neat blocks with individual landmarks like city halls, banks, schools, and hotels.[11]

Even as new transportation technologies came into use, urban areas remained relatively compact and dense. The advent of horse-drawn omnibuses, trolleys, and streetcars did allow cities to expand outward somewhat, but often this just meant that in the center of the city, houses were replaced by multistory buildings. Toward the end of the century, the construction of subways and the extension of commuter railways further expanded the city and made possible early suburbs. These technologies were built to bring people downtown from the neighborhoods and the periphery, so they also fostered tall center cities. Wherever there was a stopping place—whether a subway station or a commuter-rail terminus like Grand Central Terminal—the multitudes demanded services and shelter. The same material used to build new railways would also serve as the structural supports for the first steel-frame skyscrapers, apartment buildings, and other tall structures.[12]

Automobility fundamentally changed the nation's transportation system and the form of its cities. It began with the introduction of affordable motor vehicles, especially the Ford Model T in 1908, and the consumer credit needed to make them mass-market items in the 1920s. Change slowed during the Great Depression and World War II, but the postwar release of pent-up demand and the construction of the interstate highway system unleashed the power of the automobile to restructure the nation's built environment.

Car owners could travel wherever there were roads, and on their own schedules. Earlier modes of transportation basically carried large numbers of people over set routes and therefore tended to cluster passengers at the places where they got on and off, whether that was a pier, a streetcar stop, or a railway terminal. Cars decentralized population because drivers could head out of the city in any direction, not just where there was a rail line, and they could pull over wherever they wanted regardless of whether there was a station nearby. As a result, there were more available locations where builders could profitably build houses, stores, and offices. They therefore looked for cheaper land, often at the edge of town. Automobility also drove down population density because of the need for parking: every car required between one hundred and two hundred square feet of space reserved for it even when it was out on the road.

The effect on cityscapes was dramatic. Older commercial and industrial cities had been built in a primarily pedestrian age. Their sidewalks were wide to accommodate throngs of people on foot, and most of their streets were relatively narrow for carriages, carts, and streetcars. In downtowns, buildings were constructed close to one another and fronted directly on sidewalks, where their signs or store windows could be clearly seen and people on foot could enter and exit with ease. But land that was built up in the age of the automobile was much less dense and spread out in every direction. Money was not spent on rails but on roads. And indeed, throughout the automobile era the new parts of the country that were being built around cars and drivers—including North Dallas and the Chicago periphery—were low-density, suburban, and car-centric. In the decades after midcentury, urban sprawl was synonymous with the strip, the mall, the big, wide streets with narrow sidewalks or none at all. In this landscape, getting around on foot was all but impossible.[13]

Latin American immigration, which picked up about fifteen years after the National Highway Act of 1956 and other enactments that signaled the strong shift of the United States toward automobility over walkability, made a tremendous difference in the cityscape because these newcomers repopulated the kinds of places that were emptying out. They revitalized center cities in ways that compensated for decentralization. Their Latino urbanism was a walking culture that imported the stronger pedestrian orientation of Latin America and adapted it to the pre-automobile urban landscapes of US center cities.

THE CLEAREST EXAMPLE of how Latino walking culture reordered the cityscape could be seen in barrio business districts. There, at the neighborhood level, migrants and immigrants restored the shopping streets and storefronts that had been emptying out in favor of suburban landscapes designed around the automobile. These stores were not a new kind of commercial space, but these commercial districts became more economically active than before because they served a clientele that was growing into a substantial share of city populations. The presence of tens, sometimes hundreds, of thousands of Latinas and Latinos was enough to substantially reorder a city by countering the car-centrism of sprawl.

Nick Cordova, the owner of Charco Broilers on Jefferson Boulevard, explained that Oak Cliff's new immigrant clientele saved his family's restaurant simply by arriving on his doorstep. "There's people in this area, Hispanics mainly, who walk. They walk up to the dollar store, they walk up to Famsa to buy furniture, but then they gotta walk by us, and they're gonna get a steak or a burger or chicken or whatever. . . . I mean, it's just a difference. Not everybody's driving everywhere like your Americans are used to."[14]

In Chicago, Richard Dolejs also explicitly linked new residents' habit of walking with the economics of city land. "All over the country, what's the big thing? Malls! Everybody wants malls where you've got parking. But you see, Mexican families are still hardworking, single-car ownership." In his telling, those employed outside the neighborhood might go to work by car. But for the many with local jobs, he explained, "They don't need the parking—they walk to work." As a result, the Little Village streetscape was still heavy with pedestrians: "You go to Twenty-Sixth Street right now, I'd be willing to bet you'll find a hundred women, with their kids dragging along, walking to the store. . . . That's the phenomenon of Mexican communities that, again that the real estate moguls, or the real estate intelligentsia, they seldom ever recognize. . . . And if you stop and think about it, anybody that's been to a community like that will see it's true."[15]

The biggest Latino neighborhoods—places like Little Village and Oak Cliff, as well as older Latino districts like Los Angeles's Broadway corridor, newer ones like Miami's heavily Cuban Calle Ocho (Eighth Street), and still-emerging barrios in Denver—were only the most famous examples of a kind of urbanism that was being built wherever there were even a few thousand immigrants. Not only were these Latino business districts walkable, they offered everything people needed. There was such a variety of goods and services—from basic food shopping to restaurants and bars, from housewares and gifts to clothing and footwear, from basic personal services like hairstyling to professional providers like lawyers, bankers, and physicians—that they could attend to virtually all their needs within the community. In other words, they had re-created the kinds of locally owned and locally serving neighborhood economies that had been disappearing before they arrived.

These barrio businesses fit perfectly within the architecture of the industrial era, occupying small storefronts built before the age of the automobile. Little Village's commercial landscape dated from around the turn of the twentieth century, with small lots that fronted only twenty or thirty feet along the street. Oak Cliff's shops had mostly been built a couple of decades later, but still offered little more than curbside parking. Small shops like these were affordable to individual proprietors and their families, and because they had rooms above the store, they could serve as offices or dwellings or be rented out, generating cash to help pay the mortgage.

These commercial buildings' mixed uses also remedied a problem caused by modernist planning and identified by Jane Jacobs: the creation of superblocks and other kinds of streets used only during the

Latino entrepreneurs revitalized neighborhood economies by opening shops, offices, restaurants, and other businesses in small storefronts left vacant by English-speaking proprietors who had been driven out by big-box corporate retailers or moved to suburban malls. Photograph by the author.

day; deserted after work, they became both dull and dangerous. By contrast, the barrio's mixed-use streets operated like the older neighborhoods described by Jacobs: they were active all day and in the evening as well. Adding to the everyday hustle and bustle of Latino commercial districts was the presence of many *ambulantes*, or itinerant vendors. People sold a variety of foods from pushcarts. This kind of street retailing had long been common in Mexico and across Latin America. In Anglo America, itinerant vendors are often resented by regular shopkeepers because they compete with them but do not have to pay rent. Although this kind of conflict is not unknown in Latino America, it is much more common for store owners to welcome some *ambulantes* because they can help draw customers in their own right. Indeed, one often sees the sidewalks and parking lots of larger stores filled with various vendors of this kind. In Oak Cliff, Fiesta Mart, a predominantly Spanish-speaking supermarket, actually invited *ambulantes* and the operators of small stalls into the area in front of their store because they drew shoppers toward the store, increasing the likelihood that they might decide to go in to make a purchase.[16]

Commercial areas like these had been increasingly neglected by retailers. In the era of the walking city and the industrial city, small shops had been ubiquitous. But the rising popularity of the automobile tended to drive retailing outward, whether to peripheral commercial strips or suburban malls. This shift had begun as early as the 1910s, when the first outlying shopping centers had been constructed. Large retailing companies like department stores were quick to see the implications of the rise of automobile ownership. Like others, they sought out cheap land at the periphery of metropolitan areas and built satellite stores with the same brand names. The assumption until the postwar period, however, was that the downtown stores would be the flagships of the brand.[17]

That began to change in the 1950s under the influence of the abundant government subsidies to suburbanization. When retailers wanted to invest in new stores in the latter half of the twentieth century, and especially in the final third, they had a particular model in mind. It was not only suburban but also virtually the opposite of those small downtown shops. Executives envisioned huge stores, in the tens or hundreds of thousands of square feet. And they wanted those stores to be surrounded by parking lots, since their imagined consumer would certainly drive there. White flight to suburbia sped things up even more. By the 1960s, many retail trade journals were saying, whether in coded language or outright, that downtown stores faced a bleak future because the consumers there were people of color and therefore not desirable customers.[18]

This blueprint for suburban sprawl proliferated in part because real estate was becoming a financial product. Starting in the mid-1990s, investors worldwide learned to look for particular kinds of land development that would generate a reliable return on their capital. They found one in commercial strips and mini-malls, and as a result of their financial reliability, these kinds of car-oriented spaces were repeated over and over, creating the repetitive sprawl one now sees just about everywhere.[19]

This process accelerated even more in the last quarter of the twentieth century, for different reasons. Beginning in the 1980s, innovations in information technology, pricing practices, and organizational theory made it possible to distribute and track enormous quantities and varieties of merchandise across great distances and through highly complex supply chains. Retailers could now aggressively drive down the prices they paid to manufacturers and as a result sell at deep discounts unattainable by others. This transformation—what one historian has called "the retail revolution" and what could also be termed Walmart-ization—gave large-scale corporate retailers tremendous advantages over family-run stores and other small proprietorships. Consequently, local shopkeepers and "mom-and-pop" stores were undercut and driven out of business in one retail category after another, from groceries to hardware to sporting goods to footwear.[20]

Given all the trends against small urban retailing, how did center-city Hispanic businesses survive? One reason was simply language. Latino businesses remained viable in Little Village, Oak Cliff, and other barrios because Latin American immigrants were strongly Spanish-primary and preferred to do business in their own language. Spanish-speaking shopkeepers and professionals enjoyed exceptionally strong customer loyalty from people who for most transactions were unlikely to venture outside the neighborhood, let alone outside their language. This sheltered these businesses from competition in a way that English-speaking businesses simply were not. Indeed, there had been very active Yiddish- and Italian-language business communities in the early twentieth century, and equally strong German-language districts decades before that. Enclave economies simply worked. Studies conducted across many years have shown that small concentrations of businesspeople and customers can generate remarkable strength within cohesive communities. And much the same spatial dynamic still existed in the neighborhoods people called Little Italy and Chinatown.[21]

A related factor was that *migrantes* came from places where retailing had not yet been transformed by the same combination of factors—automobility, information technology, and finance—as in the United States. Before the 1990s, retailing in Latin America was far less consolidated than in the United States; even supermarkets had not become firmly established. In Latin America, a number of independent business types that had been decimated in the United States by the restructuring of its food marketplace—such as independent butchers, fruit and vegetable sellers, and bakeries—remained viable as small-scale, stand-alone businesses known as *carnicerías*, *fruterías*, and *panaderías*. There were also store types that operated out of small premises and served the specific needs of these immigrants: *botánicas* were shops that sold home remedies and devotional items, and before the advent of cell phones, *telecabinas* allowed immigrants to telephone their home countries without the complication and expense of having long-distance service at home. These too fit well in the kinds of small storefronts that dotted big-city and small-town shopping streets all across the nation.[22]

All these factors combined to revivify retailing in places where it had been declining, and in building types that had become less and less viable in the English-speaking United States. Noting these factors is important because of the racial subtext of much journalistic coverage. In stories about Little Village, for example, the implicit or explicit counterexample has been North Lawndale, the overwhelmingly African American neighborhood just across Cermak Road. These comparisons can quickly turn into something invidious, basically shaming black Chicagoans by asking, "These Mexicans have made themselves a nice neighborhood—why can't you?" To be sure, Little Village Latinos have worked very hard to revitalize their neighborhood, but plenty of black people in North Lawndale have tried to do the same. Despite Latinos' unmistakable challenges, significant structural advantages helped them along in ways that did not work for others.

One of these advantages was simply an expanding number of consumers. The number of *migrantes* began to rise around 1970 and soared in the 1980s and 1990s. These were the same years when the Great Migration of African Americans to the urban North ended and then reversed itself; this change in pattern had been facilitated by the Fair Housing Act of 1968, which made it possible for a rising number of black families to move to the suburbs and in some cases back to the South. As a result, at the same time that businesses operating in Spanish were gaining potential customers rapidly indeed, English-speaking stores in black neighborhoods were losing their primary clientele. For example, in the same decades that South Lawndale was gaining residents, North Lawndale saw its population plunge from 125,000 in 1950 to under 42,000 in 2000.[23]

Also essential was the opportunity, long denied to African Americans, to own homes by way of standard fixed-rate loans. This allowed Latinos with federally guaranteed mortgages to accumulate wealth in a way that was possible only through homeownership—by building equity in homes that could then be used as collateral for other kinds of credit. Indeed, the sheer lack of available credit had left black people on the West Side open to exploitation, and had dragged down much of North Lawndale and its adjacent neighborhoods. Simple, everyday varieties of discrimination such as these could quickly multiply into persistent disadvantage.

BARRIO BUSINESS DISTRICTS drew their customers from the surrounding residential streets—places with a hybrid heritage of their own. The Latinos and Latinas who settled in these areas moved into existing houses and apartments rather than building them themselves. But just as they did on the shopping streets, they brought important changes to the landscape of homes because they modified and used the space in distinctive ways.

By far the most important examples were the dwellings occupied by Mexicans and Mexican Americans. They assembled elements of both Spanish-American and Anglo-American architecture into an identifiable pattern that the cultural geographer Daniel Arreola has termed the "Mexican American housescape." This pattern was initially identified in the US Southwest, which of course was the region of greatest Hispanic habitation, but as ethnic Mexicans settled in other regions in the twentieth century they carried the basic characteristics of this housescape with them. Its most common and consequential feature was a front yard enclosed by a fence or low wall, creating space that was protected yet also visible from the sidewalk and street. Inside this perimeter, one could see the other two key features: statues or shrines of *santos* and other religious figures, and housefronts painted in bright exterior colors.[24]

These housescapes were architectural hybrids with roots that reached back centuries. At their centers were freestanding houses sitting in the middle of their lots. These were the most common type of dwelling in the United States, modeled on building traditions from medieval and early modern England. The Anglo-American forms were

Three housescapes in Little Village, 2011. In an era when so many middle-class Americans had retreated to the privacy of their backyards, US Latinos created a space they called *la yarda*—an enclosed front yard where children could safely play, supervised by adults who would chat with friends and neighbors and keep an eye on the block. Photograph by the author.

Mexicanized first and foremost by the addition of fencing to create an enclosed space: courtyard houses built up along the outer edge of a property were the standard design throughout Mexico. They were common among the elite and as the more humble dwellings of small farmers. The enclosures added to Anglo-American houses echoed the courtyard homes of Mexico and the forecourts in evidence throughout Spanish America; in this they drew on not only the mixed Spanish and Indigenous heritage of the Americas but also the Islamic and Roman origins of much of the housing in Spain. In other words, the Mexican American housescape was an architectural hybrid born of an earlier hybrid.

Not long after Mexicans moved into Oak Cliff and Little Village—places dominated by earlier housing in the Anglo tradition—they introduced key features of the housescape. The Dallas journalist Tod Robberson observed that the clearest sign of Mexicans moving into a neighborhood in the city was the appearance of chain-link fences around the front yards of their homes. Their influence was even clearer on Chicago's West Side. In Little Village you could walk for miles on the residential blocks running perpendicular to Twenty-Sixth Street and see example after example. The chain-link and wrought-iron fences on each property ran together into a single line along the sidewalk, one that included virtually every property. Even small enclosures in front of two- and three-family buildings were laid out in this way, not infrequently with small play structures for children. This configuration of space in front of homes became so frequent that it generated its own hybrid moniker: the Spanglish term *la yarda*.[25]

What was most important about housescapes like these was how they worked in everyday practice to foster strong social ties in shared public space. People spent time in front of their homes, creating active social scenes along sidewalks and streets. Children played safely in the enclosed area of the front yard, where they were supervised by parents and grandparents. The adults could chat with friends and neighbors, creating an expectation of conviviality on the block as people strolled down the street to enjoy informal outdoor visits. This social atmosphere in turn kept the public spaces of the neighborhood consistently occupied. New Urbanists had emphasized the importance of building homes with porches so that people could visit one another and create a thriving public sphere; Latino migrants and immigrants turned their front yards into exactly those kinds of spaces.[26]

Other kinds of dwellings in the Latino urban landscape also brought people out into public. Another important type of Latino space that gained prominence in this period was the Puerto Rican *casita*. This was a small house built in the same architectural style seen on the island: it was typically a brightly colored wood-frame structure with a front porch, surrounded by a yard. *Casitas* were often sited on vacant lots, where they remade the empty space into centers of community life. They usually hosted events on Puerto Rican holidays, and throughout the year they often featured productive gardens that gave local people plenty of occasions to go out and see one another in public.[27]

These features of how Latin Americans adapted Anglo-American urban space highlight one of the basic dynamics of Latino urbanism: people's need to create public spaces in a society not built around the type of Spanish-Indigenous plazas found in most of Latin America.

US Hispanics who lived in places with existing plazas—most of them found in parts of the Southwest that had been populated by Indigenous peoples and then colonized by Spain and claimed by Mexico—continued to use those spaces. In South Texas and New Mexico, for example, plazas have long been the places where Hispanos have made community life a daily public practice, through fiestas and everyday sociability. But those who moved to Anglo-American landscapes had to find other places for social and ceremonial customs.[28]

Mexican-origin people had repurposed other kinds of spaces to make them into plazas. As early as the 1920s, in Dallas's Little Mexico, recent arrivals from across the Rio Grande refashioned Pike Park into a plaza for the entire city. Anita Martínez remembered that the Pike Park "pool was right in the center . . . so the boys would go one way, and the girls would go the other way, and we'd pass little notes to one another," a description that precisely matches the paseo, a historically popular Spanish and Mexican courtship activity in which men and women promenade around the plaza in opposite directions. Jesse Tafalla, who lived in El Pozo barrio in the 1950s, similarly recalled the park as the most important destination for young people going out to socialize.[29] Decades later, people spoke of Pike Park in the same terms. At a public hearing in the 1970s, Mexican American participants called the park "a form of downtown . . . a center for our people"; noted that "people all over come to Pike to see what's happening among us Mexican Americans"; and affirmed that "if a person is new in town and wants to get to know people he soon comes to Pike."[30] In 1975, in response to Mexican Americans' requests for "a more Mexican kind of park," the Dallas Planning Department partnered with more than two dozen Hispanic civic organizations to carry out a major renovation that refurbished Pike Park's community clubhouse in a Mexican architectural style, replaced the pool with an actual plaza, and installed a *quiosco*, a type of open pavilion or bandstand that has for 150 years been one of the characteristic landscape elements of the Mexican plaza.[31] These efforts to create a distinctively Hispanic urbanism were clear examples of how *migrantes* and their descendants made the city their own.[32]

Variations on this theme became common in Latin American immigrant communities across the United States. A constant feature of

In 1975 Dallas officials partnered with local Hispanic associations to renovate a park in the city's biggest barrio. They added Mexican architectural elements, creating a proper plaza with this *quiosco* for performances. Courtesy Jay Godwin/*Dallas Morning News*.

Miami's Little Havana neighborhood was the sight of men gathered around portable tables, playing dominoes. In New York City's Washington Heights, Dominican *bodegueros*, or bodega proprietors, were located at the center of bustling street life and neighborhood-wide social networks, just as they had been in the Dominican Republic. And in the suburbs of Washington, DC, Salvadoran soccer league games became community gatherings in local parks. Urban public life in the United States was of course fantastically diverse and not limited to Latinos or immigrants. But *migrantes* constituted the largest group of new Americans and new urbanites in an era when cities desperately needed revitalization. In all these cases, a key element was how conviviality enlivened the public spaces of the neighborhood. In exactly the same years as many Anglo-American observers were bemoaning the decline of the public realm, migrants were bringing it back as they socialized on the streets of the city.[33]

The effects of Latinas' and Latinos' public presence were often misunderstood, however. A few city officials and journalists could see that immigrants had become essential players in urban revitalization, a view reflected in news items about immigrant dynamism and the occasional city report on demographics. But such attention far more commonly continued to focus on the urban crisis, key indices of which had not yet begun to improve. Even a smart observer like Grover Lewis could see "the Latino incursions of the 1970s" as a precursor of urban decline, claiming that the "two commonest signs" on Jefferson Boulevard in the early 1990s "were SE HABLA ESPAÑOL and SE ACEPTAN ESTAMPILLAS [food stamps]."[34]

Sometimes the older residents of urban neighborhoods saw Latinos' public presence as a problem. Older white ethnics in Chicago around 1960 had often called law enforcement on children who were simply playing in the park. Two decades later, a variation on this theme was included in Sandra Cisneros's acclaimed *The House on Mango Street* (1984), which is set in a Chicago barrio. "Those who don't know any better come into our neighborhood scared," the narrator explains. "They think we're dangerous. They think we will attack them with shiny knives. They are stupid people who are lost and got here by mistake. . . . All brown all around, we are safe." Rising immigration to Oak Cliff was similarly accompanied by local conflicts over the proper use of public space. Anglo overreactions to peaceable streetside gatherings were so frequent that in 1993 a Latino columnist for the *Dallas Morning News* repeated a popular joke: "the definition of a 'gang' by law enforcement officials is any gathering of five or more Hispanics."[35] And in many barrios, building codes that had been neglected for years were suddenly enforced when new immigrants moved in. This kind of behavior proved persistent: in the late 2000s a team of sociologists in Chicago found that even when an area was orderly, if it was populated by Latinos, white Anglos tended to perceive it as disorderly and unruly.[36]

Unfortunately, these kinds of misapprehensions and misperceptions were not limited to the places where Anglos encountered the barrio—they soon made their way into national politics. In 1996, the year after Republicans took control of both the Senate and the House of Representatives for the first time since 1954, Congress enacted and President Clinton signed three separate laws that created tremendous hardship for migrants and immigrants. The most important of these, the

Illegal Immigration Reform and Immigrant Responsibility Act, gave the Border Patrol greater authority to detain and deport people arriving at the border. More importantly, it reclassified numerous misdemeanors as aggravated felonies, making various nonviolent offenses into legal grounds for incarceration and deportation—and for legal permanent residents as well as undocumented ones. In other words, even if newcomers were innocent of any real wrongdoing, these laws would manufacture new categories of crime for which immigrants could be severely punished.[37]

It was only later that the closest observers of Latino America would come to realize that the arrival of these immigrants was doing more than repopulating cities and revitalizing street life. There was another effect that was recognized statistically years later: the presence of these newcomers had led to dramatic improvements in community safety and public health.

PERHAPS THE MOST remarkable turnaround in the condition of cities over the past three decades has been the dramatic drop in rates of property and violent crime. The national homicide rate, which in 1991 was nearly 10 per 100,000, had by 2015 fallen to 4.5 per 100,000, lower than it had been at any time since 1963, and lower than it had been for half the years in the 1950s. Meanwhile, the yearly crime reports compiled by the Federal Bureau of Investigation showed that in the roughly quarter century after 1990, the rate of violent crime—including such offenses as robbery, aggravated assault, and rape—dropped by nearly half. Property crimes, including auto theft and burglary, fell by 41 percent. In one remarkable measure of what all this meant in human terms, the Harvard criminologist Robert J. Sampson has estimated that thanks to the nation's plunging homicide rate, no fewer than 100,000 people who would have been killed if crime had stayed at its 1991 peak are instead alive today.[38]

In these same years, the number and proportion of immigrants, of Latinos, and of undocumented people all increased dramatically. In short, crime fell as immigrants arrived. For example, from 7.9 percent in 1990, the proportion of the foreign-born US population rose to over 13 percent by 2013—and nearly half of all these immigrants were from Latin America. Immigrants and their children were the primary drivers of the increase in the US Latino population from 9 percent in 1990 to 17.6 percent in 2015, when they totaled nearly 57 million people. In these same years, the ranks of the undocumented soared from about 3.5 million to 11.2 million people.[39]

This effect was even more pronounced in the cities where immigrants, especially those from Latin America, mostly arrived and lived. In Chicago, for example, after an all-time peak in the murder rate in 1992, when there were 943 murders in the city, the next two decades saw a steady decline. The number of murders recorded in 2014, 407, put the rate at its lowest point since 1965. In the years of these reductions in homicides, the city's Latino population had grown from 20 percent to nearly 30 percent of residents.[40]

Similar correlations were evident in the available data from Dallas. Citywide, the number of homicides per year peaked at more than 500 in 1991 before falling almost every year thereafter to 116 in 2014, the lowest number in half a century. Moreover, because Dallas's population continued to grow in these years, the murder rate dropped even more dramatically, from 48.9 per 100,000 residents in 1991 to 9.1 per 100,000 in 2014; the latter year's rate was the fourth-lowest in the seventy-five years since the city began keeping count. And this occurred as the immigration-driven Hispanic proportion of the city population rose from just over 21 percent to around 43 percent.[41]

Other big cities with fast-growing immigrant and Latino populations saw similarly dramatic declines: in New York City, murders peaked in 1990, when 2,245 homicides were recorded in the city; by 2014, that number had plunged by more than 85 percent to only 328; similarly, in Los Angeles homicides dropped by almost three-quarters, from 1,092 in 1992 to 282 by 2015. And again, since both cities gained residents in these years, the declines in the rates of killings were even steeper. Dramatic improvements in public safety were also seen in other heavily Hispanic cities like San Jose and Phoenix, as well as in predominantly Mexican-ancestry municipalities on the border, including El Paso and San Diego.[42]

The fact that crime rates fell and immigrant and Latino populations rose at the same time is intriguing, but correlation is not causation. Many other factors have been proposed to explain the drop in crime— new policing techniques, an aging population, changes in abortion law, and lower incidence of lead exposure, to name just a few—so how can we be so sure about the causal role of immigration?[43]

One key reason was that criminologists were able to track not just *when* crime began to decline, but also *who* was committing offenses and being imprisoned for them. At the national level, extensive research into infraction and incarceration records showed that the proportion of the foreign-born in prisons was much lower than the proportion in the United States as a whole. Statistical studies using the census data from 1980, 1990, and 2000 demonstrated that American-born people were between two and five times more likely to be imprisoned than immigrants. Another line of research using incarceration records yielded similar findings: for example, American-born men with less education were three times more likely to be imprisoned than similarly educated men born in Mexico, and five times more likely than such men from El Salvador and Guatemala. Yet another study, based on different data, demonstrated that immigrants who were schoolchildren in the middle of the 1990s went on to have some of the lowest rates of delinquent behavior of all youths. Further descriptions of studies of this kind could fill page after page.[44]

These trends were also visible at the level of cities and metropolitan areas. For example, Sampson led a team of investigators who performed a systematic study of crimes in Chicago. The team used the records of thousands of young Chicagoans and a survey of eight thousand city residents. They found that Mexican-origin people displayed a lower rate of violence compared with whites and black people, a difference substantially driven by the fact that many of them were foreign-born. Specifically, they found that immigrants were 45 percent less likely to engage in violence than the grandchildren of immigrants, and that the children of immigrants were 22 percent less likely to do so. The same held true of people of African ancestry and of European extraction who were immigrants.[45]

This was an intriguing set of results because it further emphasized the protective effect of immigration: not only were newcomers to the United States simply less likely to break the law, but they also managed to pass this set of behaviors on to their children and grandchildren. However, the effect was lessened in each generation: the further removed descendants were from the immigrant generation, the more they acted like the more criminally prone US-born population. Given these results, it seems more logical to ask not only what immigrants have done for this country, but also what this country has done to their descendants.

A further set of remarkable findings also emerged—one that involved not simply *when* the crime drop began and *who* was committing fewer offenses, but also *where* public safety was most improved. This became clear as criminologists plotted crime locations using geodata techniques—they mapped where and when crimes took place and then studied the social, economic, and other characteristics of high- and low-crime areas. These studies have clearly demonstrated that the presence of immigrants corresponded to significantly lower rates of many crimes. In Little Village specifically, my systematic survey of crime using detailed geodata from the period 1999 to 2001 reveals that despite being a low-income neighborhood with a young population, the homicide rate was no higher than for the city as a whole. And according to the *Chicago Tribune*'s tally of crime in the city using a scale in which the first-place neighborhood was the most dangerous, as of mid-2014 South Lawndale ranked thirty-seventh out of seventy-seven community areas with regard to violent crime, forty-first in quality-of-life crime, and fifty-fourth in property crime.[46] A separate study found that the overwhelming majority of the murders in the Little Village community area were concentrated in just four of the neighborhood's twenty census tracts; the remaining sixteen, observed the author, "had homicide rates that would rank them among the safest neighborhoods in the city." This effect was also visible in Oak Cliff. Using data from the National Neighborhood Crime Study's multicity data set for 1999–2001, I found that even though virtually every Oak Cliff tract was more socioeconomically disadvantaged than the median Dallas tract, the neighborhood's murder rate was significantly lower than expected in a neighborhood with such a low-income and disproportionately young population.[47]

Key to findings like these were two interrelated effects. First, neighborhoods where immigrants lived were safer for everybody who dwelled there, whether they were foreign- or native-born; second, while the presence of immigrants was most protective, just being near the newcomers also had a protective effect. In other words, these findings, which were measurable down to the level of census tracts, showed that crime was lower not only in sections of the city where immigrants settled but also in places adjacent to immigrant areas.[48]

Sociologists have studied this protective influence as one example of the larger category of "neighborhood effects." This school of thought holds that, as Sampson explains it, "neighborhoods are not merely settings in which individuals act out the dramas produced by autonomous and preset scripts, or empty vessels determined by 'bigger' external forces, but are important determinants of the quantity and quality of human behavior in their own right."[49]

The question is precisely *why* these neighborhoods have a protective effect with respect to crime. Some have argued that since by world standards the United States has an unusually high rate of interpersonal violence, the addition of immigrants from less violent nations not surprisingly reduces crime by simple dilution. The trouble with this interpretation is that many Latin American immigrants come from fairly violent lands, and yet their presence still reduces crime in the United States. A competing framework points to selectivity. The people who choose to come to the United States, in this explanation, are self-selected for certain qualities: they are intrepid, hardworking, and strongly motivated to avoid the kind of trouble that could lead to problems with immigration authorities. Although in many ways persuasive, these and other explanations tend to dwell on individual characteristics—just the kind of thinking that the "neighborhood effects" framework has tried to transcend.[50]

This is why it makes sense to think in terms of the built environment. The proximity effects of crime prevention indicate that this is not just about *being* an immigrant, whether from Latin America or anywhere else in the world. What if the effect is created by the neighborhood setting *created* by the foreign-born—in this case Latino urbanism? After all, in *The Death and Life of Great American Cities*, Jane Jacobs wrote at length of the importance of "eyes upon the street"—casual surveillance by people sitting on stoops, looking out of windows, and minding stores—in keeping order in urban neighborhoods. In places like Little Village and Oak Cliff, the Latinos who socialize in front of their homes and run storefront and sidewalk businesses and actively occupy public space accomplish precisely this kind of neighborhood monitoring; moreover, their participation in local clubs and transnational hometown associations fosters street presence and civic engagement.[51]

SOME OF THE most compelling evidence of exactly how Latino urbanism may have changed the way US cities work emerged out of the tragedy of the Chicago heat wave of 1995. On July 13, the temperature in the city climbed to 106 degrees, with a heat index of 126, and remained elevated for nearly a week after. As people turned up their air conditioners to stay cool, many parts of the city suffered lengthy power outages. Emergency calls multiplied, dramatically slowing ambulance response times. And Chicagoans began to die of heatstroke in such large numbers that the city morgue was overwhelmed and had to store bodies in refrigerated tractor-trailers parked outside. By the time the heat broke, more than five hundred people had lost their lives.[52]

Soon after, a young urban sociologist named Eric Klinenberg began reading through the city's official reports on the incident and noted something extraordinary: there was a massive ethnoracial disparity in the fatalities. Latinos were far less likely to have died than either black or white people. The report determined that 256 African Americans and 252 whites had perished in the heat wave, yet counted only nine deaths among Hispanics. Latinos accounted for 23 percent of all Chicagoans but only about 2 percent of the decedents—a percentage of Hispanic fatalities that a statistician might have expected to be far higher.[53]

What might explain such drastically different outcomes? After ruling out explanations based on biology, acclimation to heat, and family structure, Klinenberg considered whether the key distinction between the neighborhoods might be the quality of their urban fabric. From this view, it soon became clear that the relationship between people and their built environments played a vital role in determining the severity and distribution of the death toll. The neighborhood he selected to demonstrate how this worked was none other than South Lawndale.

The medical and statistical evidence made clear that a large proportion of the people who died in the disaster were those who remained in their homes, where there were no cooling breezes and the sweltering heat was amplified by masonry and frame walls and roofs. Going outside was thus a key determinant of survival. It was this fact that made the particular characteristics of the Little Village Latino landscape—the differences between it and the urban places occupied by African American and white Anglo Chicagoans—so crucial in what transpired.[54]

The residential landscape was the clearest link to Latino survival. In the context of the Chicago heat wave, local housescapes formed a crucial point of articulation between identity and survival, providing a site where spatial practices were protective. As we learned earlier in this chapter, Mexican American housescapes have become hugely prevalent in Little Village. They do vary somewhat from the southwestern type, since there are as many row houses as freestanding residences. But fencing at the property line is common, and on many blocks it is the rule with few exceptions. Most importantly, this architectural feature does indeed serve key purposes: adult family members, including seniors, are frequently out in front keeping an eye on children. In conditions of extreme heat, being outside would have been doubly protective. The custom of front-yard sociability would have left fewer people indoors in a position to begin overheating in the first place. Moreover, once anyone indoors found themselves in distress from the heat, there was already a place waiting for them outdoors—both literally, in that chairs, benches, or stoops would be available to sit on, and figuratively, in that it would have seemed natural to go out front to cool off, since they could expect to find family and friends there. The same was not true for black and white Chicagoans: near the peak of urban crisis crime, many African Americans (who of course had their own traditions of front-yard visiting and streetside socializing) were hesitant to venture outside for fear of being caught up in street violence, and it was whites who had most consistently abandoned public spaces.[55]

The Latino commercial landscape also played an important role. Klinenberg emphasized how Little Village shopkeepers made the "social ecology" of the neighborhood so distinctive. The neighborhood had long since become "a magnet for Mexican and Central American migrants and immigrants as well as for Mexican Americans already in Chicago," who generated a thriving "commercial economy of retailers and small local businesses." These kinds of establishments served as "places that draw people out"—they "pulled older people into public places," or "attract[ed] older and younger residents" into the streets. And specifically during the heat wave, nearby stores offered locals "safe, air-conditioned places where they could get relief from the heat." Klinenberg particularly contrasted this commercial vibrancy with the community directly to the north. "The physical landscape of North Lawndale's largest thoroughfares and many of its residential streets," he explained, was "dominated by boarded or dilapidated buildings, rickety fast-food joints, closed stores with faded signs." As a result, "residents lacked places to go in the neighborhood." Little Village had a "material substratum of busy streets, dense residential concentration, proximate family habitation, and booming commerce" that combined to draw seniors and other vulnerable people out of their homes.[56]

As it turns out, the extraordinary rate of Latino survival in the heat wave was by no means idiosyncratic—it was just one example of a much larger social phenomenon that sociologists and public health specialists have dubbed the "Latino health paradox." Numerous studies conducted over more than a decade have found that Latinos enjoy longer life expectancies and better health outcomes than similarly situated non-Hispanics. Moreover, this effect can apparently be generalized beyond matters of health. A number of researchers who have closely examined municipal- and national-level statistics have begun to define an even broader phenomenon that some have referred to categorically as the "Latino paradox"—the repeated finding that Latinos experience better outcomes than other populations of similar socioeconomic status on a variety of measures. The reasons for this are still being debated, but the findings set forth in *Heat Wave* suggest that Latinos' way of occupying and modifying the built environment will help us understand these effects.[57]

Remarkably, the "Latino paradox" holds even more profound potential when we consider that as with crime prevention, its benefits extend to non-Hispanics who live among or near large groups of Latinos. For example, Klinenberg found that the liveliness of the sidewalks and stores of Little Village was a lifesaving feature that "*protected not only the area's Latino population, but the culturally or linguistically isolated white elderly, who were at high risk of death as well.*" Other researchers have found health outcomes seemingly related to the built and enacted environments. For example, the incidence of asthma is lower among Mexican-born people than among blacks and white Anglos—but notably, no such benefit is seen among American-born people of Mexican ancestry; this and other evidence linking asthma to too much time spent indoors suggest that these health effects result from residence in immigrant-heavy pedestrian neighborhoods.[58]

These health benefits are not permanent, however: the neighborhood effect of the Latino landscape lessens over time. The grandchildren of these immigrants, for example, still have rates of criminal offense arrests that are lower than they are for other Americans in similar circumstances, but not so low as those of the first and second generations. Similarly, improved Latino health outcomes are attenuated over time, likely owing to the unhealthful US diet and the fact that native-born Hispanics tend to revert to the dominant US car culture. In other words, the improvements that come with Latino urbanism are being eroded and their benefits gradually lost.

THE EMERGENCE OF Latino urbanism and its associated public safety and health outcomes is not grounds for an uncomplicated celebration of grit and boundless opportunity. The fact that these migrants have managed to create strong communities with a vibrant public life is a testament to both their hard work and their ability to leverage small but significant advantages in the face of tremendous adversity. Latino community achievements are what they are *despite* the ongoing neglect of neighborhoods like these—the underinvestment, especially in education, and the low wages, persistent overwork, and resultant levels of poverty.

Nevertheless, Latino migrants and immigrants have been able to establish forms of city life that share many of the characteristics espoused by the New Urbanists and to attain some of the goals they set forth years ago. But rather than being the province of well-to-do elites—the most common and well-grounded criticism of New Urbanism—this has been the creation of working-class people. Latino urbanism promotes a safer, healthier public sphere, both for Latinas and Latinos and for their non-Hispanic neighbors. They have revived some of the key features of a public realm that began to disappear decades ago, creating new norms of public presence and out-of-doors sociability. And that has been a key feature that drives down some of the pathologies that characterized the urban crisis.

These *migrantes* have created a remarkable bulwark for sustainable urbanism. The question is whether their remarkable achievements can be maintained in a period of still-worsening inequality, as well as emboldened nativism and anti-Latino racism.

CHAPTER 11

A NEW URBAN AMERICA

THE NEW MILLENNIUM WAS ONLY A FEW MONTHS OLD when the curtain first went up on a show about a big-city barrio and the people living there. The play centered on Usnavi de la Vega, the young proprietor of a local bodega. An orphan, he was raised by Abuela Claudia, the wise neighborhood matriarch whose apartment window looks out on his storefront. Across the street is the taxi service owned by Kevin Rosario. Nina, his daughter, has just returned home after her first year of college; she is pursued romantically by Benny, one of her father's few non-Spanish-speaking employees. Vanessa is a hairstylist who works at Daniela's Salon next to the taxi dispatch but dreams of living downtown. These characters and others struggle to get by and consider various plans—staying in the barrio, returning to college, going back to the lands where they were born, moving to a more upscale neighborhood.[1]

In the Heights was the creation of Lin-Manuel Miranda, a Nuyorican composer and dramatist, and Quiara Alegría Hudes, a Philadelphia Puerto Rican playwright. The play is set in Washington Heights, a neighborhood at the northern tip of Manhattan. In many respects this barrio parallels places like Little Village and Oak Cliff, though with a predominantly Caribbean population. Usnavi is an immigrant

291

from the Dominican Republic. Abuela Claudia fled the Cuban Revolution when she was still a girl. Kevin left Puerto Rico as a young man when it became impossible to eke out a living in the sugarcane fields. And reflecting an emerging pan-Latino identity, one character explains, "My mom is Dominican-Cuban, my dad is from Chile and PR, which means I'm Chile-Domini-Curican, but I always say I'm from Queens!"[2]

The play's setting is a paragon of Latino urbanism, displaying many of its classic figures and features. One of the first characters introduced to the audience is Piragua Guy, an archetypal *ambulante* who calls out the day's flavors of shaved ice as he pushes his cart around the neighborhood streets. People live close together, many in apartments above the storefronts, and walk to work and shop nearby at locally owned businesses like Usnavi's bodega, Kevin's car service, and Daniela's salon. The play is suffused with dynamic street life, and most of the action takes place on the sidewalks, where people share news and gossip, conduct business, offer advice on each other's love lives, and discuss their plans and fears and hopes while enduring a heat wave and a blackout over the course of the play's running time.

Throughout the play, the people of the barrio are poised between their place in this immigrant haven and the possibility that they will have to move on. They feel at home in the neighborhood they have built together, but rising rents and opportunities elsewhere make it harder and harder for them to stay. Usnavi in particular worries that people will forget, or never even know, what the barrio represents:

> But who's gonna notice when we're gone?
> When our job's done, as the evening winds
> Down to a crawl, son. Can I ease my mind
> When we're all done? When we've resigned.
> In the long run, what do we leave behind?

Miranda and Hudes gesture toward a deeper sense of continuity in the neighborhood, presenting its Caribbean residents as the latest in a succession of striving immigrants. A stage direction calls attention to the ROSARIO CAR SERVICE sign—"Underneath is the glimmer of an older sign: O'HANRAHAN CAR SERVICE."[3]

In the Heights is certainly faithful to the history of Washington Heights. Earlier in the twentieth century, the area was populated by Irish, Polish, and Hungarian immigrants who labored in the city's abundant industrial workplaces. Later, it became home to a large community of Jews from Germany, who recognized themselves in their new neighbors. When one elderly German-Jewish resident was interviewed in 1992 about the different groups of people who called the area home, she emphasized that whatever their origins, the experience of being a migrant and a minority created a sense of community: "Whatever you went through, whatever happened, it makes you stick together. Like the Spanish people, they stick together, too." Washington Heights has seen hard times and has never been particularly prosperous: residents' ethnic backgrounds have varied greatly, but they are always resolutely working-class. Crime in the neighborhood increased along with the rest of New York, but by the early 2000s its predominantly Dominican residents presided over a neighborhood that was one of the safest in Manhattan.[4]

Washington Heights is just one of many urban neighborhoods that followed the path of Little Village and Oak Cliff. Something similar happened in the North Corona section of Queens, New York. Once a neighborhood populated by people of Italian, Irish, and German ancestry, in the last decades of the twentieth century it became overwhelmingly Hispanic, and the county became one of the most diverse out of the more than three thousand counties in the continental United States. Similar changes characterize the Mitchell Street area in Milwaukee; Barry Square in Hartford, Connecticut; vast stretches of Central, East, and South Los Angeles; and practically all of Miami. Even in Detroit, long the preeminent example of deindustrialization, population loss, and social strife, there is a story of Latino urbanism: as the city continued to lose population in the 2000s, one of the few areas of growth was Mexicantown, the Motor City's thriving and growing preeminent Hispanic community.[5]

Transformations like these have not been limited to individual barrios. In many cities overall Latino settlement includes multiple neighborhoods. For a time these were familiar mainly to barrio residents, their coethnics, and other locals in the know. But advances in digital mapping over the past decade have made it easy to see the shape and extent of Hispanic residence in any city in the nation. The extraordinary diversity and sharp segregation of urban America are displayed in maps showing the population in color-coded dots thanks to geodata projects like those set up by the *New York Times* and the University of Virginia. In Boston, there are overwhelmingly Hispanic neighborhoods in the northeast of the city around Logan Airport, and in places like South Boston Latinos have settled alongside and among longtime Irish American residents. In Houston, zones of Hispanic residence radiate out from the city center to the north and southeast, alternating with wedge-shaped areas of African American and white settlement. And in Denver, predominantly Mexican-origin people live both in a small section around Lake Street downtown and in a more extensive barrio covering much of the land to the west of Interstate 25. Each city seems to have its own distinctive pattern of Latinization.[6]

The trend also includes many cities that were smaller or had little or no previous history of Hispanic settlement. In Nashville, Tennessee, Latinos account for about one in ten of the residents counted in the last decennial census. The ethnic Mexican, Colombian, and other Hispanic communities have contributed greatly to municipal growth in the new millennium, and many considered it a sign of acceptance when the city's voters soundly defeated a proposed English-only law in 2009. The city of Allentown, Pennsylvania, was hit hard by deindustrialization and saw no net population increase for the entire second half of the twentieth century; it began growing again after an influx of mostly Puerto Rican and Dominican migrants, who now account for 43 percent of its more than 120,000 residents. And Union City, New Jersey, for more than a century celebrated as "The Embroidery Capital of the World," had reached its peak population as early as 1930; Cuban immigrants revitalized the city starting in the 1960s, forming the core of a Hispanic community that is 85 percent of a city whose population, at 70,000 residents, is now larger than at any time in its history.[7]

Latinization has also increasingly reached into suburbia, with municipalities outside cities joining the pattern of population growth. In the decade leading up to 2000, the nation's suburban Latino population increased by 72 percent. This could be seen outside Chicago in a variety of suburban municipalities, from the town of Cicero, which lies just on the other side of the city limits from Little Village, to more distant metropolitan Chicago Mexican enclaves like Aurora and Round Lake Beach. This is even more the case outside Dallas, where municipalities like Farmer's Branch, Garland, and Grand Prairie have proportions of Hispanic residents just as high as in the city itself. Another example is the New York City suburban municipality of Port Chester. Largely composed of low-density residential development, it is about 60 percent Hispanic— a proportion even higher than Los Angeles—and includes an immigrant-revived downtown with bustling sidewalks and vibrant small-scale commerce. Latino settlement has clearly reached the crabgrass frontier.[8]

Still, even the neighborhoods that benefited most from migrant re-settlement have by no means fully recovered their lost prosperity. Even before the Great Recession, the continued hollowing out of well-paid industrial and public-sector employment had reduced the job opportunities available in urban America. Cuts to education budgets and the creeping privatization of public schools have meant that many children of *migrantes* are placed in segregated and underfunded school districts. And we must not forget that reurbanization has come at great cost to Latino immigrant working people, who have endured low pay and outright wage theft, suffered elevated rates of employment-related injury and death, and experienced ongoing abuse by law enforcement.[9]

Yet despite this, Latinos and Latinas helped drive vigorous metropolitan growth around the turn of the millennium, by which time urban America had clearly turned the corner. For the first time in decades, most cities were growing. After nearly three-quarters of the nation's twenty-five most populous cities lost residents in the three decades to 1980, in the thirty years that followed almost that many *gained* population. In the 1990s alone, downtowns in Chicago, Dallas, Cleveland, San Francisco, and Atlanta all added 25 percent or more in population, and in Pittsburgh, Denver, and Seattle those gains topped 50 percent. Following the 2000s, urban growth picked up so much that all but two of the nation's fifty largest cities saw increases in their populations. At the same time, the share of the nation's gross domestic product that was produced in metropolitan areas continued to rise: by 2012, about 84 percent of new jobs and 88 percent of economic growth were generated in metropolitan areas, and half the nation's GDP was produced in just the twenty-three largest metros.[10]

Given the magnitude and extent of Latinization and the remarkable revitalization of urban America, it was only a matter of time before more people began to make connections between the two. Beyond Latinos themselves, who had already been seeing the phenomenon up close, urbanists and demographers began to work out key pieces of the puzzle of what had happened; they were followed by city officials, who began to establish new programs to make the power of immigration work for their municipalities. Political figures from both parties also got involved: most Democrats and some Republicans initially responded as one might expect—by recognizing the nation's fast-changing demographic terrain and trying to figure out how best to gain advantage. Alongside this seemingly bipartisan consensus on the benefits of immigration for metropolitan America, however, was a vocal minority who saw things very differently.

CITIES HAD REBOUNDED for a number of reasons, of course; neither Latino immigrants nor immigrants in general had done all the work themselves. Changes in the global economy had concentrated a great many well-paid jobs in urban centers—not just in the United States but worldwide—drawing large numbers of suburbanites and others back into large cities and persuading a new generation of professionals not to move out in the first place. Meanwhile, growing sectors of the economy came to depend on people and businesses being clustered in downtown areas, with nearness driving innovation in everything from advanced manufacturing to legal services to restaurants to art galleries. Even the rise of the historic preservation movement played a role by teaching the public to valorize the older urban landscape in ways that made people of means find value in industrial-era neighborhoods with "character" and "authenticity."[11]

When the time came for broad explanations of the urban recovery, however, most attention was focused on urban professionals and other educated and predominantly white Anglo populations. The leading work in this line of thinking was Richard Florida's 2002 book *The Rise of the Creative Class: And How It's Transforming Work, Leisure, Community, and Everyday Life.*[12] In it, Florida explained how one particular category of people—those who work with their minds and hands at desks in areas like consulting, advertising, art, computer programming, film and television production, teaching, and the like—had revitalized city life and held the promise of spurring further metropolitan improvement. The book quickly became a best seller, and municipal leaders from across the country hastened to read it in hopes of spurring growth and prosperity in their cities: one municipal official from Albuquerque told me in 2004 that it had become "the Bible of urban policy these days." Florida was by no means incorrect, though as he later acknowledged, he had understated the problem of inequality in his encomium to the educated and upwardly mobile. But the book focused so intently on this demographic that Latino and immigrant newcomers did not figure in his account except to the extent that ethnoracial diversity was counted as a plus in his city-by-city rankings of urban desirability.[13]

Even explanations for the urban recovery that criticized the economic changes underlying it often placed Latino migrants and other largely working-class immigrants of color in a subsidiary role. The world-famous sociologist Saskia Sassen, for example, fit migrants into her theory of globalization as people who primarily serve the needs of the professionals who work in city centers. Notably, however, she added them to the story only later, and in a way that supported her existing interpretation: she inserted a chapter on immigration into the third edition of *Cities in a World Economy* (2006) when before there had been no such material. In this sense, their migration to urban areas was simply a side effect of the new role of cities in the global economy. As she put it in her introduction, global cities are "not only the world of top-level transnational managers and professionals but also that of their secretaries and that of the janitors cleaning the buildings where the new professional class works . . . it is also the world of a whole new workforce increasingly made up of immigrant and minoritized citizens, who take on the functions once performed by the mother/wife in the older middle classes: the nannies, domestic cleaners, and dog walkers who service the households of the new professional class." Sassen is certainly correct about the global forces shaping cities. She has been a prophetic voice in urban theory and perceived the urban recovery well before others. And she is right that many immigrants, especially women, do the work of attending to the basic needs of professionals' families. But she has neglected the fact that more new immigrants worked in the manufacturing and construction sectors, and that they had begun settling in cities a decade or two before the phase of globalization to which she attributes urban transformation. The sequence of events is clear for her: capital investment and back-to-the-city professionals are the driving force, migration the aftereffect.[14]

The focus on highly educated, high-income households was even more pronounced among economists, who regularly cited key conditions for urban revitalization while making no mention of the role of Latinos and other immigrants in creating them. According to a representative survey of the literature, "Urban revival is therefore entirely driven by the rising urban share of the young and college-educated, with no contribution from general population growth." One approach emphasized the urban concentration of professional jobs in sectors like law and finance that were characterized by long hours, but without noting, as Sassen had, that these kinds of jobs require a great deal of support from childcare workers, housekeepers, and janitors, among others—work done overwhelmingly by immigrants. Another line of research cited falling crime rates as the most reliable predictors of professionals moving to center cities without noting the by-then well-documented role of immigrants in driving those crime rates down. But the most glaring example argued that the best indicator of yuppie migration to big cities was high-quality restaurants, an industry that was absolutely dominated by immigrant Latina and Latino workers, from the chefs to the sous-chefs to the prep staff to the employees who bused tables and washed dishes.[15]

A few observers did put immigrants, and Latinos specifically, at the center of a narrative of urban revitalization. Scholars living in the Los Angeles area amid the nation's biggest population of Latinos were particularly attentive to their effect on urban life. The urban planner Dowell Myers cited immigration as a "fundamental force" in city growth, an influence without parallel in defining the future of metropolitan America. The journalist Roberto Suro and the demographer Audrey Singer quantified and mapped the Hispanic presence in cities and suburbs. And the urbanist and cultural critic Mike Davis emphasized how Latinos had become some of the most urbanized of all Americans and were transforming the nature of city life. But as Davis correctly pointed out, urban theorists and others who studied cities had simply not incorporated these major changes into their thinking about life in the metropolis.[16]

Then, just as observers were refining their analyses of the urban revival and the place of immigrants in it, the most important flow of Latin American migrants began to reverse itself. Around the middle of 2006, the number of people leaving Mexico and migrating to the United States began to drop off very quickly; shortly thereafter, migration in the opposite direction began to increase as hundreds of thousands of Mexicans headed back across the Rio Grande. These countervailing trends quickly added up to a dramatic shift: between 2005 and 2010, net migration across the US-Mexico border dropped below zero as more people and their families returned home than arrived in the United States; the Mexican population in the United States had peaked in 2007. In the years that followed, departures accelerated further, with 140,000 more Mexicans leaving than arriving from 2009 to 2014.[17]

After nearly fifty years of playing the central role in the biggest human migration in both nations' histories, movement across the US-Mexico border—the most active migration corridor in the world—was running southbound. Migrants continued to arrive from elsewhere in the hemisphere and the world, and the number and proportion of the foreign-born remained near all-time highs, but the era of large-scale Mexican migration had basically run its course.

These changes quickly became apparent in US barrios. Little Village shed more than twelve thousand residents for a decline of nearly 16 percent; Oak Cliff's losses totaled nearly eleven thousand people, a decline of more than 9 percent. In Little Village, the departures were predominantly Hispanic, though about two thousand white and black residents left as well; Oak Cliff lost a few thousand each of Hispanics, African Americans, and white Anglos. More than just a matter of Latinos or immigrants leaving the neighborhood, this suggested a broader slowing of momentum in metropolitan revitalization.[18]

A number of factors contributed to the end of a decades-long surge of migration. Public attention tended to focus on the financial crisis of 2008 and the Great Recession that followed it. The resultant rise in unemployment was certainly a disincentive for prospective migrants, but the falloff in arrivals from Mexico had begun earlier. Others emphasized changes in immigration enforcement, but the overwhelming majority of people returning to Mexico did so voluntarily, with most citing the desire to reunite their families as the reason for their departure.[19]

This was not simply a year-to-year shift, however; it reflected longer-term trends. The underlying migration process had matured, with the population shifts that had driven people to relocate to cities and across borders settling into a steadier state. In one sense, this should not have been a surprise, since previous large-scale migrations had arisen, peaked, and subsided: Irish immigration had lasted a few decades before settling down at a far lower rate than in the 1840s; the same was true decades later for Italian newcomers and for Jewish immigrants from eastern Europe.[20]

Far and away the largest determinants of the migration of Mexicans that began in the 1960s and added more than sixteen million new US residents were the particular demographic and economic conditions in Mexico. Foremost among these was the high birth rate prevalent before Mexico's national contraception campaign. In 1960 the average woman in Mexico gave birth to 7.3 children during her lifetime; by 2009 that figure had plunged by over two-thirds to 2.4. As a result, there simply were fewer working-age people who might wish to go to El Norte. Also relevant was the gradual transformation of the Mexican economy: the share of rural agriculturalists had declined and the proportion of urbanized workers had grown, increasing the ranks of the country's still-small middle class. Disruptions in the Mexican countryside could still set off substantial migrations, as happened in the wake of the North American Free Trade Agreement of 1994, which flooded the country with subsidized US corn and made it impossible for Mexico's maize farmers to make a living by selling their crops. But overall the Mexican economy was performing well enough in the 2000s that the country was better able to offer employment to the rising generation of young men and women.[21]

By the early 2010s, the decline in Mexican migration and the growth of migration from Asia—sometime during 2009 the number of new arrivals from Asia surpassed the number from Latin America—meant that there were slightly more Asian immigrants in the United States (12 million) than Mexican immigrants (11.6 million). Meanwhile, the non-Mexican share of all Latin American and Caribbean immigrants (9.9 million) had risen to 46 percent of the total. Still, the total

US Latino population grew to more than 50 million by 2010, driven primarily by domestic births rather than immigration.[22]

IRONICALLY, IT WAS just as net immigration was falling to zero that it became an increasingly powerful political issue. By the mid-2000s, the Republican Party saw the chance to outflank its political opponents by reducing the Democrats' long-standing advantage with Hispanic voters. George W. Bush suffered from severe flaws as a political figure, but uneasiness with Latinos was not among them. He had adopted Texas as his political home and established ties to the 30 percent of the state's population that was Hispanic. As he sought to burnish his credentials as a "compassionate conservative," Bush had shown sympathy for Latin American immigrants, including undocumented ones. "Family values don't stop at the Rio Grande," he said frequently, often adding, "a hungry mother is going to try to feed her child." In the presidential election of 2000, he won over a third of the Latino vote, and in 2004 this proportion rose to nearly 40 percent.[23]

GOP strategists saw a new way to become the party of the majority—not by stoking nativism, but rather by appealing to Latinos. They hoped to avoid the catastrophic path of Pete Wilson, the Republican former governor of California. In his 1994 reelection campaign he had run television advertisements that ominously intoned, "They keep coming," while showing scenes of brown-skinned people crossing the border. Wilson also backed Proposition 187, which would have denied virtually all social services to undocumented immigrants, even barring their children from public schools. He won reelection, but the victory was pyrrhic: Latinos responded with an unprecedented wave of naturalizations, registrations, and voting, helping turn the home state of Richard Nixon and Ronald Reagan into a reliably blue state with a Democratic supermajority in its legislature.

Republicans attempted to strengthen Bush's inroads with Hispanic voters by leading the way on immigration. Party leaders arranged for Senator John McCain of Arizona to introduce a major immigration bill and persuaded Massachusetts senator Ted Kennedy, a longtime advocate for immigrants, to cosponsor it. The Secure America and Orderly Immigration Act of 2005 would offer a path to citizenship for many of the nation's roughly ten million undocumented people, the great majority of whom were Latino. This would involve a lengthy procedure requiring them to pay fines and back taxes, pass a background check, maintain employment, and demonstrate a basic knowledge of English and civics. The bill also included security agreements with Mexico, a guest worker program, and reimbursement for border states that had incurred substantial immigration-related expenses. While some observers saw the bill's requirements for citizenship as onerous, it won the backing of labor unions and immigrant rights organizations, which saw it as a workable solution to help millions of people come out of the shadow of illegality.[24]

The nativist base of the Republican Party quickly rose up in revolt. As news of the McCain-Kennedy bill's progress through the Senate spread more widely, it was met with a wave of anger in right-wing venues, most notably talk radio. Rush Limbaugh, for example, called undocumented Mexicans an "invasive species," later adding that they were "a renegade, potential criminal element that are poor and unwilling to work." These were of course lies, but the facts mattered little to furious nativists.[25]

This reaction should not have been surprising. While mainstream media had generally taken a welcoming tone toward newcomers to the United States, many conservative pundits had found a dedicated audience for an anti-immigrant message. For at least a decade, the best-seller lists had included books with alarmist titles like Peter Brimelow's *Alien Nation: Common Sense about America's Immigration Disaster* (1995), Pat Buchanan's *The Death of the West: How Dying Populations and Immigrant Invasions Imperil Our Country and Civilization* (2001), and the less spittle-flecked but equally pernicious *Who Are We? The Challenges to America's National Identity* (2004) by Harvard's Samuel Huntington. These books and others like them created a racist mythology centered on the Hart-Celler Act. "The Immigration Act of 1965," raged Brimelow, "triggered a renewed mass immigration, so huge and so systematically different from anything that had gone before to transform—and ultimately perhaps even destroy . . . the American nation, as it had evolved by the middle of the twentieth century." The middle of the twentieth century was, of course, the point in the previous hundred years of US history when immigrants made up the smallest percentage of the nation's population, when they were overwhelmingly from Europe, and before the dramatic growth of immigration from Latin America, Asia, and the Middle East.[26]

This opposition soon translated into action in the House of Representatives. In the fall of 2005, Wisconsin Republican James Sensenbrenner introduced the most draconian immigration bill since the National Origins Act of 1924. It included no provisions for undocumented people to regularize their status or become citizens. Instead, it focused entirely on interdiction and punishment. It required reinforcement of the US-Mexico border, including seven hundred miles of new double-walled barriers, and astonishingly, it ordered a feasibility study of a fence on the Canadian border. The bill criminalized the mere presence of undocumented people by transforming what had for decades been a misdemeanor into a second-degree felony. It also expanded the power to indefinitely imprison such people even when they could not be legally deported. The bill went so far as to threaten anybody who housed an undocumented person with a prison sentence of up to three years. In addition, it specified that local officials had "inherent authority" to enforce immigration law, making every police officer and school security guard into an adjunct of the Border Patrol. Notwithstanding the extraordinary severity of the proposed law, it passed easily that December in the House of Representatives, with 92 percent of Republicans voting for it and 82 percent of Democrats voting against. Notably, votes for the bill came disproportionately from congresspeople representing outer suburban and especially rural areas far away from the places where immigrants mostly lived.[27]

The House vote produced an immediate outcry. Human rights groups, immigrant advocates, and labor unions denounced it as cruel, economically ruinous, and likely to inspire racial harassment because local officials who attempted to enforce immigration laws had a history of selective enforcement against Hispanics and others with brown skin. But the boldest statement of opposition came from Cardinal Roger Mahony of Los Angeles, who said that if it became law, he would instruct his church's priests and laypeople to disobey it. "Christ instructs us to clothe the naked, feed the poor and welcome the stranger," he wrote in a letter to President Bush urging him to oppose the law. "Denying aid to a fellow human being violates a law with a higher authority than Congress—the law of God." But the Bush administration, faced with the anger of conservative voters, promptly jettisoned their plan to court Latinos and endorsed the bill. Now only the Senate could prevent it from becoming law.[28]

The nation's Latinos, both immigrant and native-born, responded to this threat to their families, friends, and communities by organizing some of the largest public demonstrations in US history in what came to be known as La Primavera de los Inmigrantes (the Immigrant Spring). The first major event took place on March 10 in Chicago, where at least 100,000 people marched from Union Park, not far from Little Village, into the city's downtown Loop. The size of the march surprised even its organizers, and what followed was a series of ever-larger demonstrations as immigrant communities in other cities realized their collective strength and took to the streets. Two weeks later, as many as half a million protesters thronged downtown Los Angeles chanting "*Sí se puede!*," the motto of César Chávez's United Farm Workers. On April 9, between 350,000 and half a million protesters turned out in Dallas for the largest public demonstration in the city's history. And on May 1, another Chicago protest drew between 400,000 and 750,000 marchers, including contingents from the city's Polish, Irish, Chinese, and West African immigrant communities. All told, from March to May 2006, between 3.5 million and 5 million people in more than 120 cities participated in these demonstrations.[29]

The demonstrators were both disciplined and eloquent. Having learned from controversies around immigrant marches in the 1990s, they emphasized themes of pride, patriotism, and history. American flags of every size—from handheld versions waved by small children to fifty-foot-long banners held aloft by long ranks of marchers—were everywhere, expressing their love for their adopted country. The same went for the signs they carried: WE ARE AMERICA. I LOVE THIS COUNTRY—I JUST WANT TO STAY. GOD'S LOVE HAS NO BORDERS. In Chicago, José Soberanis and his younger sister Cecilia marched with a portrait they had drawn of Martin Luther King Jr. "As the saying goes," he said, "'I have a dream.' Well, we have dreams too." The marches included citizens and legal residents, but also undocumented people who revealed themselves in a way that exposed them to arrest and deportation. Some wore banners with messages like

Downtown Chicago, May 1, 2006. As Congress debated the most draconian anti-immigration bill in more than eight decades, *migrantes* and their allies took to the streets. In some of the biggest public demonstrations in the nation's history, millions of Latinas and Latinos turned out in the cities that they had done so much to revitalize. Photograph courtesy Joseph Voves.

I DON'T WANT TO BE ILLEGAL ANYMORE or spoke of their fears for their families. "I would be separated from my two children," said one Los Angeles protester as she walked with her Mexican-born daughter and pushed her two US-born children in a stroller. In his coverage, the journalist Roberto Suro emphasized the courage of the marchers, noting that "by simply appearing, they made an existential statement, powerful for its simplicity: 'We are here. We are human, flesh and blood, parents and children.'"[30]

The marches broke the momentum of the Sensenbrenner bill, leaving the politics of immigration deadlocked. The Republicans, who controlled both houses of Congress, could see the size and coordination of the demonstrations and understood the importance of the fast-growing Latino voting bloc. The GOP Senate leadership in particular believed that it could enact piecemeal immigration legislation—a guest worker program, some regularization of the undocumented—but no path to citizenship because their electoral base was dead set against it. Meanwhile, anti-immigration Republicans still held the balance of power in the House of Representatives, and they continued to militate for their legislation militarizing the border and punishing the undocumented. These efforts continued until November 2006, when the Democrats won control of both houses of Congress, ending the threat posed to ten million undocumented immigrants by the Sensenbrenner bill.

THE POLITICS OF IMMIGRATION only intensified in the next presidential election. Republican officials who hoped to repeat the party's 2004 performance among Hispanics had been dismayed by the Bush administration's endorsement of the Sensenbrenner bill, but they hoped to minimize the damage by nominating Arizona senator John McCain, sponsor of the immigration reform bill of three years before. Under attack from the right, however, he disavowed his own bill during the primary and said that Congress should postpone any new legislation because, he claimed, "People want the border secured first."[31]

This put McCain in a poor position to compete with his general-election opponent. Barack Obama personified the nation's emerging demography, not least because his father had been an immigrant from Africa. He had also launched his political career in Chicago, whose metropolitan area was home to one of the nation's largest populations of immigrants. Obama actively courted Latino voters (as well as Asian Americans) by endorsing a path to citizenship for undocumented immigrants and highlighting his senatorial votes for the DREAM Act, which would have given legal residence and in-state college tuition rates to undocumented people who had been brought to the United States as children. On the day of the election, Latinos broke heavily for Obama, giving him their votes by a greater than two-to-one ratio and helping carry him to victory with a total of 365 electoral votes, nearly 100 more than he needed to claim the presidency. And it could be lost on nobody that Obama had won the Hispanic-heavy swing states of Florida, Colorado, Nevada, and New Mexico—all of which Bush had carried four years earlier.

The geography of the 2008 vote was as revealing as the demographics. Obama won the great majority of his votes in precisely the large metropolitan areas that Latinos and other immigrants had done so much to revitalize. This urban-rural divide had been there before, but it had grown markedly during the 2000s. Obama's electoral base was unmistakably located in the nation's largest metropolitan areas: the Democrat won all but a handful of the counties that contained the largest agglomerations of population. This, it should be noted, was true even though large proportions of these cities' residents were immigrants who were not yet eligible to become citizens or had chosen not to; their citizen neighbors, however, were resolutely blue in their electoral choices. Also important were the segments of the non-Hispanic white population among whom Obama did the best: the young, and those with more years of education, especially college degrees. In many ways this resembled nothing so clearly as the kind of urban political coalition that had made mayors out of Harold Washington, Federico Peña, Henry Cisneros, and Ron Kirk: a combination of African Americans and Hispanics and other voters of color, along with liberal whites.[32]

The GOP had clearly lost the initiative in pursuing the Latino vote. The party leadership still advised a change in tone, but the rise of the Tea Party had animated the anti-immigrant grass roots and the action soon shifted to conservative Republican-dominated state legislatures. They continued to sponsor laws hostile to immigrants, most notably Arizona's SB 1070. It required that all noncitizens register with local authorities within thirty days of arriving, and that they carry identity documents with them at all times; infractions were punishable by fines and imprisonment. It also stipulated that local officials had the power to detain anyone suspected of being undocumented, thereby deputizing entire police forces and other officials to hunt down suspected "illegals." This provision was especially suspicious in a state where the largest county's sheriff had been cited for racial profiling by the Department of Justice and whose jurisdiction had paid out tens of millions of dollars in civil rights settlements. Despite a nationwide outcry that used the phrase "Your papers, please" to invoke the authoritarian regimes of the mid-twentieth century, other states followed suit: Indiana, Georgia, South Carolina, Utah, and Alabama all passed similar laws. Much of SB 1070 was invalidated by the Supreme Court two years later, but the message sent to Latinos was clear.[33]

At the same time, however, urban electorates began to take a different approach to the immigration issue. Big-city officials became prominent supporters of migrant communities. In large part this was simply a commitment to what remained a broadly shared view of the United States as a country of immigrants, but it also reflected the recognition by mayors and other city officials that immigrants had been key to alleviating so many symptoms of the urban crisis, especially by repopulating and revitalizing city neighborhoods and metropolitan economies. In Chicago, for example, the county board of commissioners decided in 2011 to discontinue cooperation with US Immigration and Customs Enforcement (ICE) and the US Department of Homeland Security in cases where city police apprehended people who turned out to be undocumented. The following year, when the ordinance went into effect, Mayor Rahm Emanuel—who while in the House of Representatives had not fought hard against the Sensenbrenner bill and released some members of his caucus to vote for it—vocally defended immigrants and said that the new city ordinance would "make Chicago the most immigrant-friendly city in the country." The mayors of Los Angeles and New York took similar public stances in defense of immigrants, including the undocumented.[34]

This approach was not limited to cities with large immigrant populations. In Detroit, for example, the rapid population losses identified by the 2010 census—the Motor City had shed 25 percent of its population in that decade alone—prompted a coalition of civic, business, philanthropic, and academic leaders to launch Global Detroit, a local development initiative that supported research on the role of immigrants in regional growth and sought to attract new immigrants to the area. According to the Global Detroit website, "Immigration has proven, by far, to be the best American strategy to combat population loss. Detroit, a city devastated by population loss from a peak of 1.8 million residents in 1950 to below 700,000 today, is still the 18th largest city in the US, but possesses only the 135th largest foreign-born population. None of the other top 25 largest cities has a foreign-born population outside of the top 100." The Global Cleveland Initiative took a similar approach to municipal and regional growth, and in the 2010s city leaders established the WE Global Network, with the motto "Leading Rust Belt Immigrant Innovation." The network comprises more than two dozen affiliates (including organizations like Welcome Dayton, Global Pittsburgh, the St. Louis Mosaic Project, and the Immigrant Welcome Center of Indianapolis) stretching from Pennsylvania and western New York to Iowa, Minnesota, and Missouri.[35]

Urban leaders like these understood that most immigrants were people of limited means, and that they would work for modest wages and take up residence in low-rent neighborhoods. But they knew better than almost anyone that cities are made of people—and that a single block full of immigrant families contributes far more to the life of a city than a hedge-fund billionaire or nonresident petroleum oligarch who has paid tens of millions of dollars for a high-rise apartment where the lights are on for only a few nights a year.

The political divide over immigration was on display in the next presidential election. During the primary, Republican candidates used the issue to outflank each other on the right, embracing a policy of exclusion and making constant use of the term "illegals." Texas governor Rick Perry, for example, was knocked out of the primary largely because his state offered in-state college tuition rates to undocumented students. "If you say that we should not educate children who have come into our state for no other reason than they have been brought there by no fault of their own," he said in defense of his policy, "I don't think you have a heart." His rivals immediately attacked him for being "soft on immigration." Mitt Romney eagerly joined in: when asked at a January 2012 primary debate what he would do about undocumented people, he responded, "The answer is self-deportation" through strict enforcement so that "they can't find work here because they don't have legal documentation to allow them to work here." The comment created a stark contrast with Obama, who continued to support a path to citizenship and just months before had established the Deferred Action for Childhood Arrivals (DACA) program, which allowed more than 850,000 undocumented people who had been brought to the United States as minors to gain renewable two-year work permits and protection from deportation.[36]

The implications of this contrast became clear on Election Day, when Obama won 51 percent of the popular vote and 332 electoral votes to Romney's 206. Republicans had hoped that the national unemployment rate of nearly 8 percent would yield a Romney victory, since no sitting president since Franklin Roosevelt had been able to win reelection with an unemployment rate over 7.2 percent. But the result was another loss for their party, including punishing margins among Latinos, who comprised 10 percent of all voters. Obama had won a remarkable 72 percent of Hispanics, again claiming the electoral votes of Florida, Colorado, Nevada, and New Mexico. Romney's showing of 27 percent of the Hispanic vote was the second-lowest on record, and other populations with recent immigrant roots also rejected the Republican standard-bearer: his Asian American support was only 26 percent, an astonishing decline among a population that had voted majority-Republican only twenty years before.[37]

Once again, the split between urban and rural areas was dramatic. Obama won decisively in metropolitan areas with over one million people—there were fifty-one such metros, which were home to 54 percent of Americans. Obama and Romney tied in metropolitan areas between 250,000 and one million people, which held one-fifth of the population. Romney won only in the smallest cities and in rural areas, which together accounted for just under 20 percent of the population. When it came to politics, population density was one of the leading predictors of voting behavior, and the Democrats had again built a winning multiracial metropolitan coalition.[38]

STUNNED THAT OBAMA had so decisively defeated them, the Republican National Committee commissioned a study of what had gone wrong. It was formally entitled the "Growth and Opportunity Project." The ninety-seven-page document candidly acknowledged that the GOP was becoming increasingly marginalized because of demographic trends in the American electorate. Its authors were especially penitent with regard to Latino voters, pointing out the dramatic drop in the Republican percentage of the Hispanic vote from 2004 to 2012 and concluding: "If Hispanic Americans perceive that a GOP nominee or candidate does not want them in the United States (i.e. self-deportation), they will not pay attention to our next sentence . . . they will close their ears to our policies." Their suggested response included a reversal in their stance on immigration. Instead of alienating Latinos with harsh nativist rhetoric—"We've chased the Hispanic voter out of his natural home," conceded Tea Party leader and former Texas congressman Dick Armey—the GOP "must embrace and champion comprehensive immigration reform. If we do not, our Party's appeal will continue to shrink to its core constituencies only."[39]

Spurred on by the report, Republicans accelerated their efforts to court Hispanics. The following month they selected Marco Rubio to deliver the party's official response to President Obama's first post-election State of the Union speech. Rubio, the young Cuban American who had won election to the US Senate as part of the Republican wave of 2010, was seen as promising presidential material, especially since he represented Florida, the nation's fourth-most-Latino state and its most important swing state. The Republicans also featured Governor Brian Sandoval of Nevada and directed considerable campaign spending in support of Susana Martinez, who would soon be elected the first Latina governor of New Mexico. Even more importantly, they sought a deal on a comprehensive immigration reform law, sending senators from Arizona and Florida to help draft and support the Border Security, Economic Opportunity, and Immigration Modernization Act of 2013, the "Gang of Eight" bill that included a path to citizenship for the undocumented; the law passed the Senate easily by a vote of 68 to 32. With a rising cohort of Hispanic officeholders and a bipartisan effort on immigration, Republicans believed that they had moved beyond their past problems with Latino voters.[40]

Once again the party's base revolted. Conservative media personalities railed against "illegals" on radio and television and online. As immigration opponents clustered around their preferred sources of information, they increasingly reinforced each other's sense of anger and grievance. Many of them adopted the slogan "Deport the invaders" as a catchphrase to be repeated on call-in shows and Internet comment threads. Their continued thirst for anti-immigrant material made automatic best sellers of screeds like Ann Coulter's unabashedly anti-Latino book ¡Adios, America! The Left's Plan to Turn Our Country into a Third World Hellhole. Once again, Republican officeholders were quick to respond to their core voters. House Speaker John Boehner, repeatedly threatened with outright rebellion by the ultraconservative caucus, used parliamentary maneuvers to keep the bill from even coming to a vote—he knew that it would have passed with mostly Democratic votes and a significant minority of dissenting Republicans.

Even more indicative was the turnabout by Marco Rubio: he had been one of the sponsors of the bill when it was submitted in April 2013 and had voted in favor of it in June, but by October, fearing that it would doom him with primary voters, he (like McCain five years earlier) disavowed his own bill.[41]

But this was only the prelude to a shocking repudiation of the Republican Party's efforts to attract Latina and Latino voters. When Donald Trump launched his presidential campaign in 2015, he denounced the newcomers who had augmented the nation's fastest-growing demographic group: "When Mexico sends its people they're not sending their best. . . . They're bringing drugs. They're bringing crime. They're rapists. . . . It's coming in from more than just Mexico. It's coming from all over South and Latin America." At first his candidacy seemed like a lark or a joke; party officials criticized his antics and dismissed him as out of step with core conservative values. But Trump almost immediately took the lead in polling among GOP primary voters. Confounding pundits who repeatedly predicted the collapse of his campaign due to one or another of his outrageous statements, Trump won primary after primary, dispatching the party's preferred candidates—a diverse group of political figures that included two Latinos—and effectively clinched the Republican nomination by early May.[42]

The condition of the nation's cities and the place of Latinos in them was a recurrent theme in Trump's presidential campaign, one that he featured conspicuously in every major set-piece venue—from the Republican National Convention to all three presidential debates—and repeatedly at campaign rallies. The candidate constantly reiterated the idea that the nation's cities—and in particular the "inner cities," a term he used incessantly—were disaster areas, places characterized by squalor and riddled with crime. And he proposed that immigrants, especially from Latin America, were substantially to blame. In the first presidential debate, for example, he said: "We have a situation where we have our inner cities, African Americans, Hispanics are living in hell because it's so dangerous. You walk down the street, you get shot." He then blamed gangs, claiming that "in many cases, they're illegally here, illegal immigrants. And they have guns. And they shoot people." Clearly, Trump thought that this would be persuasive campaign material, or he would not have returned to it so often. What it suggested was that he, admittedly like many Americans, was still caught up in an outdated notion of ongoing urban crisis.[43]

More generally, the Trump campaign signaled the end of a period when both political parties rhetorically included Hispanics as an integral part of the nation, as they had done with previous generations of immigrant-stock "white ethnics." Now Hispanics were being ritually defamed alongside Muslims as presumptively different. Trump focused most of his accusations on undocumented Hispanics, endlessly repeating lurid tales of immigrant criminality. But this was clearly not just about legal status. Trump also attacked naturalized US citizens: he actively disparaged Alicia Machado, the Venezuelan-born former Miss Universe, on the basis of her weight, and he singled out Jorge Ramos, the most respected journalist in Latino America, by having a bodyguard push him out of a press conference. Indeed, Latinos could be declared not fully American regardless of citizenship; even the US-born could be deemed somehow foreign. This became clear when Trump publicly criticized Gonzalo Curiel, a federal judge presiding over a class-action lawsuit against Trump University, saying that he could not be impartial because, as Trump put it, "he's a Mexican." Republican officials made concerned noises about statements like these; House Speaker Paul Ryan said that Trump's words about Judge Curiel were "like the textbook definition of a racist comment." But ultimately they fell in line with their candidate and supported Trump.[44]

The results of that November's election were in some ways not so dissimilar from the one that preceded it: more than 90 percent of voters cast their ballots for the same party in 2016 as they had in 2012. Hillary Clinton won the popular vote by three million, a decline from the five-million-vote margin by which Obama had won reelection. Her majority was built on voters in large metropolitan areas, especially voters of color (though surprisingly Latino voter turnout was unchanged from four years before despite widespread expectation of a substantial increase). Clinton ran up massive margins in the leading metro areas—not just in blue states like California, Illinois, and New York, but nationwide—and reduced the Republican advantage dramatically in diverse but traditionally Republican-leaning states like Texas and Arizona.[45]

The electoral college, however, had other ideas. Trump was able to carry key states by boosting turnout among rural whites. He flipped swing states like Florida, Ohio, and Iowa back to the Republican column. And crucially, he won Pennsylvania, Wisconsin, and Michigan, traditionally Democratic states, by a total of fewer than eighty thousand votes. This was a tiny margin in an election with more than 130 million voters participating, but it was enough to claim the majority of the nation's 538 electors and the keys to the White House.

IN THE SHOCKED aftermath of the presidential election of 2016, many observers inquired into the role of immigration in the campaign. Officeholders and pundits on the right saw the outcome as a vindication of their strategy of portraying immigrants as threatening and criminally inclined. And some in the center and even on the left were wary of the role they thought immigration had played among blue-collar white voters. They worried that Democrats had been damaged by the politics of immigration and should try to neutralize the issue by agreeing to limit newcomers or fund more aggressive border enforcement. Many commentators were quick to latch on to the narrative of a Rust Belt revolt or working-class rebellion in which lower-income people economically squeezed by key symptoms of globalization, from corporate offshoring to immigrant labor competition, had declared war on out-of-touch elites who had abandoned these forgotten Americans.[46]

The economic trends that underlay this narrative were all too real. Americans' wages had barely grown since the 1970s even though productivity had increased by 75 percent. For workers toward the bottom of the pay scale, their share of wages had actually *fallen* since the late 1970s. In that decade alone, the United States lost more than thirty million jobs to relocation and disinvestment, and millions more disappeared in subsequent decades as corporations continued to move manufacturing overseas. Meanwhile, economic inequality skyrocketed: in 1965 the top executives of large corporations made about twenty times what their workers earned; by the mid-2010s, those executives took home almost three hundred times the pay of their average employee. Many people thought they saw the implications of these changes in a much-publicized 2015 paper by the Princeton economists Anne Case and Angus Deaton, who found that after 1998 the mortality of middle-aged whites had risen sharply owing to what they called "deaths of despair"—those caused by symptoms often associated with hopelessness, such as alcohol-related disease, illegal drug use, opioid addiction, and suicide. Their findings were often deployed as a way of explaining the motivations of Trump voters.[47]

What too often went unsaid, however, was that these punishing economic conditions had afflicted people of color just as much as whites, and usually much more. The predatory subprime mortgages that had helped crash the global economy, for example, were issued to African Americans and Hispanics almost twice as often as to whites, and their payments were almost one-third higher than what whites with the same credit scores were charged. By 2016 the Federal Reserve found that the median net worth of white Anglo families was more than eight times that of Hispanic families and almost ten times that of black families. Yet no other category of American workers, whether black, Hispanic, Asian American, or Native American, had responded by supporting Trump. On the contrary, blue-collar voters from all these demographics had overwhelmingly cast their ballots for Clinton. They were fewer in number than the white working class, but their contrasting political choices exposed the narrowness of vision that so often underlay the blue-collar revolt thesis.[48]

When public debate after the election focused so heavily on class without adequately noting the effects of race, white people became the default voice of "real" workers. Commentators took the predominant voting pattern of working-class whites and made it seem universal— even though in reality it was unique among an increasingly diverse group of workers. At the same time, too many observers were somehow able to cast the preferences of nonwhite voters as "identity politics." There was even a left-leaning version of this narrative that conjured up a nonexistent past when class-based appeals had somehow transcended racism and neutralized it politically—a past that would have been terrific had it ever existed.[49]

The bottom line of these accounts was always the same: they portrayed the outcome of the election of 2016 as a reasonable response by regular folks. This angle was epitomized by dozens of feature articles about rural communities and interviews with Trump voters.

Newspaper editors and television producers put out so many of these in the year after the election that the "city-based journalist meets country people in a diner" cliché soon became an inside joke among reporters themselves. People who supported Trump's policies got frequent and in-depth coverage, but the immigrants who suffered the most harm from those policies were seldom contacted by journalists—not by English-speaking ones anyway.[50]

These approaches also led observers to stereotype the white working class by treating it as an undifferentiated demographic with a shared response to economic *or* racial imperatives. In fact, there was great difference of opinion among the white working class, as well as considerable willingness among its members to change their preferences from election to election. Sometimes this stereotyping led observers to cite racism as the sole decisive factor while forgetting that Obama had won around 40 percent of white working-class people's votes in 2008. At other points it led to strenuous overemphasis on class-based voting among whites, with commentators overlooking the fact that in 2012 nearly two-thirds of white working-class voters had backed Romney, as clear a representative of predatory capital as one could have produced from central casting.[51]

In the two years after the election, however, more systematic research into voter demography and geography pointed toward other conclusions. Regression analyses of voter data files revealed that economic stress had not been a particularly reliable predictor of votes for Trump, even among non-Hispanic whites. For example, one study found that white voters earning less than the median income were actually *less* supportive of the blustering Republican than whites who enjoyed higher-than-average incomes. And more generally, a wide variety of measures of actual hardship did not correlate with greater support for Trump: people who had lost their jobs in the previous four years were not more likely to back him; neither were those whose incomes had declined or risen too slowly, nor people who thought they had been harmed by international trade. Similarly, Trump did no better than Romney in places with more factories or those with higher unemployment. Meanwhile, studies increasingly found that while income itself did not correlate with a propensity to vote for Trump among whites, other factors did: people who displayed high levels of racial resentment were significantly more likely to have supported him, as were evangelical Protestants. The simple narrative of working-class revolt, in other words, was largely without foundation.[52]

Geography also seemed to make a big difference. In addition to people of color, whites who lived in metropolitan areas with the highest proportion of immigrants were the most likely to cast their ballots for Clinton. Trump's support, by contrast, was concentrated in states with the smallest proportion of immigrants and in the peripheral suburbs, exurbs, and rural areas where most immigrants did *not* live. Trump had triumphed not among those places most transformed or even pressured by foreign-born newcomers—rather, he found the votes he needed among people who lived far away from immigrant gateways. As the columnist and academic Thomas Edsall put it, "Trump's anti-immigrant, racially loaded messages resonated most powerfully among voters living in the least diverse, most racially isolated white communities. . . . Put another way, anger, fear and animosity toward immigrants and minorities was most politically potent in the communities most insulated from these supposed threats." It is also worth noting that these rural voters were least in a position to see that Trump's linkage of immigration and crime was simply not true. After all, they had heard stories of big-city danger during the decades of the urban crisis. How were they to know that crime had plunged, since they'd long ago forsaken the cities?[53]

During its first two years, the Trump administration pushed a series of policies directed against migrants and immigrants—especially those from Latin America and the Caribbean, as well as Africa. The executive branch arbitrarily canceled DACA and ended the temporary protected status of hundreds of thousands of refugees from Haiti and El Salvador, all while the new resident of the Oval Office wondered aloud why there were so many immigrants from what he called "shithole countries" and wished that there could be more from places like Norway. The administration went on to request that Congress slash even *legal* immigration by 40 percent and ordered that the children of Central American refugees legally requesting asylum be separated from their parents—in some cases infants were torn from their mothers—and incarcerated in cages. Meanwhile, white supremacists became more vocal, planning large public events like the violent rally in Charlottesville, Virginia, in August 2017.[54]

In the run-up to the 2018 midterm elections the GOP unhesitatingly adopted Trump's trademark strategy of whipping up fear of immigrants, people of color, and religious minorities. Politicians and right-wing media figures worked together to fabricate an epidemic of immigrant criminality, spending hundreds of millions of advertising dollars to push the claim that the great proximate threat to the nation was immigrants, most notably a group of Central American refugees consisting mostly of women and children. Then these same figures pretended to be surprised when on a single October weekend an armed man attempted to enter an African American church in Louisville, Kentucky, but failed and instead shot a black man and a black woman to death in a supermarket, and a man entered a Pittsburgh synagogue with an assault rifle and three handguns and massacred eleven Jewish worshippers in the worst incident of anti-Semitic violence in the history of the United States—because, the killer wrote on social media just before entering the temple, its chapter of the Hebrew Immigrant Aid Society "likes to bring invaders in that kill our people. I can't sit by and watch my people get slaughtered. Screw your optics, I'm going in."[55]

In many respects this outbreak of xenophobia resembled the one that arose a century prior. Both eras had a vocal segment of the population with a clear loathing for newcomers, whom they imagined as fundamentally different from themselves, and media who were all too ready to feed their paranoia with exaggerated tales of threatening immigrants. The untruthful accusations of immigrant criminality echoed the charges leveled against Italians and others, with cartoons depicting violent Hispanics standing in for cartoons featuring European immigrants arriving with knives and pistols hidden behind their backs, or swimming ashore in the form of rats. The equally fallacious charges that immigrant families were not assimilating as they should were reminiscent of allegations that Jewish newcomers were clannish. Efforts to declare English the official national language reprised state statutes from the 1910s outlawing the teaching of German and other foreign languages to children. The hostility directed at cities and their cosmopolitan culture recalled the congressional investigations of the early twentieth century that emphasized urban immigrant neighborhoods as hotbeds of disease and subversion.

Also similar was the timing relative to major immigration streams. Foreign-born people made up about 13 percent of Americans in 2010, just below their proportion of over 14 percent in 1910. And in both cases, migration had peaked and fallen well before the advent of full-fledged anti-immigrant paranoia: anti-immigrant politicians could inflict a great deal of pain and sorrow on newcomers and foreign residents alike by locking the nation's gates, turning away refugees, tearing apart families, and ramping up enforcement even against un-documented people with no criminal records. What they could no longer do was stop the advent of a more diverse nation, whether that meant a population with more people descended from southern and eastern European immigrants or, a century later, from Latin America and Asia.[56]

But perhaps the most revealing similarity was the fact that in both eras an official policy of abusing and scapegoating immigrants and rejecting refugees was implemented simultaneously with massive tax cuts for the wealthy. The Revenue Acts of 1921, 1924, and 1926 slashed top marginal rates, reduced inheritance taxes, and sheltered investment income. They were echoed by the 2018 tax cuts, which made similar changes that overwhelmingly benefited rich people and corporations. Both sets of tax changes increased already-astonishing levels of economic inequality and further concentrated immense wealth in the hands of a tiny percentage of the nation's population.[57]

There has been one dramatic difference, however, between the present and the past: popular support for immigrants and immigration is widespread and increasing. In the early twentieth century, a clear majority of Americans wanted the figurative drawbridge pulled up against the alien hordes, and they elected officials who did precisely that. In the 2010s, however, this anti-immigration segment represents a clear minority—a fact that has been demonstrated in poll after poll by a variety of metrics. Three-quarters of US adults say that immigration has been good for the country overall as opposed to just one-fifth who think it has brought problems. About 60 percent of Americans say that undocumented people should be allowed to stay in the United States, and an even higher proportion say that they should be offered a path to citizenship. Those numbers rise further in the case of people brought here as children, with about 75 percent favoring their having a way to become citizens. The largest group of Americans, about four in ten, say that the current pace of immigration should be maintained, with just under three in ten saying it should be increased and the same proportion saying it should be reduced. Not only is immigration viewed more favorably, the trend is likely to accelerate because anti-immigrant attitudes are more prevalent in older people; younger people are noticeably more friendly to newcomers. In sum, despite so much hateful noise from the fringe, popular support for newcomers to the United States has been increasing in a nation that is home to nearly forty-five million foreign-born residents and citizens.[58]

TERESO ORTIZ HAD already lived in Oak Cliff for nearly half a century by the summer of 2018, when a Dallas journalist interviewed him about changes in the barrio. Ortiz had seen the neighborhood make its gradual transition from overwhelmingly Anglo to predominantly Latino—indeed, he had been a part of it. But this interview was about a different trend. "It's incredible the amount of money that property is increasing here," Ortiz explained. Developers were offering him enormous sums for the buildings and land of Casa Guanajuato, the community center he opened in 1994. "And you know why they want it? To knock it down and build apartments. That's what they want this for." Residential real estate was only part of the story; commercial development was also heating up. A friend of Ortiz's who owned the nearby Vivero Boxing Gym pointed out a neighborhood mall with a mainly Latino clientele. "You know at Wynnewood Shopping Center, they're gonna sink $30 million into it." He looked on these changes with foreboding about what this would mean for the community and the people who saved it, concluding simply: "It's coming this way."[59]

The prospect of gentrification in Oak Cliff shows that the vexed politics of immigration is not the only threat the barrio faces. The new economic incentives are straightforward: property owners can sell to developers and walk away with hundreds of thousands or even millions of dollars, while tenants face soaring rents and the likelihood of getting pushed out by people with more money. But even owners face other kinds of costs, such as higher property taxes and, more importantly, the loss of their neighbors and their clientele. Ortiz, Vivero, and many other Oak Cliff proprietors understand that they may have to move away. They look at the Bishop Arts District, the core of the gentrifying northern part of the neighborhood, as a harbinger. Hispanic businesspeople had revived commerce in the area, but in the past several years rising rents have driven many of them out. The shops on Jefferson Boulevard remain almost entirely Spanish-speaking, but that may change as more expensive stores, including national chains, seek out the neighborhood's small but very well-to-do professional class.

Others were also raising the alarm. Oak Cliff native Giovanni Valderas garnered widespread media attention beginning in early 2018 with his "Casita Triste" project. Having seen local families thrown out of affordable housing that was quickly demolished, Valderas launched a guerrilla art project in which he placed large piñatas in the form of small houses with sad faces in front of new luxury developments in the barrio. Even some gentrifiers recognized the problem. "I am that gentrification," wrote one in *D Magazine* under the headline "Oak Cliff Is Going to Hell, Thanks to Me." "I am the white woman with a weekly sourdough bread subscription. . . . I am the homeowner with a dumpster and a pallet of hand-glazed tile in the driveway." Having moved in because the neighborhood was "everything the cookie-cutter suburbs were not," she now saw the urgency of "figur[ing] out how to save the neighborhood I love, before it is lost for good."[60]

Chicago's Little Village has mostly avoided gentrification, but only because the well-to-do have focused their attention on other West Side barrios. The largest group of Mexican Americans who were pushed out of the Near West Side in the 1960s moved south and west into the Lower West Side, more commonly known as Pilsen. And that was where mostly white professionals looked for housing as the University of Illinois at Chicago continued to expand in the 1990s and 2000s. Real estate developers, seeing enormous profit potential in the area, started buying up both occupied buildings and empty lots to expand luxury rentals and high-end commercial space. The proportion of Latina and Latino residents in Pilsen began to fall, and the new landlords began to destroy key neighborhood institutions. In 2013, for example, developers bought the Casa Aztlán community center, which they planned to convert into expensive condominiums. But the true desecration came in the summer of 2017, when the new owner suddenly painted over its beautiful Chicano murals, needlessly destroying a beloved barrio landmark and sparking outrage throughout the city.[61]

Now gentrification may be coming to Little Village. In 2017, after a number of demonstrations against rising rents and evictions in the neighborhood, it was announced that a storefront on Cermak Road at the northernmost edge of the barrio would be converted into an up-scale coffee shop. Amid widespread unease, somebody spray-painted "G.T.F.O.L.V [Get the Fuck Out of Little Village]" on the glass building front. As in Oak Cliff, the people of the neighborhood are faced with cross-cutting economic pressures and incentives. According to property records, about 80 percent of Little Village lots have Spanish-surnamed owners; at the same time, however, two-thirds of the neighborhood's overwhelmingly Latina and Latino residents are renters. Owners who are willing to sell their buildings can expect to command high prices—but that will also push out tenants who cannot afford correspondingly higher rents. What may decide the future of Little Village is the attitude of the neighborhood's Latino landlords. Notably, many of them feel proud of their barrio and territorial about maintaining its character; even absentee owners who have moved away are often reluctant to sell their buildings.[62]

The question of gentrification in Oak Cliff and Little Village shows in microcosm some of the subject's broader outlines nationwide. In most of urban America, Latino populations have been increasing and barrios have been expanding. Yet there are many areas where the influx of mostly white and well-to-do householders has unmistakably driven out longtime residents of color, including Latinos. In many cases, real estate developers exploited barrios through marketing campaigns that presented Latino cultures and aesthetics as little more than amenities in upscale real estate products—the effect of which was to push up the cost of living, making it difficult for working-class Latino families to stay in the communities they created. Among the best-known examples are the Mission District in San Francisco, Los Angeles's Boyle Heights, and, most recently, the heavily Hispanic South Bronx in New York City. So even as Latino settlement has expanded, the centers of

Spanish-language enclave economies have been threatened with displacement and erasure.[63]

Other problems have also worsened in recent years. Emma Lozano, the sister of the late labor organizer and political activist Rudy Lozano, is the pastor of the Lincoln United Methodist Church, located just a few blocks beyond the eastern edge of Little Village. Lozano ministers to a congregation of primarily *migrantes* and their families, and her church has long supported immigrant rights in the community and beyond, including through the more than two-decade-old community organization Sin Fronteras (Without Borders). Beginning in the spring of 2016, Lozano's church endured repeated incidents of anti-immigrant vandalism and threats. That November, things got worse. "The moment Donald Trump was elected, our community was filled with fear," she recalled. "These massive deportations that he is threatening, with this administration, are real . . . and we need to put a plan together, how we are going to keep our families together." Most of the people living in and around Little Village were citizens or legal residents, but many families had undocumented relatives who feared that they would be targeted more aggressively for deportation. There was so much apprehension that business in stores on Twenty-Sixth Street dropped off sharply because many customers were scared to go out in public.[64]

There was good reason for these fears in places like Little Village and Oak Cliff. Headlines soon appeared in local newspapers like one from Chicago's Spanish-language *Hoy* (*Today*): "ICE Arrests Another Little Village Immigrant on His Way to Work." The story detailed the apprehension of a forty-four-year-old Mexican-born construction worker who had lived peaceably in the United States for twenty years and was the father of a DACA recipient and two US-born children. His family thought that ICE agents were in the neighborhood hunting for working people by identifying their vehicles. "I think they saw a work truck," their father explained. "I later learned that they grabbed another person driving a truck," a story that *Hoy* also reported. In Dallas, there was a high-profile case in which a deputy from a suburban municipality drove far beyond his jurisdiction to Oak Cliff, apparently to seek out and arrest people he thought might be undocumented. He apprehended a grandmother, whom he handcuffed and turned over to immigration authorities. There had been many deportations before, to be sure—it was for this reason that Univision news anchor Jorge Ramos had called Barack Obama the "Deporter-in-Chief." In response the Obama administration had shifted its approach by using prosecutorial discretion: they focused enforcement on people with warrants for serious crimes, directing agents not to expend limited resources on undocumented people who clearly posed little or no threat to the public.[65]

The Trump administration promptly discarded that policy in 2017. At the same time the White House pressured local law enforcement to cooperate with ICE in identifying, apprehending, and deporting undocumented people, expanding use of the 287(g) program created by the 1996 Illegal Immigration Reform and Immigrant Responsibility Act to deputize local officers for immigration enforcement. Immigration agents also spent more time and resources pursuing long-established community members by treating inconsequential infractions and filing errors as grounds for deportation. This increased apprehensions of individuals with no criminal record, which in turn raised ICE arrest rates to significantly higher levels than at the end of the Obama administration. The Trump administration also directed ICE to seek out stories of immigrant crimes to be used as political propaganda, but agents found little of consequence.[66]

These actions both terrorized immigrant communities and threatened to undo years of progress in crime prevention. Local officials had learned by the 2010s that it was essential to establish good relations with immigrants and their communities and political representatives because increased trust led to more cooperation with law enforcement. And indeed, criminologists confirmed that this kind of immigrant integration helped keep crime rates lower. In 2017, as the White House attacked so-called sanctuary cities for working with immigrant communities, national organizations of mayors and police chiefs issued statements opposing efforts to force police departments to give information to ICE. Undergirding messages like these was widespread concern that Trump's immigration enforcers were recklessly destroying the very factors that had made their cities so much safer for all those living there.[67]

Immigrant barrios across the nation now face two threats—one from people who have money and are drawn to these neighborhoods, the other from people who hold power and are contemptuous of them. Between the slow pressure of gentrification and the quick violence of excessive and capricious immigration enforcement, it remains to be seen whether the very people who saved so many of America's urban neighborhoods can continue to live in them.

CONCLUSION

A BRIEF CONVERSATION TOOK PLACE NOT TOO LONG AGO while José Luis Arroyo was spending time with family in their Chicago barrio. In a moment, it displayed some of the main developments in the longer history of American cities.

"This young Anglo guy comes along, and he says, '*Hola, ¿cómo estás?*' He was speaking Spanish and everything."

"'Fine, thanks. What can I do for you?'"

"He says, 'Well, this was my father's house, and I want to buy it.'"

"I tell him, 'But it's not for sale.'"

"He says, 'But I like it here. I was born here in this neighborhood.'"

"And I ask him, 'So why did you leave?'"

"He says, 'I don't know why my father moved out, he just did.'"

"But we as Latinos think: 'These Americans left because they thought we were going to destroy their neighborhood.' That was the mentality of a lot of people, no?" Arroyo thinks back on the decades since he arrived in Chicago. "When I came from Mexico to this neighborhood, these young peoples' parents got scared and moved away, and they took their children with them. And then these children grew up and became professionals and came to visit the barrio," he muses. "And now they want to move back!"[1]

OVER THE COURSE of half a century, Latino migrants and immigrants revitalized the cities of the United States, saving scores of neighborhoods from abandonment and replenishing the population in many places that would otherwise have continued to empty out. Their earnings and expenditures served as a form of large-scale urban reinvestment. As workers, they powered metropolitan economies by performing essential labor at countless offices, construction sites, restaurants, day cares, farms, hotels, and homes, while also allowing thousands of manufacturing firms to keep production in the United States rather than moving jobs overseas. As tenants and homeowners, they made distressed residential real estate viable again by renting, maintaining, and renovating countless houses and apartment buildings. As entrepreneurs and customers, they opened local businesses and served as a clientele for revived inner-city commerce, bringing activity and energy back to once-hushed streets and sidewalks. In fiscal terms, their economic activity produced a rebound in sales tax receipts, property tax revenues, and utility payments, adding billions of dollars to once-strapped city budgets and allowing municipalities to pay teachers, maintenance workers, firefighters, and police officers—though the proceeds of these greater revenues were not often spent in the neighborhoods that these newcomers had done so much to improve. Immigrants also helped reverse the crime wave of the 1970s and 1980s and make cities safer than at any time since the 1950s. In sum, they remedied a profound national crisis that most observers thought was hopeless.

Today the United States faces new challenges. The most fundamental of these is the fact that the native-born population is not reproducing itself. The birth rate of the American-born is 1.86 children per woman, and to maintain its numbers, a country needs a rate of 2.1. Not a single US-born demographic group makes babies that fast: the rates for African Americans, non-Hispanic whites, Asian Americans, and Latinas range from 1.69 to 2.01. A falling birth rate is by no means a distinctive condition—it is shared by dozens of nations, most of them with developed economies, from Japan to Russia to Italy to Germany. (A few US commentators have proposed a national effort to increase the birth rate among older-stock populations, apparently unaware that twentieth-century precedents like the Nazi Lebensborn and the Soviet Mat'-Geroinia programs amounted to genocide or ethnic cleansing, and that even on their own horrifying terms, both were failures.)[2]

It is only thanks to immigrants and their children that the population of the United States has remained stable. The nation's populace has been growing at less than 1 percent per year—a slightly lower rate than most of the past fifty years and considerably more slow than the half century before that. Nearly fifty-nine million people have arrived since 1965, and recent statistics indicate that immigrants from Latin America account for about 51 percent of the nation's foreign-born population. Of the total increase in the US population since 2000, more than half has been accounted for by Latinos and Latinas, with immigrants gradually surpassed by their native-born children as the primary source of the nation's gains.[3]

Without this growth, the United States would be unable to produce a sufficient number of workers to sustain its economy. A few years ago, the number of working-age Americans who were native-born of native-born parents began to fall. As a result, the nation has relied on immigration to maintain its labor force: the largest group of new workers are the US-born children of immigrants, followed by immigrants themselves. There are just over twenty-seven million foreign-born workers in the United States, and nearly half are from Latin America. Immigrants generally are more likely to be employed than the native-born, but this is especially true among Latin American men, who have the second-highest labor force participation rate among newcomers (after African-born men). US-born Latinas and Latinos are similarly more likely to be in the labor force than the national average. In the years after 2010 Hispanics accounted for more than two-thirds of the growth in the nation's workforce. Latinas and Latinos are also avid consumers, customers, and clients, with a total purchasing power recently estimated at more than $1.5 trillion per year. The Latino share of the nation's gross domestic product has been growing 70 percent faster than the non-Hispanic part, and if it were a country, Latino America would boast the seventh-largest economy in the world.[4]

The same goes for major national institutions. Social Security, for example, is dependent on maintaining a workforce large and productive enough to fund the benefits of retirees, a disproportionately native-born group whose ranks are projected to grow quickly in the years to come. The native-born labor force is not nearly large enough to maintain the required ratio of about three workers per retiree, making the program dependent on immigrants to remain solvent. Naturalized citizens and other authorized workers are the main supporters of the program, but the undocumented also have a distinctive role, since those working with other people's Social Security numbers are paying in for benefits they can never receive; in 2010 the Social Security Administration estimated their contributions at $13 billion per year.[5]

The US military has also come to rely on immigrants to fill its ranks. There are more than 500,000 foreign-born veterans of the nation's armed forces, and over the past two decades about 130,000 foreign-born members of the military have become citizens. Their service includes the Military Accessions Vital to the National Interest program, which was implemented in 2009 to recruit foreign-born people with essential linguistic and medical skills. In recent years Hispanics have been the fastest-growing group among the ranks of enlisted men and women, reaching 12 percent of all active-duty service members, three times their proportion in 1980. This has been especially true for Latinas: as of 2016, their presence among new recruits was higher than their share of the eligible population in all four of the main branches of the military.[6]

IT WAS IN THE CITIES that *migrantes* demonstrated how vital they were to repopulating and revitalizing American communities. Today the problems posed by depopulation are most acute in rural areas, which are afflicted by many of the same symptoms that used to be synonymous with the urban crisis.

In thousands of small cities and towns well away from metropolitan areas, jobs have disappeared, people have moved away, local businesses have closed, and treasuries have run low. If you have driven the nation's state highways and county roads, the sights are already familiar: in communities where people built the kinds of beautiful old main streets, town halls, libraries, and schools that urbanists idealize, you can also see idle mills and warehouses, shuttered businesses and empty sidewalks, conspicuously elderly residents, and silent playgrounds. Places like these are most common in the country's northern tier, but the rural crisis is present in small settlements throughout the

Cinco de Mayo parade, Jefferson Boulevard, 2012. Having done so much to remedy the urban crisis, immigrants and their families have begun to revitalize suburban municipalities and rural areas that have been losing population. Throughout the United States, immigration has become indispensable to our economy, our institutions, and the nation itself. Courtesy Louis DeLuca/*Dallas Morning News.*

nation: about half of America's rural counties lost population in every decade since 1950, with the exodus worsening over the past ten years.[7]

The economic histories of smaller cities and towns have a lot in common. Some were home to manufacturers that powered regional growth during the industrial revolution of the nineteenth century. Others gained jobs in the middle of the twentieth century as companies moved production out of cities to rural areas where the locals were willing to work for lower pay. But all gradually faded as corporations moved on, continuing their quest for cheap labor. Executives ordered newer facilities built in states and localities hostile to organized labor; later they moved those same jobs overseas. Starting in the 1980s, they took advantage of weakened employee protections, crushing the unions that remained and slashing the pay of their workers. All the while, management rewarded themselves with ever-bigger bonuses and stock options even as blue-collar wages stagnated and fell. Now, when there is growth in the economy, it increasingly happens elsewhere: in post–Great Recession Pennsylvania, for example, most of the state, and almost all its rural counties, showed zero net job gains; all the areas with employment growth were centered on the Philadelphia metropolitan area and its surrounding counties. The same is true nationwide as rural economies slow and many begin to shrink.[8]

The social and demographic results could hardly be clearer. Young people, especially those with the most education, have moved away to seek the broader opportunities and higher-paid jobs that have increasingly concentrated in large metro areas. Those left behind are most qualified for precisely the kinds of work that have been on the decline in rural areas owing to deindustrialization and the mechanization of agriculture—so the entry-level jobs available a generation or two ago are simply not there for them. Many young people succumb to hopelessness and addiction; as a result, local employers often face a labor shortage when jobs do open up because too many working-age people have become statistics in the rising rates of death and disability caused by the opioid epidemic. Meanwhile, the people living in these communities are disproportionately older, well beyond their child-raising and working years. Many small cities and towns are threatened with an irreversible downward spiral—disappearing opportunities, fewer residents, empty schools that have to be closed or consolidated, not enough customers for older local businesses, and insufficient revenues to allow the town council to turn things around.

Just as they did earlier in the nation's cities, Latino immigrants have been repopulating small-town America. Some of these *migrantes* previously lived in large cities and decided to move when the wages they earned were no longer enough to meet the cost of fast-rising rents. Others come directly from Central America or Mexico, where local economies have been flooded with cheap corn produced by government-subsidized US agribusinesses, many of which operate in the very same rural areas where the newcomers are arriving. But they all come to work, usually under conditions that are too harsh and for wages that are too low for native-born Americans to accept. Recent surveys have found that about three-quarters of the nation's agricultural workers were born in Latin America and that most of them earn less than eleven dollars an hour; the undocumented take home even less. Immigrant Latinos have also been drawn to meatpacking plants, where the pay is in the same range—half what it was when organized labor was stronger, but far higher than in their countries of birth.[9]

These newcomers to rural America have brought new life to small communities in many of the same ways their predecessors did in big cities. In town centers emptied out by depopulation and outlying shopping strips, *migrantes* patronize the remaining businesses and open their own shops. From Mississippi to Montana, old courthouse squares have come to serve as plazas for growing communities of immigrant Hispanics. They have revitalized local real estate markets by renting apartments, buying homes, and signing leases on small stores. In the process they, along with immigrants from many other parts of the world, pay sales taxes, property taxes, and assorted fees, producing revenue to fund local governments. And their children rush into parks, playgrounds, and above all schools, making it possible for teachers, custodians, administrators, and staff to keep working. Of the nearly 2,300 rural counties in the United States, 94 percent saw increases in Hispanic residents between 1990 and 2000; in more than 600 of these counties, these newcomers stemmed or reversed local population losses. From 2000 to 2010, Latinas and Latinos comprised 58 percent of all population growth in counties outside metropolitan areas.[10]

Immigrants have achieved this under circumstances even more difficult than in the centers of metropolitan areas. The labor they perform is dangerous. Farmhands work with concentrated pesticides and other hazardous chemicals that require specialized safety training, which is not always provided. Meatpacking conglomerates have sped up assembly lines to extract more labor per hour, exposing workers to uncovered chains that can snag hair or clothes and drag them into the machinery; as a result, the industry has one of the highest rates of injury and death, with tens of thousands of workers hurt on the job every year and fatalities occurring every three to four weeks on average. Outside the workplace, Latino immigrants in rural areas report feeling hypervisible because there are so few people of color in these overwhelmingly white and Anglo counties. Because they are paid so little and prefer to remain inconspicuous, they are extremely segregated residentially; many live in their own neighborhoods or in secluded trailer parks because they hope to avoid being picked on by hostile locals or picked up by immigration enforcement.[11]

Most notably and most tragically, these *migrantes* have been made into scapegoats. Politicians blame them for problems that emerged before their arrival and shamelessly try to use them as a distraction from the ongoing plunder of all working people. Voters in the nation's rural areas have provided the most consistent electoral support for officials who incite hatred against immigrants, asylum seekers, and longtime residents. Meanwhile, these same officials hand massive tax cuts to corporations, attempt to slash health and welfare programs that rural communities depend on, and facilitate further attacks on organized labor and worker health and safety. All these actions promise to make the rural crisis worse.[12]

There are people in rural America who see things more clearly. People like the Roman Catholic nuns who put up billboards across the Upper Mississippi River Valley with the words WELCOME THE IMMIGRANT YOU ONCE WERE! superimposed on photographs of recent Latin American newcomers and turn-of-the-century European immigrants. People like the small-town newspaper editors and reporters who have written so movingly about the struggles of immigrants in their towns and the essential role they play in guaranteeing their futures. And most importantly, people like the American-born children of the *migrantes* themselves, who have stayed in their small towns in hopes of becoming the next generation of homeowners, school parents, and public officials.[13]

THE FUTURE OF AMERICA has arrived and is living at the corner of *E pluribus unum* and *Aquí estamos y no nos vamos*. We can see it in the faces of the nation's schoolchildren, our neighbors, our coworkers and caretakers, our baseball players. We can taste it in the food on our plates, which would be empty were it not for the hands that planted and picked the produce, processed the meat and poultry, and worked unseen in restaurant kitchens. And we can hear it in the words of a people who, despite so many years of being dispossessed, overworked, underpaid, and falsely accused, have been among the most optimistic of all Americans.[14]

There are those who look on this future with apprehension. Some are concerned with the continuing challenge of making a nation out of disparate peoples; others plainly want to close the borders and bar the gates to those they imagine as fundamentally different from themselves. But they need not fear. America has been here before: in every century, alarmists have tried to stir up hostility against immigrants whom they warned would destroy our traditions, radicalize our body politic, mongrelize our population, wreck our economy, or balkanize our culture. Even the defamation is secondhand: every accusation now leveled against newcomers who are allegedly alien, unassimilable, clannish, or criminal is borrowed from past episodes of anti-immigrant panic. But these dark prognostications have always been wrong, as time and again the nation has renewed itself and moved forward. And as for the defamation, immigration opponents should remember that unless they are Native Americans, plenty of people in the past didn't much like the looks of their newly arrived ancestors either.[15]

A nation of immigrants is what we have been and it is what we shall remain. The United States is home to by far the largest population of foreign-born people on the planet. These newcomers traveled far to get here, and many faced danger on the journey. They trusted us to be the nation we said we were for all those years: a city on a hill, the North Star, the last best hope on the earth, Mother of Exiles. Perhaps the new Americans of today can help us recognize ourselves in them, for they are just the latest in a proud lineage of migrants seeking their promised land.[16]

ACKNOWLEDGMENTS

The origins of this book reach back to 1991, when I helped my mom move out of her New York City apartment to a town house just across the county line from the Bronx. One morning as we were unpacking, she realized that her computer printer needed a new daisy wheel, so we telephoned an office supply store in the next town over. The person who picked up the phone answered in Spanish, so my mother switched over and asked about the printer component in her native language. The voice on the line replied that they didn't have any. "So there's no office supply store there?" she asked. "No," came the amused response, "just us Mexicans!"

Mom and I had a good laugh about the exchange. It wasn't that hearing Spanish was so unexpected. After all, one could easily get by in New York without a word of English. Half of my mother's friends when I was growing up were from Spain or Cuba, and a number of my classmates were Puerto Rican—the kids I ate lunch with at a neighbor's house because the school had no cafeteria and our mothers worked, the girl who defeated me in the final round of the elementary school spelling bee, the boy who masterminded my Friday night gaming group in junior high. But it was a surprise to happen on a group of Mexican immigrants in suburbia. A little over a quarter century later, however, few people can even remember what a daisy wheel is, and Westchester County is 25 percent Latino.

The more proximate origins of this book date to the sixteen years I spent at the University of New Mexico, which included the happiest of my life so far.

I want to thank the people of the Land of Enchantment who shared them with me, especially Beth Bailey, Durwood Ball, Judy Bieber, Adam Blahut, Melissa Bokovoy, Luis Campos, Sarah Cornell, Jon Davis-Secord, Sarah Davis-Secord, David Farber, Dan Feller, Tiffany Florvil, Manuel García y Griego, Linda Hall, Heather Hawkins, Paul Hutton, Alexandro Jara, Nancy López, Erika Monahan, Gregory Montoya-Mora, the late and dearly missed Tim Moy, Anna Nogar, Dave Prior, Noel Pugach, Darren Raspa, Barbara Reyes, Mike Ryan, Enrique Sanabria, Virginia Scharff, Jane Slaughter, Jason Scott Smith, the late and invariably funny Frank Szasz, Sam Truett, María Velez, and Chris Wilson. Sincerest gratitude to and admiration for UNM's administrators, Dana Ellison, Helen Ferguson, Yolanda Martínez, Hazel Mendoza-Jayme, and Barbara Wafer, without whom everything would have ground to a halt in short order. Thanks also to Dean Mark Peceny for making it possible for me to accept a fellowship for the 2015–2016 academic year.

The Princeton University–Andrew W. Mellon Foundation Initiative in Architecture, Urbanism, and the Humanities made possible a year of uninterrupted thinking, conceptualization, and writing that immeasurably improved the project. My sincerest thanks to principal investigators Alison Isenberg and Bruno Carvalho; coordinator Aaron Shkuda; fellows Pedro Alonso, Elsa Devienne, and Joseph Heathcott; and affiliated scholars M. Christine Boyer, Purcell Carson, Beatriz Colomina, Mario Gandelsonas, Joshua Guild, Johana Londoño, Sarah Lynn López, Rosina Lozano, and Keeanga-Yamahtta Taylor. That year I also benefited tremendously from conversations with Richard Anderson, Sarah Coleman, Dylan Gottlieb, Dirk Hartog, Kevin Kruse, Beth Lew-Williams, Marta Tienda, and Julian Zelizer.

New colleagues and friends at the Pennsylvania State University have been so very generous in welcoming us to our new home. Heartfelt thanks to David Atwill, Jyoti Balachandran, Amira Rose Davis and Michael Davis, Sonia DeLuca Fernández, Lori Ginzberg, Amy Greenberg, Borja Gutiérrez, Ronnie Hsia, John Iceland, Michael Kulikowski, Melissa Landrau Vega, Jacob Lee, Dan Letwin, Eva Maczuga, Sally McMurry, Mary Mendoza, Zach Morgan, Lise Nelson, On-Cho Ng, John Ochoa, Mariana Ortega, Manuel Ostos, Victoria Prewitt-Rodríguez, Matthew Restall, Sophie De Schaepdrijver, María Schmidt,

Tatiana Seijas, Judith Sierra-Rivera, Christina Snyder, Ellen Stroud, Paul Taylor, Lyvia Valentín-Pagano, Shoba Wadhia, Susan Welch, Melissa Wright, and Cynthia Young. In the office, Lynn Hepfer, Shantelle Jones-Williams, Keshia Kennelley, Cody Miller, and Denise Poorman keep everything running. Special thanks to the students in my Introduction to Latina/o Studies classes and the Penn State Latino Caucus, especially Nicole Jara Andrade, Heidy Canales, Yesenia Cano, Camila Cepeda, Ronald Johnson Contreras, Jerrel Laureano, Rubi García Manzo, Fernando Muñoz, Eileen Peralta, Kira Robbins, Tomás Sánchez, and Jorge Zurita-Coronado.

This book would have been impossible without libraries, archives, and scholarly centers. In Chicago, I thank the Chicago Public Library's Harold Washington Library, the University of Illinois at Chicago's Richard J. Daley Library, the DePaul University Libraries, the Newberry Seminar in Borderlands and Latino Studies, the Northwestern University Libraries, the Loyola University Libraries, and the University of Chicago's Katz Center for Mexican Studies and its Center for the Study of Race, Politics, and Culture. Special thanks to Michelle Nickerson, Ben Johnson, and Tobias for letting my family spend so much time in their house, *y muchísimas gracias* to Franco Bavoni Escobedo for his extraordinary skill with the oral histories. In Dallas, thanks to the Dallas Mexican American Historical League, the Dallas Municipal Archives, especially John H. Slate, and the staff of the Dallas Public Library's Texas/Dallas History and Archives Division. Special appreciation goes to Southern Methodist University's William P. Clements Center for Southwest Studies, especially Ben Johnson, Ruth Ann Elmore, Andrea Boardman, and the late, great David Weber for giving me an office in Dallas Hall. In Mexico, thanks to the Secretaría de Desarrollo Social for being so generous with spreadsheets and other information, and to Erika Pani and the Colegio de México for inviting me across the border to speak in the fall of 2016.

Over the course of the ten years spent on this project, a great many people have read chapters, weighed claims, provided digital help, and generally aided my work as a scholar. In addition to those already mentioned, *saludos y abrazos* to Gabriela Arredondo, Daniel Arreola, Llana Barber, Leandro Benmergui, Nathan Connolly, Eduardo

Contreras, Kathleen Conzen, Raúl Coronado, Bill Disbrow, Bob Fairbanks, Lilia Fernández, Leon Fink, Brian Goldstein, Richard Griswold del Castillo, Richard Harris, Ken Jackson, Nancy Kwak, Mary Mendoza, Carl Nightingale, Mercedes Olivera, Margaret O'Mara, Darwin Payne, Pedro Regalado, James Rojas, Beryl Satter, Arijit Sen, Vanna Slaughter, Giovanni Valderas, Camilo Vergara, Sol Villasana, and Domenic Vitiello. Tom Sugrue has offered years of invaluable advice and encouragement and friendship that have made all the difference. My sincerest thanks to Matt Garcia, the first scholar in the field of Latino history to referee this material, for his faith in the project and advocacy for it. *Un montón de gracias* to the brave souls who read the entire manuscript: Xóchitl Bada, Brian Behnken, Gerry Cadava, Ramón Gutiérrez, Ben Johnson, Ari Kelman, Rosina Lozano, Michelle Nickerson, Juliet D. Samroengraja, and Amanda Seligman.

Les agradezco sinceramente y profundamente a todos los migrantes que concedieron entrevistas para este libro. Espero que este tomo represente adecuadamente sus esfuerzos durante varias décadas, y que honre todo lo que ustedes han logrado a través del vasto continente americano.

I am grateful to the National Endowment for the Humanities for its support of this project in the form of a Faculty Research Grant and the opportunity to join the freshman class of the Public Scholar Program. Without the Endowment's help, *Barrio America* might never have gotten off the ground and certainly would have taken longer to complete.

When the time came to find a publisher, Ellen Levine, my friend of many decades and literary agent of the past fifteen years, brought her world-class talents to the task of helping me write the book proposal and negotiated the deal with her customary combination of élan and sangfroid. The team at Basic Books has been just fantastic. Dan Gerstle acquired the book and provided two rounds of enormously perceptive and constructive edits. Brandon Proia's line edit greatly improved the flow of argumentation and guided me away from some of my less elegant formulations. Designer Ann Kirchner created a book cover more beautiful and compelling than I could have dreamed. Kaitlin Carruthers-Busser and Alex Colston put all the pieces together, from illustrations to permissions to captions to proofs. And Lara Heimert oversaw the entire process, shepherding the project from draft to better draft to transmission to copyedits to proofs to book, always making sure I understood what was next and exactly how much time I had, or did not have, to obsess over the text, and invariably inspiring absolute confidence that everybody at Basic Books was every bit as incredibly talented as everyone said.

Finally and most importantly, my family. My deepest love and thanks to my parents, Cecilia Sandoval Londoño and Ivan Károly Strausz, for their courage, determination, wisdom, intellectualism, and *cariño absoluto*. To los Cahill, from the centenarian matriarch to the most recent arrivals, thank you so much for being the kind of tight-knit, loud, eccentric, lovable, forward-thinking, and welcoming family that I'm so happy to be a part of. My deepest gratitude to my late Tío Alvaro and his wife, Jewell, who arrived on the scene to tell me the full history of los Sandoval and reveal that what I thought was a tiny clan actually included scores of *primos*, many in Colombia and others themselves *migrantes* across the world, all part of a family epic like something out of Gabriel García Márquez. All my love and devotion and passion and admiration to my brilliant bride, Cathleen Cahill, who makes every day funnier and cleverer and more enjoyable, and who has helped me work through this project from the beginning while also being one-third of the best reasons to just put it down and come out of my office. And to our greatest joys in the universe, Lincoln and Cecilia, I promise to stop stealing your colored pencils and pens to mark up my drafts, and to start taking you to all those places you've been asking about.

NOTES

INTRODUCTION

1. Description based on author's photographs of the federation's clubhouse and archive taken March 6, 2013.

2. Manuel Rodela Rodríguez oral history, recorded March 6, 2013, digital audio file (in the author's possession). I have translated into English the quotations from this and other interviews in Spanish. I began recording the oral histories for this book in Spanish and English in Dallas and Chicago in January-June 2010, March 2013, and July 2015. In 2015 and 2016, with the support of the Princeton-Mellon Initiative in Architecture, Urbanism, and the Humanities, I worked with Xóchitl Bada of the University of Illinois at Chicago and Franco Bavoni Escobedo, then at the University of Chicago, to record additional oral histories as part of our Mexican Hometown Association Oral History Project. Many of these oral histories are archived at the Newberry Library and available at https://www .newberry.org/mexican-hometown-association-oral-histories.

3. Manuel Rodela Rodríguez oral history.

4. Manuel Rodela Rodríguez oral history; newspaper clipping from federation archive.

5. Stuart Dybek, *The Coast of Chicago* (New York: Knopf, 1990), 130–131, 162.

6. Grover Lewis, "Farewell to Cracker Eden," *Texas Monthly* (September 1992); reprinted in Jan Reid and W. K. Stratton, eds., *Splendor in the Short Grass: The Grover Lewis Reader* (Austin: University of Texas Press, 2005).

7. Robert A. Beauregard, *Voices of Decline: The Postwar Fate of US Cities*, 2nd ed. (New York: Routledge, 2003), 118, 148, 230.

8. Beauregard, *Voices of Decline*, 230; *New York Times* editorial board, "Echoes of the Superpredator," *New York Times*, April 13, 2014; John J. DiIulio, "The Coming of the Superpredators," *Weekly Standard*, November 27, 1995; Laurie Garrett, "Murder by Teens Has Soared since '85," *New York Newsday*, February 18, 1995; William J. Bennett, John J. DiIulio, and John P. Walters, *Body Count: Moral Poverty . . . and How to Win America's War against Crime and Drugs* (New York: Simon & Schuster, 1996).

9. For an earlier version of this argument with the full scholarly apparatus, see A. K. Sandoval-Strausz, "Latino Landscapes: Postwar Cities and the Transnational Origins of a New Urban America," *Journal of American History* 101 (December 2014): 804–831. On the urban recovery, see Edward Glaeser, *Triumph of the City: How Our Greatest Invention Makes Us Richer, Smarter, Greener, Healthier, and Happier* (New York: Penguin, 2011); Richard Florida, *The Rise of the Creative Class—Revisited* (New York: Basic Books, 2012); Bruce Katz and Jennifer Bradley, *The Metropolitan Revolution: How Cities and Metros Are Fixing Our Broken Politics and Fragile Economy* (Washington, DC:

Brookings Institution Press, 2013); Domenic Vitiello and Thomas J. Sugrue, "Immigration and the New American Metropolis," in Domenic Vitiello and Thomas J. Sugrue, eds., *Immigration and Metropolitan Revitalization in the United States* (Philadelphia: University of Pennsylvania Press, 2017).

10. A. K. Sandoval-Strausz, "Migrantes, Negocios, and Infraestructura: Transnational Urban Revitalization in Chicago," in Vitiello and Sugrue, *Immigration and Metropolitan Revitalization*, 133–153; Jennifer Halperin, "Hispanics in Illinois: Neither Party Can Afford to Take Them for Granted," *Illinois Issues* (December 1994); Brigid Sweeney (text) and Manuel Martinez (photos), "Little Village, Big Business," *Crain's Chicago Business*, September 25, 2015, http://www.chicagobusiness.com/section/little-village; Alejandro Escalona, "Pride in 26th Street Marred by Reality of Little Village Violence," *Chicago Sun-Times*, March 21, 2012, 8.

11. Sandoval-Strausz, "Latino Landscapes"; William McKenzie, "Five Focus Neighborhoods, One Year Later; The Heart of Oak Cliff: Progress on Education Encouraging, but Retail Options Are Still Inadequate," *Dallas Morning News*, September 20, 2009, 4P–5P.

12. Sandra Cisneros, *The House on Mango Street* (Houston: Arte Público Press, 1984); Oscar Hijuelos, *The Mambo Kings Play Songs of Love* (New York: Farrar, Straus and Giroux, 1989); Julia Alvarez, *How the García Girls Lost Their Accents* (Chapel Hill, NC: Algonquin, 1991); Cristina García, *Dreaming in Cuban* (New York: Random House, 1992); Jaime Manrique, *Latin Moon in Manhattan* (New York: St. Martin's Press, 1992).

13. See, for example, Tom Wolfe, *The Bonfire of the Vanities* (New York: Farrar, Straus and Giroux, 1987); Richard Price, *Clockers* (New York: Houghton Mifflin, 1992); Brent Staples, *Parallel Time: Growing Up in Black and White* (New York: Pantheon, 1994).

14. Kenneth T. Jackson, *Crabgrass Frontier: The Suburbanization of the United States* (New York: Oxford University Press, 1985), 283; Eric H. Monkkonen, *America Becomes Urban: The Development of US Cities and Towns, 1780–1980* (Berkeley: University of California Press, 1988), 70–72. The urban crisis was for at least thirty years the leading subject in urban history, and most scholarly monographs touched on more than one aspect of the decline of cities; this brief introduction to a vast historiography referenced throughout this book is thus offered as a heuristic. Jackson, *Crabgrass Frontier*; Thomas J. Sugrue, *The Origins of the Urban Crisis: Race and Inequality in Postwar Detroit* (Princeton, NJ: Princeton University Press, 1996); Becky M. Nicolaides, *My Blue Heaven: Life and Politics in the Working-Class Suburbs of Los Angeles, 1920–1965* (Chicago: University of Chicago Press, 2002); Matthew D. Lassiter, *The Silent Majority: Suburban Politics in the Sunbelt South* (Princeton, NJ: Princeton University Press, 2007).

15. Barry Bluestone and Bennett Harrison, *The Deindustrialization of America: Plant Closings, Community Abandonment, and the Dismantling of Basic Industry* (New York: Basic Books, 1983); Sugrue, *The Origins of the Urban Crisis*; Jefferson Cowie, *Capital Moves: RCA's Seventy-Year Quest for Cheap Labor* (Ithaca, NY: Cornell University Press, 1999); Alison Isenberg, *Downtown America: A History of the Place and the People Who Made It* (Chicago: University of Chicago Press, 2005).

16. Ester R. Fuchs, *Mayors and Money: Fiscal Policy in New York and Chicago* (Chicago: University of Chicago Press, 1992); Joshua B. Freeman, *Working-Class New York: Life and Labor since World War II* (New York: New Press, 2000); Gerald E. Frug and David J. Barron, *City Bound: How States Stifle Urban Innovation* (Ithaca, NY: Cornell University Press, 2008); Clayton P. Gillette, "Dictatorships for Democracy: Takeovers of Financially Failed Cities," New York University Law and Economics Working Papers 369 (2014); Kim Phillips-Fein, *Fear City: New York's Fiscal Crisis and the Rise of Austerity Politics* (New York: Metropolitan Books, 2017).

17. Federal Bureau of Investigation, Uniform Crime Reports, at https://www.ucrdatatool.gov/; Patrick Sharkey, *Uneasy Peace: The Great Crime Decline, the Renewal of City Life, and the Next War on Violence* (New York: W. W. Norton, 2018). For more detail, see Chapter 4.

18. Arnold Hirsch, *Making the Second Ghetto: Race and Housing in Chicago, 1940–1960* (New York: Cambridge University Press, 1983); William Julius Wilson, *The Truly Disadvantaged: The Inner City, the Underclass, and Public Policy* (Chicago: University of Chicago Press, 1987); Michael B. Katz, *The Undeserving Poor: From the War on Poverty to the War on Welfare* (New York: Pantheon, 1990); Jennifer Halperin, "Here Comes the Neighborhood," *Illinois Issues* (January 1996); Robin D. G. Kelley, *Yo' Mama's Disfunktional! Fighting the Culture Wars in Urban America* (Boston: Beacon Press, 1997); Douglas S. Massey and Robert J. Sampson, *The Moynihan Report Revisited: Lessons and Reflections after Four Decades* (SAGE Publications, 2009); Khalil Gibran Muhammad, *The Condemnation of Blackness: Race, Crime, and the Making of Modern Urban America* (Cambridge, MA: Harvard University Press, 2010); Gil Troy, *Morning in America: How Ronald Reagan Invented the 1980s* (Princeton, NJ: Princeton University Press, 2013), 236. The "culture of poverty" discussion mostly addressed African American poverty, but its origins were in much-criticized anthropological works on Mexicans and Puerto Ricans: Oscar Lewis, *Five Families: Mexican Case Studies in the Culture of Poverty* (New York: Basic Books, 1959), and *La Vida: A Puerto Rican Family in the Culture of Poverty: San Juan and New York* (New York: Random House, 1966).

19. Saskia Sassen, *Cities in a World Economy*, 5th ed. (Thousand Oaks, CA: SAGE Publications, 2019); Richard Florida, *The Rise of the Creative Class* (New York: Basic Books, 2002); Jan K. Brueckner and Stuart S. Rosenthal, "Gentrification and Neighborhood Housing Cycles: Will America's Future Downtowns Be Rich?," *Review of Economics and Statistics* 91 (2009): 725–743; Victor Couture and Jessie Handbury, "Urban Revival in America, 2000 to 2010," National Bureau of Economic Research Working Paper 24084 (November 2017). See Chapter 11 for a more detailed discussion.

20. On the chronology behind the "world cities" globalization narrative, see Sandoval-Strausz, "Migrantes, Negocios, and Infraestructura."

21. The South Lawndale neighborhood, more commonly called Little Village, is one of Chicago's seventy-seven officially designated community areas. The statistics in this book are drawn from the decennial census tracts that correspond most closely to the official boundaries. For 2010 those tracts are 3005–3009, 3011, 3012, 3016, 3017.1, 3017.2, 3018.1, 3018.2, 3018.3, 8305, 8407, 8408, and 8417; for censuses before 2010, tract 3014 is included. I have excluded the southeasternmost tract, 8435, because nearly its entire population are inmates at the Cook County Jail, are not representative of the area's demographics, and are not local community members in the conventional sense. For Oak Cliff, to maintain a consistent frame of reference I have used the outer boundaries of the neighborhood in 1950. For 2010 those tracts are 20, 42.01, 42.02, 43–48, 50–53, 62, 63.01, 63.02, 64.01, 64.02, 65.01, 65.02, 67–69, and 199. In contemporary usage this is usually called North Oak Cliff, which distinguishes it from the more recently developed areas to the south and west. Population figures from the US Census Bureau's American FactFinder are available at https://factfinder.census.gov/faces/nav/jsf/pages/index.xhtml. The statistical material in this book is derived from US Census Bureau data accessed through the original printed volumes or via Social Explorer or both; nearly all these figures were then checked by Kendra A. Taylor, a specialist who accessed the census using a different geodata program. Note that this book's analysis of Latino population growth and influence should be seen as a cautious, conservative estimate because it is based on US Census counts, and researchers inside and outside the Census Bureau have found that it has substantially undercounted Hispanics. See Frank D. Bean and Marta Tienda, *The Hispanic Population of the United States* (Thousand Oaks, CA: SAGE Publications, 1987), 57–59; Peter Hainer, Catherine Hines, Elizabeth Martin, and Gary Shapiro, "Research on Improving Coverage in Household Surveys," Proceedings of the Fourth Annual Research Conference (Washington, DC: Bureau of the Census, 1988), 513–539.

22. US Census Bureau, American FactFinder.

23. The phrase "the seeds of the future city" is borrowed from Gabriel García Márquez, *El Amor en los tiempos del cólera* [*Love in the Time of Cholera*] (Bogotá: Editorial Oveja Negra, 1985), 5.

24. William Faulkner, *Light in August* (New York: Smith & Haas, 1932).

25. Félix M. Padilla, *Latino Ethnic Consciousness: The Case of Mexican Americans and Puerto Ricans in Chicago* (South Bend, IN: University of Notre Dame Press, 1995); Suzanne Oboler, *Ethnic Labels, Latino Lives: Identity and the Politics of (Re)Presentation in the United States* (Minneapolis: University of Minnesota Press, 1995); Clara E. Rodríguez, *Changing Race: Latinos, the Census, and the History of Ethnicity* (New York: New York University Press, 2000); Arlene Dávila, *Latinos, Inc.: The Marketing and Making of a People* (Berkeley: University of California Press, 2001); Cristina Beltrán, *The Trouble with Unity: Latino Politics and the Creation of Identity* (New York: Oxford University Press, 2010); Natalia Molina, *How Race Is Made in America: Immigration, Citizenship, and the Historical Power of Racial Scripts* (Berkeley: University of California Press, 2013).

26. G. Cristina Mora, *Making Hispanics: How Activists, Bureaucrats, and Media Constructed a New American* (Chicago: University of Chicago Press, 2014); Dávila, *Latinos, Inc.*

27. Jan Lin, *Reconstructing Chinatown: Ethnic Enclave, Global Change* (Minneapolis: University of Minnesota Press, 1998), and *The Power of Urban Ethnic Places* (New York: Routledge, 2010); Wei Li, ed., *From Urban Enclave to Ethnic Suburb: New Asian Communities in Pacific Rim Countries* (Honolulu: University of Hawai'i Press, 2006); David H. Kaplan and Wei Li, eds., *Landscapes of the Ethnic Economy* (Lanham, MD: Rowman & Littlefield, 2006); Marilynn S. Johnson, *The New Bostonians: How Immigrants Have Transformed the Metro Region since the 1960s* (Amherst: University of Massachusetts Press, 2015).

28. James R. Grossman, *Land of Hope: Chicago, Black Southerners, and the Great Migration* (Chicago: University of Chicago Press, 1989); Isabel Wilkerson, *The Warmth of Other Suns: The Epic Story of America's Great Migration* (New York: Random House, 2010).

29. For a fuller discussion of urban history and transnational history, see A. K. Sandoval-Strausz and Nancy H. Kwak, eds., *Making Cities Global: The Transnational Turn in Urban History* (Philadelphia: University of Pennsylvania Press, 2018).

30. Camilo José Vergara, *American Ruins* (New York: Monacelli Press, 1999); Dan Austin and Sean Doerr, *Lost Detroit: Behind the Motor City's Majestic Ruins* (Charlotte, NC: History Press, 2010); Matthew Christopher, *Abandoned America: The Age of Consequences* (Versailles: Jonglez, 2014); Dora Apel, *Beautiful Terrible Ruins: Detroit and the Anxiety of Decline* (New Brunswick, NJ: Rutgers University Press, 2016). For an interpretation of Latino urban history in a smaller city within the urban crisis narrative, see Llana Barber, *Latino City: Immigration and Urban Crisis in Lawrence, Massachusetts, 1945–2000* (Chapel Hill: University of North Carolina Press, 2017).

31. Louise Año Nuevo Kerr Papers, Special Collections, University Library, University of Illinois at Chicago, José Luis Loera oral history, recorded March 31 and April 1, 1996, and Rosina Magaña oral history, recorded March 17, 1996; Tereso Ortiz oral history, recorded July 12, 2010, digital audio file (in the author's possession).

CHAPTER 1: NEIGHBORHOODS ON THE EDGE

1. Richard A. Dolejs oral history, recorded July 20, 2015, digital audio file (in the author's possession).

2. Richard A. Dolejs clippings scrapbooks.

3. *Chicago Community Fact Book* 1960, 74.

4. *Chicago Community Fact Book* 1950, 126; *Chicago Community Fact Book* 1960, 75.

5. These were among the many demographic categories used in the 1960 census.

6. St. Clair Drake and Horace Cayton Jr., *Black Metropolis* (New York: Harcourt, Brace & World, 1945); Arnold R. Hirsch, *Making the Second Ghetto: Race and Housing in Chicago, 1940–1960* (New York: Cambridge University Press, 1983); James R. Grossman, *Land of Hope: Chicago, Black Southerners, and the Great Migration* (Chicago: University of Chicago Press, 1989).

7. On the Ross family, see Beryl Satter, *Family Properties: How the Struggle over Race and Real Estate Transformed Chicago and Urban America* (New York: Metropolitan Books, 2009), 247–248.

8. Gladys Priddy, "Sharp Changes Mark 2 Areas of Lawndale," *Chicago Tribune*, December 26, 1954, W3; Amanda Seligman, *Block by Block: Neighborhoods and Public Policy on Chicago's West Side* (Chicago: University of Chicago Press, 2005), 12–22, 79–87; Amanda I. Seligman, "North Lawndale," in James R. Grossman, Ann Durkin Keating, and Janice L. Reiff, eds., *Encyclopedia of Chicago* (Chicago: University of Chicago Press, 2004), 575–576.

9. Satter, *Family Properties*, 141–144.

10. James Nyka, "Lawndale-Crawford Unit Steps Up Pace in Battle with Blight," *Chicago Daily Tribune*, February 7, 1960, W1.

11. Lilia Fernández, *Brown in the Windy City: Mexicans and Puerto Ricans in Postwar Chicago* (Chicago: University of Chicago Press, 2012), 219, and chap. 6 generally; James Ritch, "Open Housing Foes to Testify on Bills," *Chicago Tribune*, August 6, 1963, 7; "Hear Foes of Open Occupancy," *Chicago Tribune*, August 7, 1963, 1; Ted Coleman, "Racist Open Housing Foes Plan to March," *Chicago Daily Defender*, September 10, 1963, 1.

12. "Holman Accuses Despres of 'Show' for Negroes," *Chicago Daily Defender*, March 28, 1961, 2; "Says Catholic Clergy Opposes New Housing," *Chicago Daily Defender*, August 7, 1963, 5; "Hear Foes," *Chicago Tribune*, August 7, 1963, 1. On Beauharnais, see "White Circle's Charter Voided for Racial Hate," *Chicago Tribune*, June 30, 1950, B11.

13. "Racists to March on City Hall," *Chicago Daily Defender*, September 10, 1963, 1.

14. Satter, *Family Properties*, 97; "Says Catholic Clergy Opposes New Housing," *Chicago Daily Defender*, 5; Coleman, "Racist Open Housing Foes," *Chicago Daily Defender*, 1; Fernández, *Brown in the Windy City*, 214–219. See also Al Camarillo, "Cities of Color: The New Racial Frontier in California's Minority-Majority Cities," *Pacific Historical Review* (2006).

15. Richard J. Dolejs oral history.

16. Richard A. Dolejs clippings scrapbooks.

17. Arthur Siddon, "South Lawndale Ponders Name Change," *Chicago Tribune*, June 14, 1964, W1; "Dick Dolejs, the Man behind the Name 'Little Village,'" *Lawndale News*, May 30, 1991, 1; Richard A. Dolejs oral history; Richard A. Dolejs clippings scrapbooks.

18. Pierre Guilmant, "W. Side Committeewoman Target of Ouster Drive," *Chicago Daily Defender*, July 19, 1969, 1.

19. Año Nuevo Kerr Papers, Guadalupe Lozano oral history, recorded March 17, 1996.

20. Guadalupe Lozano oral history; US Census Bureau, "US Censuses of Population and Housing: 1960: Census Tracts, Chicago, Ill., Standard Metropolitan Statistical Area: Final Report PHC(1)-26" (Washington, DC: US Government Printing Office, 1962), table P-1 (hereafter 1960 Census, Chicago).

21. Guadalupe Lozano oral history; Fernández, *Brown in the Windy City*, 216.

22. Fernández, *Brown in the Windy City*, 216.

23. Guadalupe Lozano oral history.

24. Fernández, *Brown in the Windy City*, 213; Guadalupe Lozano oral history.

25. Parade image from Richard A. Dolejs clippings scrapbooks.

26. Richard A. Dolejs clippings scrapbooks.

27. Ignacio M. García, ¡Viva Kennedy!: Mexican Americans in Search of Camelot (College Station: Texas A&M University Press, 2000); Mike Amezcua, "Beautiful Urbanism: Gender, Landscape, and Contestation in Latino Chicago's Age of Urban Renewal," *Journal of American History* 104 (2017), 114–117.

28. Richard A. Dolejs oral history.

29. Richard A. Dolejs oral history; Richard J. Dolejs clippings scrapbooks.

30. Josefina Velasco, interview with the author, December 12, 2015.

31. This was not a conspiracy in the technical sense of an unlawful plan carried out with others, since before 1968 discrimination in housing was not illegal in most jurisdictions.

32. Jackson, *Crabgrass Frontier*, 208; Thomas J. Sugrue, *Sweet Land of Liberty: The Forgotten Struggle for Civil Rights in the North* (New York: Random House, 2008), 203; Satter, *Family Properties*, 248. For more detail on the segregation of cities, see Chapter 3, esp. notes 38–44.

33. Satter, *Family Properties*, 3–13, and generally.

34. Satter, *Family Properties*, 248.

35. Satter, *Family Properties*, 152–154, and generally.

36. Satter, *Family Properties*, 93, 233–271, 365.

37. Richard A. Dolejs oral history.

38. Richard A. Dolejs oral history. It had long been rumored that real estate operators and others in South Lawndale had done precisely this: see Fernández, *Brown in the Windy City*, 220–221.

39. On Latinos as white, see Laura E. Gómez, *Manifest Destinies: The Making of the Mexican American Race* (New York: New York University Press, 2007); Ian F. Haney López, *White by Law: The Legal Construction of Race* (New York: New York University Press, 1996); Benjamin Heber Johnson, "The Cosmic Race in Texas: Racial Fusion, White Supremacy, and Civil Rights Politics," *Journal of American History* 98 (September 2011): 404–419. See also Chapter 3.

40. Guadalupe Lozano transcript, 14–15.

41. Guadalupe Lozano transcript, 14.

42. Guadalupe Lozano transcript, 14–18; Gordon Mantler, *Power to the Poor: Black-Brown Coalition and the Fight for Economic Justice, 1960–1974* (Chapel Hill: University of North Carolina Press, 2013).

43. 1960 Census, Chicago, table P-1; US Census Bureau, Census of Population and Housing: 1970. Census Tracts, Final Report PHC(1)-43, Chicago, Ill. SMSA (Washington, DC: US Government Printing Office, 1972), table P-1 (hereafter 1970 Census, Chicago).

44. Fernández, *Brown in the Windy City*, 218.

45. US Census Bureau, "US Censuses of Population and Housing: 1960: Census Tracts: Dallas, Tex., Standard Metropolitan Statistical Area: Final Report PHC(1)-34" (Washington, DC: US Government Printing Office, 1962), table P-1 (hereafter 1960 Census, Dallas). The 1940 and 1950 censuses found similar proportions: US Census Bureau, "Sixteenth Census of the United States: 1940: Population and Housing: Statistics for Census Tracts: Dallas, Texas, and Adjacent Area" (Washington, DC: US Government Printing Office, 1942) (hereafter 1940 Census, Dallas); US Census Bureau, "Census of Population: 1950, vol. III, Census Tract Statistics, Part 1: Akron-Dayton" (Washington, DC: US Government Printing Office, 1953) (hereafter 1950 Census, Dallas). The 1960 racial boundary is revealed by the sharp demographic contrast with tracts 34, 41, 49, and 89. See also Robert B. Fairbanks, *For the City as a Whole: Planning, Politics, and the Public Interest in Dallas, Texas, 1900–1965* (Columbus: Ohio State University Press, 1998), 29–30, 150–152, 191.

46. NO DOGS, NO NEGROES, NO MEXICANS: Lonestar Restaurant Association, Dallas, Texas. Printed JIM CROW sign, n.d., Black History Collection, Library of Congress; David Montejano, *Anglos and Mexicans in the Making of Texas, 1836–1986* (Austin: University of Texas Press, 1987); Brian D. Behnken, *Fighting Their Own Battles: Mexican Americans, African Americans, and the Struggle for Civil Rights in Texas* (Chapel Hill: University of North Carolina Press, 2011).

47. Anita Martínez, interview with the author, July 23, 2010, digital audio file (in the author's possession); Mary Jane Conde, interview with the author, March 23, 2010; Douglas K. Miller, *Indians on the Move: Native American Mobility and Urbanization in the Twentieth Century* (Chapel Hill: University of North Carolina Press, 2019).

48. Fairbanks, *For the City as a Whole*, chap. 6; W. Marvin Dulaney, "Whatever Happened to the Civil Rights Movement in Dallas, Texas?," in John Dittmer, George C. Wright, and W. Marvin Dulaney, eds., *Essays on the American Civil Rights Movement* (College Station: Texas A&M University Press, 1993), 66–95; Brian D. Behnken, "The 'Dallas Way': Protest, Response, and the Civil Rights Experience in Big D and Beyond," *Southwestern Historical Quarterly* 111, no. 1 (2007): 1–29.

49. Jim Schutze, *The Accommodation: The Politics of Race in an American City* (Secaucus, NJ: Citadel Press, 1986), 115.

50. William R. Carmack and Theodore Freedman, *Dallas, Texas: Factors Affecting School Desegregation* (New York: Anti-Defamation League of B'Nai B'rith, 1963), 20–21; Schutze, *The Accommodation*, 12–19, 110–115.

51. Behnken, "The 'Dallas Way,'" 11.

52. Dulaney, "Whatever Happened," 78–83; Behnken, "The 'Dallas Way,'" 11–12, 17.

53. Dulaney, "Whatever Happened," 76–78; Behnken, *Fighting Their Own Battles*, 49–55.

54. Borders v. Rippey, 184 F. Supp. 402 (N.D. Tex. 1960).

55. Borders v. Rippey, 184 F. Supp. 402 (N.D. Tex. 1960).

56. Dallas Citizens Council, *Dallas at the Crossroads* (1961), Texas/Dallas History and Archives Division, Dallas Public Library; Behnken, "The 'Dallas Way,'" 15–16.

57. See introduction, note 18, and Thomas J. Sugrue, "Racial Romanticism," *Democracy: A Journal of Ideas* 13 (2009).

58. Marta Tienda and Faith Mitchell, eds., *Multiple Origins, Uncertain Destinies: Hispanics and the American Future* (Washington, DC: National Academies Press, 2006), 23; US Census Bureau, "Current Population Survey: Annual Social and Economic Supplement, 2016: Table 1: Population by Sex, Age, Hispanic Origin, and Race."

CHAPTER 2: THE CITY OF YESTERYEAR

1. Campbell Gibson, Population Division, U.S. Census Bureau, "Population of the 100 Largest Cities and Other Urban Places in the United States: 1790 to 1990," Population Division Working Paper 27 (June 1998); Monkkonen, *America Becomes Urban*, 72.

2. Histories of the urban United States include Arthur Meier Schlesinger, *The Rise of the City, 1878–1898* (New York: Macmillan, 1933); Howard P. Chudacoff, Judith E. Smith, and Peter C. Baldwin, *The Evolution of American Urban History* (New York: Pearson, 2005, 2010, 2016); and Jon C. Teaford, *The Twentieth-Century American City: Problems, Promise, and Reality* (Baltimore: Johns Hopkins University Press, 1986, 1993, 2016). See also Michael Johns, *Moment of Grace: The American City in the 1950s* (Berkeley: University of California Press, 2003).

3. William Cronon, *Nature's Metropolis: Chicago and the Great West* (New York: W. W. Norton, 1991), 23–27; Michael P. Conzen and Kay J. Carr, eds., *The Illinois &*

Michigan Canal National Heritage Corridor: A Guide to Its History and Sources (DeKalb: Northern Illinois University Press, 1988).

4. Cronon, *Nature's Metropolis*, parts I and II.

5. Cronon, *Nature's Metropolis*, chap. 7.

6. Dominic Pacyga, *Chicago: A Biography* (Chicago: University of Chicago Press, 2009), chap. 6; Andrew J. Diamond, *Chicago: City on the Make: Power and Inequality in a Modern City* (Berkeley: University of California Press, 2017), 23–24. See also John Bodnar, *The Transplanted: A History of Immigrants in Urban America* (Bloomington: Indiana University Press, 1985).

7. Gabriela F. Arredondo, *Mexican Chicago: Race, Identity, and Nation, 1916–1939* (Urbana: University of Illinois Press, 2008), chap. 1; Michael Innis-Jiménez, *Steel Barrio: The Great Mexican Migration to South Chicago, 1915–1940* (New York: New York University Press, 2013), chaps. 1 and 7.

8. Perry R. Duis, "No Time for Privacy: World War II and Chicago's Families," in Lewis E. Erenberg and Susan E. Hirsch, eds., *The War and American Culture: Society and Consciousness during World War II* (Chicago: University of Chicago Press, 1996); Pacyga, *Chicago*, 273–285.

9. Ernest W. Burgess and Charles Newcomb, eds., *Census Data of the City of Chicago, 1920* (Chicago: University of Chicago Press, 1931), 605, 608–609; Martin Bulmer, *The Chicago School of Sociology: Institutionalization, Diversity, and the Rise of Sociological Research* (Chicago: University of Chicago Press, 1984); Andrew Abbott, *Department and Discipline: Chicago Sociology at One Hundred* (Chicago: University of Chicago Press, 1999).

10. Burgess and Newcomb, *City of Chicago*, map 2: "Local Communities of Chicago"; Louis Wirth and Margaret Furez, eds., *Local Community Fact Book 1938* (Chicago: Chicago Recreation Commission, 1938), "Area 30: South Lawndale."

11. Mark R. Wilson et al., "Dictionary of Leading Chicago Businesses, 1820–2000," entries for "International Harvester Co." and "Western Electric Co.," both in Grossman, Keating, and Reiff, *Encyclopedia of Chicago*, 930, 950; Sanborn Map Company, "Insurance Maps of Chicago, Illinois, circa 1901–1950" (Pelham, NY, c. 1910–c. 1950), Newberry Library, Chicago.

12. Wirth and Furez, *Local Community Fact Book 1938*, "Area 30: South Lawndale."

13. Wirth and Furez, *Local Community Fact Book 1938*, "Area 30: South Lawndale."

14. John M. Allswang, *A House for All Peoples: Ethnic Politics in Chicago, 1890–1936* (Lexington: University Press of Kentucky, 1971), 105–107.

15. Gerald Mayer, "Union Membership Trends in the United States" (Washington, DC: Congressional Research Service, 2004), appendix A, table A1; US Census Bureau, "Census of Population: 1950, vol. III, Census Tract Statistics, Part 1: Akron-Dayton" (Washington, DC: US Government Printing Office, 1953), table 2 (hereafter 1950 Census, Chicago).

16. Philip M. Hauser and Evelyn M. Kitagawa, eds., *Local Community Fact Book for Chicago 1950* (Chicago: University of Chicago Press, 1951), 126–129; *Chicago Criss-Cross Directory* (Schaumburg, IL: Haines & Company, 1950), "26th W."

17. Nelson Lichtenstein, *State of the Union: A Century of American Labor*, rev. ed. (Princeton, NJ: Princeton University Press, 2002), 56–59; Jefferson Cowie, *Stayin' Alive: The 1970s and the Last Days of the Working Class* (New York: New Press, 2010), 28–29; Ruth Rosen, *The World Split Open: How the Modern Women's Movement Changed America* (New York: Viking, 2000), 80.

18. Michelle M. Nickerson and Darren Dochuk, eds., *Sunbelt Rising: The Politics of Space, Place, and Region* (Philadelphia: University of Pennsylvania Press, 2011), 4.

19. Gibson, "Population of the 100 Largest Cities and Other Urban Places."

20. Fairbanks, *For the City as a Whole*, chap. 1.

21. Manuel García y Griego and Roberto R. Calderón, *Más Allá del Rio Bravo: Breve Historia Mexicana del Norte de Texas* (Ciudad de México: Secretaría de Relaciones Exteriores, 2013), 33–35.

22. Fairbanks, *For the City as a Whole*, chap. 2; Gibson, "Population of the 100 Largest Cities and Other Urban Places."

23. Ann R. Markusen, Peter Hall, Scott Campbell, and Sabina Deitrick, *The Rise of the Gunbelt: The Military Remapping of Industrial America* (New York: Oxford University Press, 1991).

24. Fairbanks, *For the City as a Whole*, 138–139.

25. Fairbanks, *For the City as a Whole*, 140–141.

26. Fairbanks, *For the City as a Whole*, 171–172.

27. Bruce J. Schulman, *From Cotton Belt to Sunbelt: Federal Policy, Economic Development, and the Transformation of the South, 1938–1980* (New York: Oxford University Press, 1991); Elizabeth Tandy Shermer, *Sunbelt Capitalism: Phoenix and the Transformation of American Politics* (Philadelphia: University of Pennsylvania Press, 2013).

28. Andrew Needham, *Power Lines: Phoenix and the Making of the Modern Southwest* (Princeton, NJ: Princeton University Press, 2014), 61–62.

29. On the changing landscape, see Christopher B. Leinberger, *The Option of Urbanism: Investing in a New American Dream* (Washington, DC: Island Press, 2007).

30. Gibson, "Population of the 100 Largest Cities and Other Urban Places."

31. Bill Minutaglio and Holly Williams, *The Hidden City, Oak Cliff* (Dallas: Elmwood Press, 1990), 46; Patricia Evridge Hill, *Dallas: The Making of a Modern City* (Austin: University of Texas Press, 1996), 6–7.

32. "NWIRP Dallas: A World War II and Cold War Aircraft and Missile Manufacturing Plant," n.d., National Park Service Form 10-900-a, National Register of Historic Places Continuation Sheet (in the author's possession); "Dallas Builder Cites Growth of Oak Cliff," *Dallas Times Herald*, March 23, 1957, 1B; "Oak Cliff Getting New Families Each Month," *Dallas Morning News*, April 4, 1957, pt. 1, 18.

33. "CXA-4-84," January 28, 1942, photograph, 1942 Section G8a, Aerial Photograph Collection, J. Erik Jonsson Central Library, Dallas Public Library; "DJU- 4G-7," December 11, 1950, photograph, 1950 Section G8, ibid.

34. Oak Cliff folders, Vertical Files, Texas/Dallas History and Archives Division, Jonsson Central Library; Alan C. Elliott, Patricia K. Summey, and Gayla Brooks Kokel, *Images of America: Oak Cliff* (Charleston, SC: Arcadia Publishing, 2009); *Cole Directory for Dallas and Vicinity, 1950*, 1102.

35. *Cole Directory for Dallas and Vicinity, 1950*, 1102; *Cole Directory for Dallas and Vicinity, 1961*, 269; "Towering Over the Cliff Skyline," *Dallas Times Herald*, August 16, 1964, 8.

36. 1950 Census, Dallas, tables 1 and 2.

37. Tienda and Mitchell, *Multiple Origins, Uncertain Destinies*, 19; Campbell Gibson and Kay Jung, "Historical Census Statistics on Population Totals by Race, 1790 to 1990, and by Hispanic Origin, 1970 to 1990, for the United States, Regions, Divisions, and States," Population Division Working Paper 56 (U.S. Census Bureau, February 2002).

38. Chudacoff, Smith, and Baldwin, *Evolution of American Urban History*, 157–158; Gilbert G. Gonzales, *Labor and Community: Mexican Citrus Worker Villages in a Southern California County, 1900–1950* (Urbana: University of Illinois Press, 1994), 2. See, generally, Montejano, *Anglos and Mexicans in the Making of Texas*; Ramón A. Gutiérrez, *When Jesus Came, the Corn Mothers Went Away: Marriage, Sexuality, and Power in New*

Mexico, 1588–1846 (Palo Alto, CA: Stanford University Press, 1991); David J. Weber, *The Spanish Frontier in North America* (New Haven, CT: Yale University Press, 1994); Neil Foley, *White Scourge: Mexicans, Blacks, and Poor Whites in Texas Cotton Culture* (Berkeley: University of California Press, 1999); María E. Montoya, *Translating Property: The Maxwell Land Grant and the Contest over Land in the American West, 1840–1900* (Berkeley: University of California Press, 2002).

39. Chris Wilson, *The Myth of Santa Fe: Creating a Modern Regional Tradition* (Albuquerque: University of New Mexico Press, 1997); Miguel Gandert and Enrique Lamadrid, *Nuevo Mexico Profundo: Rituals of an Indo-Hispano Homeland* (Albuquerque: Museum of New Mexico Press, 2000); Daniel Arreola, *Tejano South Texas: A Mexican American Cultural Province* (Austin: University of Texas Press, 2002); Chris Wilson and Stefanos Polyzoides, eds., and Miguel Gandert, photography, *The Plazas of New Mexico* (San Antonio: Trinity University Press, 2011); Rosina Lozano, *An American Language: The History of Spanish in the United States* (Berkeley: University of California Press, 2018).

40. Albert Camarillo, *Chicanos in a Changing Society: From Mexican Pueblos to American Barrios, 1850–1930* (Cambridge, MA: Harvard University Press, 1979); Vicki L. Ruiz, *Cannery Women, Cannery Lives: Mexican Women, Unionization, and the California Food Processing Industry, 1930–1950* (Albuquerque: University of New Mexico Press, 1987); Gonzales, *Labor and Community*, 1; Matt Garcia, *A World of Its Own: Race, Labor, and Citrus in the Making of Greater Los Angeles* (Chapel Hill: University of North Carolina Press, 2001), 14. See also Cybelle Fox, *Three Worlds of Relief: Race, Immigration, and the American Welfare State, from the Progressive Era to the New Deal* (Princeton, NJ: Princeton University Press, 2012).

41. Camarillo, *Chicanos in a Changing Society*; Richard Griswold del Castillo, *La Familia: Chicano Families in the Urban Southwest, 1848 to the Present* (South Bend: University of Notre Dame Press, 1991); George J. Sánchez, *Becoming Mexican American: Ethnicity, Culture, and Identity in Chicano Los Angeles, 1900–1945* (New York: Oxford University Press, 1993); Zaragoza Vargas, *Proletarians of the North: A History of Mexican Industrial Workers in Detroit and the Midwest, 1917–1933* (Berkeley: University of California Press, 1993); Monica Perales, *Smeltertown: Making and Remembering a Southwest Border Community* (Chapel Hill: University of North Carolina Press, 2010); Marc S. Rodriguez, *The Tejano Diaspora: Mexican Americanism and Ethnic Politics in Texas and Wisconsin* (Chapel Hill: University of North Carolina Press, 2011); Natalia Molina, *Fit to Be Citizens? Public Health and Race in Los Angeles, 1879–1939* (Berkeley: University of California Press, 2006).

42. Bean and Tienda, *Hispanic Population*, 84–88; Maggie Rivas-Rodriguez, ed., *Mexican Americans and World War II* (Austin: University of Texas Press, 2005); Elizabeth R. Escobedo, *From Coveralls to Zoot Suits: The Lives of Mexican American Women on the World War II Home Front* (Chapel Hill: University of North Carolina Press, 2013); Neil Foley, *Mexicans in the Making of America* (Cambridge, MA: Harvard University Press, 2014), chap. 4; Zaragoza Vargas, *Labor Rights Are Civil Rights: Mexican American Workers in Twentieth-Century America* (Princeton, NJ: Princeton University Press, 2005).

43. US Census Bureau, "US Censuses of Population and Housing: 1960: Final Report PHC(1)-82, Census Tracts: Los Angeles–Long Beach Standard Metropolitan Statistical Area" (Washington, DC: US Government Printing Office, 1962), table P-1, enumerated under "Spanish surname."

44. Census tract data; Hauser and Kitagawa, *Local Community Fact Book for Chicago 1950*, 126–127; 1950 Census, Chicago; 1960 Census, Chicago.

45. Mike Royko, *Boss: Richard J. Daley of Chicago* (New York: Dutton, 1971), 25.

46. Lewis, "Cracker Eden."

47. "Trolleys to Give Way to Buses in January," *Dallas Morning News*, September 15, 1955, sect. 1, p. 20.

48. "Oak Cliff Rejects Beer," *Dallas Morning News*, December 16, 1956, 1.

49. Beauregard, *Voices of Decline*, chap. 5.

CHAPTER 3: "CRACKER EDEN"

1. Lewis, "Cracker Eden."

2. Stuart Dybek, *Childhood and Other Neighborhoods* (New York: Viking, 1980), 30; Dybek, *Coast of Chicago*, 17. See also Carlo Rotella, *October Cities: The Redevelopment of Urban Literature* (Berkeley: University of California Press, 1998).

3. The literature on urban segregation is vast. Exemplary works include Hirsch, *Making the Second Ghetto*; Jackson, *Crabgrass Frontier*; David Freund, *Colored Property: State Policy and White Racial Politics in Suburban America* (Chicago: University of Chicago Press, 2007); Satter, *Family Properties*; N. D. B. Connolly, *A World More Concrete: Real Estate and the Making of Jim Crow South Florida* (Chicago: University of Chicago Press, 2014). See Chapter 3, esp. notes 38–44.

4. William H. Wilson, *Hamilton Park: A Planned Black Community in Dallas* (Baltimore: Johns Hopkins University Press, 1998), 21–31.

5. Darwin Payne, *Big D: Triumphs and Troubles of an American Supercity in the 20th Century* (Dallas: Three Forks Press, 1991), 70–71, 93–95, 200–203; Kenneth T. Jackson, *The Ku Klux Klan in the City, 1915–1930* (New York: Oxford University Press, 1967), chap. 6; Fairbanks, *For the City as a Whole*, 62, 94.

6. Payne, *Big D*, 72, 185–188.

7. Michael Phillips, *White Metropolis: Race, Ethnicity, and Religion in Dallas, 1841–2001* (Austin: University of Texas Press, 2006), 149–152; Payne, *Big D*, 254–256.

8. On Dallas's civil rights history, see Chapter 1, notes 48–49; on Atlanta and the urban South, see Lassiter, *The Silent Majority*, and Kevin M. Kruse, *White Flight: Atlanta and the Making of Modern Conservatism* (Princeton, NJ: Princeton University Press, 2005).

9. William H. Wilson, "'This Negro Housing Matter': The Search for a Viable African-American Residential Subdivision in Dallas, 1945–1950," *Legacies* 6, no. 2 (1994): 28–40.

10. Schutze, *The Accommodation*, 13–26; Payne, *Big D*, 258.

11. Foley, *White Scourge*, 13; Robert B. Fairbanks, *The War on Slums in the Southwest: Public Housing and Slum Clearance in Texas, Arizona, and New Mexico, 1935–1965* (Philadelphia: Temple University Press, 2014), 43, 99; City of Dallas, Department of Public Works, map with "Negro Section" and "Mexican Section," n.d., Dallas History and Archives Division, J. Erik Jonsson Central Library, Dallas.

12. Sol Villasana, *Dallas's Little Mexico* (Charleston, SC: Arcadia Publishing, 2011); Payne, *Big D*, 203–204; Harvey J. Graff, *The Dallas Myth: The Making and Unmaking of an American City* (Minneapolis: University of Minnesota Press, 2008), 182–184; Anita Martínez oral history, recorded July 22, 2010, digital audio file (in the author's possession); 1960 Census, Dallas, table P-1.

13. "Alamo Street Located in Little Mexico in Dallas, Texas" (between 1948 and 1955), call number PA87-1/4-45A, Dallas History and Archives Division, J. Erik Jonsson Central Library, Dallas.

14. Shirley Achor, *Mexican Americans in a Dallas Barrio* (Tucson: University of Arizona Press, 1978).

15. Geraldo L. Cadava, *Standing on Common Ground: The Making of a Sunbelt Borderland* (Cambridge, MA: Harvard University Press, 2013), 46–47, 60; Needham, *Power Lines*, 85–86; 1960 Census, Dallas, table P-1.

16. Schutze, *The Accommodation*, 70–72; Phillips, *White Metropolis*, 125–126, 131–132. For a superb summation of the racial positioning of Hispanics in Texas, see Johnson, "The Cosmic Race in Texas."

17. *Dallas Morning News*, "Mothers' Club to Hold Fiesta" (October 25, 1950), "Mexican Fiesta Decorations for Spinster Dinner Party" (June 23, 1955), "Mexican Fiesta for Sorority Group" (Feb 5, 1958), and "Mexican Party to Fete Couple" (July 24, 1958); Brian Eugenio Herrera, *Latin Numbers: Playing Latino in Twentieth-Century US Popular Performance* (Ann Arbor: University of Michigan Press, 2015); Gustavo Pérez Firmat, *Life on the Hyphen: The Cuban-American Way* (Austin: University of Texas Press, 1995), chaps. 1, 2.

18. Drake and Cayton, *Black Metropolis*; Hirsch, *Making the Second Ghetto*; Grossman, *Land of Hope*, chap. 3; Satter, *Family Properties*.

19. Drake and Cayton, *Black Metropolis* (1945), 195, 213, 319, chap. 19.

20. St. Clair Drake and Horace Cayton Jr., *Black Metropolis*, updated ed. (New York: Harper & Row, 1961), 812–816.

21. Alan Ehrenhalt, *The Lost City: The Forgotten Virtue of Community in America* (New York: Basic Books, 1995), 145; Allan Spear, *Black Chicago: The Making of a Negro Ghetto* (Chicago: University of Chicago Press, 1976), 24; Joe Trotter, *Black Milwaukee: The Making of an Industrial Proletariat, 1915–1945* (Urbana: University of Illinois Press, 2006), 179; Sugrue, *The Origins of the Urban Crisis*, 54.

22. Satter, *Family Properties*, 60–63.

23. Drake and Cayton, *Black Metropolis* (1945), 202–204, fig. 9; Ehrenhalt, *The Lost City*, 141–142.

24. Drake and Cayton, *Black Metropolis* (1945), 111, 201–202, 742; Ehrenhalt, *The Lost City*, 142–143. The sorrow, frustration, and anger that resulted were vividly evoked by the writer and poet Gwendolyn Brooks in *A Street in Bronzeville* (New York: Harper & Brothers, 1945) and *Maud Martha* (New York: Harper & Brothers, 1953).

25. Drake and Cayton, *Black Metropolis* (1945), 201.

26. Satter, *Family Properties*, 29.

27. Gladys Priddy, "Sharp Changes Mark 2 Areas of Lawndale," *Chicago Tribune*, December 26, 1954, W3; Ronald Kotulak, "South Side Super Civic Group Seen," *Chicago Tribune*, October 25, 1959, S1; Seligman, *Block by Block*, 79–87.

28. *Chicago Daily Tribune*, December 27, 1942, 22; Hirsch, *Making the Second Ghetto*, 21, 230, 239.

29. Arnold R. Hirsch, "Massive Resistance in the Urban North: Trumbull Park, Chicago, 1953–1966," *Journal of American History* 82 (1995): 522–550.

30. Drake and Cayton, *Black Metropolis* (1961), 818.

31. 1950 Census, Chicago, table 1; 1960 Census, Chicago, table P-1.

32. Fernández, *Brown in the Windy City*, chap. 2; Arredondo, *Mexican Chicago*, 39–45.

33. Amezcua, "Beautiful Urbanism," 97–119.

34. Gina M. Perez, *The Near Northwest Side Story: Migration, Displacement, and Puerto Rican Families* (Berkeley: University of California Press, 2004), 68–79. See also Ana Y. Ramos-Zayas, *National Performances: The Politics of Class, Race, and Space in Puerto Rican Chicago* (Chicago: University of Chicago Press, 2003).

35. Drake and Cayton, *Black Metropolis* (1945), 175; Amezcua, "Beautiful Urbanism," 105.

36. Alexandro Jara, "The Cross Tattoo Arrests," seminar paper, University of New Mexico, 2012; Lorrin Thomas, "Puerto Ricans in the United States," Oxford Research Encyclopedia of American History, September 2015, DOI: 10.1093/acrefore/9780199329175.013.32.

37. Drake and Cayton, *Black Metropolis* (1945), 9, 175, 180, 206, 578; Fernández, *Brown in the Windy City*, 77–81; Dybek, *Childhood and Other Neighborhoods*, 107.

38. Numerous examples are easily visible using Social Explorer (socialexplorer.com), which maps historical census data, including tract-level populations by race and ethnicity. On segregation in the North versus the South, see Sugrue, *Sweet Land of Liberty*.

39. The historical literature on metropolitan segregation is vast. For an introduction, see Hirsch, *Making the Second Ghetto*; Jackson, *Crabgrass Frontier*; Becky M. Nicolaides, *My Blue Heaven: Life and Politics in the Working-Class Suburbs of Los Angeles, 1920–1965* (Chicago: University of Chicago Press, 2002); Robert O. Self, *American Babylon: Race and the Struggle for Postwar Oakland* (Princeton, NJ: Princeton University Press, 2003); Seligman, *Block by Block*; Kruse, *White Flight*; Lassiter, *The Silent Majority*; Kevin M. Kruse and Thomas J. Sugrue, eds., *The New Suburban History* (Chicago: University of Chicago Press, 2006); Freund, *Colored Property*; Sugrue, *Sweet Land of Liberty*; Satter, *Family Properties*; Keeanga-Yamahtta Taylor, "Back Story to the Neoliberal Moment: Race, Taxes, and the Political Economy of Black Urban Housing in the 1960s," *Souls: A Critical Journal of Black Politics, Culture, and Society* (July–December 2012): 185–206; Connolly, *A World More Concrete*.

40. See, for example, Satter, *Family Properties*, 70–72; Hirsch, "Massive Resistance." See also Raymond A. Mohl, "The Second Ghetto and the 'Infiltration Theory' in Urban Real Estate, 1940–1960," in June Manning Thomas and Marsha Ritzdorf, eds., *Urban Planning and the African American Community: In the Shadows* (Thousand Oaks, CA: SAGE Publications, 1997), 58–74.

41. Freund, *Colored Property*, 92–95.

42. Jackson, *Crabgrass Frontier*, 241–243; Fairbanks, *For the City as a Whole*, 29–30.

43. Jackson, *Crabgrass Frontier*, chap. 11. For recent research and visualization of these practices, see Richard Marciano, Nathan Connolly, Rob Nelson, and LaDale Winling, "Mapping Inequality: Redlining in the United States," https://dcicblog.umd.edu/mapping-inequality/. See also Chapter 4, note 17.

44. Kruse, *White Flight*, 42–51; Thomas J. Sugrue, "Crabgrass-Roots Politics: Race, Rights, and the Reaction Against Liberalism in the Urban North, 1940–1965," *Journal of American History* 82 (1995); Hirsch, "Massive Resistance in the Urban North."

45. Haney López, *White by Law*; David Montejano, "The Beating of Private Aguirre: A Story about West Texas during World War II," in Maggie Rivas-Rodriguez, ed., *Mexican Americans and World War II* (Austin: University of Texas Press, 2005); Eric V. Meeks, *Border Citizens: The Making of Indians, Mexicans, and Anglos in Arizona* (Austin: University of Texas Press, 2007); David Montejano, *Quixote's Soldiers: A Local History of the Chicano Movement* (Austin: University of Texas Press, 2010); Cecilia Márquez, "The Strange Career of Juan Crow: Latino/as and the Making of the US South, 1940–2000," PhD thesis, University of Virginia (2016).

46. Mauricio Mazón, *The Zoot Suit Riots: The Psychology of Symbolic Annihilation* (Austin: University of Texas Press, 1984); Edward Escobar, *Race, Police, and the Making of a Political Identity: Mexican Americans and the Los Angeles Police Department, 1900–1945* (Berkeley: University of California Press, 1999); Luis Alvarez, *The Power of the Zoot: Youth Culture and Resistance during World War II* (Berkeley: University of California Press, 2008).

47. Bean and Tienda, *Hispanic Population*, 84–88.

CHAPTER 4: BUILDING THE URBAN CRISIS

1. Miguel Villa and Jorge Rodriguez, "Demographic Trends in Latin America's Metropolises, 1950–1990," in Alan Gilbert, ed., *The Mega-City in Latin America* (New York: United Nations University Press, 1996).

2. Beauregard, *Voices of Decline*, chap. 5.

3. Bluestone and Harrison, *The Deindustrialization of America*; Cowie, *Capital Moves*; Jefferson Cowie and Joseph Heathcott, *Beyond the Ruins: The Meanings of Deindustrialization* (Ithaca, NY: ILR Press, 2003).

4. Cowie, *Capital Moves*.

5. Mark H. Rose, *Interstate: Express Highway Politics, 1939–1989* (Lawrence: University of Kansas Press, 1979); Owen Gutfreund, *Twentieth-Century Sprawl: Highways and the Reshaping of the American Landscape* (New York: Oxford University Press, 2004); Shane Hamilton, *Trucking Country: The Road to America's Wal-Mart Economy* (Princeton, NJ: Princeton University Press, 2012).

6. Aaron Shkuda, *The Lofts of Soho: Gentrification, Art, and Industry in New York, 1950–1980* (Chicago: University of Chicago Press, 2016), 27.

7. 1943 Chicago Plan Commission map, fig. 12 in Fernández, *Brown in the Windy City*; 1950 Census, Chicago, table 3.

8. Listed as "craftsmen, foremen, and kindred workers" and "operatives and kindred workers"; US Census Bureau, "Sixteenth Census of the United States: 1940: Population and Housing: Statistics for Census Tracts: Chicago, Ill. (Washington, DC: US Government Printing Office, 1942) (hereafter 1940 Census, Chicago), table 3; 1950 Census, Chicago, table 2; 1960 Census, Chicago, table P-3: all for the Chicago tracts indicated in introduction, note 21; Barbara Marsh, *A Corporate Tragedy: The Agony of International Harvester Company* (New York: Doubleday, 1985).

9. Listed as "craftsmen, foremen, and kindred workers" and "operatives and kindred workers," 1940 Census, Dallas, table 3; 1950 Census, Dallas, table 2; 1960 Census, Dallas, table P-3: all for the Dallas tracts indicated in introduction, note 21.

10. Seligman, *Block by Block*, 73–79; Chicago Plan Commission, *Master Plan of Residential Land Use of Chicago* (Chicago: City of Chicago, 1943), table 5.

11. Seligman, *Block by Block*, 73–79; Hirsch, *Making the Second Ghetto*, chap. 5.

12. Fairbanks, *For the City as a Whole*, 126–135; Fairbanks, *The War on Slums in the Southwest*, 88–89, 218n79.

13. Fairbanks, *For the City as a Whole*, 126–135; Fairbanks, *The War on Slums in the Southwest*, 131–132.

14. On renewal policies, see Samuel Zipp, *Manhattan Projects: The Rise and Fall of Urban Renewal in Cold War New York* (New York: Oxford University Press, 2010); Christopher Klemek, *The Transatlantic Collapse of Urban Renewal: Postwar Urbanism from New York to Berlin* (Chicago: University of Chicago Press, 2011); Elihu Rubin, *Insuring the City: The Prudential Center and the Postwar Urban Landscape* (New Haven, CT: Yale University Press, 2012); Francesca Russello Ammon, *Bulldozer: Demolition and Clearance of the Postwar Landscape* (New Haven, CT: Yale University Press, 2016).

15. Thomas W. Hanchett, "The Other 'Subsidized Housing': Federal Aid to Suburbanization," *Journal of Housing and Community Development* 58 (2001): 18–29.

16. Jackson, *Crabgrass Frontier*, chap. 11.

17. Jackson, *Crabgrass Frontier*, 205–218; Hanchett, "The Other 'Subsidized Housing,'" 22. See also David Freund, "Marketing the Free Market: State Intervention and the Politics of Prosperity in Metropolitan America," in Kruse and Sugrue, *The New Suburban History*, 11–32. For recent research and visualization of these practices, see Marciano et al., "Mapping Inequality."

18. Jackson, *Crabgrass Frontier*, 206; Hanchett, "The Other 'Subsidized Housing,'" 44–46.

19. Mark Gelfand, *A Nation of Cities: The Federal Government and Urban America, 1933–1965* (New York: Oxford University Press, 1975), 106–110; Wendell E. Pritchett, "The 'Public Menace' of Blight: Urban Renewal and the Private Uses of Eminent Domain,"

Yale Journal of Law and Public Policy 21 (2003); Klemek, *The Transatlantic Collapse of Urban Renewal*, 3–6, 143–148.

20. Chicago alderman Ben Lewis quoted in Arnold R. Hirsch, "Chicago: The Cook County Democratic Organization and the Dilemma of Race, 1931–1987," in Richard M. Bernard, ed., *Snowbelt Cities: Metropolitan Politics in the Northeast and Midwest since World War II* (Bloomington: Indiana University Press, 1990), 80; Ammon, *Bulldozer*, 164–165.

21. Herbert J. Gans, *The Urban Villagers: Group and Class in the Life of Italian-Americans* (New York: Free Press, 1962), epilogue; Eric Avila, *Popular Culture in the Age of White Flight: Fear and Fantasy in Suburban Los Angeles* (Berkeley: University of California Press, 2006), chap. 5; Zipp, *Manhattan Projects*, 200–214; Lydia R. Otero, *La Calle: Spatial Conflicts and Urban Renewal in a Southwest City* (Tucson: University of Arizona Press, 2010), chap. 4; Connolly, *A World More Concrete*, 211–213.

22. Rose, *Interstate*; Clay McSahane, *Down the Asphalt Path: The Automobile and the American City* (New York: Columbia University Press, 1994); Gutfreund, *Twentieth-Century Sprawl*.

23. Robert A. Caro, *The Power Broker: Robert Moses and the Fall of New York* (New York: Vintage, 1975), chap. 36; Eric Avila, *The Folklore of the Freeway: Race and Revolt in the Modernist City* (Minneapolis: University of Minnesota Press, 2014).

24. Thomas Hanchett, "US Tax Policy and the Shopping-Center Boom of the 1950s and 1960s," *American Historical Review* 101 (1996): 1082–1110.

25. Robert B. Kent, *Latin America: Regions and People* (New York: Guilford Press, 2006), 246; Gilbert, *The Mega-City in Latin America*.

26. Michael Kulikowski, *Late Roman Spain and Its Cities* (Baltimore: Johns Hopkins University Press, 2004); Jorge E. Hardoy, *Pre-Columbian Cities* (New York: Walker, 1973); Philip II, Ordenanzas hechas para los decubrimientos, nuevas poblaciones y pacificaciones: Bosque de Segovia, July 13, 1573, esp. ordinances 33, 37, 39, 89–92, 99–107, and 110–135, sourced and partially translated in Zelia Nuttall, "Royal Ordinances Concerning the Laying Out of New Towns," *Hispanic American Historical Review* 4 (November 1921); Domingo Faustino Sarmiento, *Facundo: Civilización y barbarie* (Santiago: Imprenta del Progreso, 1845); José Luis Romero, *Latinoamerica: Las ciudades y las ideas* (Buenos Aires: Siglo XXI, 1976); Angel Rama, *La ciudad letrada* (Hanover, 1984).

27. Edgar J. Dosman, *The Life and Times of Raúl Prebisch, 1901–1986* (Montreal: McGill-Queen's University Press, 2008); Victor Bulmer-Thomas, *The Economic History of Latin America since Independence* (Cambridge: Cambridge University Press, 2014).

28. Rubén Hernández-León, *Metropolitan Migrants: The Migration of Urban Mexicans to the United States* (Berkeley, 2008), 3–5, and generally.

29. Leslie Bethell, ed., *Mexico since Independence* (New York: Cambridge University Press, 1991), 323–332.

30. Hector Guillen Romo, *Origenes de la crisis en México* (Mexico City: Ediciones Era, 1984); José Valenzuela Feijoo, *El Capitalismo mexicano en los ochenta* (Mexico City: Ediciones Era, 1986); David Barkin, *Distorted Development: Mexico in the World Economy* (Westport, CT: Westview Press, 1990).

31. Carmen Teresa Whalen, *From Puerto Rico to Philadelphia: Puerto Rican Workers and Postwar Economies* (Philadelphia: Temple University Press, 2001), chaps. 2 and 4.

32. Jesse Hoffnung-Garskof, *A Tale of Two Cities: Santo Domingo and New York after 1950* (Princeton, NJ: Princeton University Press, 2008), chap. 2.

33. James R. Scobie, *Argentina: A City and a Nation* (New York: Oxford University Press, 1964); Jorge Hardoy and Richard Schaedel, *Las ciudades de América Latina y sus áreas de influencia a través de la historia* (Buenos Aires: Ediciones SIAP, 1975); Jorge Hardoy, *Urbanization in Latin America: Approaches and Issues* (Garden City, NY: Anchor

Press, 1975); Richard M. Morse and Jorge E. Hardoy, *Repensando la ciudad de América Latina* (Buenos Aires: Grupo Editor Latinoamericano, 1988); Gilbert, *The Mega-City in Latin America*, 1–21, 173–183.

34. Fairbanks, *The War on Slums in the Southwest*, 131–140.

35. Fairbanks, *The War on Slums in the Southwest*, 137–138; Fairbanks, *For the City as a Whole*, 221–233.

36. Fairbanks, *The War on Slums in the Southwest*, 131.

37. Leonor and Ronnie Villareal oral history, recorded July 14, 2010, digital audio file (in the author's possession); Jesse Tafalla oral history, recorded July 22, 2010, digital audio file (in the author's possession).

38. Joe Sherman, "New Schools Slated in Area," *Dallas Times Herald*, August 16, 1964, 14; "'Conspiracy' Seen by Cliff Council," *Dallas Times Herald*, June 23, 1965, 27; Behnken, *Fighting Their Own Battles*, 210–211.

39. *Dallas Times-Herald*, August 21, 1965; Schutze, *The Accommodation*, 163.

40. Seligman, *Block by Block*, 5–9, and generally.

41. Seligman, *Block by Block*, chap. 4; Richard Anderson, "'We Had Tied That Noose around Our Necks': Urban Renewal, Grassroots Planning, and the Battle to Build the University of Illinois–Chicago, 1947–1965," unpublished paper in the possession of the author; US Census 1960 Chicago, table H-2; US Census 1970 Chicago, table H-1.

42. Fernández, *Brown in the Windy City*, chaps. 3, 6.

43. Art Peters, "North Phila. Tension Seethes in Wake of Youth's Shooting," *Philadelphia Tribune*, October 29, 1963, 2; Matthew Countryman, *Up South: Civil Rights and Black Power in Philadelphia* (Philadelphia: University of Pennsylvania Press, 2006); Chris Perry, "False Killing Rumor Triggered Riot," *Philadelphia Tribune*, September 1, 1964, 1; *Report of the National Advisory Commission on Civil Disorders* (New York: Bantam Books, 1968), 37. On Harlem and Watts, see Otto Kerner et al., *Report of the National Advisory Committee on Civil Disorders* (Washington, DC: US Government Printing Office, 1968), 20, 38. On the civil disorders generally, see Sugrue, *Sweet Land of Liberty*, chap. 10.

44. James Patterson, *Grand Expectations: The United States, 1945–1974* (New York: Oxford University Press, 1996), 663; Kerner et al., *Report of the National Advisory Committee on Civil Disorders*, chap. 1; Sugrue, *The Origins of the Urban Crisis*, conclusion.

45. Kerner et al., *Report of the National Advisory Committee on Civil Disorders*, 1.

46. Roger Biles, *Richard J. Daley: Politics, Race, and the Governing of Chicago* (DeKalb: Northern Illinois University Press, 1995), 145–147; David Farber, *Chicago '68* (Chicago: University of Chicago Press, 1988), chap. 6; Sugrue, *Sweet Land of Liberty*, 324–327.

47. Beauregard, *Voices of Decline*, 169–181; Michael W. Flamm, *Law and Order: Street Crime, Civil Unrest, and the Crisis of Liberalism in the 1960s* (New York: Columbia University Press, 2005), chap. 5; Sugrue, *Sweet Land of Liberty*, chap. 10.

48. Phillips, *White Metropolis*, 167; Campbell Gibson and Kay Jung, "Historical Census Statistics on Population Totals by Race, 1790 to 1990, and by Hispanic Origin, 1970 to 1990, for Large Cities and Other Urban Places in the United States," Population Division Working Paper 76 (US Census Bureau, February 2005).

49. Gibson and Jung, "Historical Census Statistics" (2005).

50. Jonathan Mahler, *Ladies and Gentlemen, the Bronx Is Burning: 1977, Baseball, Politics, and the Battle for the Soul of a City* (New York: Farrar, Straus and Giroux, 2002). Neither Cosell nor his cohost used those words. Phillips-Fein, *Fear City*, 229–230; "The Nation: Arson for Hate and Profit," *Time*, October 31, 1977.

51. "How Much Time Do We Have? . . . No Time," *Chicago Tribune*, May 10, 1981, 1; Graff, *The Dallas Myth*, 295–296; Cowie and Heathcott, *Beyond the Ruins*, ix.

52. "City Trying to Take Hold of Its Future," *Chicago Tribune*, December 13, 1981, 1; Isenberg, *Downtown America*.

53. Margaret Pugh O'Mara, *Cities of Knowledge: Cold War Science and the Search for the Next Silicon Valley* (Princeton, NJ: Princeton University Press, 2004); Louise A. Mozingo, *Pastoral Capitalism: A History of Suburban Corporate Landscapes* (Cambridge, MA: MIT Press, 2011).

54. See introduction, note 16.

55. Self, *American Babylon*, chap. 3; Isenberg, *Downtown America*, chap. 5.

56. Self, *American Babylon*, 316–323; Frank Van Riper, "Ford to City: Drop Dead!" *Daily News*, October 30, 1975, 1; Phillips-Fein, *Fear City*, 177–189.

57. FBI Uniform Crime Reports, available by city at https://www.fbi.gov/services/cjis /ucr; "Chicago Homicide Data since 1957," *Chicago Tribune*, March 2, 2016, at https:// www.chicagotribune.com/news/local/breaking/ct-chicago-homicides-data-since-1957 -20160302-htmlstory.html; Dallas Police Department, "City Council Retreat, January 15, 2015,"at http://dallascityhall.com/government/DCH%20documents/DpD_Retreat2015-R _011515.pdf.

58. Patricia J. Williams, *The Alchemy of Race and Rights* (Cambridge, MA: Harvard University Press, 1991), chap. 7.

59. See the works cited in Chapter 1, note 18; Gary Peller, "Race-Consciousness," in Kimberlé Crenshaw, Neil Gotanda, Gary Peller, and Kendall Thomas, *Critical Race Theory: The Key Writings That Formed the Movement* (New York: New Press, 1995); Stephen Steinberg, *Turning Back: The Retreat from Racial Justice in American Thought and Policy* (Boston: Beacon Press, 1995); Self, *American Babylon*; Premilla Nadasen, *Welfare Warriors: The Welfare Rights Movement in the United States* (New York: Routledge, 2005); Kruse, *White Flight*.

60. Edward H. Miller, *Nut Country: Right-Wing Dallas and the Birth of the Southern Strategy* (Chicago: University of Chicago Press, 2016); Graff, *The Dallas Myth*, 26.

61. Graff, *The Dallas Myth*, 11–17.

62. Brian D. Behnken, "'We Want Justice!': Police Murder, Mexican American Community Response, and the Chicano Movement," in Dan Berger, ed., *The Hidden 1970s: Histories of Radicalism* (New Brunswick, NJ: Rutgers University Press, 2010).

63. "Chicago: City on the Brink," *Chicago Tribune*, May 10–14, 1981; *Chicago Tribune*, May 14, 1981, 1.

64. *Chicago Tribune*, May 10, 1981, 1.

CHAPTER 5: NINETEEN SIXTY-FIVE

1. Irving Bernstein, *Guns or Butter: The Presidency of Lyndon Johnson* (New York: Oxford University Press, 1996), 258.

2. *Public Papers of the Presidents of the United States: Lyndon B. Johnson, 1965*, vol. II (Washington, DC: US Government Printing Office, 1966), 1037–1040.

3. On the 1965 immigration act, see David M. Reimers, *Still the Golden Door: The Third World Comes to America*, 2nd ed. (New York, 1992); Daniel J. Tichenor, *Dividing Lines: The Politics of Immigration Control in America* (Princeton, NJ: Princeton University Press, 2002); Mae Ngai, *Impossible Subjects: Illegal Aliens and the Making of Modern America* (Princeton, NJ: Princeton University Press, 2004); Aristide Zolberg, *A Nation by Design: Immigration Policy in the Fashioning of America* (New York: Russell Sage Foundation, 2006); María Cristina García, Madeline Hsu, and Maddalena Marinari, *A Nation of Immigrants Reconsidered: US Society in an Age of Restriction, 1924–1965* (Champaign: University of Illinois Press, 2018).

4. On the era of immigration restriction, see Chapter 5, note 3, and John Higham, *Strangers in the Land: Patterns of American Nativism, 1860–1925* (New Brunswick, NJ: Rutgers University Press, 1955); Robert A. Divine, *American Immigration Policy, 1924–1952* (New Haven, CT: Yale University Press, 1957); Roger Daniels, *Guarding the Golden Door: American Immigration Policy and Immigrants since 1882* (New York: Hill and Wang, 2004); Katherine Benton-Cohen, *Inventing the Immigration Problem: The Dillingham Commission and Its Legacy* (Cambridge, MA: Harvard University Press, 2018); Paul Kramer, "The Geopolitics of Mobility: Immigration Policy and American Global Power in the Long Twentieth Century," *American Historical Review* 123 (2018): 393–438; Maddalena Marinari, *Unwanted: Italian and Jewish Mobilization against Restrictive Immigration Laws, 1882–1965* (Chapel Hill: University of North Carolina Press, 2019).

5. Divine, *American Immigration Policy*, 14–15; *Congressional Record*, US House of Representatives, April 8, 1924, 5868; Higham, *Strangers in the Land*, 141–142; Knights of the Ku Klux Klan, "Proceedings of the Second Imperial Klonvokation," Kansas City, MO, September 23–26, 1924, 114.

6. Higham, *Strangers in the Land*; Alexandra Minna Stern, *Eugenic Nation: Faults and Frontiers of Better Breeding in North America* (Berkeley: University of California Press, 2006); Robert L. Fleegler, *Ellis Island Nation: Immigration Policy and American Identity in the Twentieth Century* (Philadelphia: University of Pennsylvania Press, 2013); Douglas Bayton, *Defectives in the Land: Disability and Immigration in the Age of Eugenics* (Chicago: University of Chicago Press, 2016). See also Erika Lee, *America for Americans: A History of Xenophobia in the United States* (New York: Basic Books, 2018).

7. Kelly Lytle Hernandez, *Migra! A History of the US Border Patrol* (Berkeley: University of California Press, 2010), chap. 1; Rachel St. John, *Line in the Sand: A History of the US-Mexico Border* (Princeton, NJ: Princeton University Press, 2011), 178–187; Divine, *American Immigration Policy*, 57; Mary E. Mendoza, "Unnatural Border: Race and Environment at the US-Mexico Divide," PhD thesis, University of California–Davis (2015).

8. William E. Leuchtenberg, *The Supreme Court Reborn: The Constitutional Revolution in the Age of Roosevelt* (New York: Oxford University Press, 1996), chap. 1; Meyer v. Nebraska, 262 U.S. 390 (1923); Pierce v. Society of Sisters, 252 U.S. 510 (1925); Joel T. Braslow, "In the Name of Therapeutics: The Practice of Sterilization in a California State Hospital," *Journal of the History of Medicine and Allied Sciences* 51 (1996): 29–51; James Q. Whitman, *Hitler's American Model: The United States and the Making of Nazi Race Law* (Princeton, NJ: Princeton University Press, 2017); Harry Bruinius, *Better for All the World: The Secret History of Forced Sterilization and America's Quest for Racial Purity* (New York: Alfred A. Knopf, 2006), 315–316.

9. Tichenor, *Dividing Lines*, chap. 5; Marinari, Hsu, and García, *Nation of Immigrants Reconsidered*, introduction.

10. David S. Wyman, *Paper Walls: America and the Refugee Crisis 1938–1941* (New York: Pantheon, 1984); Leonard Dinnerstein, *Uneasy at Home: Antisemitism and the American Jewish Experience* (New York: Columbia University Press, 1987), chap. 6; Tichenor, *Dividing Lines*, 160–167.

11. Marinari, *Unwanted*; Kramer, "The Geopolitics of Mobility"; Slotkin, "Thinking Mythologically," *European Journal of American Studies* 12, no. 2 (2017); Meredith Oyen, *The Diplomacy of Migration: Transnational Lives and the Making of US-Chinese Relations in the Cold War* (Ithaca, NY: Cornell University Press, 2015); Carl J. Bon Tempo, *Americans at the Gate: The United States and Refugees during the Cold War* (Princeton, NJ: Princeton University Press, 2008); Daniel Tichenor, "Lyndon Johnson's Ambivalent Reform: The Immigration and Nationality Act of 1965," *Presidential Studies Quarterly* 46, no. 3 (2016): 691–705.

12. President's Commission on Immigration and Nationalization, *Whom We Shall Welcome* (Washington, DC: US Government Printing Office, 1953); Ngai, *Impossible Subjects*, 242; Tichenor, *Dividing Lines*, chap. 7.

13. Maddalena Marinari, "Divided and Conquered: Immigration Reform Advocates and the Passage of the 1952 Immigration and Nationality Act," *Journal of American Ethnic History* 35, no. 3 (2016): 9–40; Reimers, *Still the Golden Door*, 139.

14. "Kennedy Record on Immigration," John F. Kennedy Presidential Library, Pre-Presidential Papers, Presidential Campaign Files 1960, 1–3.

15. García, *¡Viva Kennedy!*; Jackson, *Ku Klux Klan in the City*, 20–21, 307; "Address of Senator John F. Kennedy Accepting the Democratic Party Nomination for the Presidency of the United States," July 15, 1960.

16. Letter from Williams to Kennedy, July 26, 1960, Papers of John F. Kennedy, Pre-Presidential Papers, Presidential Campaign Files, 1960, Speeches and the Press; Press Secretary's Subject File, 1960, DNC Nationalities Conference and Division, quoted in Gregory Montoya-Mora, "Viva Kennedy? The Role of the Democratic Nationalities Division in the Election of 1960," seminar paper, University of Chicago (2014).

17. Montoya-Mora, "Viva Kennedy?," 3–8.

18. On the racial politics of Hispanic identity, see introduction, note 25; "Nuestro Líder es Kennedy," Box 38, Folder 15, Series II, Subseries 1, Richard J. Daley Collection, Special Collections and University Archives, University of Illinois at Chicago, cited in Montoya-Mora, "Viva Kennedy?," 9.

19. Robert A. Caro, *The Years of Lyndon Johnson: The Passage of Power* (New York: Alfred A. Knopf, 2012), chap. 5; "Remarks at the Welhausen Elementary School, Cotulla, Texas," November 7, 1966; Julie Leininger Pryor, *LBJ and Mexican Americans* (Austin: University of Texas Press, 1997), 18.

20. Adam Cohen and Elizabeth Taylor, *American Pharaoh: Mayor Richard J. Daley: His Battle for Chicago and the Nation* (Boston: Little, Brown, 2000), 265; 1960 Census, Chicago, table P-2.

21. Bill Minutaglio and Steven L. Davis, *Dallas 1963* (New York: Twelve, 2013), 58–66; Matt Schudel, "Bruce Alger, Firebrand Republican Congressman from Texas, Dies at 96," *Washington Post*, April 25, 2015.

22. *Public Papers of the Presidents of the United States: John F. Kennedy, 1963* (Washington, DC: US Government Printing Office, 1964), 596–597. For detailed accounts of the passage of the Immigration and Nationality Act of 1965, see Reimers, *Still the Golden Door*, chap. 3; Daniel J. Tichenor, "Lyndon Johnson's Ambivalent Reform: The Immigration and Nationality Act of 1965," *Presidential Studies Quarterly* (2016); Ngai, *Impossible Subjects*, chap. 7; Zolberg, *Nation by Design*, 327–333; Daniels, *Guarding the Golden Door*, chap. 7; Maddalena Marinari, "'Americans Must Show Justice in Immigration Policies Too': The Passage of the 1965 Immigration Act," *Journal of Policy History* 26 (2014): 219–245.

23. Johnson, "State of the Union," January 4, 1965.

24. Reimers, *Still the Golden Door*, 96; "Immigration Bill Backed by Carey at Hearing," *Washington Post, Times Herald*, March 16, 1965, A2. See also Brian Burgoon, Janice Fine, Wade Jacoby, and Daniel Tichenor, "Immigration and the Transformation of American Unionism," *International Migration Review* 44, no. 4 (2010): 933–973.

25. Marinari, "'Americans Must Show Justice'"; Tichenor, "Ambivalent Reform."

26. Robert A. Caro, *The Years of Lyndon Johnson: Master of the Senate* (New York: Random House, 2002), 867.

27. Hearings on H.R. 770 before Subcommittee No. 1 of the Committee on the Judiciary, US House of Representatives, 88th Cong., 2nd sess., August 5, 6, 7, 10, 11, 14, 20,

and 21, September 2, 3, 11, and 17, 1964, Part III, Serial 13 (Washington, DC: US Government Printing Office, 1964), 672.

28. Hearings on S. 500, to "Amend the Immigration and Nationality Act, and for Other Purposes," before the Subcommittee on Immigration and Naturalization of the Committee on the Judiciary, US Senate, 89th Cong., 1st sess., February 10–August 3, 1965, vol. 1 (Washington, DC: US Government Printing Office, 1965), 162; ibid., 689.

29. See, for example, *Congressional Record-House* (Washington, DC: US Government Printing Office, 1965), August 24, 1965, 21572 and August 25, 1965, 21773–21774; *Congressional Record-Senate* (Washington, DC: US Government Printing Office, 1965), September 17, 1965, 24235 and August 22, 1965, 24773; Hearings on S. 500, to "Amend the Immigration and Nationality Act, and for Other Purposes," Part 1, 18–19, and Part II, 484, 813.

30. Daniels, *Guarding the Golden Door*, 130–132; Tichenor, "Ambivalent Reform," 699–703; Bon Tempo, *Americans at the Gate*, 96.

31. Tichenor, "Ambivalent Reform," 700.

32. 89th Cong., 1st sess., Public Law 89-236, October 3, 1965; in federal code, 79 Stat. 911; quotation is from section 2(a).

33. Ngai, *Impossible Subjects*, chap. 7.

34. Foley, *Mexicans in the Making of America*, chap. 2; Roger Daniels, *Coming to America: A History of Immigration and Ethnicity in American Life*, 2nd ed. (New York: HarperCollins, 2002), 19–21, 27–28; Thomas J. Archdeacon, *Becoming American: An Ethnic History* (New York: Free Press, 1983), 139.

35. David FitzGerald, *A Nation of Emigrants: How Mexico Manages Its Migration* (Berkeley: University of California Press, 2008), 39–48.

36. Bethell, *Mexico since Independence*, 327–329, 341, 350–351, 359; Pablo Landa, María Margarita Segarra Lagunes, et al., for the Instituto Nacional de Bellas Artes, *Despliegues y ensambles* [*Unfoldings and assemblages*], Bienniale di Venezia (Mexico City: Secretaría de Cultura, 2016), 33–57, and generally.

37. Manuel García y Griego, "The Importation of Mexican Contract Laborers to the United States, 1942–1964," in Peter G. Brown and Henry Shue, eds., *The Border That Joins: Mexican Migrants and US Responsibility* (Totowa, NJ: Rowman & Littlefield, 1983); Deborah Cohen, *Braceros: Migrant Citizens and Transnational Subjects in the Postwar United States and Mexico* (Chapel Hill: University of North Carolina Press, 2011); Foley, *Mexicans in the Making of America*, chap. 4.

38. Michael C. Meyer and William L. Sherman, *The Course of Mexican History*, 4th ed. (New York: Oxford University Press, 1991), 589–592; William H. Beezley and Michael C. Meyer, eds., *The Oxford History of Mexico* (New York: Oxford University Press, 2010), 552–554. See also Guillen Romo, *Origenes de la crisis*; Valenzuela Feijoo, *Capitalismo mexicano*; Barkin, *Distorted Development*.

39. Tanalís Padilla, *Rural Resistance in the Land of Zapata: The Jaramillista Movement and the Myth of the Pax Priísta, 1940–1962* (Durham, NC: Duke University Press, 2008), 1–2; Tore C. Olsson, *Agrarian Crossings: Reformers and the Remaking of the US and Mexican Countryside* (Princeton, NJ: Princeton University Press, 2017), 188, 196–197.

40. Beezley and Meyer, *The Oxford History of Mexico*, 552–554.

41. Olsson, *Agrarian Crossings*, 196–197; FitzGerald, *Nation of Emigrants*, 55–56.

42. Juan González, *Harvest of Empire: A History of Latinos in America*, rev. ed. (New York: Penguin Books, 2011).

CHAPTER 6: *BIENVENIDOS A* OAK CLIFF

1. Ray P. Browne and Pat Browne, eds., *The Guide to United States Popular Culture* (Madison: University of Wisconsin Press, 2001), 217–218.

2. Gibson, "Population of the 100 Largest Cities and Other Urban Places."

3. Gibson, "Population of the 100 Largest Cities and Other Urban Places."

4. Tereso Ortiz oral history, recorded July 21, 2010, digital audio file (in the author's possession).

5. 1960 Census, Dallas, table P-1; US Census Bureau, "US Census of Population and Housing: 1970: Census Tracts, Dallas, Tex., Standard Metropolitan Statistical Area: Final Report PHC(1)–52" (Washington, DC: US Government Printing Office, 1972), tables P-1 and P-2 (hereafter 1970 Census, Dallas).

6. Tasby v. Estes, 342 F. Supp. 945 (N.D. Tex. 1971); Behnken, *Fighting Their Own Battles*, 210–211; 1970 Census, Dallas, tables P-1 and P-2; US Census Bureau, "US Census of Population and Housing: 1980: Census Tracts, Dallas–Fort Worth, Tex., Standard Metropolitan Statistical Area, PHC 80-2-131" (Washington, DC: US Government Printing Office, 1983), table P-7.

7. 1970 Census, Dallas, table P-3; Tereso Ortiz oral history; Francisco Rojas oral history, recorded March 26, 2016, and Florina Jayme oral history, recorded March 26, 2016, digital audio files (in the author's possession).

8. Mexican Migration Project, "Graph 14: Occupation on First Trip by Migration Period," https://mmp.opr.princeton.edu/results/014ftoccupation-en.aspx.

9. Whalen, *From Puerto Rico to Philadelphia*, chap. 3; María Cristina García, *Havana, USA: Cuban Exiles and Cuban Americans in South Florida, 1959–1994* (Berkeley: University of California Press, 1996), chap. 1.

10. See, for example, Matt Garcia, *From the Jaws of Victory: The Triumph and Tragedy of César Chávez and the Farm Worker Movement* (Berkeley: University of California Press, 2012), 16–19; Minian, *Undocumented Lives*, 56–57, 212.

11. Tereso Ortiz oral history; Douglas Massey, Rafael Alarcón, Jorge Durand, and Humberto González, *Return to Aztlán: The Social Process of International Migration from Western Mexico* (Berkeley: University of California Press, 1987), 271–273. See also Salvador Balleños oral history, recorded July 15, 2016, and Leodegario Torres oral history, recorded August 3, 2016, digital audio files (in the author's possession).

12. 1970 Census, Dallas, table H-2.

13. Minian, *Undocumented Lives*, 112–115; Massey et al., *Return to Aztlán*, 271–273; Tereso Ortiz oral history. See also Douglas Massey, Jorge Durand, and Nolan J. Malone, *Beyond Smoke and Mirrors: Mexican Immigration in an Era of Economic Integration* (New York: Russell Sage Foundation, 2002), fig. 6.3.

14. Tereso Ortiz oral history.

15. Tereso Ortiz oral history; Gustavo López Castro, *El Rio Bravo Es Charco: Cancionero del Migrante* (Zamora, Michoacán: El Colegio de Michoacán, 1995).

16. Tereso Ortiz oral history.

17. Tereso Ortiz oral history.

18. Tereso Ortiz oral history.

19. Tereso Ortiz oral history.

20. See, for example, Dámaso Ramírez oral history, recorded June 14, 2016, Manuel Correa oral history, recorded March 31, 2016, Manuel Barbosa oral history, recorded June 15, 2016, and Isidro Arroyo oral history, recorded June 8, 2016, digital audio files (in the author's possession); Massey et al., *Return to Aztlán*, 270–276.

21. Minian, *Undocumented Lives*, 42, 89–90, 230–232. For deaths in a later period, see Massey, Durand, and Malone, *Beyond Smoke and Mirrors*, fig. 6.3.

22. Massey et al., *Return to Aztlán*, 272–273. See also Orner, *Underground America*.

23. Miguel Pinedo, Xóchitl Castañeda, and Suzanne Teran, "Occupational Health and Safety among Latinos in the United States" (fact sheet), November 2011, Health Initiative of the Americas, University of California at Berkeley, School of Public Health, http://lohp .org/docs/pubs/Occupational%20Fact%20Sheet_HIA.pdf.

24. Leo R. Chávez, *The Latino Threat: Constructing Immigrants, Citizens, and the Nation*, 2nd ed. (Palo Alto, CA: Stanford University Press, 2013), 28–38; Andrew MacDonald (pseud.), *The Turner Diaries* (National Vanguard Books, 1999), chaps. 5, 9; Stephen Tropiano, *Saturday Night Live FAQ: Everything Left to Know about Television's Longest-Running Comedy* (Milwaukee: Applause, 2013), 35–38.

25. The most systematic of these is the Mexican Migration Project (MMP), initiated in 1982 by Jorge Durand and Douglas S. Massey. Its data are available to the public at https://mmp.opr.princeton.edu/. Research findings based on the MMP's data are listed at https://mmp.opr.princeton.edu/databases/pdf/Cumulative%20Bibliography%20as%20 of%20July%202007.pdf.

26. Massey et al., *Return to Aztlán*, 172–182; Donna Gabaccia and Vicki Ruiz, eds., *American Dreaming, Global Realities: Rethinking US Immigration History* (Urbana: University of Illinois Press, 2006), 533.

27. Sandoval-Strausz, "Migrantes, Barrios, and Infraestructura," 144–145; Massey et al., *Return to Aztlán*, 182, 209.

28. Camarillo, *Chicanos in a Changing Society*; Mario Barrera, *Race and Class in the Southwest: A Theory of Racial Inequality* (South Bend, IN: University of Notre Dame Press, 1979); Montejano, *Anglos and Mexicans in the Making of Texas*; Benjamin Heber Johnson, *Revolution in Texas: How a Forgotten Rebellion and Its Bloody Suppression Turned Mexicans into Americans* (New Haven, CT: Yale University Press, 2003); William D. Carrigan and Clive Webb, *Forgotten Dead: Mob Violence against Mexicans in the United States, 1848–1928* (New York: Oxford University Press, 2013); Monica Muñoz Martínez, *The Injustice Never Leaves You: Anti-Mexican Violence in Texas* (Cambridge, MA: Harvard University Press, 2018).

29. 1960 Census, Dallas, tables P-3 and P-5; 1970 Census, Dallas, tables P-2, P-3, P-7, and P-8; 1980 Census, Dallas, tables P-10, P-20, and P-21.

30. 1950 Census, Dallas, table 2; 1960 Census, Dallas, tables P-3 and P-5; 1970 Census, Dallas, tables P-2, P-3, P-7, and P-8; 1980 Census, Dallas, tables P-10, P-20, and P-21. This is just one example of the broader tendency of immigrants to generate jobs in the areas to which they move. For a national-level study on immigrant-driven job creation, including in the manufacturing sector, see Jacob Vigdor, "Estimating the Impact of Immigration on County-Level Economic Indicators," in Vitiello and Sugrue, *Immigration and Metropolitan Revitalization*, 25–38.

31. 1970 Census, Dallas, tables P-4 and P-8; 1980 Census, Dallas, tables P-11 and P-21.

32. 1960 Census, Dallas, tables P-3 and P-5; 1970 Census, Dallas, tables P-2, P-3, P-7, and P-8; 1980 Census, Dallas, tables P-10, P-20, and P-21.

33. 1980 Census, Dallas, tables P-21 and P-11.

34. Tereso Ortiz oral history.

35. 1970 Census, Dallas, tables H-1 and H-2; 1980 Census, Dallas, tables H-1 and H-8.

36. 1980 Census, Dallas, tables H-1 and H-8; US Census Bureau, "US Census of Population and Housing: 1990: Population and Housing Characteristics for Census Tracts and Block Numbering Areas, Dallas–Fort Worth, Tex., CMSA. CPH-3-125A" (Washington, DC: US Government Printing Office, 1993), tables 9 and 33 (hereafter 1990 Census, Dallas).

37. 1980 Census, Dallas, table P-21; 1990 Census, Dallas, table 19.

38. John J. Betancur, "The Settlement Experience of Latinos in Chicago: Segregation, Speculation, and the Ecology Model," *Social Forces* 74 (June 1996): 1315–1316.

39. Tereso Ortiz oral history.

40. Tereso Ortiz oral history.

41. Tereso Ortiz oral history.

42. Rubén Chávez oral history, recorded July 21, 2016, digital audio file (in the author's possession); Isidro Arroyo oral history; José Juan Estrada oral history, recorded September 4, 2016, digital audio file (in the author's possession); Manuel Barbosa oral history; Leodegario Torres oral history; Susana Hernández oral history, recorded March 26, 2016, digital audio file (in the author's possession); Mercedes Olivera, "Rebirth in Oak Cliff: Hispanics Revitalize Jefferson Boulevard," *Dallas Morning News*, March 2, 1986, 33a.

43. Tereso Ortiz oral history; Olivera, "Rebirth in Oak Cliff."

44. 1960 Census, Dallas, table H-2; 1970 Census, Dallas, tables H-1 and H-2; 1980 Census, Dallas, tables H-1 and H-8; 1990 Census, Dallas, tables 9 and 33. Precisely this kind of housing-driven revitalization by immigrants has been demonstrated in nationwide studies: see Gary Painter, "Immigrants, Housing Demand, and the Economic Cycle," in Vitiello and Sugrue, *Immigration and Metropolitan Revitalization*. This is just one example of the tendency of immigrants to generate jobs in the areas to which they move. For a national-level study on immigrant-driven job creation, including in the manufacturing sector, see Jacob Vigdor, "Estimating the Impact of Immigration on County-Level Economic Indicators," in Vitiello and Sugrue, *Immigration and Metropolitan Revitalization*, 39–64; Albert Saiz, "Immigration and Housing Rents in American Cities," *Journal of Urban Economics* 61 (2006), 345–371.

45. *Cole Cross-Reference Directory for Greater Dallas, 1970*, 335–336; *Cole Cross-Reference Directory for Greater Dallas, 1980*, 426–427; Olivera, "Rebirth in Oak Cliff."

46. Olivera, "Rebirth in Oak Cliff."

47. Olivera, "Rebirth in Oak Cliff."

48. Olivera, "Rebirth in Oak Cliff."

49. Olivera, "Rebirth in Oak Cliff."

50. Olivera, "Rebirth in Oak Cliff."

51. William K. Black, *The Best Way to Rob a Bank Is to Own One: How Corporate Executives and Politicians Looted the S&L Industry* (Austin: University of Texas Press, 2005); Peter Elkind, "Rock Bottom," *Texas Monthly* (June 1989); John O'Keefe for the Division of Research and Statistics, Federal Deposit Insurance Corporation, "The Texas Banking Crisis: Causes and Consequences, 1980–1989," July 1990, https://fraser.stlouisfed.org/files/docs/publications/texasbankcrisis_1980_1989.pdf; Jody Grant, "The 1980s Banking Crash Humbles Dallas," *D Magazine* (January 2010): 48–50.

52. Black, *The Best Way to Rob a Bank Is to Own One*, chap. 5; Elkind, "Rock Bottom"; Grant, "The 1980s Banking Crash Humbles Dallas."

53. 1970 Census, Dallas, table P-2; 1980 Census, Dallas, table P-7.

54. Gibson and Jung, "Historical Census Statistics" (2002).

CHAPTER 7: THE WINDY CITY PITCHES THE WOO

1. City of Chicago, Department of Development and Planning, *Chicago's Spanish-Speaking Population* (September 1973), ii, 1.

2. Chicago 21 Corporation, *Chicago 21: A Plan for the Central Area Communities* (September 1973).

3. Gibson, "Population of the 100 Largest Cities and Other Urban Places."

4. *Chicago's Spanish-Speaking Population*, iii, 1–4.

5. *Chicago's Spanish-Speaking Population*, 1.

6. Gibson, "Population of the 100 Largest Cities and Other Urban Places."

7. *Chicago 21*.

8. Cohen and Taylor, *American Pharaoh*, 293, 530.

9. Emma Lozano and Slim Coleman, interview for Rita Hernández dissertation, recording no. 2, Loyola University Library Special Collections; Pilsen Neighbors handbill, Chicago Collection, Special Collections, De Paul University Libraries.

10. Louise Año Nuevo Kerr Papers, José Luis Loera oral history.

11. Massey et al., *Return to Aztlán*, 172–173. Dollar equivalents calculated using Economic History Association, "Measuring Worth," http://eh.net/howmuchisthat/.

12. Año Nuevo Kerr Papers, Margarita Arredondo oral history, recorded April 11, 1996.

13. Año Nuevo Kerr Papers, Miguel Ramírez oral history, recorded March 29, 1996.

14. Año Nuevo Kerr Papers, Rosina Magaña oral history.

15. 1970 Census, Chicago, tables P-1 and P-2; US Census Bureau, "US Census of Population and Housing: 1980: Census Tracts, Chicago, Ill., SMSA, PHC 80-2-119" (Washington, DC: US Government Printing Office, 1983), tables P-7 and P-9 (hereafter 1980 Census, Chicago).

16. Año Nuevo Kerr Papers: Jesus Serrato oral history, recorded April 1, 1996; Rosalio Torres oral history, recorded April 8, 1996; Agustín Delgado oral history, recorded April 1, 1996; Bertha Martinez oral history, recorded April 14, 1996; Miguel Ramírez oral history, recorded March 29, 1996; Eustolia Martínez oral history, recorded March 15 and 17, 1996; José Pérez oral history, recorded April 3, 1996.

17. 1960 Census, Chicago, table P-3; 1970 Census, Chicago, table P-3; 1980 Census, Chicago, table P-10.

18. 1970 Census, Chicago, table P-4; 1980 Census, Chicago, table P-11; 1970 Census, Chicago, table P-4; 1980 Census, Chicago, table P-11; Janet Abu-Lughod, *New York, Chicago, Los Angeles: America's Global Cities* (Minneapolis: University of Minnesota Press, 1999), 323; Vigdor, "Estimating the Impact of Immigration."

19. John J. Betancur, Teresa Cordova, and Maria de Los Angeles Torres, "Economic Restructuring and the Process of Incorporation of Latinos into the Chicago Economy," in Rebecca Morales and Frank Bonilla, eds., *Latinos in a Changing Economy: Comparative Perspectives on Growing Inequality* (Newbury Park, CA: SAGE Publications, 1993), 134.

20. Morales and Bonilla, *Latinos in a Changing Economy*; Gordon K. Mantler, *Power to the Poor: Black-Brown Coalition and the Fight for Economic Justice, 1960–1974* (Chapel Hill: University of North Carolina Press, 2013), and Mantler, "Rainbow Reformers: Black-Brown Activism and the Election of Harold Washington," in Brian Behnken, ed., *Civil Rights and Beyond: African Americans and Latino/a Activism in the Twentieth-Century United States* (Athens: University of Georgia Press, 2016).

21. 1980 Census, Chicago, tables P-13 and P-21; Morales and Bonilla, *Latinos in a Changing Economy*, 30.

22. Howard A. Tyner, "Our Vulnerable Illegal Aliens," *Chicago Tribune*, April 29, 1981, 1.

23. Tyner, "Our Vulnerable Illegal Aliens"; Miguel Ramírez oral history.

24. Massey et al., *Return to Aztlán*, 172–173.

25. Tyner, "Our Vulnerable Illegal Aliens."

26. 1960 Census, Chicago, table H-1; 1970 Census, Chicago, table H-1; 1980 Census, Chicago, table H-1; US Census Bureau, "US Census of Population and Housing: 1990: Characteristics for Census Tracts and Block Numbering Areas, Chicago, Ill., PMSA" (Washington, DC: US Government Printing Office, 1993), table T-73 (hereafter 1990 Census, Chicago).

27. Melaniphy & Associates for the City of Chicago, *Chicago Comprehensive Neighborhood Needs Analysis: South Lawndale Community Area*, vol. II (1982), 18, 22–23. On

immigrant-driven urban revitalization through the housing market, see Saiz, "Immigration and Housing Rents."

28. 1980 Census, Chicago, table H-8; Tyner, "Our Vulnerable Illegal Aliens."

29. 1950 Census, Chicago, table 5; 1960 Census, Chicago, table H-1; 1970 Census, Chicago, table H-1; 1980 Census, Chicago, table H-1; 1990 Census, Chicago, table 27.

30. Satter, *Family Properties*, 335–337.

31. 1950 Census, Chicago, table 5; 1980 Census, Chicago, table H-1, for North Lawndale, the area coterminous with the 2010 tracts numbered 2909, 2912, 2916, 2922, 2924, 2925, 8386, 8387, 8414, 8415, 8416, 8430, 8431, 8433, and 8434.

32. Isidro Arroyo oral history.

33. *Chicago Criss-Cross Directory* (Schaumburg, IL: Haines & Company, 1980), "26th W."

34. Melaniphy & Associates, *Chicago Comprehensive Neighborhood Needs Analysis*, 18, 28.

35. Armando Triana, "General Characteristics of Latino Businesses in the City of Chicago" (held at Harold Washington Library), tables 1 and 2.

36. "An Oasis of Harmony in the Inner City," *Chicago Tribune*, January 16, 1977; "Two Sides of 26th Street Renewal," *Chicago Tribune*, May 20, 1979; "Old Mexico Is a Hit in Old Chicago," *Chicago Tribune*, September 6, 1987; "Enterprising Immigrants Converge on Little Village," *Chicago Tribune*, September 6, 1987.

37. Lois Wille, *At Home in the Loop: How Clout and Community Built Chicago's Dearborn Park* (Carbondale: Southern Illinois University Press), 110.

38. Wille, *At Home in the Loop*, 112, 157–158, 185–187, jacket copy.

39. Wille, *At Home in the Loop*, 173, 185–186.

40. "Arch to Be Built on 26 St. as 'Tourism Attraction,'" *Lawndale News*, June 22, 1986, 1; "Mexican President to Visit Little Village," *Lawndale News*, January 17, 1991, 5.

41. 1970 Census, Chicago, table P-2; 1980 Census, Chicago, table P-7.

42. 1970 Census, Chicago, table P-2; 1980 Census, Chicago, table P-7; 1990 Census, Chicago, table 8.

CHAPTER 8: *LA POLÍTICA*

1. Milton L. Rakove, *We Don't Want Nobody Nobody Sent: An Oral History of the Daley Years* (Bloomington: Indiana University Press, 1979).

2. Douglas Knox, "Ward System," in Grossman, Keating, and Reiff, *Encyclopedia of Chicago*, 857.

3. John M. Allswang, *A House for All Peoples: Ethnic Politics in Chicago, 1890–1936* (Lexington: University Press of Kentucky, 1971), chap. 8.

4. Mike Royko, *Boss: Richard J. Daley of Chicago* (New York: Dutton, 1971), 60–77; Cohen and Taylor, *American Pharaoh*, 155–163. See also Biles, *Richard J. Daley*.

5. Fairbanks, *For the City as a Whole*, chaps. 1 and 2.

6. Allswang, *House for All Peoples*; Thomas Kessner, *Fiorello H. LaGuardia and the Making of Modern New York* (New York: McGraw-Hill, 1989).

7. Fairbanks, *For the City as a Whole*, 15–23; Phillips, *White Metropolis*, 62–63.

8. Pierre Guilmant, "W. Side Committeewoman Target of Ouster Drive," *Chicago Daily Defender* (weekend edition), July 19, 1969, 1.

9. Teresa Córdova, "Harold Washington and the Rise of Latino Electoral Politics in Chicago, 1982–1987," in David Montejano, ed., *Chicano Politics and Society in the Late Twentieth Century* (Austin: University of Texas Press, 1999), 36–37.

10. William J. Grimshaw, *Bitter Fruit: Black Politics and the Chicago Machine* (Chicago: University of Chicago Press, 1992), 15–40; Cohen and Taylor, *American Pharaoh*, 95–98; Roger Biles, *Mayor Harold Washington: Champion of Race and Reform in Chicago* (Urbana: University of Illinois Press, 2018), 55.

11. John T. McGreevy, *Parish Boundaries: The Catholic Encounter with Race in the Twentieth-Century Urban North* (Chicago: University of Chicago Press, 1996); René Luis Alvarez, "'A Community That Would Not Take "No" for an Answer': Mexican Americans, the Chicago Public Schools, and the Founding of Benito Juarez High School," *Journal of Illinois History* 17 (2014): 78–98.

12. Cohen and Taylor, *American Pharaoh*, 554–558.

13. Gary Rivlin, *Fire on the Prairie: Chicago's Harold Washington and the Politics of Race* (New York: Henry Holt, 1992), 68.

14. Biles, *Mayor Harold Washington*, 58–59; Mantler, "Rainbow Reformers," 223.

15. Mantler, "Rainbow Reformers," 220–224; Emma Lozano and Slim Coleman, interview for Rita Hernández dissertation.

16. Mantler, "Rainbow Reformers," 220–222.

17. Mantler, "Rainbow Reformers," 223–228.

18. Biles, *Mayor Harold Washington*, 17–29.

19. Mantler, "Rainbow Reformers," 228–230; Rivlin, *Fire on the Prairie*, 349.

20. Córdova, "Harold Washington and the Rise of Latino Electoral Politics in Chicago," 40; Mantler, "Rainbow Reformers," 228–230; Lozano and Coleman interview.

21. Biles, *Mayor Harold Washington*, 87–104; Año Nuevo Kerr Papers, Carlos Cortez oral history, recorded April 15, 1996. See also Jakobi Williams, *From the Bullet to the Ballot: The Illinois Chapter of the Black Panther Party and Racial Coalition Politics in Chicago* (Chapel Hill: University of North Carolina Press, 2013), chap. 6.

22. Rivlin, *Fire on the Prairie*, 350–352; Mantler, "Rainbow Reformers," 230.

23. Kevin Klose, "Upset in Chicago," *Washington Post*, February 24, 1983, 1; Córdova, "Harold Washington and the Rise of Latino Electoral Politics in Chicago," 40.

24. Biles, *Mayor Harold Washington*, 87–104. See also Rivlin, *Fire on the Prairie*, "Book Two: Council Wars."

25. Melvin G. Holli and Paul M. Green, *Bashing Chicago Traditions: Harold Washington's Last Campaign: Chicago, 1987* (Grand Rapids, MI: Eerdmans, 1989), 27–30.

26. Córdova, "Harold Washington and the Rise of Latino Electoral Politics in Chicago," 42–48.

27. Rivlin, *Fire on the Prairie*, 352–353; Biles, *Mayor Harold Washington*, 239–241.

28. Biles, *Mayor Harold Washington*, 238–244; Rivlin, *Fire on the Prairie*, 398–400; Mantler, "Rainbow Reformers," 230–232.

29. Holli and Green, *Bashing Chicago Traditions*, chap. 5; Biles, *Mayor Harold Washington*, 248–269; Córdova, "Harold Washington and the Rise of Latino Electoral Politics in Chicago," 50–54.

30. David K. Fremon, *Chicago Politics Ward by Ward* (Bloomington: Indiana University Press, 1988), 148.

31. Payne, *Big D*, 336.

32. Behnken, *Fighting Their Own Battles*, 93–96.

33. Behnken, *Fighting Their Own Battles*, 123–126.

34. Payne, *Big D*, 338.

35. Behnken, *Fighting Their Own Battles*, 109–113, 188, 225–231.

36. Behnken, *Fighting Their Own Battles*, 215–223.

37. Lipscomb v. Wise, 399 F. Supp. 782 (N.D. Tex. 1975).

38. Lipscomb v. Wise, 399 F. Supp. 782 (N.D. Tex. 1975).

39. Williams v. City of Dallas, 734 F. Supp. 1317 (N.D. Tex. 1990), 1322.

40. Ruth P. Morgan, *Governance by Decree: The Impact of the Voting Rights Act in Dallas* (Lawrence: University Press of Kansas, 2004), 148, 166.

41. *Dallas Morning News*, October 11, 1981; November 10, 1981; February 24, 1982.

42. Payne, *Big D*, 391–392.

43. Williams v. City of Dallas, 734 F. Supp. 1317 (N.D. Tex. 1990), 1325–1327.

44. Payne, *Big D*, 392; Domingo García, "Dallas Adopts 14-1," *D Magazine* (January 2010): 11.

45. Williams v. City of Dallas, 734 F. Supp. 1317 (N.D. Tex. 1990); García, "Dallas Adopts 14-1," 11.

46. García, "Dallas Adopts 14-1," 11.

47. Jim Schutze, "Is Ron Kirk Inevitable?" *D Magazine* (April 1995).

48. Phillips, *White Metropolis*, 168–169; Graff, *The Dallas Myth*, 11–13, 241–242.

49. Ron Kirk, "Dallas Elects Its First Black Mayor," *D Magazine* (January 2010): 18–19; Schutze, "Is Ron Kirk Inevitable?".

50. Montejano, *Quixote's Soldiers*, 251–254.

CHAPTER 9: TRANSNATIONAL CITIES

1. Gloria Rubio oral history, recorded July 19, 2010, digital audio file (in the author's possession); María Cristina García, *Seeking Refuge: Central American Migration to Mexico, the United States, and Canada* (Berkeley: University of California Press, 2006), 21–25, 175n36. See also Cecilia Menjívar, *Fragmented Ties: Salvadoran Immigrant Networks in America* (Berkeley: University of California Press, 2000).

2. Carlos Henriquez Consalvi, *Broadcasting the Civil War in El Salvador: A Memoir of Guerrilla Radio* (Austin: University of Texas Press, 2010), 139; Jemera Rone, Aryeh Neier, and Anne Nelson for the Americas Watch, *Settling into Routine: Human Rights Abuses in Duarte's Second Year: Eighth Supplement to the Report on Human Rights in El Salvador* (New York: Americas Watch Committee, 1986), 153; Marielos Ramirez, "Gloria Rubio: Una salvadoreña que conquistó el paladar de los anglosajones," *El Salvador Magazine* (October 2, 2012).

3. David Harvey, *A Brief History of Neoliberalism* (Oxford: Oxford University Press, 2007); Alejandro Portes and Kelly Hoffman, "Latin American Class Structures: Their Composition and Change during the Neoliberal Era," *Latin American Research Review* 38 (February 2003).

4. Portes and Hoffman, "Latin American Class Structures," 41–82; Rubén Hernández-León, *Metropolitan Migrants: The Migration of Urban Mexicans to the United States* (Berkeley: University of California Press, 2008), 3–5; Demetrios G. Papademetriou, John J. Audley, Sandra Polaski, and Scott Vaughan, "NAFTA's Promise and Reality: Lessons from Mexico for the Hemisphere," *Migration Policy Institute Report* (2004): 17, 21.

5. García, *Seeking Refuge*, chap. 1.

6. 1980 Census, Chicago, table 13; 1990 Census, Chicago, table 13; "Census 2000 summary file 1 (SF 1), QT-3: Race and Hispanic or Latino," table created from data at US Census Bureau, American Fact Finder, http://factfinder2.census.gov (hereafter 2000 Census, Chicago); 1980 Census, Dallas, table 13; 1990 Census, Dallas, table 13; 2000 Census, Dallas, tables 14 and 15.

7. 1990 Census, Chicago, table 14; 2000 Census, Chicago, table 18; 1990 Census, Dallas, table 14; "Census 2000 summary file 1 (SF 1), QT-3: Race and Hispanic or Latino," table created from data at US Census Bureau, American Fact Finder, http://factfinder2.census.gov (hereafter 2000 Census, Dallas).

8. Massey, Durand, and Malone, *Beyond Smoke and Mirrors*, 42–47.

9. Lawrence Fuchs, "The Corpse That Would Not Die: The Immigration Reform and Control Act of 1986," *Revue Européenne des Migrations Internationales* 6 (1990): 113; Select Commission on Immigration and Refugee Policy, "US Immigration Policy and the National Interest," March 1, 1981.

10. On the path to the 1986 act, see Harris N. Miller, "The Right Thing to Do: A History of Simpson-Mazzoli," *Journal of Contemporary Studies* 7 (1984): 253–275; Bill Ong Hing, *Defining America through Immigration Policy* (Philadelphia: Temple University Press, 2004), chap. 9; Zolberg, *Nation by Design*, 354–376; Fuchs, "The Corpse That Would Not Die."

11. Christine M. Sierra, "In Search of National Power: Chicanos Working the System on Immigration Reform, 1976–1986," in Montejano, *Chicano Politics and Society*, 131–153; Fuchs, "Corpse That Would Not Die," 115–116.

12. Jason DeParle, "The Anti-Immigration Crusader," *New York Times*, April 17, 2011; John Tanton, "Witan Memo III," Southern Poverty Law Center, October 10, 1986, https://www.splcenter.org/fighting-hate/intelligence-report/2015/witan-memo-iii. See also Southern Poverty Law Center, "John Tanton," https://www.splcenter.org/fighting-hate/extremist-files/individual/john-tanton.

13. "The Candidates Debate: Transcript of the Reagan-Mondale Debate on Foreign Policy," *New York Times*, October 22, 1984; Fuchs, "The Corpse That Would Not Die," 118.

14. Zolberg, *Nation by Design*, 365–366; Fuchs, "The Corpse That Would Not Die," 124–125.

15. Fuchs, "The Corpse That Would Not Die," 111, 125.

16. 99th Cong., Public Law 99-603 (enacted November 6, 1986), 100 Stat. 3359.

17. Robert Pear, "President Signs Landmark Bill on Immigration," *New York Times*, November 7, 1986; Muzaffar Chishti and Charles Kamasaki, "IRCA in Retrospect: Guideposts for Today's Immigration Reform," *Migration Policy Institute Issue Brief* 9 (January 2014), 1.

18. Chishti and Kamasaki, "IRCA in Retrospect," 6–7.

19. Xóchitl Bada, Oscar A. Chacón, and Jonathan Fox, eds., "Latino Immigrants in the Windy City: New Trends in Civic Engagement," *Reports on Latino Immigrant Civic Engagement* 6 (Washington, DC: Woodrow Wilson International Center for Scholars, January 2010), 13; interview with Vanna Slaughter, April 30, 2010.

20. Interview with Vanna Slaughter.

21. Zolberg, *Nation by Design*, 371; Bada, Chacón, and Fox, "Latino Immigrants in the Windy City," 13; Dallas estimate based on relative sizes of Chicago and Dallas immigrant populations and share of Dallas in US Hispanic population.

22. Frank De Avila oral history, recorded May 5, 2016, digital audio file (in the author's possession); Frank Trejo, interview with the author, February 21, 2010; interview with Vanna Slaughter.

23. David S. North and Anna Mary Portz, *The US Alien Legalization Program* (Washington, DC: TransCentury Development Associates, 1989); Cecilia Muñoz, *Unfinished Business: The Immigration Reform and Control Act of 1986* (Washington, DC: National Council of La Raza, 1990).

24. Jorge Durand, Douglas S. Massey, and Emilio A. Parrado, "The New Era of Mexican Migration to the United States," *Journal of American History* 86 (1999): 523–525. See also Douglas Massey, "Understanding America's Immigration 'Crisis,'" *Proceedings of the American Philosophical Society* 151 (2007): 309–327.

25. López Castro, *El Rio Bravo Es Charco*.

26. Maria de Lourdes Villar, "Rethinking Settlement Processes: The Experience of Mexican Undocumented Migrants in Chicago," *Urban Anthropology and Studies of Cultural Systems and World Economic Development* 19 (1990): 73–74.

27. Durand, Massey, and Parrado, "New Era of Mexican Migration," 518–536; Douglas S. Massey and Kristin E. Espinosa, "What's Driving Mexico-US Migration? A Theoretical, Empirical, and Policy Analysis," *American Journal of Sociology* 102 (1997): 939–999. See also Massey, "Understanding America's Immigration 'Crisis.'"

28. Shirley J. Smith, Roger G. Kramer, and Audrey Singer, *Characteristics and Labor Market Behavior of the Legalized Population Five Years Following Legalization* (Washington, DC: US Department of Labor, 1996); Mary G. Powers, William Seltzer, and Jing Shi, "Gender Differences in the Occupational Status of Undocumented Immigrants in the United States: Experience before and after Legalization," *International Migration Review* 32 (1998): 1015–1046; Ellen Percy Kraly, William Seltzer, and Mary G. Powers, "US Immigration Policy and Immigrant Immigration: Occupational Mobility among the Population Legalizing under IRCA," in Lydio F. Tomasi and Mary G. Powers, eds., *Immigration Today: Pastoral and Research Challenges* (New York: Center for Migration Studies, 2000), chap. 7; Rob Paral & Associates, *Economic Progress via Legalization: Lessons from the Last Legalization Program* (Washington, DC: Immigration Policy Center, 2009); Silvia Helena Barcellos, "Legalization and the Economic Status of Immigrants," WR-7 54 (RAND Corporation, March 2010); Fernando A. Lozano and Todd A. Sorensen, "The Labor Market Value to Legal Status," Discussion Paper 5492, Institute for the Study of Labor (February 2011).

29. Durand, Massey, and Parrado, "New Era of Mexican Migration," 527–528.

30. General Accounting Office, "Immigration Reform: Employer Sanctions and the Question of Discrimination: Report to Congress" (March 1990); Katharine M. Donato and Douglas S. Massey, "The Effect of the Immigration Reform and Control Act on the Wages of Mexican Migrants," *Social Science Quarterly* 74 (September 1993); Deborah A. Cobb-Clark, Clinton R. Shiells, and B. Lindsay Lowell, "Immigration Reform: The Effects of Employer Sanctions and Legalization on Wages," *Journal of Labor Economics* 13 (July 1995); Durand, Massey, and Parrado, "New Era of Mexican Migration," 526–529; Carlos Arango, videotaped interview, held at DePaul University Special Collections; Nicholas De Genova, *Working the Boundaries: Race, Space, and "Illegality" in Mexican Chicago* (Durham, NC: Duke University Press, 2005), chap. 5.

31. General Accounting Office, "Immigration Reform"; B. Lindsay Lowell, Jay Teachman, and Zhongren Jing, "Unintended Consequences of Immigration Reform: Discrimination and Hispanic Employment," *Demography* 32 (November 1995); Nicholas De Genova and Ana Y. Ramos-Zayas, *Latino Crossings: Mexicans, Puerto Ricans, and the Politics of Race and Citizenship* (New York: Routledge, 2003), chap. 3; "Mexican Leader Criticized for Comment on Blacks," *CNN*, May 15, 2005, http://www.cnn.com/2005/US/05/14/fox.jackson/.

32. Durand, Massey, and Parrado, "New Era of Mexican Migration," 525–527.

33. Durand, Massey, and Parrado, "New Era of Mexican Migration," 526–527.

34. 1980 Census, Chicago, tables P-53 and P-60; 1990 Census, Chicago, tables 43 and 46; 2000 Census, Chicago, tables 93 and 94; 1980 Census, Dallas, tables P-53 and P-60; 1990 Census, Dallas, tables 43 and 46; 2000 Census, Dallas, tables 93 and 94. These and other statistical measures of improvement over time likely underestimate the economic advances of migrants because some of them moved to more prosperous neighborhoods and were succeeded in Little Village and Oak Cliff by new arrivals just starting in entry-level jobs.

35. Frank De Avila oral history, and see also Alberto Salazar oral history, recorded March 31, 2016, digital audio file (in the author's possession); Daniel Immergluck, "Focusing In: Indicators of Economic Change in Chicago's Neighborhoods," report prepared for the Woodstock Institute (May 1994), held at the Harold Washington Library, Chicago.

36. 1950 Census, Chicago, table 3; 1960 Census, Chicago, table H-1; 1970 Census, Chicago, table H-1; 1980 Census, Chicago, table H-1; 1990 Census, Chicago, table T-73; 2000 Census, Chicago, table T-156; 1950 Census, Dallas, table 3; 1960 Census, Dallas,

table H-1; 1970 Census, Dallas, tables H-1 and H-2; 1980 Census, Dallas, table H-1; 1990 Census, Dallas, table T-73; 2000 Census, Dallas, table T-156.

37. 1960 Census, Chicago, table H-1; 1970 Census, Chicago, table H-2; 1980 Census, Chicago, table H-1; 1990 Census, Chicago, tables T-80 and T-82; 2000 Census, Chicago, tables T-163, T-166, and T-167; 1960 Census, Dallas, table H-1; 1970 Census, Dallas, tables H-1 and H-2; 1980 Census, Dallas, tables H-1 and H-8; 1990 Census, Dallas, tables 9 and 33.

38. 1980 Census, Chicago, table H-8; 1990 Census, Chicago, table T-83; 2000 Census, Chicago, table T-166; 1980 Census, Dallas, table H-8; 1990 Census, Dallas, table T-83; 2000 Census, Dallas, table T-166.

39. Federal Reserve Bank of St. Louis, "30-Year Fixed Rate Mortgage Average in the United States," https://fred.stlouisfed.org/graph/?g=NUh (accessed April 2019).

40. Frank De Avila oral history.

41. Frank De Avila oral history; Gloria Rubio oral history.

42. Gloria Rubio oral history.

43. Gloria Rubio oral history.

44. Gloria Rubio oral history; Marielos Ramírez, "Gloria Rubio: Una salvadoreña que conquistó el paladar de los anglosajones," *El Salvador Magazine*, October 2, 2012.

45. Rebeca Raijman and Marta Tienda, "Immigrants' Pathways to Business Ownership: A Comparative Ethnic Perspective," *International Migration Review* 34 (2000): 695; Marta Tienda and Rebecca Raijman, "Promoting Hispanic Immigrant Entrepreneurship in Chicago," *Journal of Developmental Entrepreneurship* 9 (2004): 4.

46. Raijman and Tienda, "Immigrants' Pathways to Business Ownership"; Tienda and Raijman, "Promoting Hispanic Immigrant Entrepreneurship." See also Rebeca Raijman and Marta Tienda, "Training Functions of Ethnic Economies: Mexican Entrepreneurs in Chicago," *Sociological Perspectives* 43 (2000): 439–456; Research and Training Associates, "Growth Paths of Larger Hispanic Businesses," report prepared for Department of Economic Development, City of Chicago, March 25, 1985.

47. Robert Kemper et al., "From Undocumented Camionetas (Mini-Vans) to Federally Regulated Motor Carriers," *Urban Anthropology* 36 (2007): 382–384, 405, 409–410; Michael Peter Smith and Matt Baker, *Citizenship across Borders: The Political Transnationalism of El Migrante* (Ithaca, NY: Cornell University Press, 2008), 61; Mary Sutter, "Mexicanal Added to DTV," *Variety*, July 27, 2005.

48. Teresa Gubbins, "How Supermarkets Cater to the Neighborhood," *Dallas Morning News*, September 29, 1993, 1F; Teresa Gubbins, "Special Extras," *Dallas Morning News*, September 29, 1993, 6F; Waltrina Stovall, "Global Groceries," *Dallas Morning News*, July 31, 1994, "Dallas Life" section, 10; "Global Groceries," *Dallas Morning News*, July 31, 1994; Jenalia Morena, "Retailer Pushes North," *Houston Chronicle*, August 20, 2006, 1B; U.S. Dept. of Commerce, International Trade Commission, Office of Trade and Economic Analysis, "Metropolitan Area Exports: An Export Performance Report on over 250 U.S. Cities, 1993–1998" (Washington, DC: US Government Printing Office, 1999), 23. This expansion was of course facilitated by the North American Free Trade Agreement.

49. Nick Cordova oral history, recorded July 20, 2010, and Rosario Gaytan oral history, recorded July 23, 2010, digital audio files (in the author's possession).

50. Tienda and Raijman, "Promoting Hispanic Immigrant Entrepreneurship," 8.

51. Richard T. Herman and Robert L. Smith, *Immigrant, Inc.: Why Immigrant Entrepreneurs Are Driving the New Economy* (New York: Wiley, 2010), 184–185.

52. Xóchitl Bada, *Mexican Hometown Associations in Chicagoacán: From Local to Transnational Civic Engagement* (New Brunswick, NJ: Rutgers University Press, 2014). Bada's indispensable book includes a bibliography on hometown associations.

53. David Waldstreicher, *In The Midst of Perpetual Fetes: The Making of American Nationalism, 1776–1820* (Chapel Hill: University of North Carolina Press, 1997),

128–130; Tyler Anbinder, "Moving Beyond 'Rags to Riches': New York's Irish Famine Immigrants and Their Surprising Savings Accounts," *Journal of American History* 99 (December 2012): 741–770; Bruno Ramírez, *On the Move: French-Canadian and Italian Migrants in the North Atlantic Economy, 1860–1914* (Toronto: McClelland and Stewart, 1990); Gregor Benton and Hong Liu, *Dear China: Emigrant Letters and Remittances, 1820–1980* (Berkeley: University of California Press, 2018). The definitive work on remittances and the built environment is Sarah Lynn Lopez, *The Remittance Landscape: Spaces of Migration in Rural Mexico and Urban USA* (Chicago: University of Chicago Press, 2015).

54. Bada, *Mexican Hometown Associations in Chicagoacán*, 48; *The Other Side of the Border*, dir. Ginny Martin (KERA Dallas/Fort Worth, 1987) (videotape, PBS Video).

55. Rudoph J. Vecoli, "*Contadini* in Chicago: A Critique of *The Uprooted*," *Journal of American History* 51 (December 1964), 412–414; Pacyga, *Chicago*, 118–122; Innis-Jiménez, *Steel Barrio*, 117–123; Bada, *Mexican Hometown Associations in Chicagoacán*, chap. 2.

56. César Valenciano Vazquez, email communication with the author, December 1, 2012.

57. Bada, *Mexican Hometown Associations in Chicagoacán*, 48–50; Natasha Iskander, *Creative State: Forty Years of Migration and Development Policy in Morocco and Mexico* (Ithaca, NY: Cornell University Press, 2010), chaps. 7–9.

58. Smith and Baker, *Citizenship across Borders*, 31–41.

59. Smith and Baker, *Citizenship across Borders*, 31–41; Manuel Rodela, interview by the author, March 6, 2013, digital audio (in the author's possession); Federación de Clubes Zacatecanos del Norte de Téxas, "Zacatecas, Patrimonio Cultural de la Humanidad" (Dallas, 2002), 10, 11, 22. The FCZNT archive is not cataloged.

60. Smith and Baker, *Citizenship across Borders*, 31–41; FCZNT archive photo collection (in Rodela's possession).

61. FCZNT, "Zacatecas, X Aniversario (Zacatecas, tenth anniversary)" (Dallas, 2007); FCZNT, "Zacatecas, XII Aniversario (Zacatecas, twelfth anniversary)" (Dallas, 2009); FCZNT, "Zacatecas, XV Aniversario (Zacatecas, fifteenth anniversary)" (Dallas, 2012).

62. Secretaría de Desarrollo Social (SEDESOL) (Department of Social Development), spreadsheets from 2004, 2009, 2010, and 2011, received from Roberto Joaquin Galíndez, SEDESOL Eastern Zone representative, in emails to the author, November 26, December 10, 2012, and January 9, 2013 (in the author's possession); SEDESOL, "Logros Programa 3x1 para Migrantes" (Achievements of the 3x1 Program for Migrants) (Mexico City, 2012), 3. The peso-dollar exchange rate in this period varied from about nine-to-one to thirteen-to-one. See Board of Governors of the Federal Reserve System, "Foreign Exchange Rates—H.10: Historical Rates for the Mexican Peso," http://www.federalreserve.gov/releases/h10/hist/dat00_mx.htm.

63. SEDESOL, spreadsheets from 2004, received from Roberto Joaquin Galíndez on January 9, 2013; Bada, *Mexican Hometown Associations in Chicagoacán*, 54.

64. SEDESOL, spreadsheets from 2004, 2009, 2010, and 2011, received from Roberto Joaquin Galíndez on November 26 and December 10, 2012, and January 9, 2013; SEDESOL, "Logros Programa 3x1 para Migrantes," 3. The peso-dollar exchange rate in this period was about twelve-to-one.

65. Nicolás Argueta, former ACA president, personal communication with the author, March 13, 2013; SEDESOL, "Memoria del Programa 3x1 para Migrantes, 2007–2012" (Mexico City, 2012), sect. A2; Carolina Stefoni, "Migración, remesas, y desarrollo," *Polis* 30 (2011): 5; Manuel Orozco, with Julia Yansura, "Migration and Development in Central America: Perceptions, Policies, and Further Opportunities" (Washington, DC: InterAmerican Dialogue, 2013), 22–25.

66. On migrantes and the question of agency, see Michael Peter Smith and Luis Eduardo Guarnizo, "Global Mobility, Shifting Borders, and Urban Citizenship," *Tijdschrift voor Economische en Sociale Geografie* 100, 5 (2009): 614.

CHAPTER 10: BUILDING LATINO URBANISM

1. José Angel N., *Illegal: Reflections of an Undocumented Immigrant* (Urbana: University of Illinois Press, 2014), 41; Frank Trejo, interview with the author, February 21, 2010.

2. Richard Sennett, *The Fall of Public Man* (New York: Alfred A. Knopf, 1977); Ehrenhalt, *The Lost City*; Robert D. Putnam, *Bowling Alone: The Collapse and Revival of American Community* (New York: Simon & Schuster, 2000). See also Elaine Tyler May, *Homeward Bound: American Families in the Cold War Era* (New York: Basic Books, 1988); Jeff Wiltse, *Contested Waters: A Social History of Swimming Pools in America* (Chapel Hill: University of North Carolina Press, 2007).

3. Jane Jacobs, *The Death and Life of Great American Cities* (New York: Random House, 1961); Congress for the New Urbanism, "Charter of the New Urbanism," https://www.cnu.org/who-we-are/charter-new-urbanism.

4. James Rojas, "The Enacted Environment: The Creation of 'Place' by Mexicans and Mexican Americans in Los Angeles," master's thesis, Massachusetts Institute of Technology, 1991; Gustavo Leclerc, Raúl Villa, and Michael J. Dear, eds., *Latino Urban Cultures: La Vida Latina en LA* (Thousand Oaks, CA: SAGE Publications, 1999); Victor M. Valle and Rodolfo D. Torres, *Latino Metropolis* (Minneapolis: University of Minnesota Press, 2000); Mike Davis, *Magical Urbanism: Latinos Reinvent the US Big City* (London: Verso, 2000); David R. Díaz, *Barrio Urbanism: Chicanos, Planning, and American Cities* (New York: Routledge, 2005); Michael Mendez, "Latino New Urbanism: Building on Cultural Preferences," *Opolis* 1 (2005); David R. Díaz and Rodolfo D. Torres, *Latino Urbanism: The Politics of Planning, Policy, and Redevelopment* (New York: New York University Press, 2012); Michael Rios, Leonardo Vázquez, and Lucrezia Miranda, eds., *Diálogos: Placemaking in Latino Communities* (New York: Routledge, 2012).

5. Dora P. Crouch, Daniel J. Garr, and Axel I. Mundigo, *Spanish City Planning in North America* (Cambridge, MA: MIT Press, 1982); Wilson, Polyzoides, and Gandert, *The Plazas of New Mexico*.

6. Wilson, Polyzoides, and Gandert, *The Plazas of New Mexico*, 11. See also Setha M. Low, *On the Plaza: The Politics of Public Space and Culture* (Austin: University of Texas Press, 2000); Lawrence A. Herzog, *Return to the Center: Culture, Public Space, and City Building in a Global Era* (Austin: University of Texas Press, 2006).

7. Tereso Ortiz interview; Rosario Gaytán, interview by the author, July 22, 2010, digital audio file (in the author's possession). See also Achor, *Mexican Americans in a Dallas Barrio*, 71.

8. US Census 1990, tables 42 and 44 divided by tables 6 and 7 for each tract listed in introduction, note 21.

9. Joyce Dargay, Dermont Gately, and Martin Sommer, "Vehicle Ownership and Income Growth, Worldwide, 1960–2030," *Energy Journals* 28 (2007): 146, 147.

10. Robert Kemper, *Migration and Adaptation: Tzintzuntzán Peasants in Mexico City* (Beverly Hills, CA: SAGE Publications, 1977), 25.

11. Jackson, *Crabgrass Frontier*, 14–17; John W. Reps, *Bird's Eye Views: Historic Lithographs of North American Cities* (Princeton, NJ: Princeton Architectural Press, 1998).

12. Jackson, *Crabgrass Frontier*, chap. 2; Carol Willis, *Form Follows Finance: Skyscrapers and Skylines in New York and Chicago* (Princeton, NJ: Princeton Architectural Press, 1997), introduction.

13. On sprawl, see McShane, *Down the Asphalt Path*; Gutfreund, *Twentieth-Century Sprawl*; Andres Duany, Elizabeth Plater-Zyberk, and Jeff Speck, *Suburban Nation: The Rise of Sprawl and the Decline of the American Dream* (New York: North Point Press, 2000); Dolores Hayden and Jim Wark, *A Field Guide to Sprawl* (New York: W. W. Norton, 2004). For a contrary view, see Robert Bruegmann, *Sprawl: A Compact History* (Chicago: University of Chicago Press, 2005).

14. Nick Cordova oral history.

15. Richard A. Dolejs oral history.

16. Jacobs, *The Death and Life of Great American Cities*, part 2; Rojas, "The Enacted Environment," 51–56; Camilo José Vergara, "Los Paleteros," in Gustavo Leclerc, Raúl Villa, and M. J. Dear, *Urban Latino Cultures: La Vida Latina in LA* (Thousand Oaks, CA: SAGE Publications, 1999); "Special Extras" and "How Supermarkets Cater to the Neighborhood," *Dallas Morning News*, September 29, 1993.

17. Lizabeth Cohen, "From Town Center to Shopping Center: The Reconfiguration of Community Marketplaces in Postwar America," *American Historical Review* 101 (October 1996): 1050–1081; Richard Longstreth, *City Center to Regional Mall: Architecture, the Automobile, and Retailing in Los Angeles, 1920–1950* (Cambridge, MA: MIT Press, 1997).

18. Leinberger, *The Option of Urbanism*, chap. 2; Isenberg, *Downtown America*, chaps. 5 and 6.

19. Leinberger, *The Option of Urbanism*, chap. 3.

20. Nelson Lichtenstein, *The Retail Revolution: How Wal-Mart Created a Brave New World of Business* (New York: Henry Holt, 2009), esp. chap. 2.

21. Alejandro Portes and Robert L. Bach, *Latin Journey: Cuban and Mexican Immigrants in the United States* (Berkeley: University of California Press, 1985); Marta Tienda and M. Rosenfeld, "Labor Market Implications of Mexican Migration: Economies of Scale, Innovation, and Entrepreneurship," in Frank D. Bean, Rodolfo de la Garza, Bryan Roberts, and Sidney Weintraub, eds., *At the Crossroads: Mexico and US Immigration Policy* (New York: Rowman & Littlefield, 1997), 177–199; Ivan Light and Steven J. Gold, *Ethnic Economies* (San Diego: Academic Press, 2000).

22. Thomas A. Reardon and Julio A. Berdegue, "The Rapid Rise of Supermarkets in Latin America: Challenges and Opportunities for Development," *Development Policy Review* 20 (2002): 371–388.

23. Amanda Seligman, "North Lawndale," in Grossman, Keating, and Reiff, *Encyclopedia of Chicago*, 575–576.

24. Daniel D. Arreola, "Mexican American Housescapes," *Geographical Review* 78 (July 1988): 299–315.

25. Tod Robberson, interview by the author, January 15, 2010, notes (in the author's possession); A. K. Sandoval-Strausz, "Latino Vernaculars and the Emerging National Landscape," *Buildings and Landscapes* 20 (2013): 7.

26. Rojas, "The Enacted Environment," 78–83.

27. Joseph Sciorra and Martha Cooper, "'I Feel Like I'm in My Country': Puerto Rican Casitas in New York City," *TDR* 34, no. 4 (1990): 156–168.

28. Daniel D. Arreola, *Tejano South Texas: A Mexican American Cultural Province* (Austin: University of Texas Press, 2002), esp. 78–80, 117–119; Wilson, Polyzoides, and Gandert, *The Plazas of New Mexico*; Low, *On the Plaza*; Herzog, *Return to the Center*.

29. Jesse Tafalla oral history.

30. Dallas Department of Planning, *El Barrio Study Phase 1: City of Dallas* (1978), 56, "Planning Department Publications and Related Materials, 1966–1990," Box 4, Folder 24, Dallas Municipal Archives.

31. Texas Historical Commission, "Marker Report for Pike Park," July 17, 1981; Arreola, *Tejano South Texas*, 78–79.

32. Anita Martínez oral history; Arreola, *Tejano South Texas*, 79–80, 117–119; Jesse Tafalla oral history; Dallas Department of Planning, *El Barrio Study Phase 1*, 56; Texas Historical Commission, "Marker Report for Pike Park."

33. Alejandro Portes and Alex Stepick, *City on the Edge: The Transformation of Miami* (Berkeley: University of California Press, 1993), 110–111; Christian Krohn-Hansen, *Making New York Dominican: Small Business, Politics, and Everyday Life* (Philadelphia: University of Pennsylvania Press, 2012); see also Pedro A. Regalado, "From Familia to Market: The Puerto Rican Merchants Association (PRMA) and Latinx Entrepreneurship in East Harlem, Brooklyn, and the South Bronx, 1940–1980," chap. 2 of "Where Angels Fear to Tread: Latina/os, Work, and the Making of New York" (PhD Thesis, Yale University, 2019); Marie Price and Courtney Whitworth, "Soccer and Latino Cultural Space: Metropolitan Washington Fútbol Leagues," in Daniel Arreola, ed., *Hispanic Spaces, Latino Places: Community and Cultural Diversity in Contemporary America* (Austin: University of Texas Press, 2004), 167–186. See also the rest of the Arreola volume as well as Rios, Vázquez, and Miranda, *Diálogos*.

34. See, for example, Judy Hevrdejs, "Hispanic Chicago: A Time and Place for Celebration," *Chicago Tribune*, September 14, 1990, 30A; Melita Garcia and Constanza Montana, "Hispanic Areas on the Grow: Dreams of Owning Homes, Businesses Helping These Communities to Flourish," *Chicago Tribune*, September 11, 1991, G24; Enrique Rangel, "The Will to Live Again," *Dallas Morning News*, November 19, 1990, 19A; Frank Trejo, "Lasting Imprint: From Markets to Marketing, Hispanic Culture Increasingly Apparent in Aspects of Daily Life," *Dallas Morning News*, June 15, 1992; Lewis, "Farewell to Cracker Eden."

35. "Police Invasion of Oak Cliff Dampens Hispanic Fete," *Dallas Morning News*, October 21, 1993.

36. Guadalupe Lozano transcript, 12–13; Cisneros, *The House on Mango Street*, "Those Who Don't"; "Police Invasion of Oak Cliff Dampens Hispanic Fete," *Dallas Morning News*, October 21, 1993; Robert J. Sampson, "Rethinking Crime and Immigration," *Contexts* 7, no. 1 (2008): 29–30.

37. 110 U.S. Statutes at Large 3009; Walter A. Ewing, Daniel E. Martínez, and Rubén G. Rumbaut, "The Criminalization of Immigration in the United States," American Immigration Council Special Report (July 2015), 13–14; Christina Gerken, *Model Immigrants and Undesirable Aliens: The Cost of Immigration Reform in the 1990s* (Minneapolis: University of Minnesota Press, 2013).

38. Robert J. Sampson, "Immigration and the New Social Transformation of the American City," in Vitiello and Sugrue, *Immigration and Metropolitan Revitalization*, 13; Ewing, Martínez, and Rumbaut, "The Criminalization of Immigration in the United States," 1; Robert J. Sampson, keynote address at the "Immigration and Metropolitan Revitalization" conference, University of Pennsylvania, May 19, 2014.

39. Ewing, Martínez, and Rumbaut, "The Criminalization of Immigration in the United States," 1.

40. Chicago Police Department, "Chicago Police Statistical Report" or "Chicago Police Statistical Summary," issued yearly and available at https://home.chicagopolice .org/inside-the-cpd/statistical-reports/annual-reports/; Chicago Police Department, "Chicago Murder Analysis 2011." Note that the peak rate was influenced by the city's gradually declining population. Note also the questions raised about crime reporting in the city: David Bernstein and Noah Isackson, "The Truth about Chicago's Crime Rate," *Chicago*, April 7, 2014.

41. Figures cited or calculated from "Dallas Police Homicide Report," January 9, 2012, at http://www3.dallascityhall.com/committee_briefings/briefings0112/PS_Dallas PoliceHomicideReport_010912.pdf; Tristan Hullman, "Dallas Murder Rate Falls to Lowest

Point since 1930," *Dallas Morning News*, January 7, 2015; 1990 Census, Dallas, table 1; US Census Bureau, United States: 2010; Summary Population and Housing Characteristics—2010 Census of Population and Housing, CPH-1-1 (Washington, DC: US Government Printing Office, 2013), tables 2, 37, summary file 1 (hereafer 2010 Census, Dallas).

42. FBI Uniform Crime Reports at https://ucr.fbi.gov/crime-in-the-u.s; Sampson, "Immigration and the New Social Transformation," 12–14.

43. Steven D. Levitt, "Understanding Why Crime Fell in the 1990s: Four Factors That Explain the Decline and Six That Do Not," *Journal of Economic Perspectives* 18 (2004): 163–190; Kevin Drum, "An Updated Lead-Crime Roundup for 2018," *Mother Jones* (February 2018); Sharkey, *Uneasy Peace*.

44. Ewing, Martínez, and Rumbaut, "The Criminalization of Immigration in the United States." See also John Hagan and Alberto Palloni, "Sociological Criminology and the Mythology of Hispanic Immigration and Crime," *Social Problems* 46 (November 1999): 617–632; Ramiro Martínez Jr. and Matthew T. Lee, "On Immigration and Crime," in Gary LaFree, ed., *The Nature of Crime: Continuity and Change*, vol. 1, National Institute of Justice Report 182408 (July 2000), 485–524; Tim Wadsworth, "Is Immigration Responsible for the Crime Drop? An Assessment of the Influence of Immigration on Changes in Violent Crime between 1990 and 2000," *Social Science Quarterly* 91 (June 2010): 531–553; Christopher J. Lyons, María B. Vélez, and Wayne A. Santoro, "Neighborhood Immigration, Violence, and City-Level Immigrant Political Opportunities," *American Sociological Review* 78 (August 2013): 604–632.

45. Sampson, "Rethinking Crime and Immigration," 29.

46. Ruth D. Peterson and Lauren J. Krivo, "The National Neighborhood Crime Study, 2000," Inter-University Consortium for Political and Social Research, University of Michigan (2010); "Crime in Chicago: Explore Your Community," *Chicago Tribune*, January 9, 2018, http://crime.chicagotribune.com/chicago/community (accessed August 18, 2014).

47. I worked with criminologist María Vélez using the data from Peterson and Krivo, "The National Neighborhood Crime Study, 2000"; "Crime in Chicago: Explore Your Community," *Chicago Tribune*; Roberto Vargas, *Wounded City: Violent Turf Wars in a Chicago Barrio* (New York: Oxford University Press, 2016), 15.

48. For additional citations on these phenomena, see Robert J. Sampson, *Great American City: Chicago and the Enduring Neighborhood Effect* (Chicago: University of Chicago Press, 2012), 251–260; Sampson, "Immigration and the New Social Transformation," 15–20.

49. Sampson, *Great American City*, 21–22.

50. See, for example, Mitchell Duneier, "Ethnography, the Ecological Fallacy, and the 1995 Chicago Heat Wave," *American Sociological Review* 71, no. 4 (2006): 679–688; Sampson, *Great American City*, 39–40.

51. Jacobs, *The Death and Life of Great American Cities*, 35–36, 53–56, 77–78; A. K. Sandoval-Strausz, "Latino Landscapes: Immigration and Urbanism, 1945–2010," paper presented at the annual meeting of the Vernacular Architecture Forum, Butte, MT, June 13, 2009; Claudia Kolker, *The Immigrant Advantage: What We Can Learn from Newcomers to America about Health, Happiness, and Hope* (New York: Free Press, 2011), 139.

52. Eric Klinenberg, *Heat Wave: A Social Autopsy of Disaster in Chicago* (Chicago: University of Chicago Press, 2002), 1–11.

53. Klinenberg, *Heat Wave*, 19.

54. Klinenberg, *Heat Wave*, 53–64, 84.

55. Sandoval-Strausz, "Latino Vernaculars and the Emerging National Landscape," 5–7; Klinenberg, *Heat Wave*, 90–109. My interpretation differs slightly from Klinenberg's because I emphasize the Latin American and Latino origins of the Little Village landscape;

he presents its "cultural practices" as the dependent variable, "effects" of the "social ecology" of the area.

56. Klinenberg, *Heat Wave*, 90–94, 109–110, 116.

57. Kyriakos Markides and Jeannine Coreil, "The Health of Hispanics in the Southwestern United States: An Epidemiologic Paradox," *Public Health Reports* 101, no. 3 (1986): 253–265; David E. Hayes-Bautista et al., "Latino Health in California, 1985–1990: Implications for Family Practice," *Family Medicine* 26, no. 9 (1994): 556–562; Sampson, *Great American City*, 251–260; Pamela Balls Organista, Gerardo Marín, and Kevin M. Chun, *Multicultural Psychology*, 2nd ed. (Lanham, MD: Rowman & Littlefield, 2018), 100, 219–220.

58. Kathleen A. Cagney, Christopher R. Browning, and Danielle M. Wallace, "The Latino Paradox in Neighborhood Context: The Case of Asthma and Other Respiratory Conditions," *American Journal of Public Health* 97 (2007): 919–925.

CHAPTER 11: A NEW URBAN AMERICA

1. Quiara Alegría Hudes and Lin-Manuel Miranda, *In the Heights: The Complete Book and Lyrics of the Broadway Musical* (New York: Applause Libretto Library, 2013). The earliest version of the show was performed at Wesleyan University.

2. Hudes and Miranda, *In the Heights*, 118.

3. Hudes and Miranda, *In the Heights*, 146, 148–149.

4. James Bennet, "The Last of Frankfurt-on-the-Hudson: A Staunch, Aging Few Stay On as Their World Evaporates," *New York Times*, August 27, 1992; Rose Hackman, "The Last Affordable Neighborhoods in Manhattan: 'The Air Is Fresher Up Here,'" *Guardian*, August 29, 2016; New York Police Department crime statistics by precinct available at https://www1.nyc.gov/site/nypd/stats/crime-statistics/compstat.page.

5. The demographic shifts in these and any other American neighborhoods as recorded by the US Census Bureau can be quickly surveyed at socialexplorer.com by selecting the corresponding census tracts at any decennial census and selecting categories such as race, nativity, and foreign born–place of birth.

6. "Mapping Segregation," *New York Times*, July 8, 2015, https://www.nytimes.com /interactive/2015/07/08/us/census-race-map.html; "The Racial Dot Map," https://demo graphics.virginia.edu/DotMap/.

7. Jamie Winders, *Nashville in the New Millennium: Immigrant Settlement, Urban Transformation, and Social Belonging* (New York: Russell Sage Foundation, 2013); Edgar Sandoval, *The New Face of Small-Town America: Snapshots of Latino Life in Allentown, Pennsylvania* (University Park: Pennsylvania State University Press, 2010); Yolanda Prieto, *The Cubans of Union City: Immigrants and Exiles in a New Jersey Community* (Philadelphia: Temple University Press, 2009). For a national metropolitan demographic perspective, see John Iceland, *Where We Live Now: Immigration and Race in the United States* (Berkeley: University of California Press, 2009).

8. Teaford, *The Twentieth-Century American City* (2016), 197; Audrey Singer, Susan W. Hardwick, and Caroline B. Brettell, *Twenty-First Century Gateways: Immigrant Incorporation in Suburban America* (Washington, DC: Brookings Institution Press, 2008); population statistics from the US Census Bureau, American Fact Finder, https://factfinder .census.gov/faces/nav/jsf/pages/index.xhtml; Michael B. Katz, Mathew J. Creighton, Daniel Amsterdam, and Merlin Chowkwanyun, "Immigration and the New Metropolitan Geography," *Journal of Urban Affairs* 32, no. 5 (2010): 523–547.

9. Pinedo, Castañeda, and Teran, "Occupational Health and Safety among Latinos in the United States"; Mark Hugo Lopez and Gretchen Livingston, "Hispanics and

the Criminal Justice System: Low Confidence, High Exposure," Pew Research Center: Hispanic Trends Project, April 7, 2009, http://www.pewhispanic.org/2009/04/07/hispanics-and-the-criminal-justice-system/.

10. US Census Bureau, "Statistical Abstract of the United States: 2003; No. HS-7: Population of the Largest 75 Cities: 1960–2000" (Washington, DC: US Government Printing Office, 2003); 2010 Census, table 2 and summary file 1; Teaford, *The Twentieth-Century American City* (2016), 184; Vitiello and Sugrue, *Immigration and Metropolitan Revitalization*, 1; United States Conference of Mayors, "U.S. Metro Economies: Outlook—Gross Metropolitan Product, and Critical Role of Transportation Infrastructure (July 2012), 1; United States Bureau of Economic Analysis, "Gross Domestic Product by Metropolitan Area, 2012 and Revised 2001–2011," September 17, 2013, https://www.bea.gov/news/2013/gross-domestic-product-metropolitan-area-2012-and-revised-2001-2011.

11. Glaeser, *Triumph of the City*; Katz and Bradley, *The Metropolitan Revolution*; Vitiello and Sugrue, *Immigration and Metropolitan Revitalization*; Brueckner and Rosenthal, "Gentrification and Neighborhood Housing Cycles"; Suleiman Osman, *The Invention of Brownstone Brooklyn* (New York: Oxford University Press, 2011); Shkuda, *The Lofts of SoHo*.

12. Richard Florida, *The Rise of the Creative Class: And How It's Transforming Work, Leisure, Community, and Everyday Life* (New York: Basic Books, 2002).

13. Florida, *The Rise of the Creative Class*; Richard Florida, *The New Urban Crisis* (New York: Basic Books, 2017), xvi–xvii. See also Alec MacGillis, "The Ruse of the Creative Class," *American Prospect* (January 4, 2010).

14. Sassen, *Cities in a World Economy*, 2. Sassen's book has been through five editions since 1994. On immigrant workers' job sectors in Chicago, see Sandoval-Strausz, "Migrantes, Negocios, and Infraestructura."

15. Victor Couture and Jessie Handbury, "Urban Revival in America, 2000 to 2010," National Bureau of Economic Research Working Paper 24084 (November 2017), 1–3, 9. A useful survey of the literature is Brueckner and Rosenthal, "Gentrification and Neighborhood Housing Cycles." See also Edward Glaeser, Jed Kolko, and Albert Saiz, "Consumer City," National Bureau of Economic Research Working Paper 7790 (July 2000).

16. Dowell Myers, "Immigration: Fundamental Force in the American City," *Housing Facts and Findings* 1 (1999); Roberto Suro and Audrey Singer, "Latino Growth in Metropolitan America: Changing Patterns, New Locations," Brookings Institution Center on Urban and Metropolitan Policy and Pew Hispanic Center Survey Series (July 2002); Davis, *Magical Urbanism*.

17. Ana Gonzalez-Barrera, "More Mexicans Leaving Than Coming to the US," Pew Research Center, November 19, 2015, https://www.pewhispanic.org/2015/11/19/more-mexicans-leaving-than-coming-to-the-u-s/.

18. 2000 Census, Chicago, tables 14 and 15; 2010 Census, Chicago, tables 2, 37, summary file 1; 2000 Census, Dallas, tables 14 and 15; 2010 Census, Dallas, tables 2, 37, summary file 1.

19. Francisco Alba, "Mexico: The New Migration Narrative," Migration Policy Institute profile, April 24, 2013; Douglas S. Massey, ed., "Immigration & the Future of America," *Daedalus* special issue, Summer 2013; Ana Gonzalez-Barrera, "More Mexicans Leaving Than Coming to the US," Pew Research Center report, November 19, 2015; Jorge Durand, *Historia mínima de la migración México-Estados Unidos* (Ciudad de México: El Colegio de México, 2016), chaps. 7, 8.

20. Douglas Massey, Katharine Donato, John Hiksey, and Jorge Durand, *Continental Divides: International Migration in the Americas* (Thousand Oaks, CA: Sage Publications, 2010), special issue of the *Annals of the American Academy of Political and Social Science*;

Nancy Foner, "Immigration Past & Present," in Massey, ed. "Immigration & the Future of America."

21. Alba, "Mexico: The New Migration Narrative;" Gonzalez-Barrera, "More Mexicans Leaving Than Coming to the US."

22. Mary C. Waters and Marisa Gerstein Pineau, eds., *The Integration of Immigrants into American Society*, National Academies of Sciences, Engineering, and Medicine, Committee on Population (Washington, DC: National Academies Press, 2015), 11, 28; Gustavo López, Kristen Bialik, and Jynnah Radford, "Key Findings about US Immigrants," Pew Research Center, November 30, 2018, https://www.pewresearch.org/fact-tank/2018/11/30/key-findings-about-u-s-immigrants/.

23. George W. Bush video clip, 1999, aired on *Anderson Cooper 360*, May 16, 2006; Jonathan Chait, "The GOP's Smart Plan to Avoid Change," *New York*, March 18, 2013; Roberto Suro, Richard Fry, and Jeffrey S. Passel, "How Latinos Voted in 2004," Pew Research Center, June 27, 2005, https://www.pewhispanic.org/2005/06/27/iv-how-latinos-voted-in-2004/.

24. S. 1033, 109th Cong., 1st sess., introduced May 12, 2005.

25. Julie Leininger Pycior, *Democratic Renewal and the Mutual Aid Legacy of US Mexicans* (College Station: Texas A&M University Press, 2014), 147.

26. David M. Reimers, *Unwelcome Strangers: American Identity and the Turn against Immigration* (New York: Columbia University Press, 1998), 112, quoting Brimelow, *Alien Nation*, introduction.

27. H.R. 4437, 109th Cong., 1st sess., introduced December 6, 2005; for the House roll call, see "Final Vote Results for Roll Call 661," December 16, 2005, http://clerk.house.gov/evs/2005/roll661.xml; Joel S. Fetzer, "Why Did House Members Vote for H.R. 4437?," *International Migration Review* 40, no. 3: 698–706.

28. Amalia Pallares and Nilda Flores-González, eds., *¡Marcha!: Latino Chicago and the Immigrant Rights Movement* (Urbana: University of Illinois Press, 2010), introduction; Roger Mahony, "There Is a Higher Law: Welcome the Stranger," *New York Times*, March 22, 2006.

29. Jonathan Fox, Andrew Selee, and Xóchitl Bada, eds., *Invisible No More: Mexican Migrant Participation in the United States* (Washington, DC: Woodrow Wilson International Center for Scholars, 2007), table 8.1.

30. Oscar Avila and Antonio Olivo, "A Show of Strength," *Chicago Tribune*, March 11, 2006; Daniel Hernández, "Stirring the Other LA," *LA Weekly*, March 27, 2006; Roberto Suro, "Out of the Shadows, into the Light," in Kim Voss and Irene Bloemraad, eds., *Rallying for Immigrant Rights: The Fight for Inclusion in 21st Century America* (Berkeley: University of California Press, 2011).

31. John McCain, appearing on *CNN*, *American Morning*, January 31, 2008.

32. William H. Frey, *Diversity Explosion: How New Racial Demographics Are Remaking America*, 2nd ed. (Washington, DC: Brookings Institution, 2018), 221–224.

33. Theda Skocpol and Vanessa Williamson, *The Tea Party and the Remaking of Republican Conservatism* (New York: Oxford University Press, 2012); Arizona v. United States, 567 U.S. 387 (2012).

34. Julia Preston and Steven Yaccino, "Obama Policy on Immigrants Is Challenged by Chicago," *New York Times*, July 10, 2012; Christina Boyle, "Mayor Bloomberg: New York Is Most Immigrant-Friendly City in the Country," *New York Daily News*, April 25, 2012; Catherine Saillant, "Mayor Wants City to Issue Photo IDs," *Los Angeles Times*, October 13, 2012.

35. Global Detroit, "About," http://www.globaldetroit.com/about/; Global Detroit, "For City Builders," http://www.globaldetroit.com/city-builders/; Welcoming Economies Global Network, "Leading Rust Belt Immigrant Innovation," https://www.weglobal

network.org/. See also Waters and Pineau, *The Integration of Immigrants into American Society*, 236.

36. Reid Wilson, "Texas to Debate Ending In-State Tuition for Undocumented Immigrants," *The Hill*, November 18, 2016; Mitt Romney, Republican primary debate, Tampa, FL, January 23, 2012.

37. Binyamin Applebaum, "Employment Data May Be the Key to the President's Job," *New York Times*, June 1, 2011; Frey, *Diversity Explosion*, 221–224; John Sides and Lynn Vavreck, *The Gamble: Choice and Chance in the 2012 Presidential Election* (Princeton, NJ: Princeton University Press, 2013).

38. Ruy Teixeira and John Halpin, "The Obama Coalition in the 2012 Election and Beyond," Center for American Progress (December 2012), 9–17.

39. Henry Barbour, Sally Bradshaw, Ari Fleischer, Zori Fonalledas, and Glenn McCall for the Republican National Committee, *Growth and Opportunity Project* (2013), 8.

40. S. 744, 113th Cong., 1st sess., introduced April 16, 2013; for the Senate roll call, see "S.744: Border Security, Economic Opportunity, and Immigration Modernization Act," https://www.congress.gov/bill/113th-congress/senate-bill/744.

41. Ginger Gibson, "Boehner: No Vote on Senate Immigration Bill," *Politico*, July 8, 2013; Jeremy W. Peters and Ashley Parker, "Marco Rubio's History on Immigration Leaves Conservatives Distrustful of Shift," *New York Times*, November 14, 2015.

42. Donald J. Trump presidential campaign announcement, June 16, 2015.

43. First presidential debate, Hempstead, NY, September 26, 2016.

44. Gia Tolentino, "Trump and the Truth: The 'Mexican' Judge," *New Yorker*, September 20, 2016; Katie Reilly, "Paul Ryan: Donald Trump's Comments Are 'Textbook Definition of a Racist Comment,'" *Time*, June 7, 2016.

45. CNN Exit Poll of the 2016 presidential election, at https://www.cnn.com/election/2016/results/exit-polls/national/president; Larry Sabato, Kyle Kondik, and Geoffrey Skelley, *Trumped: The 2016 Election That Broke All the Rules* (Lanham, MD: Rowman & Littlefield, 2017), especially chaps. 1, 2, 8; Chad Shearer, "The Small Town–Big City Split That Elected Donald Trump," Brookings Metropolitan Policy Program report, November 11, 2016; Ronald Brownstein, "How the Election Revealed the Divide Between City and Country," *Atlantic*, Nov 17, 2016.

46. Nicholas Carnes and Noam Lupu, "It's Time to Bust the Myth: Most Trump Voters Were Not Working Class," *Washington Post*, June 5, 2017.

47. Sarah A. Donovan and David H. Bradley for the Congressional Research Service, "Real Wage Trends, 1979 to 2017," Report 45090, March 15, 2018; Paul Krugman, *The Great Unraveling: Losing Our Way in the New Century* (New York: Norton, 2003), 58; Joseph E. Stiglitz, *The Price of Inequality: How Today's Divided Society Endangers Our Future* (New York: Norton, 2012), 81–82, 383; Cowie and Heathcott, *Beyond the Ruins*, ix; Lawrence Michel and Alyssa Davis, "Top CEOs Make 300 Times More Than Typical Workers; Pay Growth Surpasses Stock Gains and Wage Growth of Top 0.1 Percent," Economic Policy Institute (June 21, 2015); Anne Case and Angus Deaton, "Rising Morbidity and Mortality in Midlife among White Non-Hispanic Americans in the 21st Century," *Proceedings of the National Academies* 112, no. 49 (December 8, 2015): 15078–15083.

48. Justin P. Steil, Len Albright, Jacob S. Rugh, and Douglas S. Massey, "The Social Structure of Mortgage Discrimination," *Housing Studies* 33 (2018): 759–776; Lisa J. Dettling, Joanne W. Hsu, Lindsay Jacobs, Kevin B. Moore, and Jeffrey P. Thompson, "Recent Trends in Wealth-Holding by Race and Ethnicity: Evidence from the Survey of Consumer Finances," *FEDS Notes* (September 27, 2017); CNN Exit Poll.

49. Rob Hoffman, "How the Left Created Trump," *Politico*, November 20, 2016; Mark Lilla, "The End of Identity Liberalism," *New York Times*, November 18, 2016.

50. See, for example, Ryan Cooper, "The Media Is Blinded by Its Obsession with Rural White Trump Voters," *The Week*, December 28, 2017; James Wolcott, "The 'Left Behind' Trump Voter Has Nothing More to Tell Us," *Vanity Fair*, September 7, 2018.

51. Andrew Gelman and Josh Sides, "Stories and Stats," *Boston Review*, September 10, 2009, http://bostonreview.net/gelman-sides-stories-and-stats; Daniel Cox, Juhem Navarro-Rivera, and Robert P. Jones, "2012 Post-Election American Values Survey," PRRI (November 15, 2012).

52. See, for example, John Sides, Michael Tesler, and Lynn Vavreck, *Identity Crisis: The 2016 Presidential Campaign and the Battle for the Meaning of America* (Princeton, NJ: Princeton University Press, 2018); Daniel Cox, Rachel Lienesch, and Robert P. Jones, "Beyond Economics: Fears of Cultural Displacement Pushed the White Working Class to Trump," *PRRI/The Atlantic*, May 9, 2017; Diana C. Mutz, "Status Threat, Not Economic Hardship, Explains the 2016 Presidential Vote," *Proceedings of the National Academy of Sciences* 115, no. 19 (May 2018): E4330–E4339; Amy Walter, "Getting to Know White Voters," *Cook Political Report*, August 29, 2018, https://cookpolitical.com/analysis/national /national-politics/getting-know-white-voters, citing Pew Research Center, "An Examination of the 2016 Electorate, Based on Validated Voters," August 2018, at https://www.people-press .org/2018/08/09/an-examination-of-the-2016-electorate-based-on-validated-voters/; Zack Beauchamp, "White Riot: How Racism and Immigration Gave Us Trump, Brexit, and a Whole New Kind of Politics," *Vox*, January 20, 2017, https:// www.vox.com/ 2016/9/19/129 33072/far-right-white-riot-trump-brexit. For a historical perspective, see Carol Anderson, *White Rage: The Unspoken Truth of our Racial Divide* (New York: Bloomsbury USA, 2016) and Ta-Nehisi Coates, "The First White President," *Atlantic*, October 2017.

53. Thomas B. Edsall, "White-on-White Voting," *New York Times*, November 16, 2017.

54. Josh Dawsey, "Trump Derides Protections for Immigrants from 'Shithole' Countries," *Washington Post*, January 12, 2018; David Nakamura, "Study: White House Plan Slashes Legal Immigration Rates by 44 Percent—22 Million Fewer Immigrants over a Half-Century," *Washington Post*, January 29, 2018.

55. Michelle Ye He Lee and Anu Narayanswamy, "Despite Record Spending, 2018 Midterms Highlighted the Limits of Campaign Cash," *Washington Post*, November 7, 2018; Zak Cheney-Rice, "When White Supremacists Target the Black Elderly," *New York*, October 28, 2018; Masha Gessen, "Why the Tree of Life Shooter Was Fixated on the Hebrew Immigrant Aid Society," *New Yorker*, October 27, 2018.

56. US Census Bureau, "The Foreign-Born Population in the United States: 2010," *American Community Survey Reports* (May 2012); Campbell J. Gibson and Emily Lennon, "Historical Census Statistics on the Foreign-Born Population of the United States: 1850–1990," US Census Bureau Population Division Working Paper 29 (February 1999).

57. Roy G. Blakey, "The Revenue Act of 1926," *American Economic Review* 16 (1926): 401–425; Tax Cuts and Jobs Act of 2017, 115th Cong., Public Law 115-97, 131 Stat. 2054.

58. Jon Schuppe, "Most Americans Don't Want Undocumented Immigrants to Leave, Poll Says," *NBC News*, November 24, 2016; Jonathan Easley, "Poll Finds Broad Support for Path to Citizenship for DACA Recipients," *The Hill*, February 26, 2018; Megan Brenan, "Record-High 75% of Americans Say Immigration Is Good Thing," *Gallup Politics*, June 21, 2018. More generally, see Matt A. Barreto, "Trump Thinks He's Still Winning on Immigration, Never Mind What the Election Results Say," *New York Times*, December 18, 2018; Francis Wilkinson, "Trump Is Making Americans More Immigrant-Friendly," *Bloomberg Opinion*, December 19, 2018; Bradley Jones, "Majority of Americans Continue to Say Immigrants Strengthen the US," Pew Research Center (January 31, 2019).

59. Roberto José Andrade Franco, "Boxing Gyms Fight to Save Oak Cliff," *D Magazine* (October 2018).

60. Rachel Stone, "'Casita Triste' Art Project Spotlights Lack of Affordable Housing," *Oak Cliff Advocate*, January 4, 2018; Kathy Wise, "Oak Cliff Is Going to Hell, Thanks to Me," *D Magazine* (October 4, 2018).

61. Jacqueline Serrato, "'Casa Aztlan' Developer Promises to Recreate Mural in Pilsen," *Chicago Tribune/Hoy*, June 23, 2017; Leonard G. Ramírez et al., *Chicanas of 18th Street: Narratives of a Movement from Latino Chicago* (Urbana: University of Illinois Press, 2011), front cover, 13, 18, 24, 76, 86, 89, 116.

62. Jackie Serrato, "Little Village Tenants Protest Evictions: 'We Will Not Be Gentrified!'" *DNAInfo*, August 17, 2016, https://www.dnainfo.com/chicago/20160817/little-village/little-village-tenants-protest-evictions-we-will-not-be-gentrified/; Stephen Gossett, "'F**K Yr Coffee': Vandals Tag Little Village Cafe amid Gentrification Anxieties," *Chicagoist*, October 2, 2017, https://chicagoist.com/2017/10/02/fk_yr_coffee_vandals_tag_little_vil.php; Shannon Pimmel, "Residential Property Records," report on Little Village based on the Cook County Recorder of Deeds and the Cook County Property Tax Portal (in the author's possession); Marcia Soto oral history, recorded April 13, 2016, Heraclio García oral history, recorded April 1, 2016, Juan Rojas oral history, recorded June 7, 2016, and José Luis Arroyo oral history, recorded April 11, 2016, digital audio files (in the author's possession).

63. Arlene R. Dávila, *Barrio Dreams: Puerto Ricans, Latinos, and the Neoliberal City* (Berkeley: University of California Press, 2004); Johana Londoño, "Latino Design in an Age of Neoliberal Multiculturalism: Contemporary Changes in Latin/o American Urban Cultural Representation," *Identities* 17 (2010); Nancy Raquel Mirabal, "Gentrification," in Oxford Bibliographies in Latino Studies, http://www.oxfordbibliographies.com/obo/page/latino-studies.

64. Trina Orlando, "Chicago Church Vandalized for 6th Time This Year, Pastor Says," *NBC Chicago*, October 3, 2016, https://www.nbcchicago.com/news/local/Chicago-Church-Vandalized-For-6th-Time-This-Year-Pastor-Says-395756701.html; "Inside a Church at the Forefront of Chicago's Sanctuary Movement," *PBS*, https://www.pbs.org/video/inside-church-forefront-chicagos-sanctuary-move-chfhll/; Marwa Eltagouri, "Little Village Streets, Restaurants Quiet as Deportation Fears Rise," *Chicago Tribune*, February 19, 2017.

65. Jacqueline Serrato, "ICE Arresta a un 'Raitero' de La Villita Mientras Iba al Trabajo," *Hoy*, August 10, 2018, and "ICE Arresta a Otro Inmigrante de La Villita que Iba en Camioneta de Trabajo," *Hoy*, August 11, 2018; Julieta Chiquillo, "Are Dallas County Constables Quietly Rounding Up Unauthorized Immigrants for ICE?" *Dallas Morning News*, July 31, 2018; Ramos was echoing the words of Janet Murguía of the National Council of La Raza. Muzaffar Chishti, Sarah Pierce, and Jessica Bolter, "The Obama Record on Deportations: Deporter in Chief or Not?," Migration Policy Institute, January 26, 2017, https://www.migrationpolicy.org/article/obama-record-deportations-deporter-chief-or-not; Shoba Sivaprasad Wadhia, *Beyond Deportation: The Role of Prosecutorial Discretion in Immigration Cases* (New York: New York University Press, 2015), chap. 5.

66. John Kelly, "Enforcement of the Immigration Laws to Serve the National Interest," Department of Homeland Security memorandum, February 20, 2017, https://www.dhs.gov/sites/default/files/publications/17_0220_S1_Enforcement-of-the-Immigration-Laws-to-Serve-the-National-Interest.pdf; "Enhancing Public Safety in the Interior of the United States," Executive Order 13768, January 25, 2017; Randy Capps, Muzaffar Chishti, Julia Gelatt, Jessica Bolter, and Ariel G. Ruiz Soto, "Revving Up the Deportation Machinery: Enforcement under Trump and the Pushback," Migration Policy Institute (May 2018); US Immigration and Customs Enforcement, "Fiscal Year 2018 ICE Enforcement and Removal Operations Report"; TRAC Immigration, "Tracking over 2 Million ICE Arrests: A First Look," September 24, 2018, https://trac.syr.edu/immigration/reports/529/; Noah Lanard, "ICE Cold: How a Loyal Obama Bureaucrat Became the Face of Trump's Deportation Force," *Mother Jones*, April 13, 2018. See also Adam Goodman, "Mexican

Migrants and the Rise of the Deportation Regime, 1942–2014" (PhD thesis, University of Pennsylvania, 2015).

67. Lyons, Vélez, and Santoro, "Neighborhood Immigration, Violence, and City-Level Immigrant Political Opportunities"; Tom Jackman, "Police Chiefs' Immigration Task Force Outlines Opposition to Trump Policy," *Washington Post*, March 1, 2017. See also Jonathan Blitzer, "A Veteran ICE Agent, Disillusioned with the Trump Era, Speaks Out," *New Yorker*, July 24, 2017.

CONCLUSION

1. José Luis Arroyo oral history.

2. William H. Frey, *Diversity Explosion: How New Racial Demographics Are Remaking America* (Washington, DC: Brookings Institution Press, 2015), chap. 2, 258n2; Gretchen Livingston, "Births Outside of Marriage Decline for Immigrant Women," Pew Research Center (October 2016); T. J. Matthews and Brady E. Hamilton, "Total Fertility Rates by State and Race and Hispanic Origin: United States, 2017," *National Vital Statistics Reports* 68, no. 1 (January 10, 2018). On the Lebensborn, see the United States Holocaust Memorial Museum's Holocaust Encyclopedia at https://encyclopedia.ushmm.org/content /en/article/ss-and-nazi-policy and https://www.ushmm.org/learn/students/learning-materials -and-resources/poles-victims-of-the-nazi-era/expulsions-and-the-kidnapping-of-children. On the Mat'-Geroinia, see Mie Nakachi, "N. S. Khrushchev and the 1944 Soviet Family Law: Politics, Reproduction, and Language," *East European Politics, Societies, and Cultures* 20 (2006), 40–68.

3. US Census Bureau Population Division, Population Estimates Program, "Historical National Population Estimates: July 1, 1900, to July 1, 1999," April 11, 2000, https:// www.census.gov/population/estimates/nation/popclockest.txt; William Frey, "US Population Growth Hits 80-Year Low, Capping Off a Year of Demographic Stagnation," Brookings, December 21, 2018, https://www.brookings.edu/blog/the-avenue/2018/12/21 /us-population-growth-hits-80-year-low-capping-off-a-year-of-demographic-stagnation/; US Census, "2013–2017 American Community Survey 5-Year Estimates: Percent of Foreign-Born People Born in Latin America"; Waters and Pineau, *The Integration of Immigrants into American Society*, 28.

4. Jeffrey S. Passel and D'Vera Cohn, "Immigration Projected to Drive Growth in US Working-Age Population through at Least 2035," Pew Research Center, March 8, 2017; US Bureau of Labor Statistics, "Labor Force Characteristics of Foreign-Born Workers," USDL-18-0786, https://www.bls.gov/news.release/forbrn.toc.htm; Werner Schink and David Hayes-Bautista, "Latino Gross Domestic Product Report: Quantifying the Impact of American Hispanic Economic Growth," Latino Donor Collaborative (June 2017). For analogous findings, see Gonzalo Huertas and Jacob Funk Kierkegaard, "The Economic Benefits of Latino Immigration: How the Migrant Hispanic Population's Demographic Characteristics Contribute to US Growth," Peterson Institute for International Economics working paper (February 2019).

5. Gayle L. Reznik, Dave Shoffner, and David A. Weaver, "Coping with the Demographic Challenge: Fewer Children and Living Longer," *Social Security Bulletin* 66, no. 4 (2005/2006): 40; Stephen Goss, Alice Wade, J. Patrick Skirvin, Michael Morris, K. Mark Bye, and Danielle Huston, "Effects of Unauthorized Immigration on the Actuarial Status of the Social Security Trust Funds," Social Security Administration Actuarial Note 151 (April 2013), 3.

6. Jie Zong and Jeanne Batalova, "Immigrant Veterans in the United States," Migration Policy Institute (October 13, 2016), https://www.migrationpolicy.org/article

/immigrant-veterans-united-states; US Citizenship and Immigration Services, "Military Naturalization Statistics," https://www.uscis.gov/military/military-naturalization-statistics (updated December 6, 2018); US Department of Defense, "Military Accessions Vital to National Interest (MAVNI) Recruitment Pilot Program," https://dod.defense.gov/news /mavni-fact-sheet.pdf; Kim Parker, Anthony Cilluffo, and Renee Stepler, "6 Facts about the US Military and Its Changing Demographics," Pew Research Center, April 13, 2017, http://www.pewresearch.org/fact-tank/2017/04/13/6-facts-about-the-u-s-military-and-its -changing-demographics/; George M. Reynolds and Amanda Shendruk, "Demographics of the US Military," Council on Foreign Relations, April 24, 2018, https://www.cfr.org /article/demographics-us-military.

7. John Cromartie, Christiane von Reichert, and Ryan Arthun, "Factors Affecting Former Residents' Returning to Rural Communities," US Department of Agriculture, Economic Research Service, Economic Research Report 185 (May 2015), 1; United States Department of Agriculture, Economic Research Service, "Rural America at a Glance," Economic Information Bulletin 182 (November 2017), 1.

8. Cowie, *Capital Moves*; Thurston Domina, "What Clean Break? Education and Nonmetropolitan Migration Patterns, 1989–2004," *Rural Sociology* 71 (2006): 373–398; Patrick J. Carr and Maria J. Kefalas, *Hollowing Out the Middle: The Rural Brain Drain and What It Means for America* (Boston: Beacon Press, 2009); Kenneth M. Johnson, "The Continuing Incidence of Natural Decrease in American Counties," *Rural Sociology* 76 (2011): 74–100; Alana Semuels, "The Graying of Rural America," *Atlantic*, June 2, 2016; Theodore R. Alter, Theodore E. Fuller, Gretchen Seigworth, and Tessa Sontheimer, "Pennsylvania Employment on the Move: 2001–17," Penn State Center for Economic and Community Development report, April 2018; Enrico Moretti, *The New Geography of Jobs* (New York: Houghton Mifflin Harcourt, 2012); Richard Florida, *The New Urban Crisis: How Our Cities Are Increasing Inequality, Deepening Segregation, and Failing the Middle Class—and What We Can Do About It* (New York: Basic Books, 2017).

9. William Kandel and John Cromartie, "New Patterns of Hispanic Settlement in Rural America," US Department of Agriculture, Economic Research Service, Rural Development Research Report 99 (May 2004); William Kandel and Emilio A. Parrado, "Restructuring of the US Meat Processing Industry and New Hispanic Migrant Destinations," *Population and Development Review* 31 (September 2005): 447–471; Patrick J. Carr, Daniel T. Lichter, and Maria J. Kefalas, "Can Immigration Save Small Town America? Hispanic Boomtowns and the Uneasy Path to Renewal," *Annals of the American Academy of Political and Social Science* 641 (May 2012): 40–42; US Department of Labor, "Findings from the National Agricultural Workers Survey (NAWS) 2015–2016: A Demographic and Employment Profile of United States Farmworkers," Research Report No. 13 (January 2018), 1.

10. Kandel and John Cromartie, "New Patterns of Hispanic Settlement," 11; Waters and Pineau, *The Integration of Immigrants into American Society*, 225–227.

11. US Bureau of Labor Statistics, "Workplace Injuries and Illnesses" (Washington, DC: US Department of Labor, 2005); Lise Nelson, "Racialized Landscapes: Whiteness and the Struggle over Farmworker Housing in Woodburn, Oregon," *Cultural Geographies* 15 (2008): 41–62; Gerardo Francisco Sandoval and Marta Maria Maldonado, "Latino Urbanism Revisited: Placemaking in New Gateways and the Urban-Rural Interface," *Journal of Urbanism* 5 (2012): 193–218; Faranak Miraftab, *Global Heartland: Displaced Labor, Transnational Lives, and Local Placemaking* (Bloomington: Indiana University Press, 2016).

12. Steve King of Iowa's 4th Congressional District is a prime example. He has consistently voted to cut or weaken educational, medical, welfare, and retirement programs; against organized labor and civil rights; and in favor of reducing taxes on business and

high incomes: see https://steveking.house.gov/legislation/voting-record. Meanwhile, even though for nearly two decades Iowa's population growth has been entirely attributable to Latino migrants and their families, King has consistently blamed Hispanic immigrants for various problems. In early 2019, shortly after his constituents reelected him to a ninth term, King's statements on white supremacy became too much for the GOP House leadership to bear, and they stripped him of his committee assignments, including on the agriculture subcommittee—leaving him even less able to serve the constituents of his predominantly rural and agricultural district. Trip Gabriel, Jonathan Martin, and Nicholas Fandos, "Steve King Removed from Committee Assignments over White Supremacy Remark," *New York Times*, January 14, 2019. On rural political culture more generally, see Katherine J. Cramer, *The Politics of Resentment: Rural Consciousness in Wisconsin and the Rise of Scott Walker* (Chicago: University of Chicago Press, 2016); Jonathan M. Metzel, *Dying of Whiteness: How the Politics of Racial Resentment Is Killing America's Heartland* (New York: Basic Books, 2019).

13. Carr, Lichter, and Kefalas, "Can Immigration Save Small Town America?" 45–46; Diana R. Gordon, *Village of Immigrants: Latinos in an Emerging America* (New Brunswick, NJ: Rutgers University Press, 2015); Art Cullen, "My Iowa Town Needs Immigrants," *New York Times*, July 30, 2018; Gus Bova and Christopher Collins, "These Rural Panhandle Towns Should Be Shrinking. But Thanks to Immigrants, They're Booming," *Texas Observer*, January 3, 2019.

14. Southern Poverty Law Center, "Injustice on Our Plates," November 8, 2010, https://www.splcenter.org/20101107/injustice-our-plates; Trevor Tompson and Jennifer Benz, "The Public Mood: White Malaise but Optimism among Blacks, Hispanics," *Associated Press*–NORC Center for Public Affairs Research (July 2013), exhibit 1; Carol Lee Graham and Sergio Pinto, "Unequal Hopes and Lives in the US: Optimism, Race, Place, and Premature Mortality," *Journal of Population Economics* 687 (January 2018). This may have changed, however: see Mark Hugo Lopez, Ana Gonzales-Barrera, and Jens Manuel Krogstad, "Latinos Have Become More Pessimistic about Their Place in America," Pew Research Center, October 25, 2018, https://www.pewhispanic.org/2018/10/25/latinos-have-become-more-pessimistic-about-their-place-in-america/.

15. Erika Lee, *America for Americans: A History of Xenophobia in the United States* (New York: Basic Books, 2019).

16. On the phrase "a nation of immigrants," see Marinari, Hsu, and García, *Nation of Immigrants Reconsidered*, introduction and afterword; Roxanne Dunbar-Ortiz, *An Indigenous Peoples' History of the United States* (Boston: Beacon Press, 2014), 13, 50–51. John Winthrop, "A Model of Christian Charity" (drawn from Matthew 5:14), 1630. The North Star was used by enslaved Americans to guide them toward freedom, becoming a symbol so widely recognized and powerful that Frederick Douglass chose it as the name of the antislavery newspaper he published beginning in 1847. Abraham Lincoln, annual message to Congress, December 1, 1862; Emma Lazarus, "The New Colossus," 1883.

INDEX

A. K. Sandoval-Strausz is director of the Latina/o Studies Program and associate professor of history at Penn State University. He is the author of *Hotel: An American History* and coeditor of *Making Cities Global*. He lives in State College, Pennsylvania.